PLOTS AND CHARACTERS
IN THE FICTION
OF WILLIAM DEAN HOWELLS

THE PLOTS AND CHARACTERS SERIES

Plots and Characters in the Fiction of Henry James, with an introduction by Oscar Cargill

Plots and Characters in the Fiction and Narrative Poetry of Herman Melville, with a foreword by Harrison Hayford

Plots and Characters in the Fiction and Sketches of Nathaniel Hawthorne, with a foreword by Norman Holmes Pearson

Plots and Characters in the Fiction and Poetry of Edgar Allan Poe, with a foreword by Floyd Stovall

Plots and Characters in the Works of Mark Twain, with a foreword by Frederick Anderson

ROBERT L. GALE
General Editor

PLOTS AND CHARACTERS
IN THE FICTION
OF WILLIAM DEAN HOWELLS

George C. Carrington, Jr.

and

Ildikó de Papp Carrington

with a foreword by
George Arms

Archon Books

1976

© 1976 by George C. Carrington, Jr.
and Ildikó de Papp Carrington
First published 1976 as an Archon Book by
The Shoe String Press, Inc.
Hamden, Connecticut 06514

Library of Congress Cataloging in Publication Data

Carrington, George C
    Plots and characters in the fiction of William Dean
Howells.

    (The Plots and characters series)
    "Chronological list of Howells' fiction": p. 1. Howells,
William Dean, 1837–1920—Plots. 2. Howells, William
Dean, 1837–1920—Characters. I. Carrington, Ildikó de
Papp, 1929– joint author. II. Title.
PS2037.P54C3   813'.4   75-45257

ISBN 0-208-01461-6

Printed in the United States of America

CONTENTS

FOREWORD

Just ten years ago *The Immense Complex Drama: The World and Art of the Howells Novel,* by George C. Carrington, Jr., appeared. It was and is an important and exciting book, one among the first half-dozen at least that everybody turns to when reading or rereading a novel by Howells. Now, with Ildikó de Papp Carrington, his wife, Mr. Carrington has written a second work on Howells that seems to me also important and exciting, though in a different way. In *Plots and Characters in the Fiction of William Dean Howells* we have detailed summaries of all Howells' fictional works that for various readers will serve special uses, perhaps principally as a reminder of what they have read or as a pleasant invitation to read what they have missed. Also, as the Carringtons suggest in their preface, through the summaries and the listing of characters we may also see new connections and relationships in the "immense complex" of Howells' "world and art."

Though the title of the "Plots and Characters" series echoes Aristotle's observation that plot is "the soul" (of tragedy specifically) and that character "holds the second place," as the series has developed there has been a broadening of these aspects. Thus, while the summaries are based upon action, we receive a constant sense of that action as emerging from the characters who participate in it and as having an intensely personal meaning for the author and the reader. Though the Carringtons properly warn us that the plot does not substitute for the whole work of fiction, they still manage to give hints of the sensibility that informs the novels. As an example, the references to the "I" narrator of *Their Wedding Journey* give the context as they recount his independent action in Chapter IV of that novel. Their concluding remarks about the true tragedy of Don Ippolito convey as well as restricted space allows the closing paragraph of *A Foregone Conclusion.* The references to the Civil War monument in *Annie Kilburn* typically note the significant images that appear in their rendering of plots. Throughout the summaries we are also reminded of the reappearance of characters — known by many readers in the frequently present Basil and Isabel March, but perhaps forgotten by most with Bromfield Corey's appearing in three novels after *The Rise of Silas Lapham.* Though these reappearances are cross-referenced only as appropriate in the summaries, in the list of characters we have a complete record.

In this book we are given not only the novels but the shorter stories (of which Howells wrote many more than are generally remembered) and sketches with fictional characteristics. Of the latter, an unexpected but most welcome addition is that of ninety-eight "Addisonian sketches," eighty-four of them in the "Editor's Easy Chair." These are mostly dialogues between Howells in various fictional guises and others, occasionally the author again with another fictive mask. Written between 1900 and 1916, years when Howells was writing fewer novels than earlier, the "Easy Chair" sketches round out his career as writer of fiction with an impressiveness that has generally been overlooked. Indeed, I should like to see them gathered as a book—following Howells' own precedent of reprinting some in two collections—and hope that the Carringtons will give priority to this desirable editorial project.

George Arms

University of New Mexico, Albuquerque
January, 1976

PREFACE

This handbook is one of a series on American authors begun by Robert L. Gale and now under his general editorship. This book is not intended to serve as a substitute for the actual works of William Dean Howells, but as a useful tool for students, at all levels, of this prolific American author. Readers interested in tracing a theme or topic through Howells' work should find the summaries useful, especially when trying to decide whether it is worthwhile to make a special effort to obtain rare or minor works. By referring to the main alphabetical list of characters, a reader can find the work or works in which a character figures, and can trace the use and development of characters such as Basil March and Bromfield Corey who appear in several works. The alphabetical list at the end of each summary should help in the study of the characters in a given novel.

By examining first the chronological list of Howells' fiction, and then the summaries in the light of that list, a good deal can be learned about Howells' development from the awkward apprentice of the 1850s to the mature master of the realistic novel and then to the more occasional writer of the last years. (In the chronological list, dates in parentheses are of first book publication, and subtitles have been dropped unless essential for clarity.) Through the chronology of Howells' life, the student can begin to gauge the effect on Howells' work of such events as the Haymarket massacre and the tragic illness of his daughter Winifred. Finally, we hope that use of these research tools will stimulate the student to examine Howells' works themselves, and the rich biographical and critical literature on Howells.

An overview of the Howells canon through this book should suggest his great range as a writer of fiction. Many are familiar with Howells the novelist; few are aware of his achievement, especially in his later years, in the genre of the Addisonian sketch, which develops a thesis through symbolic or allegorical fictional action or through a dialogue or a symposium of fictional characters. In four "Editor's Studies," ten "Life and Letters," and eighty-four "Editor's Easy Chairs" (in addition to the sketches of his early career), Howells reveals his ability to use this genre in innumerable ways. Other little-known facets of this versatile writer can be seen in his amusing children's stories and in his psychological tales of the turn of the century.

With a writer of Howells' range it is necessary to define the term "fiction" carefully. We have included all published works by Howells which are entirely or predominantly narrated imaginary actions in prose or verse. (We omit translations by Howells.) We have had little trouble defining Howells' conventional novels or stories, even those like *A Traveller from Altruria* that include symposia and other essay elements. There are four epistolary novels, one in verse (*No Love Lost*) and three in prose (*Letters Home*, "Letters of an Altrurian Traveller," and *Through the Eye of the Needle*). The latter two Altrurian works, being collections of fictional letters unified mostly by point of view, somewhat stretch our definition. There is a chapter ("The Father") from a collaborative novel (*The Whole Family*). The serialized "The Independent Candidate" (1854), Howells' first long work of fiction, is a clumsy affair, but it is clearly a novel. Howells himself did not consider *Their Wedding Journey* a novel, but by our contemporary yet more old-fashioned standards it is as much a novel as its ancestor, *A Sentimental Journey*. Several mature works, such as *A Parting and a Meeting*, and *Miss Bellard's Inspiration*, are no longer than many of James's novellas, but were published as books and must be classified as novels.

In the case of sketches, we have included as works of fiction any in which a fictional persona takes part, alone or with others, in a fictional action which includes or dominates the entire sketch. (Some "Easy Chairs," for example, begin as straight book reviews but then turn into stories.) To define Howells' fiction negatively, we have omitted all plays, whether stage plays (like his well-known farces) or closet dramas; we have omitted sketches based entirely or predominantly on actual events and with a nonfictional narrator (e.g., "Jubilee Days"), and sketches (e.g., hundreds of "Easy Chairs" and "Editor's Studies") in which the narrator is a fictional persona ("we," "the Easy Chair," etc.) but the form is nonfiction (a book-review rather than a symposium on books, a travel sketch rather than a narrative of imaginary or fictionalized travel). Although many of Howells' sketches are by these definitions fiction, most of them, certainly, are not. We have made no effort to force any Howells work into the mold of fiction; indeed, we have omitted many bits of fiction embedded in essays that are decidedly not works of fiction. We do not try to differentiate short stories from sketches. Howells' short fictions lie along a broad spectrum from obvious short stories like "Editha" to obvious sketches like "Doorstep Acquaintance," with many mixed works in between, and for the purposes of this handbook a classification of the parts of the spectrum seemed arbitrary and needless.

According to our definition of Howells' fiction, he wrote 43 novels and 160 short stories and fictional sketches. In these totals we include stories originally published in collections (e.g., *Christmas Every Day*) if such stories have value as separate works, but we do not include separately published episodes from novels (e.g., certain sections of *The Flight of Pony Baker*); we do have cross-references from these episodes. We have treated "Letters of an Altrurian Traveller" as a single work, because it is now most widely available as such a work, in *The Altrurian Romances* (1968), ed. Clara and Rudolf Kirk. For the same reason we treat *Through the Eye of the Needle* as a single work, although parts of it originally appeared in the serialized "Letters of an Altrurian Traveller," and we have entered "The Selling and the Giving of Dinners" as a separate work, although it was originally part of Letter IX of the same serial. (For a full discussion of Howells' complex handling of his Altrurian materials, see the Kirks' introduction to *The Altrurian Romances*.)

The list of characters consists of all names and namable persons (fictional or historical), animals, and personified things or abstractions who appear in Howells' published fiction and who are of significance in the light of what they are or what they do. The list also includes unnamed characters when they are of similar significance. A "significant" character is one who affects the plot or the meaning of the work. We omit characters of no significance — e.g., background characters or characters who perform routine services. Without these omissions the list of characters would be impossibly long, because many Howells works, especially those involving travel, contain endless numbers of gondoliers, porters, doorkeepers, sailors, soldiers, railroad employees, hotel clerks and guests, diners-out, society ladies, and so on, who are not significant apart from their background occupational functions. Even so, the character list includes 1240 characters. The list includes turkeys, steam engines, and pumpkinseeds, and a number of ghosts, spirits, and muses. The insignificant and unnamed characters have been lumped together arbitrarily under two headings, "Americans" and "Europeans," which indicate their significance en masse to the characters who observe them. We have gone to considerable lengths to identify narrative personae. To a critic examining Howells' use of narrative techniques, there are meaningful differences between "we" and "the Easy Chair" as narrators, or between a named "I" and an unnamed "I" as narrator, or between "I" as narrator-protagonist and "I" as narrator-listener.

In the alphabetical lists characters with first names are listed before characters with the same surname and no first names (e.g., Frank Baker, Baker). In the case of a group of characters with the same surname and no first names, the order is men, married women, and unmarried women, regardless of their relationship. In the summaries subtitles have been dropped unless meaningful or essential for clarity. Chapter numbers and titles have been almost entirely dropped, and our paragraph divisions have no necessary relation to divisions between chapters or groups of chapters. Chapter titles have been kept where they seemed to us to be essential to Howells' effect (e.g., *Their Wedding Journey*). Part numbers have been kept (e.g., *The Quality of Mercy*). There is no necessary connection between the length of a summary and the length of the Howells work summarized. The connection, if any, is to the importance of the original work. Thus, for example, *A Woman's Reason,* a long but minor novel, is summarized more briefly than *The Shadow of a Dream,* a short but important novel.

The major bibliographical authority for Howells' published works is William Gibson and George Arms, *A Bibliography of William Dean Howells.* Gibson and Arms make no attempt to suggest the fictional qualities of many "Easy Chairs" and similar works; for that reason this handbook may be a helpful supplement to Gibson and Arms.

We have abbreviated the names of months, when they appear repeatedly in the same context; we use "ES" for "Editor's Study," "EEC" for "Editor's Easy Chair," and "L and L" for "Life and Letters."

We wish to acknowledge with gratitude the assistance of Mr. Samuel Huang and Mrs. Myrtie Podschwit, of the Interlibrary Loan Department of the Northern Illinois University Library, in obtaining Howells materials.

We are especially grateful to Prof. George Arms for contributing the foreword, and for bringing to our attention "Incident," recently unearthed by Prof. George Hendrick. Our thanks to the latter for consenting to our publishing a summary of "Incident" before his republication of the sketch.

The authors divided up the Howells material equally, but after much discussion, mutual review, and multiple revisions, both authors must be held responsible for all of the summaries and the character descriptions. We hope that this handbook will stimulate readers to go to the actual works in all their rich variety, and will enable readers to approach those works with some advance knowledge.

G. C. C., Jr.
I. de P. C.

Northern Illinois University
Dekalb, Illinois

CHRONOLOGY

1837 William Dean Howells born, second son and second child, to William Cooper Howells and Mary Dean Howells, in Martins Ferry, Ohio, March 1.

1840 Family moves to Hamilton, Ohio (Howells' "Boy's Town"), where father runs a printing office and a newspaper.

1849 Newspaper having failed, because of father's unpopular abolitionist and political views, family moves to Dayton, Ohio, where father runs another newspaper that fails for same reasons. Howells begins work as printer's apprentice, while educating himself in literature and foreign languages.

1850 Family moves to Eureka Mills, Ohio (Howells' "New Leaf Mills"), and lives in log cabin.

1851 Family moves to Columbus, Ohio, where father is legislative reporter for *Ohio State Journal*. Howells publishes his first literary work, a poem.

1852 Family moves to Ashtabula, Ohio, where father successfully edits *Ashtabula Sentinel*.

1853 Family and newspaper move to nearby Jefferson. Howells' first published fiction, "A Tale of Love and Politics. Adventures of a Printer Boy."

1854 First long work of fiction, "The Independent Candidate," begins to appear in *Sentinel*.

1856 Suffers nervous breakdown.

1857 Begins annual work as legislative reporter in Columbus. Works briefly as city editor of *Cincinnati Gazette*.

1858 Suffers from attacks of vertigo. Becomes city editor of *Ohio State Journal*.

1859 First book, *Poems of Two Friends*, with John J. Piatt.

1860 Writes a campaign biography of Lincoln. Visits East; meets New England literati and New York bohemians.

1861 Made consul to Venice.

1862 Marries Elinor Mead, of Brattleboro, Vermont, in Liverpool, and takes her to Venice.

1863 Daughter Winifred born.

1865 Returns to America. Works in New York for the *Nation*.

1866   Becomes assistant editor of *Atlantic Monthly;* gradually
            becomes *de facto* editor. Lives in Cambridge, in first
            of several houses there. *Venetian Life.*
1868   Son John Mead born. Mother dies. Refuses first of sev-
            eral offers of professorships.
1869   Meets Mark Twain. *No Love Lost.*
1871   Becomes, officially, editor of *Atlantic. Suburban Sketches.*
1872   Daughter Mildred born. *Their Wedding Journey.*
1873   *A Chance Acquaintance.*
1875   *A Foregone Conclusion.* "Private Theatricals" (serialized
            only, in 1875–76).
1877   *Out of the Question.*
1878   Moves to new house in Belmont, near Boston.
1879   *The Lady of the* Aroostook.
1880   Winifred Howells begins to show signs of illness. *The
            Undiscovered Country.*
1881   Resigns from *Atlantic;* arranges for regular publication
            with James R. Osgood and Company. Nervous break-
            down during writing of *A Modern Instance.* Moves to
            Boston. *Dr. Breen's Practice.*
1882   Travels to Canada and Europe. *A Modern Instance.*
1883   Rents house in Louisburg Square, Boston. *A Woman's
            Reason.*
1884   Buys house at 302 Beacon Street, Boston.
1885   After Osgood goes bankrupt, signs contract for one
            novel a year (and for minor items) with Harper and
            Brothers. Because of Winifred's illness (believed psy-
            chological), moves out of Boston to suburban residen-
            tial hotel, first of many moves in next few years. Be-
            comes influenced by Tolstoy. *The Rise of Silas Lapham.*
1886   Begins "Editor's Study" in *Harper's Monthly.* Visits
            Washington, D.C. *Indian Summer.*
1887   Supports, in print, men condemned for Haymarket mas-
            sacre in Chicago. *The Minister's Charge.*
1888   Lives in Buffalo, New York City, and Nahant (Mass.) in
            efforts to help Winifred. *April Hopes.*
1889   Winifred dies, of organic causes. Wife begins decline
            into invalidism. *Annie Kilburn. A Hazard of New
            Fortunes.*
1890   Lives briefly in Boston. *The Shadow of a Dream. A Boy's
            Town.*

1891   Moves permanently from Boston; establishes pattern of winters in New York and summers in mountains or at shore. *Criticism and Fiction. An Imperative Duty.*

1892   Quits "Editor's Study" and arrangement with Harper and Brothers. Briefly editor of *Cosmopolitan.* Becomes free lance. *The Quality of Mercy.*

1893   *The World of Chance. The Coast of Bohemia. My Year in a Log Cabin.*

1894   Father dies. *A Traveller from Altruria.*

1895   Begins three years of writing "Life and Letters" for *Harper's Weekly. Stops of Various Quills* (poems).

1896   *Impressions and Experiences.*

1897   *The Landlord at Lion's Head. Stories of Ohio.*

1898   Opposes Spanish-American War. Begins year of writing "American Letter" in *Literature. The Story of a Play.*

1899   *Their Silver Wedding Journey. Ragged Lady.*

1900   Signs long-term contract with recently reorganized Harper and Brothers. Begins "Editor's Easy Chair" in *Harper's Monthly;* does other columns for *Harper's Weekly, Harper's Bazar,* and *North American Review.*

1901   Litt. D., Yale.

1902   *The Kentons.*

1904   Litt. D., Oxford. Elected one of first seven members, and first president, of American Academy of Arts and Letters. *The Son of Royal Langbrith.*

1905   Litt. D., Columbia.

1907   *Through the Eye of the Needle.*

1910   Wife dies. Mark Twain dies. *My Mark Twain.*

1911   First six (and only) volumes of projected Library Edition of works published.

1912   Litt. D., Princeton.

1913   *New Leaf Mills.*

1916   *The Leatherwood God. Years of My Youth.*

1920   Dies, May 11. *The Vacation of the Kelwyns.*

1921   *Mrs. Farrell,* originally "Private Theatricals."

1928   *Life in Letters of W.D. Howells,* ed. Mildred Howells.

1968 — A Selected Edition of W.D. Howells.

CHRONOLOGICAL LIST OF HOWELLS' FICTION

"A Fearful Responsibility" (1881)
A Fearful Responsibility
1882 *A Modern Instance*
1883 "Niagara Revisited" (1884, 1887)
A Woman's Reason
1884 *Niagara Revisited* (pirated)
1885 *The Rise of Silas Lapham*
1886 "Christmas Every Day" (1893)
"Editor's Study," Jan.
Indian Summer
1887 *The Minister's Charge*
Their Wedding Journey (enlarged)
1888 *April Hopes*
1889 *Annie Kilburn*
A Hazard of New Fortunes
1890 "Editor's Study," Dec.
The Shadow of a Dream
1891 "Editor's Study," Dec.
An Imperative Duty
1892 "Editor's Study," March.
The Quality of Mercy
1893 *Christmas Every Day and Other Stories Told for Children*
The Coast of Bohemia
"Letters of an Altrurian Traveller" (1896, 1907, in part; 1968)
The World of Chance
1894 *A Traveller from Altruria*
1895 "A Circle in the Water" (1901)
"Life and Letters," July 6, July 13, Aug. 10, Aug. 24, Dec. 14
1896 *The Day of Their Wedding*
Impressions and Experiences
"Life and Letters," April 25 (1902), May 9 (1902), Dec. 19
A Parting and a Meeting
1897 *The Landlord at Lion's Head*
"Life and Letters," Jan. 23 (1902), Dec. 25
An Open-Eyed Conspiracy
"A Pair of Patient Lovers" (1901)
1898 "The Abandoned Watermelon Patch" (1902)
The Story of a Play

Through the Eye of the Needle

1908   "Editor's Easy Chair," Jan. (1910), April, June, July
        (1910), Oct., Dec. (1910)

Fennel and Rue

The Whole Family (in part)

1909   "Editor's Easy Chair," Jan. (1910), Feb. (1910), March
        (1910), April, May (1910)

    "The Mother-Bird" (1916)

1910   "Editor's Easy Chair," June (as "Table Talk," 1916), July,
        Sept., Oct., Nov., Dec.

Imaginary Interviews

1911   "The Daughter of the Storage" (1916)

    "Editor's Easy Chair," Jan., Feb., April, Sept., Oct., Nov.

    Library Edition, first (and only) six volumes, including
        A Hazard of New Fortunes and *The Landlord at Lion's
        Head*

1912   "Editor's Easy Chair," Feb., March, May, June, July,
        Aug., Oct., Nov., Dec.

    "The Fulfilment of the Pact"

1913   "The Critical Bookstore" (1916)

    "Editor's Easy Chair," Feb., April, Nov.

New Leaf Mills

1914   "The Archangelic Censorship"

    "Editor's Easy Chair," April, June, July, Sept., Oct.

The Seen and the Unseen at Stratford-on-Avon

1915   "Editor's Easy Chair," July, Oct. (as "A Feast of Rea-
        son," 1916), Nov., Dec.

    "An Experience" (1916)

    "The Return to Favor" (1916)

    "Somebody's Mother" (1916)

1916   "The Boarders" (1916)

Buying a Horse

The Daughter of the Storage

    "Editor's Easy Chair," Feb. (as "The Escapade of a
        Grandfather," 1916), July, Nov., Dec.

The Leatherwood God

    "The Pearl"

    "The Rotational Tenants"

1917   "Editor's Easy Chair," Jan., March, Sept., Oct.

    "A Tale Untold"

1918	"Editor's Easy Chair," Jan., May, Sept.
1919	"Editor's Easy Chair," Jan., April, July, Sept., Nov.
1920	"Editor's Easy Chair," Feb., April
	The Vacation of the Kelwyns
1921	*Mrs. Farrell*
1928	*Life in Letters of William Dean Howells,* ed. Mildred Howells
1968	*The Altrurian Romances,* ed. Clara and Rudolf Kirk
1968 —	A Selected Edition of W.D. Howells

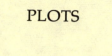

PLOTS

"The Abandoned Watermelon Patch." See *The Flight of Pony Baker*.

"*The Amigo*," 1905 (in *The Daughter of the Storage*, 1916).
  On a ship sailing from Ecuador to France, "I," the narrator, observes two Ecuadorian passengers, Perez Armando Aldeano, a devilishly mischievous nine-year-old boy who addresses everyone as "amigo," and his dark and silent adult companion, either his tutor or his uncle. The boy, whom everyone calls "the amigo," behaves well when he is with this man, but is very bad the rest of the time. Nobody can stay angry with him for long, but finally an elderly off-duty ship captain spanks him. Disembarking at Plymouth, the narrator feels sorry to leave his bad little "amigo" behind.

  Perez Armando Aldeano (the "amigo"), German-American
  boy, off-duty ship captain, Ecuadorian, "I" (the narrator),
  passengers on the ship.

"The Angel of the Lord," 1901 (in *Questionable Shapes*, 1903).
  At a New York club, Wanhope, Minver, Rulledge, and Acton (the narrator) discuss the concept of the personification of natural forces.

Wanhope believes that the personification of death still survives in the unconscious and can be brought out in a crisis. He refers to the case of the Ormonds, both recently dead. Ormond had a lifelong fear of death, and he and his wife quarreled often. When the Ormonds lived in a country house, she was nervous and lonely, and he was maniacally happy; later, his happiness became calm and radiant.

In early fall Ormond became obsessed with the idea of "The Angel of the Lord" in the Bible and even saw a wandering tramp as possibly such a being. During a drive the Ormonds talked of death and then decided to move back to the city. They saw the tramp again, after which Mrs. Ormond found that she had lost her hat. When Ormond found it, near where they had seen the tramp, Ormond suddenly started running through the woods and calling out. Mrs. Ormond found him dead, with a broken neck, below a rock; the tramp was standing beside him. Discussing the affair, Rulledge is convinced, Minver jeers, and Wanhope is skeptical.

> Acton, Minver, Ormond, Mrs. (Jenny) Ormond, Rulledge, tramp, Wanhope.

Annie Kilburn, 1889.

After her father's death in Rome, Annie Kilburn decides to return at once to America, after eleven years away. When he died, Kilburn was seventy-eight and a widower; Annie is thirty-one. To the puzzlement of the American colony in Rome, Annie decides to live in the old farm homestead where the family once spent its summers, near Hatboro', Massachusetts, a flourishing mill town. Annie hopes that she will be able to be of some use to the world in Hatboro', but can't help feeling some misgivings about her decision to plunge into contemporary America. For years she lived a quiet, comfortable life with her father, who had retired to Rome after being a Congressman and practicing law in Washington. Along with her aspirations she has retained a distrust of her own nature and desires.

When she returns, Annie finds that despite its factories Hatboro', with its neighboring resort town South Hatboro', is still a quiet, leafy New England village. She flinches at the sight of the pretentious Civil War monument, which she admired when she had it made for the town in Rome. At the old Kilburn home, her caretaker,

Bolton, a local farmer, tells her about the controversial new Orthodox (Congregational) minister, Julius W. Peck. Bolton has allowed
Peck to board, with his small daughter, Idella, in the Boltons' part of
the house. (Peck has been a widower for a year.)

Annie finds the old house musty and redolent of her distant
childhood. Because the town never felt the Kilburns to be permanent residents, Annie is welcomed slowly. After a while she is
visited by three grown-up girlhood friends, Mrs. Ellen Putney, Mrs.
Emmeline Gerrish, and Mrs. Lyra Wilmington, all much better
dressed than Annie, and rather condescending. She finds them
blunt and small-townish. Gerrish is a rising, conceited merchant;
Wilmington, the owner of a stocking mill; and Putney, a lawyer and
occasional alcoholic. Annie wonders if her fate will simply be to
grow older like her friends, and if she is really an old maid. She feels
very much alone.

Then Percy Brandreth, a young man from South Hatboro', asks
Annie to join in the lively social life there, and thus bridge the gap
between the two Hatboro's. He wants her to lead in establishing a
Social Union for the workers and to help put on theatricals to help
pay for the Union. All this vaguely depresses Annie; she considers
it trivial. Wanting to do something for Peck, Annie invites Idella to
midday dinner, but Annie's clumsy manner puts the child off and
eventually she has hysterics. Still determined, Annie tries to interest
Peck, a dry, gaunt man, in the Social Union. To Annie's chagrin, he
regards it as a typical meaningless gesture of the rich. He approves
of the theatricals, but refuses any part in the affair when he realizes
that the working class will be kept out of the socializing to follow
the theatricals. Annie finds herself awkwardly defending the para-
dox of advancing social union through social separation. Peck
calmly points out that only shared experience, not money, can buy
fraternity. When he leaves, he forgets his child and has to come back
for her.

Next day Annie feels vaguely grumpy at Peck for upsetting her.
Mrs. Munger, a large, self-confident woman and the social leader of
South Hatboro', agrees with her that Peck is absurd, but says they
had better drop the social side of the theatricals, and bears Annie off
to see Annie's Hatboro' friends. Annie and Mrs. Munger visit the
Gerrishes at his flourishing dry-goods store, which Gerrish runs
with an iron hand. The social chatter soon becomes a conceited lecture by Gerrish, attacking unions and praising himself. He strongly

opposes dropping the reception and inviting the lower classes. Putney comes in and sardonically asks how they would get rid of the
lower classes after the theatricals. Dr. Morrell also drops in, and after
he laughingly refuses to give a definite opinion on the subject, the
group breaks up. Later, at the Wilmingtons' house, Annie meets
Jack Wilmington, Lyra's surly nephew, whom Lyra Wilmington casually flirts with, to Annie's distress. Lyra, a handsome woman who
was a mill hand before she was married, dislikes the idea of not inviting her former workmates to the reception.

By May, as the summer folk begin to arrive in South Hatboro',
Annie is deeply involved in the theatricals, which push the Social
Union itself into the background. Annie finds South Hatboro' dis-
turbingly raw and *nouveau riche*, the Brandreths' house tiresomely
quaint, and the summer people boring, but wonders if she and her
life are really any better. At tea at Putney's house Annie learns that
several years ago Putney, when drunk, crippled his son by dropping him down the stairs. Putney says that Hatboro' is now a
sprawling town full of immigrants, and that as one of the old in-
habitants, he is tolerated in his eccentric ways and radical opinions.
Putney wants to get Annie and Peck together; he calls Peck a man
without emotion but with deep insights into people. Annie finds
Dr. Morrell charming and sympathetic, and confides in him her desire to do good. He suggests that she not worry about Peck and his
ideas of social equality. Annie gets to know the daughters of J. Milton Northwick, a rich Boston businessman who commutes to a farm
near South Hatboro'; the older daughter is stiff, the younger (Sue)
beautiful and haughty. Lyra Wilmington introduces Annie to her elderly husband at his ugly mill and describes her indolent life to
Annie.

Annie misses the old, simple, small-town life with its earnest in-
tellectualism, and regrets that money is now the basic social stan-
dard. She and Dr. Morrell find each other strange but interesting,
and talk a good deal. She worries about the unemployed during the
slack season at the mills; Dr. Morrell suggests that she send some
poor sick children to the seaside, but this ideas backfires when one
of them, the Savor child, dies and Mrs. Savor illogically but naturally blames Annie. She feels utterly discouraged and useless, but
finally pulling herself together returns to the idea of the Social
Union. She finds all the local ministers except Peck agreeable to the
idea and to the theatricals. Finally she apologizes to him for her dif-

ferences with him, but is rather surprised to find that he doesn't seem to have been upset. He tells her that she shouldn't feel guilty for the death of the Savors' child, because she meant well, and he reiterates that it is hard for those who don't need help to give it.

At Putney's suggestion, Annie attends Peck's church. As summer wanes, Brandreth prepares for the theatricals in September. At the theatricals, held on Mrs. Munger's tennis court, the working class (those who buy special tickets) mingle with their betters. The crowd applauds an elaborate minuet followed by an abridged performance of *Romeo and Juliet*. Annie holds Peck's little girl, Idella, and only reluctantly gives her to the bereaved Mrs. Savor. After the play Mrs. Munger persuades Peck, the Savors, and certain representatives of the working class to stay for the reception. Sue Northwick and Lyra Wilmington compete silently for the attentions of Jack Wilmington. The different classes are ill at ease with each other, especially after they all go into Mrs. Munger's house and are thrown closer together. At the end of the evening, when most people have left, Putney gets drunk, reproaches Mrs. Munger for serving punch, and verbally attacks Gerrish and others. Finally Mrs. Putney gets him away. Peck judges Mrs. Munger harshly for tempting Putney to drink.

When Peck absentmindedly leaves Idella at the Munger house, Annie takes her home for the night. Mrs. Munger comes next day to attack Putney and Peck, and to ask for Annie's support, but Annie agrees with them that Mrs. Munger is at fault, whereupon the latter huffily withdraws from the Social Union. Dr. Morrell, however, comes in and manages to josh her out of her angry mood. Alone with Annie, Dr. Morrell says that Putney is in bad shape, and agrees with Annie's idea that she take Idella into her house. Later Lyra Wilmington says that everyone thinks Annie is after Peck or Dr. Morrell is after her; she ridicules Annie's anxious comments about herself and Jack Wilmington. Peck does let Annie have Idella for a time. She finds the child's company and devotion intensely enjoyable. Annie is amused by Peck's failure to teach Idella not to covet or to possess selfishly; Annie herself is satisfied to make the child ladylike. Peck is sure that inequality, like slavery, can be eliminated, but thinks that the Social Union is not the right approach. He does agree finally to leave Idella with Annie for an indefinite time.

One Sunday Annie dresses Idella elegantly and takes her to Peck's church, to the astonishment of the congregation. Using the text "I am the Resurrection and the Life," Peck preaches on the need for

America to proceed from social liberty to social equality and justice. The Gerrishes get up and walk out. After church Putney and the Boltons tell Annie that Gerrish means to put Peck out at the church's business meeting, and has a large party behind him. Dr. Morrell agrees with Annie that Peck's position is serious. They puzzle over his coldness and his apparent indifference to Idella. Annie says that she agrees with Peck that charity, now useless, must be replaced with justice, and she is bothered that Morrell doesn't take her earnestness seriously.

A great crowd, of church members and non-members, gathers for the business meeting, which Peck attends. Gerrish moves that a committee examine Peck's suitability for his charge, and speaks unctuously of his own virtues and of Peck's error in preaching Christ as a life as well as a spirit. Mr. Gates, the local grocer, mildly defends Peck. Mr. Wilmington says that he thinks Gerrish misunderstood Peck's sermon, and asks him to withdraw the motion and confer with Peck. Gerrish agrees, but to irritate him Putney won't let him withdraw the motion (which Putney himself seconded in order to get the argument going). Putney attacks Gerrish with harsh irony, and asks the group to decide what it thinks of Peck's preaching. No one votes for Gerrish's resolution, and most shout no. Peck says that he intended no personal references in his sermon, but thinks that his ministry has failed, for reasons he will give next Sunday. He says he plans to resign. Everyone is startled and many oppose the idea. Putney is angry with Peck for leaving the feeling that Gerrish's attack contained some truth.

After the meeting Peck calls on Annie, who urges him to stay, but he says he is going to Fall River to teach in a public school and apply his ideas wherever else he can. He plans to leave Idella with the Savors for the time being and then bring the Savors and Idella to Fall River. Sadly Annie must agree that the loss of Idella is an expiation for her. Then she exultantly says that she will come to Fall River too, though deep down she is revolted by the idea. Peck does his best to dissuade her, but fails. Next day Annie is so worried and confused that she sends for Dr. Morrell, who says that he, Putney, and other supporters of Peck have spent the day cooling off Gerrish and persuading Peck to stay over a day at least before going for a day to Fall River. He is amazed to find Annie upset by this news, and more amazed when she tells him what she said to Peck the night before.

Putney arrives to say that Peck has decided to go at once to Fall River after all.

The next night Savor tells Annie and the doctor that Peck has been hit by a train after arriving at the station from Fall River. Annie gathers up Idella and rushes to the Savors' house, where Peck lies dying. While others are managing to remain cheerful and useful in the face of Peck's inevitable death, Annie is speechless and helpless. After the funeral Annie takes Idella to the Savors, and goes home to collapse. Late at night she is awakened by strange noises and finds that Idella has come back to her. Now Annie refuses to give up the child.

The town continues to gossip about the Peck case, and finds plenty to disapprove of. Idella has a bad illness, thus reuniting Annie and the doctor. Annie begins to feel reconciled to her failures, finding them trivial in relation to the ordered largeness of the universe. Brandreth says that the feeling is that the money from the theatricals should be used to beautify the Civil-War monument, and asks Annie to handle the matter. Dr. Morrell suggests that instead she carry out Peck's plan to establish a cooperative boardinghouse run by the Savors, but in Hatboro' rather than Fall River. Annie gets the Peck Social Union going and continues to help it. Putney still gets drunk occasionally. After a long and roundabout courtship, which the town observes with amusement, Annie and the doctor are happily married.

> Olive Bolton, Pauline Bolton, Percy Brandreth (Sr.), Mrs. Brandreth, Miss (Bella) Chapley, Gates, Emmeline Gerrish, William Gerrish, Annie Kilburn, Rufus Kilburn, lady, Colonel Marvin, Dr. James Morrell, Jim Munger, Mrs. Munger, J. Milton Northwick, Miss Northwick, Sue Northwick, Idella Peck, Rev. Julius W. Peck, Ellen Putney, Ralph Putney, Winthrop Putney, Maria Savor, William Savor, George Wilmington, Jack Wilmington, Lyra Wilmington.

April Hopes, 1888.

At a Class Day celebration at Harvard, Elbridge G. Mavering, a middle-aged alumnus, and his son Dan, a graduating senior aged twenty-three, are introduced by John Munt, a mutual friend, to a

Mrs. Pasmer and her pretty daughter Alice, aged twenty-one. Dan invites Mrs. Pasmer to go to some "spreads" (student parties) with him, but she is dubious because she can't place the Maverings. Neither can Alice, but she likes Dan. Eventually all leave the deserted Gym and join mutual friends, Prof. Saintsbury and his wife. Dan and Alice stroll off to other spreads, while the others follow slowly. The day, the college, and the people, especially Dan, are all radiant. At the spreads Alice is much admired, while Mrs. Pasmer more than ever wonders who the Maverings can be. In Dan's room they meet his friend Boardman, and Dan changes into old clothes for the Tree-ritual. At the Tree in the Yard, a brilliant crowd watches while the classes file in, cheer their favorite classmates and teachers, and then struggle for a garland of flowers put around the trunk well above the ground. Dan gets a big bunch and gives them to his father.

Two days later Mrs. Saintsbury tells Mrs. Pasmer that the Maverings are wealthy wallpaper makers from Ponkwasset Falls, N.H., that Mrs. Mavering is bedridden, and that there are two daughters in addition to the one son, Dan. Mrs. Pasmer is satisfied that Dan is acceptable in both of the elevated and quite different social worlds of Cambridge and Boston. The Pasmers have lived for years in France and England, and, rather straitened financially, have returned to Boston for Alice's sake. In Boston society Mrs. Pasmer exploits her prudence, her talent for flattery, and her family name (Hibbins). Mr. Pasmer is a coldly quiet man of leisure who leaves all decisions to Mrs. Pasmer as long as she makes him comfortable. A few days later Dan and his friend Boardman call at the Pasmers' flat and discuss Campobello, N.B., a new summer resort where the Pasmers go, Mrs. Pasmer all the time fishing for more of Dan's background.

At Campobello later in the summer Mrs. Pasmer finds an active hotel life, and as usual far too few young men. Alice makes friends with the old ladies on the hotel piazza and with a vivacious New York girl, Julia Anderson. Suddenly Mr. Munt and Dan Mavering arrive, to the Pasmers' secret joy. In a round of picnics and other amusements on the foggy island the unacknowledged affair of Dan and Alice takes its leisurely course, eagerly followed by the piazza ladies. Dan is undecided about his future but clearly interested in Alice.

On a big picnic at the beach Dan is the life of the party. While he and Alice gather blueberries, they have a long talk. She is earnest, moralistic, and unworldly; he is easygoing and lively, and ridicules her girlish dream of entering an Anglican sisterhood. Back at the hotel Mrs. Pasmer with her husband's permission decides to let the affair go on, even though the thought of losing Alice upsets her. She asks Alice to be aware of what is happening to her and Dan. Alice is embarrassed but deep down knows that she loves Dan. Mrs. Pasmer finds the whole business troubling because not quite Bostonian. That night, during some amateur theatricals at the Trevors' cottage, Dan "goes on" too much with Julia Anderson, and Alice is offended in her stiff way. Next day Dan is repentant, abases himself to Alice, and finally blurts out that he loves her. Forcing herself into cold-ness, she says that everything is over between them, and refuses to give a reason, even to her mother, who is somewhat amused by her tragic pose. The piazza ladies discuss the matter as Dan leaves the island.

At Portland, Dan, utterly wretched, runs into Boardman and tells all to his drily sympathetic friend; they both sing Alice's praises. Staying on to see a yacht race that Boardman is covering for his Bos-ton newspaper, the *Events*, Dan meets and escorts to the race Mrs. Frobisher and her sister Miss Wrayne, two charming Portland ladies whom he met at Class Day. In Boston he tells his father that he doesn't want to go to Harvard Law School and doesn't want to look after Mavering's affairs in Boston. His father realizes that Dan's love affair has gone wrong and suggests that he eventually spend a year in Europe acquiring background for the aesthetic side of the wallpa-per business. Dan agrees, plunges into work, and begins to recover.

In October Dan returns to Boston on business, meets Alice by ac-cident at the Art Museum, and is instantly reconciled with her. When she learns that he went there to meet Mrs. Frobisher and Miss Wrayne, Alice is not disturbed since Dan says he forgot all about the other ladies when he saw Alice. Alice rushes in to tell her mother the good news, but finds her calmly adding up the bills, and ex-plodes in tears. Finally she manages to tell her startled and rather amused mother that she is engaged. In the evening Dan pays his respects to Mr. and Mrs. Pasmer, who are very pleasant to him. While doting on Dan, Alice says he must apologize to the Portland ladies for not meeting them at the museum. When she learns that Dan enjoyed himself at the yacht race, Alice feels a resentment which she manages to swallow. Before breakfast next morning Dan, still in ecstasies, brings Alice roses, to Mrs. Pasmer's amazement.

Alice, in a solemnly practical mood, insists that Dan go home that day and tell his family. He is still in a happy daze but assents.

Back home, Mrs. Mavering and Dan's sisters, Eunice and Minnie, are much less enthusiastic than Dan hoped. After dinner the family go upstairs to see Mrs. Mavering, who has been an invalid since shortly after Dan's birth; she is gay when her pain is dulled (by opium), but cruelly sharp-tongued when it is not. Tonight she is not in pain, receives Dan's news agreeably, and asks Dan to invite the Pasmers for a visit. She wants him to live at home; he doesn't tell her that he wants to take Alice abroad and has told Mrs. Pasmer so with the latter's approval.

A week later, after the Maverings visit the Pasmers, the Pasmer ladies return the visit. Mrs. Pasmer examines the house coolly, to Alice's embarrassment, and pronounces it masculine and vulgarly showy. The Maverings sympathize with Alice's agitation. Alice shrinks from Mrs. Mavering instinctively, but the invalid doesn't notice, and their meeting is friendly. Afterwards Mrs. Mavering tells Dan that Mrs. Pasmer is a cat but that Alice is sublime although too intense. Mrs. Mavering still assumes that Dan will bring his bride to live in the Mavering house. Meanwhile, Mrs. Pasmer tells Alice that Mrs. Mavering is so strong-willed that it's a good thing Alice won't be living in Ponkwasset Falls. Mrs. Pasmer considers the Maverings self-satisfied and provincial but Dan a good match anyway. Alice is vaguely troubled in realizing that she means little to the Maverings.

At Mrs. Bellingham's reception in Boston, a few days later, Mrs. Brinkley, the most sardonic of the piazza ladies, discusses the engagement with John Munt. Bromfield Corey, now almost senile, is there too. Later in the evening Dan introduces Mrs. Frobisher and Miss Wrayne to Mrs. Brinkley and Corey. Charles Bellingham, Corey's cousin, already knows them, but the other Bostonians ignore them. Later a bewildered Dan is seen taking Miss Wrayne in to supper. Next morning he shows Boardman a letter from Alice in which she returns his ring because, she says, he hasn't given her his full heart. Puzzled, Dan explains that at the reception he asked Alice to help him with the Portland ladies, she refused, he introduced them to Corey and Bellingham, Alice remained cold the rest of the evening, he had to go on being polite to the ladies, and in the morning he got the note and the ring. Boardman says that Dan must go to see Alice at once. Mrs. Pasmer doesn't know what Alice has done, and is inclined to laugh when Dan shows her the note. She decides to help Dan get Alice back. Alice appears, very tragic, and solemnly gives him up to the Portland ladies. Irritated and amused, Dan asks which one, and points out that neither of them wants him. Alice finally sees the absurdity of the situation, and they are reconciled.

Dan being careful not to joke about the tiff, he and Alice are very harmonious, and their engagement is finally made public. Dan senses her hardness, which her exterior gentleness conceals. One evening Dan dances with a Miss Langham, a friend of Alice; she falls and hurts herself, and Dan feels lucky to escape Alice's disapproval. When Alice decides to write Mrs. Mavering in diary form, Dan conceals, with trepidation, the fact that he has not settled the residence question with his mother. During this period Alice talks everything over with Miss Cotton, a middle-aged spinster, who encourages Alice's severe idealism. Then Alice gets a letter from Mrs. Mavering that makes her send for Dan.

Frightened by Alice's note, Dan rushes to her and reads Mrs. Mavering's letter, which makes it clear that she expects the couple to settle in Ponkwasset Falls. Alice solemnly orders Dan to leave forever, but he has had enough of this sort of thing, and argues back. They quarrel with real heat, Alice speaking largely in phrases taken from novels. Dan finally walks out. Furious at Alice, Mrs. Pasmer takes Dan's side and tells her daughter not to be silly and cruel. Dan turns, as usual, to Boardman, who is sympathetic, but says frankly that Dan and Alice are incompatible. Dan feels bitter, but, to his own embarrassment, glad to be free. At home, he tells his sisters and is irritated to find them joyful. His father points out that Dan was to blame for letting things run on without a decision. Mrs. Mavering is glad it's over, sorry for both Dan and Alice, and still angry at Mrs. Pasmer, who she thinks caused the breakup intentionally. Dan feebly tries to defend Mrs. Pasmer, whom he realizes he resembles in his easygoing sociability. All Boston buzzes, meanwhile, over the breakup of the engagement. Alice gets Miss Cotton to agree with her, but Mrs. Brinkley tells Miss Cotton that Alice really wants Dan back and that Alice isn't good enough for him — she is imperceptive and impatient.

Dan stays at home, hears nothing from Boston, and helps his father at the mill. Mr. Mavering sympathizes with Dan but feels that his son is better off now. By and by, while Dan is in Washington on business, he meets Julia Anderson and her aunt, Miss Van Hook.

Going with them to several official receptions, Dan is impressed by Julia's charm and sophistication, though he feels twinges of guilt for seeing her so much. Eventually he tells Julia all about the affair with Alice. Julia says that Alice was morbid, but seems to be concealing other emotions. Julia and her aunt eventually go off to Old Point Comfort, leaving Dan oddly troubled.

At the Hygeia Hotel in Old Point Comfort, Mrs. Brinkley and Miss Van Hook discuss Dan and Julia. It seems that Julia has been engaged for a long time to a Lt. Willing; they have largely lost interest in each other, but she is unable to break off the affair and has shown no interest in other men until meeting Dan. When Dan writes Julia asking if he may come down to see her, she asks him not to, and says she will soon marry Lt. Willing. Next day the New York ladies leave and the Pasmer ladies arrive. Mrs. Brinkley, sparring with Mrs. Pasmer, tells her that Dan was seen constantly with Julia in Washington. Mrs. Brinkley is sure that the Pasmers have come with dark designs on Dan, but feels some sympathy with their evident misery. Mr. Brinkley carelessly lets Alice see that Mrs. Brinkley has received a letter from Dan. Mrs. Brinkley telegraphs Dan not to come, and tells the wretched Mrs. Pasmer that he is not coming. Later Mrs. Brinkley worries about her entanglement in the affair and wonders if perhaps Dan isn't Alice's rightful prey after all. Alice now snubs Mrs. Brinkley, who begins to feel that she deserves it. Suddenly Dan arrives. Mrs. Brinkley doesn't know what to do or think, but at last she leaves Dan alone on the hotel verandah, just as Alice comes around the corner.

The following June Alice and Dan get married. They will live abroad for a year and then live at the Falls. Mrs. Brinkley still feels that Alice is a hard egotist. As Dan and Alice leave the church after the wedding, she is asking him with passionate seriousness always to be frank and open, and he is wondering what to tell her about Julia; thus, as they begin married life, neither one has changed, and the potential for disaster is still there.

Julia Anderson, Charles Bellingham, Jane (Mrs. James) Bellingham, Boardman, Brinkley, Mrs. Brinkley, Bromfield Corey, Miss Cotton, Mrs. Frobisher, Joe, Lily Langham, Daniel Mavering, Elbridge G. Mavering, Eunice Mavering, Minnie Mavering, Mrs. Mavering, Mrs. Secretary Miller, John Munt, Alice Pasmer, Mrs. Jenny Pasmer, Pasmer, Pat,

Mrs. Etta Saintsbury, Prof. Saintsbury, Mrs. Stainwell, Mr. and Mrs. Trevor, Miss Van Hook, Mrs. Whittington, Miss Wrayne.

"The Archangelic Censorship," 1914.
The angels in heaven discuss the beginning of World War I.
Angels.

"At the Sign of the Savage," 1877 (in *A Fearful Responsibility*, 1881).
Just after the Civil War, two Americans, Colonel Edward Kenton and Mrs. Bessie Kenton, take the train from Paris to Vienna, en route to Italy. Kenton humorously refuses to believe that the drab wintry places he sees are really the romantic places mentioned in the guidebooks. At 3 A.M. they arrive in Vienna and tell the cab-driver to take them to the Kaiserin Elisabeth Hotel. After a good rest at the hotel, Kenton visits the American consul to get some American papers. The consul turns out to be Davis, an old Army friend. The two men tour Vienna after sending a note about their plans to Mrs. Kenton. Their sleigh breaks down in the country and they walk back, very late, to the hotel—but it is not the hotel Kenton was at and Mrs. Kenton is in. The dishonest cabdriver had taken them to another hotel. Davis is vastly amused, but Kenton is more and more furious as they go from hotel to hotel. Finally they are reminded that the police have Kenton's hotel registration. He is registered, they learn, at the Gasthof zum Wilden Mann. A nervous Kenton is relieved to find his wife not at all upset by his absence. She still thinks that she is in the Kaiserin Elisabeth, and Davis and Kenton are afraid to tell her the truth until much later.

Cabdrivers, *concierges*, Davis, Mrs. Bessie Kenton, Colonel Edward Kenton, a *Lohndiener*, policemen, porters.

"The Bag of Gold," 1863.
With a poor Italian woman innkeeper, Madonna Lucrexia, three ruffians leave a bag of gold, obviously a stolen one, and make her vow to return it only to all three, but one of them secretly returns and takes it. When the other two take her to court, the young lawyer

Lorenzo Martelli, the lover of her daughter Gianetta, gets her off by demanding that according to the original oath all three men step forward and make their claim.

Gianetta Lucrexia, Madonna Lucrexia, Lorenzo Martelli, three ruffians.

"The Boarders," 1916 (in *The Daughter of the Storage*, 1916).

In the mid-1850's three young men, boarders at Mrs. Betterson's small-town boardinghouse, are discussing the departure of Phillips, a divinity student, who has left because the food is so bad. Afraid to confront Mrs. Betterson, he has left his carpetbag with his roommate, Briggs, a young newspaperman. When Phillips throws some gravel at the window, Briggs is to sneak out of the house and give Phillips his bag. Mrs. Betterson is an elderly widow with two daughters: Minervy, a pretty pianist courted by a Mr. Saunders, and Jenny, a sick little drudge. Wallace, a medical student, and Blakely, a law student, agree that Phillips had every right to leave, because he paid his board. Returning from his errand, Briggs is caught on the stairs by Mrs. Betterson and Jenny, savagely tells them why Phillips has left, and rushes up to his room to start packing, too. But then the three young men overhear Jenny sobbing downstairs and Mrs. Betterson trying to console her by saying that maybe Mr. Saunders will marry Minervy. Chagrined, Briggs decides to stay, and Wallace goes downstairs to offer Mrs. Betterson an advance on his board.

Jenny Betterson, Minervy Betterson, Mrs. Betterson, Blakely, Briggs, Phillips, Saunders, Wallace.

"Bobby. Study of a Boy," 1858.

Bobby, an energetic scamp of twelve, has survived numerous boyhood accidents, and is now a pest to his older and younger siblings and other relatives, except for his grandmother. His main occupation is the circus in which he stars himself. A little girl admires him, but he loathes her. He is very aggressive with other boys, but bashful in adult company. At present he lives a happy animal life; in the future, the narrator ("I") thinks, he will probably turn out all right.

Bobby, "I" (the narrator).

"Braybridge's Offer," 1906 (in *Between the Dark and the Daylight*, 1907).

In the Turkish room, a lounge in a dining club in New York, the narrator (Acton, a novelist) joins Wanhope the psychologist, Rulledge the man of leisure, and Minver the painter before dinner. They discuss the general question of assigning responsibility for initiative in love affairs, and a particular case, narrated by Wanhope, involving Braybridge and Miss Hazelwood. These two, both bashful, met in the Adirondacks at the house of the Welkins, who later told Wanhope the story. Braybridge wanted to leave the party, which he found uncongenial, but Mrs. Welkin wouldn't allow it; he and Miss Hazelwood were subsequently thrown together and have recently become engaged. Halson enters; he says that Miss Hazelwood, an orphan, was brought up half wild on a Western ranch, brought recently to New York, and pushed into society against her will. At a picnic during the house party, Halson says, she and Braybridge became lost, he turned his ankle, and she gave him no help; the next day he was leaving in a huff when she told him that she acted indifferent out of delicacy toward him, he was instantly enchanted, and by some shy remark she showed that she cared for him. After Halson leaves, Minver, always a skeptic, maintains that Halson imagined the whole thing, and the group is left wondering what is fact and what is fiction and how one separates the two.

Acton, Braybridge, Halson, Miss Hazelwood, Minver, Rulledge, Wanhope, Welkin, Mrs. Welkin.

"Butterflyflutterby and Flutterbybutterfly," in *Christmas Every Day and Other Stories Told for Children*, 1893.

A papa tells his small nephew and niece of Prince Butterflyflutterby and Princess Flutterbybutterfly, orphan royalty of a fantastic kingdom. The Khan and Khant of Tartary, twin brother and sister, come to marry them, but nobody can tell the sex of either visitor until the Khant is frightened by a cow and the Khan isn't.

Butterflyflutterby, Flutterbybutterfly, Khan, Khant, nephew, niece, court officials, papa.

"Buying a Horse," 1879 (in *A Day's Pleasure and Other Sketches*, 1881, and *Buying a Horse*, 1916).

Being about to move from Charlesbridge, a Boston suburb, into more open country, the friend of the narrator blithely sets out to buy a horse and equipage. On the advice of a friend, a professor, he goes to a dealer who has, he says, just sold the very horse he would have wanted. Thereafter, dealers and owners constantly descend on the friend with horses that have every kind of fault. After several weeks he knows a great deal about horses, but has no horse. Then he sees a good mare for sale, but the owner mysteriously turns inaccessible and won't sell. Advertising fails. The friend moves, and has to rent a horse, but then his carpenter recommends a firm that sells horses on trial, and the friend gets a horse named Billy, along with a phaeton. Billy seems perfect—until he runs away and destroys the phaeton. Billy is sold, at a loss. The friend is now the laughingstock of the area. Finally a neighbor helps him buy an old but competent horse named Frank. When the snow comes the friend has no use for Frank and reluctantly sells him. Now the friend is meekly awaiting whatever horse fate sends him next.

Billy, carpenter, dealer, farmer, Frank, friend of the narrator, neighbor, professor.

"By Horse-Car to Boston," 1870 (in *Suburban Sketches*, 1871).

"I," the narrator, observes people, customs, bad manners, scenery, and the many indignities of travel during a horsecar ride from suburban Charlesbridge to Boston.

Conductors, "I" (the narrator), horsecar passengers.

"A Case of Metaphantasmia," 1905 (in *Between the Dark and the Daylight*, 1907).

At a New York dining club Newton, a guest of Halson, tells a group (Wanhope the psychologist, Minver the painter, and Acton the novelist and narrator) about an odd experience he had on a Pullman, many years earlier. There he met his old Harvard roommate, Melford, who in college had had the same nightmare over and over. After a talk and after seeing a girl who resembled a girl Newton had known, the two men went to their berths, opposite one another; the girl was in a stateroom. Later Newton heard Melford bellowing in the throes of his nightmare; then the girl started crying "Help! Burglars!" Then everyone in the car, including the porter, started running up and down and shouting about burglars and robbers, until the conductor came in and calmed everyone down. Wanhope thinks that Melford's dream could have been transferred to other minds; the others in the group think that Newton dreamed the whole thing.

Acton, conductor, girl, Halson, Melford, Minver, Newton, porter, Rulledge, travelers, Wanhope.

A Chance Acquaintance, 1873.

On a boat about to leave Quebec for a cruise up the Saguenay River, Kitty Ellison, a young woman from Eriecreek in western New York State, thinks how kind it is of her cousins Colonel and Fanny Ellison, of Milwaukee, to invite her to join them and thus stretch her brief trip to Niagara Falls into a journey to Montreal, Quebec, and home via Boston and New York. She also looks forward to seeing her new friends the Marches in Boston. The only flaw in the plan is that Kitty has few and plain clothes and must borrow better ones from Fanny. We learn Kitty's history. After her father, an ardent Abolitionist, had been killed in Kansas by Jayhawkers and her mother died, Kitty became the ward of her uncle, Dr. Ellison, in Eriecreek, and the pet of her numerous cousins. She acquired the family's "wholesomely fantastic," good-humored sense of life, along with its idealized respect for Boston and its people.

Kitty's boat is held up for an elegant young man whom every one takes for an Englishman, but who is really Mr. Miles Arbuton, of Harvard and Boston. Kitty realizes that he is the handsome stranger she noticed at Niagara. Arbuton decides at once to avoid all these vulgar people, but manages despite himself to take some interest in the St. Lawrence and its scenery. Standing at the rail beside Arbuton and thinking he is the Colonel, Kitty absentmindedly takes his arm; he simply stares at her and says nothing as she draws back in confusion. At Tadoussac Arbuton realizes her embarrassment, introduces himself to Col. Ellison, and apologizes to him and later to Kitty, who waxes facetious about the matter, to Arbuton's bafflement and confusion.

At Ha-Ha Bay, in the Saguenay, Arbuton joins the Ellisons in a tour and provokes Kitty by his cold indifference to the local people. When Mrs. Ellison turns her ankle and must stay in the cabin, Kitty is able to wear her fine clothes, and finds herself thrown more closely together with Arbuton. Kitty's good-hearted innocence, a product of her simple background, clashes more and more with Arbuton's stiff and narrow snobbishness. The characters and the narrator admire the scenery of the Saguenay, but Arbuton finds it unhistorical and too big; however, he surprises himself and the others by throwing a stone at a cliff, after which he relapses into an even greater chilliness.

The ship returns to Quebec, which is crowded, but the Ellisons find some charming rooms in an old house, and Arbuton, driven by a feeling he is hardly aware of, surprises himself again by staying on, at the same house. Kitty projects her romanticism onto the quaint sights of Quebec. After the doctor says that Mrs. Ellison must rest her ankle in bed for a week or two, Arbuton escorts Kitty about the old town. At the cathedral his cold criticisms of the admittedly second-rate pictures put her off and make him alien to her. His kindness to a beggar raises her opinion of him, but she still cannot make up her mind about him. After a week in Quebec Kitty writes home about the charm of the town, and about "our Bostonian," who is not at all like the Ellison family's imagined perfect democrat from Boston, but stuffy and humorless, though oddly impressive all the same. Mrs. Ellison draws out Kitty on the subject of Arbuton, who still irritates Kitty with his stiffness and his need to be not so much respected as revered. Kitty has a new vision of Boston, a smugly fastidious and Europeanized Boston. Unlike Fanny, Kitty can't see a novel in Arbuton and herself. She is tired of the situation, but not of him. She half-wishes he would go, but he finds himself more and more charmed, and can't tear himself away, although he still doesn't know why.

On a stroll, Kitty tells Arbuton of a plotless novel that she likes; he says he knows the author, a Bostonian, who is agreeable, but not a gentleman. Kitty is first impressed by Arbuton's knowing the author, but then annoyed by his superior airs, and attacks "the idea of a gentleman," to Arbuton's amazement. In the old lower town Arbuton saves Kitty from a savage dog by intercepting the dog's leap with his own body, at the cost of his elegant topcoat. In and through this noble act Arbuton realizes that he loves Kitty, although he doesn't say so, and baffles Kitty with his changed behavior—for example, he now laughs at her sallies. At first amused by Arbuton's changed conduct, Kitty repents and is kind to him as he remains enraptured, as much by his own feelings as by her. The days pass in a happy dream for the pair.

After Arbuton and Kitty are taken for a married couple, Arbuton proposes. After putting him off—because, she says, this is real life, not a story—Kitty discusses the matter with Fanny, who in turn tells the bewildered colonel what he should think. Wondering if Arbuton has been deceived by her clothes borrowed from Fanny, Kitty decides to wear her own simple clothes henceforth. During a picnic in the country, Arbuton and Kitty have a long intimate talk. Kitty relates her family history and insists on her difference from Boston girls. Arbuton, in turn, insists on his love, but agrees to wait until he sees Kitty in Boston.

Next day the four visit Lorette and its Huron village. Arbuton courts Kitty warmly, but when two Boston ladies appear suddenly, he leaves Kitty, talks to the ladies at length, within sight of Kitty, and, tortured by embarrassment and confusion, ignores her, even when the older of the ladies makes cutting remarks about her that she overhears. (Given the etiquette of the time, Arbuton can't introduce the ladies to Kitty or vice versa; he should excuse himself as quickly as possible and return to Kitty.) Numbed, Kitty is forced to recognize the unbridgeable gap between Arbuton and herself, between Boston and Eriecreek. Arbuton sees the ladies to their carriage, thus leaving Kitty completely alone. Enraged, she rushes off, but Arbuton returns and clumsily tries to right matters. He can't deny to himself or to her, however, that he was ashamed of her before those ladies, and that the affair is irretrievably ruined.

Next day Kitty sees a man wearing Arbuton's torn topcoat, which he left at the scene of the attack by the dog. Thus reminded of Arbuton's risking his life to save her from serious injury, Kitty leaves Quebec more miserable than ever. She will return to Eriecreek and work out her destiny there.

Miles Arbuton, ship captain, cooper, English couple, Fanny Ellison, Kitty Ellison, Colonel Richard Ellison, French-Canadian guide, two Boston ladies, nuns.

"The Chick of the Easter Egg," 1906 (in *Between the Dark and the Daylight,* 1907).

At a New York club, Newton, Halson's friend from Boston, reminisces about the Easter eggs of his Southwestern boyhood, and tells an incident from his Boston years. In search of a milder March climate and curious about the Moravians, he took his family to Bethlehem, Pa. On Easter morning Newton went, alone, to the sunrise ceremonies at the old Moravian cemetery. Later he took his family around the old town and showed them Easter eggs and rabbits. The children received eggs as gifts and "fought" them, by banging them together until one was left as uncracked champion. They took that one back to Boston and put it under a hen even though it was a hard-boiled egg. When it was eaten by a predator, Newton bought his wife a hat, with his children's connivance. The hat was the "chick." The confirmed bachelors at the club enjoy this desultory family story.

Acton, Minver, Newton, Rulledge, Wanhope.

"Christmas Every Day," 1886 (in *Christmas Every Day and Other Stories Told for Children,* 1893).

A papa tells his small daughter a story about a little girl who wants it to be Christmas every day of the year. The day before Christmas the Christmas Fairy answers her letter and grants her request. The little girl is very happy and finds eternal Christmas wonderful at first, but the adults find the repetitions of Christmas ever more boring, and the national economy is turned topsy-turvy by the endless demand for trees, turkeys, and presents. Eventually everyone becomes very cross, and the little girl wishes she could withdraw her request. Finally, on the next true Christmas Day, the Fairy relents and lets Christmas come just once a year.

Christmas Fairy, little girl in the story, little girl to whom the story is told, Mother, papa.

"A Circle in the Water," 1895 (in *A Pair of Patient Lovers,* 1901).

On a dreary November day (probably in the 1880's), Basil March, the narrator, broods by a pool at an old ruin near his rented New England country cottage; he dwells on the mortality of fame and good, and the seeming immortality of infamy and evil. Spreading and dying circles in the water, apparently made by a leaping fish, seem to support his feeling, until he sees a man throwing stones into the water. The man turns out to be Tedham, who, one learns little by little, worked in March's Boston insurance agency, embezzled money, tried to put the blame on March, was caught and convicted, served a ten-year term, and has just been released. Long a widower, Tedham wants to see his daughter, who was nine when he went to prison, but March doesn't know where she is and doesn't want to help Tedham find her by inquiring of Tedham's sister-in-law, Mrs. Hesketh, who lives near Boston and has been caring for the girl. March feels that he has done all that he can for Tedham by forgiving him, but Tedham sees March as his only friend.

When March takes Tedham home, Isabel March is very severe against Tedham, but politely invites him to stay for dinner. Tedham says that he hasn't seen or heard from his daughter for ten years, has expiated his crime, and feels that he has a right to see the girl, but Isabel refuses to intercede for him with Mrs. Hesketh. Arguing for the solidity of families, Basil says that she should help, and finally she agrees. When the Marches see Mrs. Hesketh, she says that she is over her once implacable loathing for Tedham, but still can't bear to see him. She tells the Marches that after Tedham's conviction she moved to Canada for four years to get away from the notoriety and left Tedham's daughter in a convent school there; later she felt guilty about thus separating the girl from her father. Eventually Mrs. Hesketh agrees to let Tedham come to see the girl the next night.

Tedham shocks the Marches by saying that he now agrees with them that he shouldn't see his daughter. Isabel tries to argue him into doing so, or into letting his daughter make the decision, but Tedham is adamant, and tells the Heskeths so. Next evening the Heskeths startle the Marches by calling with Tedham's daughter, a ladylike beauty who is pathetically eager to see her father. The Marches are miserable, and Hesketh is sure that he and his wife erred in keeping the girl from her father. Suddenly Tedham arrives and confronts his daughter.

Later they meet from time to time, but live apart. Several years later the girl marries a young Englishman she met in Canada; they live in England, with Tedham. The Marches agree that evil can be killed by love, man thus getting a glimpse of the universal divine compassion.

Daughter of Basil and Isabel March, daughter of Tedham, Hesketh, Mrs. Hesketh, Basil March, Isabel March, Tedham.

The Coast of Bohemia, 1893.

At the county fair in Pymantoning, Ohio, Walter Ludlow, a young artist from New York staying with his friends the Burtons, enjoys the colorful outdoor scene, but is pained by the amateur sketches on display. He sees a young girl in a red dress tearing up her drawings over her mother's objections. She tells him that her daughter, Cornelia, who is only fifteen, has been drawing since childhood. Ludlow says that with his help Cornelia could get into a New York art school, the Synthesis of Art Studies. Cornelia, however, feels that Ludlow is simply making fun of her. The Burtons tell Ludlow that she is Cornelia Saunders and her mother a widowed dressmaker. Though Cornelia's work shows talent, Ludlow says he would rather see her happily married than studying art.

Ludlow's painting of the fair does not sell. Five years pass. Cornelia has a minor love affair (with J. B. Dickerson, an art-goods salesman who marries someone else) and teaches school for a while, but finally, after many hesitations, decides to go to New York. Mrs. Burton, who has been urging her on, does not reveal that she has written to Ludlow, who told her to keep Cornelia at home. Ludlow does arrange lodgings for Cornelia with a Mrs. Montgomery. At the station in New York the bewildered Cornelia is met by Ludlow (by arrangement with Mrs. Burton), and is grateful, yet vexed at being treated like a child. Ludlow then rushes off to dinner with General Westley and his beautiful second wife (at whose house the characters often meet later).

Accepted in the lowest grade at the Synthesis, Cornelia has an awkward time at first, but makes friends with Charmian Maybough, a rich student, and begins to feel more at home. At the Mayboughs' elegant apartment she meets Plaisdell, their decorator, and Wetmore, a portrait painter, who arrives with Ludlow. Cornelia finds Ludlow very handsome and feels awkward with him. She refuses an invitation to his studio, but, even so, the romantic Charmian starts rumors about the two. When Ludlow shows that he respects Cornelia as an artist, she likes him better, and (chaperoned) visits his studio. Later, while upset by an encounter with the now-divorced Dickerson, Cornelia refuses Ludlow's invitation to paint Charmian along with him, but finally accepts, at Charmian's insistence, and enjoys the Bohemian atmosphere and the discussions with Ludlow in Charmian's studio.

When the two girls look at Ludlow's painting of Charmian, they realize that it is actually a portrait of Cornelia; so does Wetmore. Mrs. Westley tells Ludlow that Cornelia is so beautiful that if she were painting Charmian she would be afraid of putting Cornelia into the picture; later Wetmore admits to Ludlow what he saw. Ludlow says that he has seen the resemblance himself and has painted it out. He now tells Cornelia that he has abandoned the portrait as a failure, and offers to help her exhibit her own work, but the two find themselves embarrassed and alienated. Ludlow tells Mrs. Westley that perhaps Mrs. Maybough should take Cornelia's portrait of Charmian, since his personal feelings ruin his portraits of women. When Ludlow asks Cornelia to go on with Charmian's portrait, she is uncertain, and he feels rebuffed.

As Dickerson begins to pursue her again, Cornelia resumes her work on Charmian's portrait under Ludlow's supervision. After sketching Charmian again, he tells Cornelia that he realizes why his earlier portrait looked like Cornelia, and confesses his love, but she says she doesn't care for him and runs away. She feels that she gave Dickerson the impression that she cared for him and therefore she has made any relationship with Ludlow impossible. She writes Ludlow confessing her love but insisting that she can't see him and can't tell him why.

Submitted to the Exhibition on Ludlow's advice, Cornelia's portrait of Charmian is rejected. When Ludlow comes to apologize for his mistaken advice, he and Cornelia end up in each other's arms. Later Cornelia wishes she had told him about Dickerson. Dickerson writes Ludlow a nasty letter referring to his "little affair" with Cornelia. Ludlow sends Cornelia the letter, but the next morning he calls, and tells her he doesn't believe Dickerson's letter; she confesses the whole story, and they are reconciled. They are married in Pymantoning. He paints a picture of her as he first imagined her, half girl and half crimson hollyhock, and sells the picture to Mrs. Maybough, which makes Cornelia angry. The artists in New York

recognize the identity of the beautiful hollyhock and tell Cornelia
that she will be in all of her husband's paintings from now on.

> Agnew, Dr. Brayton, James Burton, Mrs. Polly Burton, J. B.
> Dickerson, janitress, Katy, Lida, Walter Ludlow, Charmian
> Maybough, Mrs. Maybough, Mrs. Montgomery, Plaisdell,
> Mrs. Rangeley, Cornelia Saunders, Mrs. Saunders, General
> Westley, Mrs. Westley, Wetmore, Mrs. Wetmore.

"The Critical Bookstore," 1913 (in *The Daughter of the Storage* 1916).

Frederick Erlcort asks Miss Prittiman, a sales girl in a New York
department-store bookshop, to recommend a good book. Miss
Prittiman suggests a novel, but when Erlcort asks whether he can
return it if he is dissatisfied, she consults Mr. Jeffers, the floorwalker. He says a book that has been read is a used article which
cannot be returned like other merchandise. Erlcort reads the publisher's glowing advertisement, buys the book, and starts reading it
on the subway, but it is so boring that he gives it to the subway
guard.

Erlcort visits Margaret Green, a painter friend, and tells her about
his plan for a critical bookstore. He will read all the new books to see
whether they are worth stocking. He buys a hardware store from an
"old codger," and Margaret helps him to decorate it. A "Leading
Society Woman at the Intellectual Club" invites Erlcort to speak
about his project, and a girl journalist writes it up for the Sunday
supplement. Erlcort begins his reading, and also consults the critics;
he finds their judgment good, but he realizes that book buyers pay
little attention to reviews. When he opens his shop, he finds out
that customers want to buy what *they* want, not what he recommends as worthwhile. He also has trouble with volunteer readers;
they are offended if he does not accept their recommendations.
However, one lady customer is very pleased with his stock, and he
begins to sell books. But then he has problems with authors who
come to see whether their books are stocked and occasionally argue
when they are not. Erlcort longs for a visit from Margaret. When she
comes she suggests that he stock the major magazines. Though they
sell very well, he is worried by their mixture of good and bad material and finally censors one issue with printer's ink. When Margaret
tells him that he is going crazy, he agrees, tells her he is selling the

store to the author of a best seller, and asks her to marry him. The new owner plans to have customers vote for the best books.

> An author, authors, the old codger, lady customers, four elderly men customers, Frederick Erlcort, little girl, Margaret Green, subway guard, Jeffers, girl journalist, young novelist, Miss Pearsall, Miss Prittiman, volunteer readers, the Leading Society Woman.

"The Daughter of the Storage," 1911 (in *The Daughter of the Storage,* 1916).

Ambrose Forsyth, a painter, and his wife are taking some of their things out of storage to send them to the country. Tata, their little daughter, unpacks a trunkful of toys in the corridor of the Constitutional Storage Safe-Deposit Warehouse. In the next room of the warehouse, Mrs. Bream, a wealthy woman, is putting her things into storage. Peter, her little boy, unpacks a trunkful of his toys and offers them all to Tata, but the little girl seems to ignore him. The Forsyths are embarrassed. That evening when Mrs. Forsyth asks Tata why she wouldn't give any of her toys to Peter, the child says that she wanted to give him all of them but couldn't decide whether she should give away her parents' gifts.

During the next ten or twelve years the Forsyths keep storing things in the warehouse. Tata, now called Charlotte, always knows what her mother wants to put in or take out of the trunks, but she can never decide about her own possessions. When Charlotte is almost eighteen she meets Peter Bream again in the warehouse. He tells Mrs. Forsyth that he admires her husband's paintings, and she invites him to tea. Charlotte and Peter keep seeing each other at the warehouse and elsewhere. Peter tells her that he has been in love with her since the day she wouldn't give him any of her toys, but she rejects his proposal. When he sails for England, she sends him a letter changing her mind. After his mother's death in England, he returns to New York, but Charlotte cannot decide when to get married; then one day she decides that they must get married immediately. They ask Rev. Vanecken, an old acquaintance at the warehouse and a Presbyterian minister, to perform the ceremony. Since it is too late for a church wedding that day, they get married in the reception room of the warehouse.

Peter Bream, Mrs. Bream, Ambrose Forsyth, Charlotte ("Tata") Forsyth, Mrs. Forsyth, the manager, Rev. Vanecken, Mrs. Vanecken, the Misses Vanecken.

The Day of Their Wedding, 1896.

As her train arrives in Fitchburg, Mass., Sister Althea Brown, a pretty, shy girl, is joined by Lorenzo Weaver, a gauche young man. Rejecting the Shaker doctrine of celibacy, they have run away from the Shaker Family at Harshire, where they have both lived since childhood, to get married. She is very nervous about leaving the Family; he reassures her with an air of great confidence, largely assumed. They are headed for Saratoga Springs, New York, where they will be married, after which Lorenzo will work with a patent-medicine manufacturer.

At Saratoga Springs they walk timidly about, eat breakfast in a dingy café, and in ignorance fail to tip the waiter. Lorenzo buys Althea some elegant clothes, and lets an impudent carriage driver show them the town, which thrills and scandalizes them. After some impertinences he obeys Lorenzo's orders to take them to a minister, who questions them closely to make sure they really want to be married, and to learn about Shaker life. The minister's defense of marriage makes Althea more nervous than ever, and she insists that they go off and reconsider.

On the street they are set upon by the same carriage driver, who is sure they are now married and insists on taking them to the Grand Union Hotel. Listening awestruck to the band in the hotel courtyard, they meet a Mrs. George Cargate, a vivacious young woman on her honeymoon whose husband has been called away for a few days. Lorenzo registers, awkwardly. Althea doesn't want to take her hat off and enter the dining room of the hotel, because she is shy about her short hair. Mrs. Cargate reassures her and helps them. They dine, but again Lorenzo leaves no tip and Mrs. Cargate must enlighten them about tipping. Then Mrs. Cargate takes Althea off to go shopping.

After Althea returns late in the day, they sit in a park and reminisce about the Shaker Family and the ways in which they came to love each other. Althea tells Lorenzo what Mrs. Cargate said about her lightning courtship; Lorenzo finds it faintly disgusting. They are embarrassed to realize that they first fell in love with each other's looks. Lorenzo says that their love must begin with the outside, and that they will love each other's souls more and more. Mollified, Althea pulls him off toward the minister's. He fetches his wife and marries Lorenzo and Althea. Althea is upset that it's so simple.

As they leave the minister's house, Lorenzo finds that he is almost penniless. They decide to return to Fitchburg at once. At the hotel Althea puts her Shaker garb back on and says that the Family influence is too strong for her to leave it. After a painful discussion, they decide to return and live in the Family separately.

> Althea Brown, Mrs. George Cargate, hotel clerk, carriage driver, old man, minister, minister's wife, Pullman porter, saleswomen, waiters, Lorenzo Weaver.

"A Day's Pleasure," 1870 (in *Suburban Sketches*, 1871).

I. The Morning. After long planning, a family in Charlesbridge, a Boston suburb, begin a day trip to the outer reaches of Boston Harbor. The mother stays home, but Cousin Lucy and Aunt Melissa go along. "I," the narrator, comments and digresses throughout. The group takes an early train to Boston. After rushing across town, they find that they have just missed the Nantasket boat and must wait five hours for the next one.

II. The Afternoon. The family travels by boat across Boston Harbor to Nantasket in order to see the beach. They have a good picnic lunch on board. At Nantasket it is cool, so they stay on board and never get to the beach. The boat goes aground but finally gets away and returns to Boston.

III. The Evening. The family returns home to find a lost child there, tended by Sallie, the mother of the family. Frank, the father of the family, notifies the police. The child's father finally turns up, thus making the day a success despite its many disappointments.

> Frank's small child, a lost child, slum children, the father of the lost child, Frank, "I" (the narrator), Cousin Lucy, Aunt Melissa, the nurse of Frank's child, fellow passengers, police officers, Sallie, ticket sellers.

"A Difficult Case," 1900 (in *A Pair of Patient Lovers*, 1901).

Clarence Ewbert is a minister in the New England town of Hilbrook, originally West Mallow, renamed for Josiah Hilbrook, a native who became rich in New York and left his money to establish Hilbrook University in his home town. Ewbert is of Hilbrook's sect, nicknamed the "Rixonites," after the founder seventy years earlier, Rev. Adoniram Rixon. Mrs. Ewbert mildly dislikes the nickname and the sect, though she has dutifully joined it. She wants her husband to proselytize among the university faculty, but he is preoccupied with Ransom Hilbrook, Josiah's now elderly cousin, who lives as a recluse in the family homestead. The sight of battlefield dead in the Civil War killed his belief in immortality, but he knows a great deal of religious philosophy, as Ewbert found out when he tried and failed to argue Hilbrook into belief.

Mrs. Ewbert now finds Hilbrook a burden on Ewbert; indeed, Hilbrook's doubts have begun to disturb Ewbert's own beliefs. Arguing the question at length, again, Hilbrook says that everything, including souls, wears out, and that he doesn't want to live again anyway, but is afraid to die because of the possibility that there might really be an afterlife, a repetition of life. Ewbert sympathizes with Hilbrook but still believes that there will be a worthwhile afterlife. Later Hilbrook says that he now believes that there is some kind of permanent soul in him, but that he still wants to be shown that afterlife will be better than life. Ewbert argues that our souls in any kind of afterlife will be simpler and better than now. He is worn out by these arguments with Hilbrook, who seems rejuvenated, as if he is draining force from Ewbert. Finally Hilbrook accepts the afterlife and thanks Ewbert. Now Mrs. Ewbert will not let her husband see Hilbrook at all. She sends Ewbert to the seacoast for a rest.

After he returns he finds that Hilbrook has rejected everything he agreed to earlier. Hilbrook becomes apathetic, refuses to eat, wastes away, and dies. Mrs. Ewbert regrets the time that Ewbert spent on Hilbrook, but Ewbert feels that he had to make the effort.

> Doctor, Rev. Clarence Ewbert, Mrs. Emily Ewbert, fish man, Ransom Hilbrook, Mrs. Stephson.

Dr. Breen's Practice, 1881.

Jocelyn's is a pleasant, quiet New England coastal resort, consisting of a hotel, a beach, and lots laid out but never built on after

the hard times of the 1870's. Staying there with her friend and patient, Louise Maynard, from Wyoming, is Grace Breen, M.D., a
newly qualified homeopathic physician who rather dislikes medicine but turned to it with puritan determination to do good and to
occupy herself after an unhappy love affair. At twenty-eight, she
has given up hope of enjoying life. Being well off, she treats Mrs.
Maynard out of an often-strained sense of duty and friendship. Mrs.
Maynard, a silly, complaining woman who met Dr. Breen at an Eastern boarding school, has come to Jocelyn's to get away from her irritating husband and to be looked after by Dr. Breen at the latter's
expense. Dr. Breen's mother is also with her.

Mrs. Maynard talks with indelicate intimacy with Mr. Libby, a
handsome young visitor in the neighborhood. Mrs. Maynard also
chats with Barlow, the garrulous handyman, and with Dr. Breen;
she accuses the latter of being, as a doctor, more unconventional
than she is. Dr. Breen is troubled by this but keeps her temper and
advises Mrs. Maynard to avoid intimacy with Mr. Libby. The latter,
after some sparring with Dr. Breen, takes Mrs. Maynard sailing.
Dr. Breen does not want her to go; and therefore, with puritan logic,
forces her to go. Dr. Breen tells her mother she finds Mrs. Maynard a
burden and would prefer her cherished scheme of practicing among
the poor in Fall River. She discusses at length the problems of being
a woman doctor. In the afternoon a storm comes up, Libby's boat is
overturned off shore, but after some perilous moments he and Mrs.
Maynard are rescued. Dr. Breen blames herself and accepts Mrs.
Maynard's accusations.

Next day Mrs. Maynard coughs up blood and demands a doctor,
"a man doctor." Dr. Breen considers the blood trivial, and refuses to
consult with another physician, but is willing to relinquish the case
completely to the local allopathic physician. Wearing a friend's evening clothes, Libby comes to inquire about Mrs. Maynard. Dr.
Breen is contrite about getting him into this clothesless fix; Libby is
contrite about not calling her "Doctor," though she prefers "Miss."
He invites her for a buggy ride, but offends her by making fun of
Mrs. Maynard. The latter grows quite ill, and Dr. Breen, watching
her through the night, is dismayed.

Next morning Miss Gleason, a feminist boarder, urges Dr. Breen
not to call in a male doctor, though all the other women boarders
want her to. Libby drives Dr. Breen to Corbitant, the nearest town,
to consult with Dr. Mulbridge, an allopath. Enroute Libby is skepti-

cal about the seriousness of Mrs. Maynard's condition, and takes
Mr. Maynard's side against her. At Corbitant Dr. Mulbridge puts
Dr. Breen off with his cool, sardonic manner. Finally she realizes
that he has not looked at her card, does not know that she is a physician, and thinks that she is the patient. After she sets him straight,
he is apologetic but amused, and agrees to come to see Mrs. Maynard. When he hears that Dr. Breen is a homeopath, however, he
refuses to come, for "disciplinary" reasons. Dr. Breen's cold disapproval of his attitude and manner flusters him greatly. Finally,
because she believes that Mrs. Maynard is very ill, she relinquishes
the case, and Dr. Mulbridge agrees to take over with Dr. Breen acting as nurse. Mrs. Maynard objects to having Dr. Mulbridge, but
submits to his expert diagnosis, which indicates pneumonia. Libby
telegraphs to Mr. Maynard to come East. The lady boarders dissect
the situation. Dr. Breen confesses to Dr. Mulbridge that she insisted
on Mrs. Maynard's going out in the sailboat; Dr. Mulbridge ridicules her feelings of responsibility, and orders her to rest.

Libby's friends leave, but he stays on, and waits upon Dr. Breen
tactfully. He takes her in his sailboat to Leyden, a nearby coastal
town. She enjoys the sail, and they grow more intimate. At Leyden
they hear that Maynard has just started East from Cheyenne. On the
return sail they discuss their plans and hopes for the future. In an
emotional moment Libby blurts out that he loves her; much dis-
composed, she tries to make him drop the subject. The wind dies,
and she blames him for it. In the emotion of the moment they settle
that neither of them believed there would be a storm on the day of
Mrs. Maynard's disastrous sail. He vows to leave Jocelyn's now that
Dr. Breen has rejected him, but to the embarrassment of both he
must carry her ashore when the tide falls and leaves them stranded.
Dr. Breen discusses Libby with her mother, who censures them
both. Dr. Breen finds Mrs. Maynard quite ill and even more crabby
than usual; she even looks forward to her husband's arrival. She
grows worse, and Dr. Breen and Libby help the skilful Dr. Mulbridge through the long crisis. That past, Mrs. Maynard graciously
forgives Dr. Breen for causing (she thinks) the illness.

Maynard arrives. He turns out to be not an ogre but a pleasant,
disheveled Westerner who suffers from insomnia and indigestion.
Libby goes, as agreed earlier, and Dr. Breen finds herself strangely
lonely. Dr. Mulbridge and his sterile village life are described. He
comes from an old New England family of hard, solitary skeptics.

His mother dislikes Dr. Breen, but he begins to praise her highly, and finally tells his mother that he wants to marry her. His mother thinks that Dr. Breen won't find him socially good enough; that angers Dr. Mulbridge and hardens his intention to propose.

During her convalescence Mrs. Maynard is reconciled with her husband. Dr. Breen finds Maynard uncouth but likable. He plans to take Mrs. Maynard back West to recuperate, and suggests that Dr. Breen come along and practice there. He tells of Libby's self-effacing courage in saving the lives of two climbers in the Alps. During a long talk with Dr. Mulbridge, Dr. Breen tells him that she has given up medicine; she never liked it, and Mrs. Maynard's rejection of her convinced her that women would never trust her as a doctor (she assumes that most of her patients would be women). Dr. Mulbridge proposes to her on the basis that she would continue practice and with his help would succeed. She declines; she feels that she does not and cannot love him, and could not be of professional help to him. In his overbearing way Dr. Mulbridge tries to convince her of his respect for her. She feels frightened and unsure of herself, and forces him to hold the matter in abeyance. Dr. Breen talks Dr. Mulbridge over with her mother, who regrets her daughter's new indifference to serious life and her yearnings for frivolity. Dr. Breen tries to get in touch with Libby, who is somewhere nearby, no one is sure where. She writes him a note, but lacks the courage to send it. She sits in Libby's dory and waits for the daily carryall from the depot so she can send the letter to Libby. He arrives unexpectedly in the carryall. In an emotional, confused conversation she asks him for advice on what to do about Dr. Mulbridge, and finally blurts out that she loves Libby. He still loves her, of course, but had been too discreet to offer himself a second time.

Next day Dr. Mulbridge reappears and won't accept Dr. Breen's repeated refusals. Finally she drives him away by saying that she is engaged to Libby. Dr. Mulbridge returns home in a daze. The loafers in the general store in Corbitant exchange sardonic remarks about his case. Mrs. Maynard is astounded at Dr. Breen's news; she was sure that Dr. Breen would marry Dr. Mulbridge. Some time later, after marriage and travel in Europe, the Libbys settle in the New Hampshire mill town where Libby's father has bought mills for Libby to manage and where Dr. Libby practices medicine not out of enthusiasm but out of a puritan need to keep busy and do good works.

Mrs. Alger, Barlow, Dr. Grace Breen, Mrs. Breen, Mrs. Frost, Miss Gleason, Jane, Libby, Bella Maynard, Louise Maynard, Maynard, Mrs. Merritt, Dr. Mulbridge, Mrs. Mulbridge, Mrs. Scott, telegraph operator, townsfolk at the general store, wagon driver.

"Doorstep Acquaintance," 1869 (in *Suburban Sketches*, 1871).

"I," the narrator, ruminates about the many people who come to his house and street in the quiet Boston suburb of Charlesbridge. Most of them are Italians.

"I" (the narrator), old Genoese lady, organ-grinders, scissors grinder, a Triestine, a genteel war veteran, a starch-peddling war veteran, "Widow" of Giovanni Cascamatto.

"Editha," 1905 (in *Between the Dark and the Daylight*, 1907).

War is in the air, and Editha Bascom, a lovely young woman, is eager for it, as she awaits her lover George Gearson at lunch time in a small town in New York State. When he arrives he says that war has been declared; she is ecstatic but he is thoughtful. She has never been able to understand his contempt for war; she feels that a man who wins her must do something to deserve her, but George never has. Now is his chance and hers, she feels. She parrots jingoistic newspaper phrases at him; he insists on being rational and ironic. Eventually he concludes that he should want what she wants, but he goes back to work with nothing decided.

Editha's mother hopes that George won't go, but Editha hopes that he will. To persuade him she plans to send back her engagement ring and mementoes with a letter telling him to keep them until he enlists, but she decides to hold the package for a while in case George does the right thing. She is justified in this decision when George arrives that evening with the news that he has willy-nilly led the pro-war speakers at the town meeting and is to be the captain of the local volunteers. He is almost hysterical with a mixture of mob feeling and self-disgust. When he leaves she gives him the letter, to show him how serious she has been. Now they are almost strangers to each other. Editha's father is amused by George's excitement and pooh-poohs the idea of war. Next day George, much calmer, asks Editha to help his widowed mother, who opposes war.

When George leaves, he again asks Editha not to forget his mother. Editha writes Mrs. Gearson, who is not well enough to reply. Then word comes that George is dead, killed in one of the first skirmishes. Editha pines, but to her surprise doesn't die, and eventually goes with her father to Iowa to see Mrs. Gearson, who surprises Editha with her cold bitterness and irony. Mrs. Gearson derides Editha's eagerness to send George off to kill other young men, and Editha's assumption that George would suffer only some trifling glamorous wound and return to her in glory. Mrs. Gearson concludes that she is glad that George was killed before he could kill, and attacks Editha for wearing mourning.

That summer a visiting lady painter consoles Editha: the war was good for the country, Editha's behavior was exemplary, and Mrs. Gearson was "vulgar." At this final word Editha has an epiphany; her misery falls away, and she is able once again to live in the ideal.

> Editha Bascom, Bascom, Mrs. Bascom, George Gearson, Mrs. Gearson, lady painter.

"Editor's Easy Chair," *Harper's Monthly*, December 1900 — April 1920.

Only those "Easy Chairs" are summarized that are basically or preponderantly fictional. Many "Easy Chairs" were reprinted, some under different titles, in *Imaginary Interviews* (1910) and *The Daughter of the Storage* (1916); see "Chronological List of Howells' Fiction."

D 00. With the Easy Chair itself, "I" (Howells) chats about his feelings upon resuming the Chair after its eight-year absence from the magazine.

Ap 03. The Unreal Editor talks to a rejected contributor who wrote an essay about vaudeville.

S 03. At various stages in their marriage Florindo and Lindora vacation at the seashore or boarding farms, in the mountains or Europe, or in their own cottage. Beforehand they often quarrel about their vacations, and afterwards they are never fully satisfied with them.

My 04. The editor imagines that a reader accompanies him to *L'Elisir d'Amore* and reacts to it as the editor did when he first saw it forty years earlier in Venice.

N 04. Eugenio, a famous author, advises young writers that the secret of writing fiction is hard work, especially patient attention to the process of writing, which cannot be mechanical, but must develop organically.

My 05. Eugenio comments on the criticism of his (Howells') work. He wonders if he is repeating himself in his fiction. He would prefer his critics to be older ones, familiar with all his work. As a critic himself, he has never been completely satisfied with his reviews of other writers.

Jl 05. Eugenio tells the Easy Chair that as a beginning writer he ran out of subjects because he felt that only he was interesting, but he found plenty of topics when he realized that all people are interesting. An essayist, he thinks, can have the same experience because his subject matter is so large.

Ag 05. Eugenio eavesdrops on a pair of young lovers, an unemployed fictional hero and heroine, conversing on a park bench. They complain that short-story writers are no longer interested in nice, middle-class American ladies and gentlemen, but in foreign or abnormal or lower-class characters. Eugenio longs to reassure them that normal heroes and heroines will be popular again.

Jl 06. At a famous seaside resort Eugenio finds nothing in the guests to kindle his imagination. A friend points out that all the old American types have been replaced by a new type, the "world-bourgeoisie."

Ag 06. The Veteran Novelist's great-niece has just finished reading one of his stories and criticizes its lack of epigrams and passion. He confesses to her that as an old man he has outlived love and perhaps ought to write love stories only from an old man's point of view.

D 06. Imagining himself to be a "Greek of the mind," the Easy Chair observes many different types of people during a trip in New England.

Mr 07. Two old poets wonder if good poems are lost in the mass of mediocre poems published in magazines, but a careful survey of many magazines fails to turn up any good poems.

My 07. The Easy Chair and an imaginary famous author discuss ways that unknown writers can get into print.

Jl 07. The Easy Chair, a poet, and the poet's muse discuss spring, youth, and old age.

S 07. The Easy Chair and a visiting friend discuss the fact that one's conscience always accuses him when he does wrong but never praises him when he does good.

O 07. The Easy Chair pretends to be a young reporter assigned to cover the arrival of a liner and trying to describe the scene at the pier. Halfway through, he abandons this persona because the reporter is too young to remember what he remembers about the emotions of homecoming Americans.

Ja 08. The Editor and the satirical reader discuss the difficulty of civilities between employers and servants, and agree that employers ought to treat their servants as human beings.

Ap 08. Eugenio recalls in detail a voyage on the Great Lakes.

Je 08. He and she discuss the mixed motives of those trying to help the poor through organized charity.

Jl 08. When the Easy Chair and the veteran observer discuss "mental sclerosis" in critics, the former defends himself against the charge of having stiffened in his critical opinions.

O 08. Meeting in England, and comparing English and American life as material for fiction, the young novelist says that English social life is richer than American, and the old novelist insists that psychologically Americans are the most interesting people in the world.

D 08. "We" (the Easy Chair) and a friend just returned from Europe discuss the "caressing irony" of American manners, which European immigrants quickly acquire, and also discuss the fact that Americans who have been abroad develop even worse manners than they already have.

Ja 09. "We" (the Easy Chair) and a friend who has been in Boston discuss the way its puritan character persists in spite of the immigration there, and continues to beautify the city. New York, they agree, is just too big to be beautiful.

F 09. "We" (the Easy Chair) and a friend try to define the components of New York's "sublimity."

Mr 09. "We" (the Easy Chair) and the Howadji, his traveling friend, discuss the fact that living is cheaper in New York City than in the capitals of Europe.

Ap 09. "We" (the Easy Chair) and the Howadji discuss the problems of housing and household help in New York City, which would be the cheapest of great cities if rents weren't so high.

Je 09. "We" (the Easy Chair) and a visitor discuss the question of female suffrage and the position of women.

Jl 09. In an essay about music at mealtime, the Easy Chair shifts to a narrative of an elderly brother and sister on a steamboat on Long Island Sound who observe their fellow passengers at a concert.

Ja 10. Sitting on a park bench, two friends compare the Stoic and the Christian ideals of duty and analyze the way that conscience serves these ideals.

F 10. In the railroad station in Portland, Maine, a friend of the Easy Chair eavesdrops on a elderly village couple who yearn to ride in a parlor car. The incident makes him think about his European traveling experiences, which he later discusses with "we," the Easy Chair.

Mr 10. The Easy Chair's friend tells him a story about "Smith," a Scotch ex-convict who appeared at his house on Christmas Eve asking for money to live on until he could get back to Scotland. The friend gave "Smith" some money, but felt that he should have been paid by the state for his work in prison. The Easy Chair argues ironically that his unpaid labor was his punishment and a deterrent from future crime. When "Smith" returns to ask for more money, the friend concludes that perhaps he isn't really an ex-convict.

Ap 10. After the friend of "we" (the Easy Chair) has overheard two girls in the park discussing a gentleman caller, the friend and the Easy Chair imagine the caller as a poet, and then discuss New York City as a source of poetic inspiration.

My 10. The Easy Chair and his other self discuss writers and books about smart society.

Je 10. At a dinner party, the host, the hostess, an elderly bachelor, a girl, a stopgap guest, two husbands, and two ladies discuss marriage and divorce; later the wife of the stopgap guest wonders what the hostess thought of her husband's peculiar opinions.

Jl 10. The friend of "we" (the Easy Chair) describes a couple of thirtyish lovers he saw in the park, and the two men speculate about whether the pair were a divorced couple or not.

S 10. Continuing to discuss the lovers that the friend of "we" (the Easy Chair) saw in the park, the friend and the Easy Chair weave a story around the woman's brother, the lovers' bored chaperon.

O 10. The Easy Chair dreams that in London he and a young Bostonian observe the pretty riders in Hyde Park and discuss a suffragist meeting.

N 10. In a Scottish hotel the Easy Chair and a young Bostonian discuss a woman's book about hunting and conclude that hunting isn't something that women should be proud of enjoying.

D 10. With one of its oldest "separable selves," the Civil-War-era consul at Torcello, the Easy Chair recalls crossing the Atlantic during the Civil War. The consul refuses to remember anything dramatic enough for a Christmas number.

Ja 11. The Easy Chair and the ex-consul at Torcello discuss past and present ship travel, and the air travel of the future.

F 11. The Easy Chair and "our other self" discuss E. C. Stedman.

Ap 11. The Easy Chair and the reader discuss autobiographies, in general, and one by an American businessman.

S 11. With the poet, the philosopher, the novelist, and the editor, the Easy Chair discusses Havelock Ellis and his ideas of romantic love.

O 11. With the Good Citizen, the Easy Chair discusses the easy availability of firearms in America and the consequent rash of killings.

N 11. With the Cynic, the Easy Chair discusses implications, in a novel by Valdés, about the American system of justice.

F 12. With the Cynic the Easy Chair discusses women's suffrage.

Mr 12. As part of a discussion of American fiction, the Easy Chair describes a very old author who is upset by criticism of his work.

My 12. The Reviewer and the Easy Chair discuss ethical values in a capitalistic system.

Je 12. The Reviewer and the Easy Chair discuss publishing and an assortment of recent books.

Jl 12. The Cynic, the Reviewer, the Muse of Poetry, and the Easy Chair discuss the differences between poetry and prose.

Ag 12. At a Spanish hotel, American ladies, an American bachelor, an American pessimist, an American housekeeper, and a young artist conclude that America like Europe has the *mañana* habit.

O 12. At a New England mountain resort, guests discuss the automobile and its effects on modern life; one guest, Alverly, whose doctor accompanies him, once killed a child with his car, as he tells a philosophic guest.

N 12. In the presence of listeners, the Easy Chair, a lady, a suffragist, and a theorist discuss spiritualistic phenomena.

D 12. From the eighteenth century the Easy Chair calls up a Chinese philosopher to discuss the recent election.

F 13. Two travelers, an American and a European, discuss the conditions of travel in the two regions.

Ap 13. With the Easy Chair, the First and Second Citizens, both Americans, discuss Arnold Bennett's recent travel book about America, and earlier works in that genre.

N 13. With a favorite author the Easy Chair discusses the effect on readers of newspaper reports of murders and other horrors.

Ap 14. Observing and then identifying with an elderly man (aged fifty-eight) and an old man (aged eighty-five), the Easy Chair travels to London and notes similarities to and differences from the England of the past.

Je 14. An uncle and his niece discuss charities and doing good.

Jl 14. With the reader the Easy Chair discusses Romance and Realism in American literature as suggested by several recent books.

S 14. The Idealist tells the Easy Chair about the good treatment of a wrongly convicted person in the Commonwealth of Barataria.

O 14. Florindo and Lindora, an elderly pair, rent a summer cottage and try in vain to save money by buying everything direct from manufacturers; a philosophic native points out their errors.

Jl 15. The Easy Chair and an elderly sage discuss the staying power of books, and conclude that books live only as long as they are read.

O 15. Florindo and Lindora give a foodless party, to the dismay of their guests.

N 15. With the elderly sage the Easy Chair discusses recent novels of many nations and concludes that the best ones are American.

D 15. The week before Christmas the Easy Chair finds his study invaded by the Motley Crew, stereotyped characters in old-fashioned Christmas stories, with names like "the Homeless Boy" and "the Heartless Miser." They complain that they are out of work because magazine editors no longer take such stories. Their case is presented by the Psychosociologist, who lists the kinds of adventure plots such characters appear in. The Easy Chair promises to ask his contributors to go over Christmas stories of the past and give the Motley Crew work next year. They refuse the meal tickets that he offers them.

F 16. An elder sage, over eighty, and a younger sage chat in Central Park until the elder's granddaughter arrives with her young man and scolds him for not staying on the bench where he promised to wait.

Jl 16. The elder and the younger sage meet in Central Park and discuss the effects of being out of the city during the winter.

N 16. With an apparition, the nondescript presence, the Easy Chair discusses the ideas about republics in the October "Easy Chair."

D 16. During their summer at Lobster Cove, Florindo and Lindora enjoy the new state roads, which the hated motorcar has given them, and talk to an old gentleman and his daughter at the Pine Cone Inn, a country hotel.

Ja 17. Continuing their motor tour of Maine, Florindo and Lindora talk at another hotel with the old gentleman and his daughter, about the idea of state-run hotels for automobile travelers.

Mr 17. An elderly essayist discusses solecisms with a lady and his niece.

S 17. The Easy Chair and a sage discuss ways of talking about the War.

O 17. After having his pocket picked twice, twenty-three years apart, a train traveler thinks about thieves and their punishments, past and present, in reality and in fiction. He recalls that Christ said that money is the root of all evil, but very few people act as if they believed that.

Ja 18. The Easy Chair is visited by a lively lady, a young man, and other characters from modern Christmas stories, and discusses frankness in fiction with them.

My 18. With Citizens (First, Second, Third, etc.) the Easy Chair discusses various problems of cleanliness in public places.

S 18. In this thinly veiled allegory of World War I Altruria defeats Egoria and ends poverty through socialist legislation.

Ja 19. The younger sage and the older sage discuss the latter's passion for light reading and happy endings.

Ap 19. On their park bench the younger and the older octogenarian discuss the qualities of postwar life as suggested by the recent report of the Secretary of the Interior.

Jl 19. A returned winterer in the South discusses with the Easy Chair the American and European plans in hotels past and present.

S 19. The Easy Chair and a friend discuss implications of the Easy Chair's idea that people always get what they want when they want it.

N 19. After receiving an invitation to join a home-correspondence writing course, an aged author broods on ways of learning to write, and discusses the matter with a magazine editor.

F 20. "I," a friend of the editor, recalls his faithful servant Maria in San Remo. She was a hard-working sixty-year-old widow, who would tell her employers stories of her life. When they left they gave her what they couldn't take with them, hoping that these gifts redressed some of the inequalities between rich and poor.

Ap 20. A Martian couple visits "we" (the Easy Chair). They don't understand the recent World War because there has never been any war on Mars. The Martian lady thinks that American women consider shopping, like voting, the exercise of a public function, but the Easy Chair tells her that women aren't interested in politics. At the Easy Chair's suggestion the Martians give a public lecture. Although the Easy Chair warns them to confine themselves to a physical description of Mars, the Lady Martian starts lecturing on the Martian socialist government, the audience starts breaking up the hall, police arrest the Martians, and they are deported to Russia as Bolshevists.

Alverly, young artist, audience, aged author, famous author, very old author, American bachelor, elderly bachelor, young Bostonian, young Bostonian, brother of a young woman, elderly brother and sister, characters in modern Christmas fiction, first citizen, the good citizen, second citizen, citizens, rejected contributor, the Motley Crew, "the Cynic," daughter of old gentleman, doctor at a resort hotel, the Editor's Easy Chair, Editor, magazine editor, the unreal editor, elderly essayist, Eugenio, ex-consul for Torcello, Florindo, friend of the Easy Chair, friend of Eugenio, two friends, Martian gentleman, old gentleman, girl, two girls in Central Park, granddaughter, grandfather, the novelist's great-niece, a stopgap guest, guests at Lindora's party, guests at a resort hotel, "he," unemployed fictional hero and heroine, host and hostess, American housekeeper, "the Howadji," two husbands, "I," the Idealist, John and his wife, American ladies, two ladies, lady, lady, lively lady, Martian lady, Lindora, listeners, lovers, man aged eighty-five, man aged fifty-eight, young man, young man, Maria, Muse of poetry, the poet's Muse, philosophic native, niece, niece of elderly essayist, novelist, the old novelist, the Veteran Novelist, the young novelist, the veteran observer, older and younger octogenarians, the padrona, American pessimist, philosopher, eighteenth-century Chinese philosopher, poet, poet, two old poets, policemen, the nondescript presence, the Psycho-sociologist, the reader, the satirical reader, young reporter, the Reviewer, a sage, an elder sage, elderly sage, the sage, the younger sage, elder and younger sages, older and younger sages, our other self, "she," Smith, suffragist, theorist, train traveler, American and European travelers, uncle, visitor, "we", returned winterer.

"Editor's Study," *Harper's Monthly*, January 1886—March 1892.

Only those "Editor's Studies" are summarized that are basically or preponderantly fictional.

Ja 86. The unreal editor describes his gorgeous study, which overlooks the whole world and its literature, and gives his plans for conducting this department of the magazine.

D 90. Peering out its windows, the Study sees a vision of the future America, the Synthetized Sympathies of Altruria. Critics and Creative Authors, now friends, pass in review. Scrooge's boy (from *A Christmas Carol*) tells the Study that a decrepit but youthfully dressed man is the Last of the Romanticists, and an armored man firing blank cartridges at authors is the Anonymous Critic. Copyright laws, the boy says, now protect all authors. The Real and the Ideal, and the True and the Beautiful, perform allegorical dances. The Last of the Romanticists defends his kind of fiction. Visiting (foreign) and creative (Altrurian) authors embrace, celebrating copyright. Then the Study wakes up.

D 91. As Christmas approaches, the Study drowses off and finds himself looking out on a city square in the United Sympathies of Altruria where a celebration is going on. The Christmas Boy arrives with presents and tells the Study that the year is 2091, the bicentennial of the International Copyright Law, which protects literary property for fifty years. Every fifty years all property changes hands, on Christmas Day, because Altrurians believe that human equality is linked to limited tenure of property. The Study notes the relief of those renouncing property and the solemn air of responsibility of those receiving it. The latter, the boy explains, must share the enjoyment of the property with the former. The boy disappears and the Study awakes, happy to know that in 1891 everybody still keeps his property forever — except authors, who can keep theirs only for forty-two years.

Mr 92. On leaving the magazine, the Study observes the paulo-post-future, helped by the Christmas Boy, removing from the office all evidence of literary realism (e.g., a bust of Tolstoy) and replacing it with symbols of romanticism (e.g., a bust of Thackeray).

> Creative and visiting authors, Christmas boy, Scrooge's boy, anonymous critic, dramatic and literary critics, the Unreal Editor, the paulo-post future, the Last of the Romanticists, the Editor's Study.

"The Eidolons of Brooks Alford," 1906 (in *Between the Dark and the Daylight*, 1907).

At a club Wanhope tells a group of the strange experiences of Alford. After a morning watching the spray of falling shot during target practice at a coastal fort, Alford is telling others about it at lunch at the hotel when he sees the spray before him as an eidolon (realistic apparition). After discussing it with a Mrs. Yarrow, a widow, he goes to his room and sees an eidolon of her sitting there. On the train a few weeks later Alford sees, out the window, a scene from his earlier life, and when he turns away from the window, sees the whole car filled with eidolons, which vanish when the train stops and he meets Mrs. Yarrow. He begins to see her as his solace and to love her, but the summer passes and he says nothing, though he sees no more eidolons. After he leaves, he sees eidolons of her everywhere, and he disintegrates. His doctor suggests that he marry Mrs. Yarrow. He visits her, tells her about the visions, and proposes to her, adding that she helps him eliminate the visions. Rather irritated at being a prescription, she sends him away, but after talking with Alford's doctor, she accepts him.

> Brooks Alford, Dr. Enderby, Minver, Rulledge, Wanhope, gossipy women, Mrs. Yarrow.

"The Emigrant of 1802. A Chapter from an Unpublished History," 1854.

Signed "Lereo." M., a New England farmer, leaves his rocky native soil for fertile wilderness land in "New Connecticut" (the Western Reserve). Sadly yet cheerily Mrs. M. parts with her home. After a grueling winter journey the family arrive at their beautiful land on the shores of a lake (Erie), live in a crude log cabin, and with great efforts and some suffering establish their farm. (Based roughly on the migration of the Howellses to Ohio.)

Bragg, farmers, Lereo, M., Mrs. M.

"Entertaining on Thirty-Five Hundred a Year," 1903.
The higher journalist and his friend discuss the question of whether a man and his wife can entertain on $3500 a year. The journalist says that as long as they have no children they can afford a simple supper at home or a dinner for a dozen people in an unpretentious French restaurant. His friend retorts that in that case they ought to have children and not entertain.

The higher journalist's friend, the higher journalist.

"The Escapade of a Grandfather," in *The Daughter of the Storage* (1916). See "Editor's Easy Chair," February, 1916.

"An Experience," 1915 (in *The Daughter of the Storage*, 1916).
On a very hot, humid day "I," the narrator, an editor in a publisher's office, vaguely notices an insurance agent enter the large room where he and several other people are working. He returns to the manuscript he is reading. The hero of the story dies suddenly, and the editor muses on the subject of sudden death. The insurance agent has left the room, but suddenly he comes back, dazed by the heat, and collapses. Somebody runs for a doctor and finds one, but the man gradually stops breathing. The editor feels that the man's sudden death is not tragic, but dignified.

Insurance agent, doctor, employees in a publisher's office,
"I" (the narrator, an editor in a publisher's office).

"The Father," 1907 (in *The Whole Family*, 1908).
The father is Cyrus Talbert, the owner of the Plated-Ware Works

of Eastridge, and the benevolent despot of the village. He and the first-person narrator, Ned Temple, the owner of the Eastridge *Banner*, are neighbors. Over the fence they discuss the engagement of Talbert's daughter Peggy to a young man who hopes to be a professor. The engaged couple are students at a coeducational college. Temple describes Mr. Talbert and the other Talbert children — his elder and younger sons, and his older, married daughter.

Al, Dr. Denbigh, Mrs. Evarts, Cyrus Talbert, Mrs. Talbert, Peggy Talbert, Ned Temple, Mrs. Temple.

A Fearful Responsibility, 1881.

At the beginning of the Civil War, Owen Elmore, a history professor in a small college at Patmos, New York, loses his job when everyone enlists and the college closes. Elmore has bronchitis and can't enlist. With his wife he sails for Europe to write a history of Venice. Working in the libraries of Venice, Elmore soon realizes that it will take him many years to write a good history of the city. Venice is quiet, because the patriots are boycotting public activities, though the Austrians are polite. The Elmores reluctantly associate only with Venetians, who are dull, especially to Mrs. Elmore.

After eighteen months in Venice they learn that Lily Mayhew, a girl from Patmos, is coming to Venice for her health. Mrs. Elmore is pleased at the prospect of having company; Elmore gloomily considers it a fearful responsibility. They plan to go to Genoa to meet Lily, but Mrs. Elmore has a sick headache, and Elmore arranges to hire Cazzi, a *valet de place*, to bring her from the ship. He is helped in this arrangement by Hoskins, the American consul, who has recently replaced Ferris (see *A Foregone Conclusion*). Hoskins is a sculptor who has been invalided out of the war. Lily arrives, and Mrs. Elmore enjoys her company immensely, though Lily is six years younger. From Lily's gossip about Patmos, Elmore is disturbed to hear that America is vigorous and prosperous despite, indeed because of, the war. Lily tells Mrs. Elmore that she talked in the train with a dashing Austrian officer, Captain Ernst von Ehrhardt, who followed her all the way to Venice and gave her his card. The Elmores, much disturbed, hope to discourage anything further; the meeting was highly irregular by European standards, and besides, if the Elmores receive an Austrian, they will lose all their Italian friends.

Elmore glimpses Mrs. Elmore and Lily talking to an Austrian officer in the street. Mrs. Elmore tells him that she and Lily, while doing
their errands, met the officer, Lily's new acquaintance, in front of
the Stadt Gratz, a hotel. Elmore objects to their talking to the officer;
Mrs. Elmore defends it and him. Elmore speaks to Hoskins about it,
and Hoskins agrees to talk to the Austrian military governor and
have the officer reprimanded. Now that the affair is, he thinks,
squelched, Elmore feels more charitable toward Captain Ehrhardt
and the ladies. But then, to Elmore's consternation, Lily receives a
letter from Capt. Ehrhardt; the English is atrocious but the sentiments unmistakable. Elmore points out to Lily that if she were a European girl, an officer would write to her father, not to her. With
Lily's consent Elmore writes to the captain telling him to leave Lily
alone, and over Mrs. Elmore's objection that the letter is needlessly
harsh, sends it to him. Much relieved, Elmore shows Lily around
the usual tourist sights of Venice. Mrs. Elmore chides him for not
giving Lily parties and dances. Elmore objects that anything of that
sort is impossible because it would involve them with Austrians,
but consents to take the two ladies to dinner at the Hotel Danieli. At
the *table d'hôte* they see the British painter Rose-Black (from *The
Lady of the* Aroostook) and meet young Herbert Andersen, a shy
Dane smitten with Lily, and Andersen's aunt. Next morning Mr.
Rose-Black calls, coolly makes himself at home, and acts mad-
deningly superior to Americans.

In a letter Ehrhardt asks Elmore for Lily's hand. After much worried discussion the Elmores decide to speak to Lily about the matter.
She talks it over in a mature way, but her refusal of the Austrian is
full of ambiguities and agitation that Elmore fails to appreciate.
Elmore starts to write Ehrhardt a refusal, but Mrs. Elmore's lack of
strong support for his position irritates him, and he is glad to realize
that for a refusal Ehrhardt's letter requires no answer. But Mrs. Elmore continues to seem to support Ehrhardt in a devious way, and
Elmore, utterly exasperated, fires off a curt refusal to Ehrhardt.
Though the matter is now apparently settled, Elmore is still uneasy
at the fearful responsibility laid on him, which eventually drives
him to his bed. While he is ill the ladies see Rose-Black and the An-
dersens. Shortly after Elmore recovers, young Mr. Andersen calls on
Elmore, hands flowers and a souvenir turtle to him, talks to Lily on
the balcony, and then leaves suddenly. To Elmore's horror, his wife
tells him that the presents were for Lily, and that Andersen has pro-

posed to Lily and been refused. Elmore feels crushed by his responsibility for Lily, and broods about the pointlessness of human courtship.

Rose-Black's obnoxiousness gives the Elmores and Howells the chance to vent some anti-British opinions. When Rose-Black tries to flirt with Lily, she rebuffs him sharply, and he leaves for good. Elmore still worries about Ehrhardt. As time passes quietly, Hoskins escorts his American friends about the city. Elmore innocently compliments Hoskins on the American quality of a female figure in an allegorical statuary group that Hoskins has just finished. Another *faux pas*! As Mrs. Elmore severely tells her husband, Hoskins based the statue on Lily, and everyone except Elmore knew it and was trying to ignore the fact.

Hoskins helps Lily get an invitation to an elaborate masquerade ball. She dresses as Hoskins' allegorical figure "Westward," and does not return until late the morning after the ball, literally "danced to rags." After a talk with Lily, Mrs. Elmore describes the ball to her husband. Lily danced with a masked officer who seemed smitten and eventually kissed her hand. Elmore thinks it was Ehrhardt and is annoyed, but nothing more is heard of the matter. Now Lily is moody, Elmore doesn't know why. Reopening, Patmos University offers Elmore its presidency. Mrs. Elmore is eager to go; Elmore is reluctant to leave, but feels he could never write a really adequate history of Venice, and therefore accepts. Just before the three leave, Hoskins proposes to Lily. At first Elmore declines to write a letter of refusal for Lily, but eventually he gives in. They say a friendly goodbye to Hoskins at the station. During the long halt at Peschiera, where Ehrhardt is stationed, Elmore is nervous lest the Austrian appear, but he never does.

Back in Patmos, Elmore does his university work and publishes a slight book on Venetian history. Lily refuses her old American flame, whom she has outgrown. As she approaches thirty, Lily begins to have bad health and acts reproachful to Elmore, who feels that he erred in dismissing Ehrhardt so abruptly. Mrs. Elmore justifies his behavior, but still he is tortured. Lily takes a teaching position in Omaha, eventually marries a clergyman there, and lives quite happily. Elmore is the only one left worrying about Ehrhardt.

Herbert Andersen, Andersen's aunt, Captain Ernst von Ehrhardt, Mrs. Celia Elmore, Owen Elmore, Ferris, gondoliers, Hoskins, Lily Mayhew, an unknown Austrian officer, Austrian officers, Russian princess, Rose-Black.

"A Feast of Reason," in *The Daughter of the Storage* (1916). See "Editor's Easy Chair," October, 1915.

Fennel and Rue, 1908.

After years of struggle, Verrian, a serious writer living in New York with his mother, becomes a success with a serialized novel whose bitter quality attracts many letters, mostly from women. One such letter, from a young invalid, asks to know now the outcome of the story, because the writer may die before the ending is published. Verrian's mother agrees with him that he must show the letter to Armiger, his editor. Armiger reluctantly says they should make the girl prove her bona fides; she might be a crafty journalist or simply a fake. Armiger's firm has a little paragraph about the letter printed in the papers. Verrian hopes the girl doesn't see it; his mother wonders how simple the girl really is.

The girl, Jerusha Peregrine Brown, as she calls herself, writes Armiger saying that she wrote the letter to Verrian with a friend on a dare and now feels apologetic. Verrian, his vanity hurt, is furious. Verrian writes the girl a sharp, insulting letter and sends hers back to her. Mrs. Verrian condemns her son's vindictiveness. Though Verrian wanted to crush the girl, he still hopes for a reply. Meanwhile, his story is more popular than ever, and his publishers plan to bring it out as a book. Mrs. Verrian continues to worry that the girl's feelings may be hurt.

Verrian's novel earns him not only recognition both from knowledgeable readers and from the general public but also an invitation to a house party by a Mrs. Westangle, a stranger to Verrian. He goes to her house, Seasands, with Miss Julia Macroyd, an airy socialite; a well-dressed but ill and feeble young woman is also on the train. After Miss Macroyd commandeers the Westangle carriage at the station, Verrian shares a hired carriage to Seasands with the sickly girl, who is a Miss Shirley. She says she has not been out for six months, and is going to Seasands to work. Miss Shirley will be Mrs. Westangle's director of amusements. She is distressed when

Verrian doesn't change to a carriage sent to pick him up. At Mrs. Westangle's Verrian feels awkward until he attaches himself to Julia Macroyd and chats about the girl on the train.

Verrian feels awkward with Julia for coming with Miss Shirley from the station, but joins in the social chatter before dinner. Next morning Mrs. Westangle proposes a snow battle at a snow fort. Evidently, Verrian realizes, this is Miss Shirley's idea. After Verrian helps to get things going, the guests have great fun storming the snowcastle. Everyone congratulates Mrs. Westangle on her bright idea. Miss Shirley sends Verrian a note thanking him for his help at the fort. Verrian is annoyed with Miss Shirley for writing the note, and even more annoyed when Julia says that the others think he is Verrian the matinee idol (for whom the name is a stage name). He surprises Miss Shirley in the library arranging the stunt of having people react to a "ghost." After the two talk, Verrian finds himself puzzled and pleased with her. Next day Verrian finds that Miss Shirley plans a tea on the ice. A thaw threatens, but doesn't happen; the ice tea is a great success, and Mrs. Westangle a great success as a hostess. Mrs. Westangle, thinking Verrian is a newspaper writer, irritates him by asking him to help Miss Shirley get another engagement as social director. Bushwick, a guest and a real-estate man, says that Julia told him Mrs. Westangle has a professional assistant. Verrian tells Bushwick the truth; Bushwick says that he will try to help Miss Shirley succeed. At the ghost affair people are permitted to ask questions of the "ghost." Bushwick irritates Verrian by introducing the affair facetiously, but the guests take the questioning and the solemn answers more and more seriously. After a girl, Miss Andrews, asks earnestly if a falsehood can ever be undone, and after Verrian says he has no question, the "ghost" figure faints.

Having returned to the city, Verrian tells his mother that he has seen the girl who wrote the letter. Miss Shirley confessed that she was Jerusha Brown, or rather that she had written the first letter with a Jerusha Brown, a girl in the village where Miss Shirley was vacationing, and had herself written the second, apologetic letter, in Jerusha's name. Miss Shirley's guilt made her ill, and she had been unable to get well until she confessed to Verrian. His mother is deeply jealous of Miss Shirley. Later Verrian and his mother meet Miss Andrews and her mother. Mrs. Verrian finds Miss Andrews innocent and noble, and wants Verrian to marry her. He visits Miss

Andrews often, and hears that Bushwick is seeing Miss Shirley. When Verrian goes to see his namesake in a play, he finds himself sitting next to Miss Shirley; later she tells him that she is engaged to Bushwick, and that he, Verrian, was cruel for the letter he sent her and the sufferings that followed from it. With Verrian there she tells Bushwick all about the letter episode. Bushwick is angry at Verrian and stalks off with Miss Shirley. Verrian is upset, but is impressed with Miss Shirley, and refuses to follow his mother's wish and console himself with the earnest Miss Andrews.

Miss Andrews, Armiger, Jerusha Peregrine Brown, Bushwick, Julia Macroyd, Miss Shirley, Mrs. Stage, Verrian, Mrs. Verrian, Mrs. Westangle.

The Flight of Pony Baker. A Boy's Town Story, 1902.

In Howells' Boy's Town, in southwestern Ohio about 1850, Frank Baker, a boy of eight or nine nicknamed Pony because of his small size, feels entitled to run off because his mother is over-solicitous and his father won't let him have a gun or try to learn to smoke. Finally comes the last straw: his father makes Pony stay in school even though the teacher is mean to him. All the boys offer Pony advice on running off; Jim Leonard, a wily, imaginative, fatherless boy, suggests that Pony go live with the Indians. Once, when Jim took refuge on top of his mother's stable during a spring flood, the stable and Jim were washed away down the river, but Jim's panicky screams of "Fire!" aroused the town, and a man named Blue Bob rescued him. Later Jim Leonard persuaded the boys to raid Bunty Williams' watermelon patch, which he said (falsely) was abandoned. They all enjoyed themselves except for Pony, who thought it wasn't right, and Jim, who was nervous. When Bunty Williams chased them, they all escaped. Later in the day Pony got sick after cooking food over a fire with Jim. Now Jim advises Pony to run away, via canal, to an Indian reservation in northern Ohio. The boys urge Pony to take the canal boat owned by Piccolo Wright's father, but Pony thinks that's wrong.

One day several boatloads of Indians, being moved by the government, pass through Boy's Town, and Jim advises Pony to go with them; however, Pony forgets about running off when July 4 comes and he has a fine time. On one Fourth, Pony's cousin Frank went, as he told Pony, with his friend Jake Milrace to the farm of Dave Black's father at Pawpaw Bottom. They helped pile fence rails, and then had a good time playing in the fields and the river, but were perplexed to see several times a strange, elusive boy. Later, a Mrs. Foyle in Boy's Town said that she felt the presence of her dead son Wilford all day, and the boys realized whom they had seen.

In late July, Pony, again at odds with his mother, who is very jumpy for some unknown reason, decides to run away for sure, with the circus this time. A man with the circus teasingly tells Pony to be ready to go with them at 1 A.M., and Pony feels bound to do so, though he feels better about his mother now. After the circus performance, which Pony can't enjoy, Jim helps him pack. He and his mother are fully reconciled. He oversleeps and misses the circus, though he dreams that he goes out to join it and encounters a nightmare figure. His friends tease him about his failure. Pony now gets along fine with his parents, and would be content not to run off, but Jim keeps urging him to. Meanwhile Frank Baker is the talk of the town, for bringing $2,000 in cash home to the town from the nearby city, as a favor for a local merchant. Frank had numerous troubles en route, including a terrific storm and runaway horses, and was more anxious about the money than about his small brother, whom he had with him.

As September approaches, Jim is still after Pony to run off—on a raft, this time, down the river to the Ohio and thence to New Orleans. He makes Pony hide food in the hayloft and train his dog not to dig the food out. When another boy in the town runs off, Jim says Pony must do the same at once, and start alone. Jim himself keeps backing out. The evening before he is to run off, Pony feels wretched, and resentful of Jim. Late at night he creeps out to the barn and tries to sleep there, but only cries. His parents look for him all over town and finally find him in the hayloft. At dawn Mr. Baker finds Jim sneaking to the barn and takes him home to his mother, who makes him confess everything. Pony now gets along better with his parents. Instead of babying him, his mother babies his new little brother.

Frank Baker, Frank ("Pony") Baker, Henry Baker, Lucy Baker, Baker, Mrs. Baker, Hen Billard, Dave Black, Black, Blue Bob, Bushell, Mrs. Fogle, Archy (Old) Hawkins, Jim

Leonard, Mrs. Leonard, circus man, Jake Milrace, Trip, Bunty Williams, Piccolo Wright.

"Flitting," 1870 (in *Suburban Sketches*, 1871).

After a residence of four years, "I," the narrator, leaves Benecia Street, in suburban Charlesbridge, with much regret, and ruminates about moving in general.

"I" (the narrator).

A Foregone Conclusion, 1875.

In Venice, during the Austrian occupation and the early days of the American Civil War, Don Ippolito, a priest, visits Mr. Ferris, the American consul, in an attempt to get an American passport and sell America an ingenious cannon. Though sympathetic, Ferris points out that the passport can be given only to American citizens and that the ingenious cannon would blow up. Don Ippolito does know something practical—a little English—and hopes to get to America somehow. We learn that Ferris is consul solely because as a young painter he needed money, the position was open, and no one else wanted it. Ferris is baffled by Don Ippolito but doesn't let that feeling interfere with his pleasure in Venice as he goes to visit Miss Florida Vervain and her mother. Miss Vervain is the beautiful, proud daughter, aged seventeen, of an American army officer, now dead, who named her after the state where he had fought and been stationed. Mrs. Vervain is forty-eight, fragile, and rather scatterbrained. Ferris escorts them on a gondola trip across the lagoon to the island of San Lazzaro, where they visit the Armenian convent in which Byron once lived and studied. Mrs. Vervain asks Ferris to find an Italian teacher for Florida. Ferris mentions Don Ippolito, but thinks him unsuitable. As the day goes on, Florida takes a dislike to Ferris for teasing her mother.

In his laboratory Don Ippolito broods over the useless inventions that have eaten up his small income and earned him the derision of his colleagues. Having lost a long-time pupil, he needs money and dreams of emigrating to America. Ferris comes, and after admiring Don Ippolito's paintings and laboratory, and his absurd inventions, offers him the position as Florida's instructor. The priest accepts eagerly and considers the matter settled. Troubled and amused because he has just offered a job to a man he declared unsuitable the day before, Ferris calls on the Vervains and persuades them to accept the priest. He brings Don Ippolito to the Vervains for breakfast in their charming, decaying palazzo, with its beautiful hidden garden. Mrs. Vervain is pleased with him; Florida, as usual, seems indifferent.

Ferris makes himself at home with the Vervains, as does Don Ippolito, who becomes neater and more Americanized every day. Ferris observes them all, and paints the priest. Florida, who takes Don Ippolito very seriously, silently rebukes his lapses from her ideal of pious propriety. The priest praises Florida to Ferris, who replies that he mistrusts her temper. Don Ippolito is oddly both glad and troubled to hear that Ferris does not love Florida. Ferris speaks clumsily to Florida of his undefinable uneasiness about Don Ippolito. Florida is upset that Ferris has no concrete opinions, evidence, or advice. The two part coldly.

Ferris unwillingly joins Florida, Mrs. Vervain, and Don Ippolito for lunch and a boat ride up the Brenta Canal into the countryside. The party enjoys the lagoon, the canal, and the villas that line it. Ferris teases Florida, as usual, and sketches her, giving her a proud expression. She grows more and more sullen. Defending her, the priest says that she is not proud and is always good to her mother. Florida brutally tells him not to comment on her or her relations with her mother. The day is ruined for all. On the return, at night, the party is detained at the customs because their gondoliers have stolen a rope from some fishermen. After this matter is cleared up, near midnight, the gondola runs aground near an Austrian fort with a suspicious sentry. Don Ippolito pushes them off, and they finally return wretchedly to Venice. Florida awkwardly apologizes to the priest for her rudeness; he is overcome.

Next day the exhausted Mrs. Vervain collapses. Florida sits up all night with her, and then turns to Ferris for help in finding a doctor. Ferris now feels drawn to Florida, although he still is bothered by her temper and the contradictions in her character. Thinking she likes him, he calls on her, only to find her indifferent; he is angry, and vows to avoid the Vervains.

Don Ippolito and Florida apologize to and compliment each other, while Mrs. Vervain sleeps. Don Ippolito speaks bitterly to Florida of the frustrations of being a priest. Florida is distressed to hear that Don Ippolito became a priest although he really wanted to be an inventor, and is amazed to learn that he is an agnostic.

The Vervains coax the grumpy consul back, and Florida treats him so gently that he forgets his pique. She questions him at length about priests and the problems of an unbelieving priest. Ferris says that such a priest should leave the Church. Ferris doesn't dream that Florida is applying his general remarks to Don Ippolito's case. The three Americans watch the ecclesiastical parade in St. Mark's Square. Ferris jests at the parade, and teases Florida as usual. They see a sad, pious priest, who turns out to be Don Ippolito, much to everyone's surprise. In a long talk later Florida commiserates with Don Ippolito and urges him to leave the Church and go to America.

Don Ippolito tells Ferris he still dreams of going to America; Ferris says he would starve there. Ferris is amazed to hear the priest say that Florida has encouraged him to leave the priesthood, and even more amazed to hear Don Ippolito say he loves Florida. Don Ippolito can't understand why Ferris is so upset by all this. Ferris can't understand Florida's position in the matter, and can't decide what to do. In the evening Mrs. Vervain tells Ferris that she and Florida are leaving and taking the priest with them. She sends him to fetch Florida from the garden. Taking leave of Don Ippolito while Ferris is inside talking to Mrs. Vervain, Florida encourages the priest and is indignant to hear that Ferris says he should not go to America. Don Ippolito then involuntarily discloses his love for Florida. She recoils, but then feels sorry for him and treats him gently. She confesses she loves Ferris. In a fit of pity she hugs the priest just before he leaves. In the darkness Ferris sees this and assumes that Florida and Don Ippolito are in love. He rushes off in a fury. Returning to the house, Florida tells her bewildered mother that Don Ippolito is not going with them. Mrs. Vervain wonders what happened to Ferris after she sent him out to get her daughter. Florida is troubled to realize that he disappeared, but she can't imagine why. Next day, before the two women depart from Venice, Mrs. Vervain leaves a lightly scolding note at Ferris's house, and has a pointless final chat with a gloomy Don Ippolito. Florida won't speak to him.

Ferris returns home after a day of mad wandering about Venice and the lagoon. He reads Mrs. Vervain's note and assumes that the priest has left Venice with the ladies, but a later note from Mrs. Vervain says he hasn't. Utterly bewildered, and racked by the loss of

Florida, Ferris tries to kill time, and fails. He is glad when he is informed shortly that a new consul has been appointed. Learning that the priest is ill, Ferris visits him, and hears the full story, ending with Florida's rejection of him. Don Ippolito vows to become a Carmelite friar. He tells Ferris that Florida loves him, Ferris, and straightens out the confusion about the hug in the garden. Ferris, to his own shame, still can't believe that Florida embraced the priest solely out of sympathy. Having convinced himself anew that the priest has lied, and that he and Florida did love one another, Ferris returns to the priest's house, only to learn that he is dead.

Ferris returns to America, finds the Vervains' house empty, joins the army, serves two years, is badly wounded, and returns convalescent to New York. With the help and persuasion of his friends he exhibits his unfinished study of Don Ippolito at a general salon. One day he finds Florida, in mourning, standing before the sketch. He tells her of the priest's last conversation. Suddenly he blurts out his love for her. She is still bitter with him, and they work out their feelings slowly. Florida tells him that her mother died in Europe. They are about to part when she takes the initiative in removing the remaining suspicions between them. They are fully reconciled and get married at once. Years later, they revisit Venice, where Ferris remembers Don Ippolito as a self-deceiving romantic. Thus the priest's final tragedy is to be misunderstood and forgotten while the others live on happily.

> Aide to the Governor of New York, Henry Ferris, fishermen, gondoliers, Nina, customs officers, priests, Don Ippolito Rondinelli, soldiers, Don Ippolito's uncle, Veneranda, Florida Vervain, Mrs. Vervain, old Venetian woman.

"The Fourth-of-July Boy." See *The Flight of Pony Baker.*

"The Fulfilment of the Pact," 1912.
    At their club, four men — the narrator ("I"), Minver, Rulledge, and Wanhope — discuss the question of whether Ormond, a man who has recently died, appeared after death to his wife as she says he did. Wanhope tells them that Ormond and Mrs. Ormond agreed

that whichever died first would come back to tell the other one what it was like. When Ormond died, his wife went into the room where he was laid out, and his spirit appeared (she said) at the head of his corpse and communicated wordlessly with her. He told her that he had some difficulty in coming back, but had been allowed to fulfill his promise because of his love for her. At their next meeting she also saw other dead relatives, and Ormond told her that it was she who was in the spiritual world, not he in the material one. She was impatient to know what eternity was like, but the only thing he could tell her was that life on earth is not a trick but God's pledge of eternal life. Seeing a great host of other spirits, she wanted to question them but could not. Eager to join her husband, she said she would commit suicide, but Ormond warned her not to and said she would be with him soon. As they parted, he told her that now he knew only love and perfect trust. His wife feels that they have never been parted since. Minver concludes that Ormond must have loved his wife.

"I" (the narrator), Minver, Mrs. Jenny Ormond, Ormond, Rulledge, Wanhope.

A Hazard of New Fortunes, 1889 (dated 1890).

Part I. On an autumn day in Basil March's Boston insurance office, his friend Fulkerson, a live-wire journalist and syndicator, urges him to give up business, which Fulkerson knows he dislikes, and accept Fulkerson's offer of the editorship of a new literary magazine to be published in New York and financed by a millionaire Fulkerson knows. The magazine will appear fortnightly and the contributors will be paid shares of the profits of each issue. Fulkerson likes March, whom he met on the Quebec boat several years before, and offers him $4,000 a year, $1,000 more than March now makes. As they part, with March interested but undecided, Fulkerson says that he will call the magazine *Every Other Week*. At home March tells his wife Isabel of Fulkerson's offer. She thinks he should accept, because the insurance company may replace March at any time, but she abruptly changes her mind when March says that the magazine will be published in New York, which she loathes. March, who likes his adopted home of Boston, agrees to drop the matter.

March feels, however, that Isabel has pushed him into rejecting

Fulkerson's offer. For twenty years he has lived a narrow and frustrated life, though a dignified one, drudging at the office and writing an occasional poem. Isabel begins to regret her opinion, but March angrily says the matter is closed. Next morning she urges him to accept, but he can't believe that she is entirely serious, and they quarrel. The next day, the insurance company notifies March that he is to be replaced, by his pushy clerk Watkins, March believes. March is offered the editorship of the company's house organ, in New York and at a lower salary. March rejects the offer and telegraphs his acceptance to Fulkerson, who shows up in person to thank March and to enlist Isabel's support.

After finding a tenant for their Boston house, the Marches go to New York to look for a place to live. Their journey amuses them somewhat, but much less than it would have in their earlier days (cf. *Their Wedding Journey*, Chapter I). In New York the Marches stay at their accustomed quiet hotel and then set out gaily to find the perfect ten-room flat—cheap, furnished, and sunny. They look at dozens, of all sorts, but each one has something wrong with it, especially Mrs. Grosvenor Green's flat, which is crammed with what March mockingly calls "Jamescracks." Next day the Marches continue their wearying and fruitless search, far into the night. As the days pass they come to know the city well. March finds it lively; his puritan wife says that they forget death in New York. Once the Marches pass through a slum, which once they would have considered merely picturesque, but which now seems horrible, though March pretends to be facetious about it. Now the Marches look at houses rather than flats. On the street they see a man eating food out of garbage heaps. Mrs. March is so upset that she insists on going back to Boston and letting March rent a place. Hoping to rent her flat to them, Mrs. Green calls; Isabel puts her off, warns March against her, and leaves for Boston, after an entertaining ride on the new elevated railway to the station.

At a restaurant Fulkerson tells March about Dryfoos, their backer. He is a middle-aged Pennsylvania Dutchman who moved to western Ohio, farmed there for many years, and reluctantly sold out when natural gas was discovered on his land. He moved to the county seat, gradually became seduced by the sport of money-making, made a fortune, and moved to New York, mainly to satisfy his daughters' eagerness to get into society. Fulkerson, who met

Dryfoos while reporting the gas boom in Ohio, ran into him in New York, and sold him on the prestige to be gotten from backing Fulkerson's magazine, with Dryfoos's unworldly son Conrad as nominal publisher. In the restaurant March sees Lindau, a German refugee of 1848 who taught March German in Indianapolis a generation before. March is pained to see that Lindau is poor and that he lost an arm in the Civil War. Fulkerson shows March the magazine's office, a remodeled house.

Then March rents the Green flat, knowing as he does so that he is doing wrong. When she left him, Isabel was sure that he would make a mess of things. He feels hemmed in now by his family's needs and by the presence of Fulkerson and the Dryfooses on the magazine. Fortunately Isabel becomes reconciled to the Green flat, after she has cleared out the Jamescracks. March at once finds his editorial work absorbing and rewarding. Fulkerson publicizes the magazine shamelessly among his wide acquaintance. March has plenty of manuscripts but no illustrations, until Fulkerson says that he has found an artist.

Part II. The Marches looked at and rejected lodgings in a boarding house run by a widow, Mrs. Leighton, and her pretty daughter Alma. After the death of Rev. Archibald Leighton they came to New York from St. Barnaby, a small summer-resort town, so that Alma could study art while they supported themselves by taking in boarders in their rented house. At St. Barnaby Alma was encouraged to paint by a handsome young summer visitor, an artist named Angus Beaton. Alma is now in Mr. Wetmore's class, for which Lindau is currently the model. The Leightons are distressed that Beaton has not yet come to see them in New York. Their first boarders arrive: Col. Woodburn, a dignified reactionary Virginian, and his vivacious daughter Madison.

In his studio Beaton models a bust of Lindau, in the intervals between writing and painting; he has talent for all the arts, he believes when he is not in one of his fits of self-disgust. Beaton has been writing syndicate letters for Fulkerson; he is also supported by his poor old father in Syracuse. Fulkerson now asks Beaton to be the art department of *Every Other Week,* and pays no attention to Beaton's objections and refusal. Beaton then goes to a reception at the house of Mrs. Horn, a gracious socialite, who inquires patronizingly about the Leightons, thus embarrassing Beaton for his neglect of them. Finally he calls on them. Alma snubs Beaton severely for his neglect. He feels very put upon, and perversely he decides to work for Fulkerson. At the magazine office he meets March and Dryfoos, whom he treats with lofty indifference as they discuss the first issue. March finds Beaton irritating, but Fulkerson says he's a good man when he's not an ass. Fulkerson suggests that they have Lindau do translations. Conrad wants the magazine to crusade for good; March still takes New York poverty lightly, and can't grasp Conrad's moral passion.

The Marches call on the Dryfoos ladies. The Dryfoos house is expensively but tastefully decorated, not by the Dryfooses but by Mrs. Mandel, a genteel widow whom Fulkerson has hired to civilize the Dryfooses. The Dryfoos girls are vulgar and countrified. Christine, the older, is dark, intense, and catty; Mela is friendly and silly. Mrs. Dryfoos is plain and quiet. Fulkerson arrives with Beaton in tow. Fulkerson jokes with everybody and makes Christine show the group the intaglio ring that he brought from Italy and gave to her. Beaton has her put it on a different finger. She is instantly enamored of him; he is grave and dreamy-eyed with her. Later Fulkerson tells the Marches that it was he who found Mrs. Mandel and installed her at the Dryfoos house. He adds casually that he is now eating at the Leightons. Brooding in his room, Beaton thinks of Christine and sketches her for the cover of *Every Other Week*. He is sure that Alma Leighton still likes him, and next day he calls on the Leightons. Alma refuses to be impressed with the sketches for *Every Other Week* which, as Beaton knows, are really her sketches which he borrowed once and is secretly using. Col. Woodburn lectures the group on the commercialization of society and the superiority of the Southern slave system if its flaws had been purged. He is trying to publish a book of his ideas. Beaton goes to an elegant reception at Mrs. Horn's and talks to her niece, Margaret Vance, an earnest, aesthetic society girl.

Later, as the magazine take shape, March resists Fulkerson's efforts to sensationalize it, e.g., with an attack on Bevans, a controversial novelist who resembles Howells, or with a paper by Col. Woodburn defending slavery, or with advertising by sandwich-board men. On his way to see the ailing Lindau, March admires the teeming East Side. He is distressed to find Lindau apparently in extreme poverty, and offers him translating work. Lindau says that he moved to the slums because he was forgetting the poor. He and March discuss the economic system, which Lindau says is plain robbery; March is superficial and facetious, and finds Lindau's intensity distressing.

March has never considered labor agitators and socialists sincere, and is glad to turn from Lindau to the first issue of *Every Other Week*, which he finds very good, thanks largely to Beaton's art work. Fulkerson pushes the magazine vigorously. The New York papers give it mixed reviews; they seem to dislike its being neither newspaper, book nor magazine. The first number is a great hit with readers, especially outside New York. Fulkerson flirts with Madison Woodburn and flatters Col. Woodburn, though he offends the old man by praising Beaton, whom the Colonel can't stand. Fulkerson plans a little dinner for the staff and contributors of *Every Other Week*. Alma Leighton tells her mother she once cared for Beaton, but doesn't like or trust him now.

Part III. March begins to realize that Fulkerson is daunted and impressed by Dryfoos, especially by his luck and his *sangfroid*. Dryfoos visits the office to meet March. Both men are nervous, though Dryfoos soon feels himself superior, as a worldly and a rich man. Dryfoos doesn't look at or even ask about the magazine; this indifference irritates March. In Conrad's presence Dryfoos speaks contemptuously to March of Conrad's desire to be a preacher, and March begins to dislike Dryfoos. Fulkerson's arrival in the office relieves the tension. He jocosely argues the success of the magazine, but Dryfoos is contemptuous of its projected profits. Fulkerson later explains Dryfoos's stiffness as the result of differences with Conrad and not as directed at March personally. March finds Dryfoos a distressing example of the way money makes Americans mean and unpleasant. Isabel regrets that March must associate with Dryfoos, and tells March never to knuckle under to Dryfoos in any way.

In the Dryfoos house Mrs. Dryfoos reproaches Dryfoos for selling the family burial plot in Ohio; meanwhile, Beaton flirts with Christine in the drawing room, to Dryfoos's irritation. Both of the old people complain that wealth has dislocated their lives, with no real compensations, even for the children. The magazine is for Conrad, to help him learn business in a congenial way, but the tactic doesn't seem to have worked. Conrad, to his parents' consternation, wants to be an Episcopalian priest.

Beaton finds a wild charm in Christine, but cares more for Alma, who still treats him coolly, and chides him for trifling with the Dryfoos girls. Beaton admires Alma, finds her adapting rapidly to New York, and sees her at his side in a dim vision of the future. At a reception Beaton meets Margaret Vance and, half facetiously, encourages her to help the Dryfooses socially. The Marches meet and admire Margaret. As they leave the Horn house, the sight of a prostitute on the street makes March wonder if society doesn't pay too high a price for the rare Margaret Vances. Mrs. Horn looks askance at Margaret's plan to visit the Dryfooses, especially since attempts at relations with the Leightons didn't work out. Not knowing quite why, Margaret calls on the Dryfoos girls, listens patiently to their inane bragging about the gas country, and invites them to a musicale at Mrs. Horn's. Margaret thinks the Dryfoos girls are flattered by her advances, but they are too narrow and ignorant to feel anything except condescension for her. Mrs. Mandel can't make them see how lucky they are to be invited to Mrs. Horn's. Dryfoos agrees with the girls. He once believed in things beyond money, but no more; money making is the drug which dulls the recurring pain of the loss of two children years before, of his farm, and of his old life. After much bickering at the Dryfoos table it is agreed that Conrad will go to the musicale with the girls.

Over Mrs. Mandel's protests the girls arrive late at the musicale. While Christine monopolizes Beaton, Mela has a grand time, as she says, talking to a young writer, Kendricks; she doesn't realize that he is studying her as a case. Beaton finds Christine unbearably catty and conceited, but manages to conceal his feelings. When Christine hears that Margaret already knows Conrad, she suspects her of plotting to marry him and get the Dryfoos money. Afterward, Mrs. Horn vents her disgust at the newly rich; Isabel again warns March not to truckle to Dryfoos, while March muses on the utter self-assurance of the vulgar in good society; the Dryfoos girls discuss the evening in placid ignorance of their gaucheries; and Conrad walks home in a daze of love for Margaret.

Part IV. As spring comes, Fulkerson tirelessly urges on Dryfoos the idea of the *Every Other Week* dinner, to be held at Dryfoos's house. Dryfoos rejoices in the idea of being publicly connected with the magazine; Conrad resents the idea, because he works there unwillingly. March concludes that Dryfoos and his money could be used and abused for worse purposes than publicizing *Every Other Week*. Fulkerson thinks that Col. Woodburn's paper advocating serfdom will be a hit; March is dubious. Fulkerson, meanwhile, is more and more smitten with Madison Woodburn and the idea of married life. March has Lindau to the house a good deal, to the well-concealed distress of Isabel, who finds Lindau's violent political opinions unsettling. She feels that he will bring trouble to March.

The Marches meanwhile enjoy the peculiar tang of life in New York, especially the immigrant quarters, with their groceries and restaurants. They find the anonymity of New York life largely refreshing. Greenwich Village and its nearby piers always fascinate March. He views the poverty with detachment and is upset to find his son Tom condemning it, thanks to Lindau's influence. The Marches find the prosperous uptown districts agreeable but dull after the teeming life of downtown. At the Battery they try to renew their first impression of New York (see *Their Wedding Journey*), but are instead struck by the immigrants at Castle Garden. They often ride the elevated railroad through the city and out to the ends of the lines, in the rapidly urbanizing country. The Marches no longer regard the city as a spectacle; they see it as a living organism in which they are willy-nilly involved. New York bothers March, but on a visit to Boston he finds it by contrast a kind of living death. His editorial work absorbs him. The contributors themselves, mostly young men, he finds rather insipid. After much argument about vacations the Marches stay in New York for the summer and see much of the Leightons and their circle.

Following Fulkerson's advice, the Dryfoos ladies in August go to Saratoga, where they chafe at their well-dressed isolation. Christine is still enamored of Beaton, and realizes that she attracts him, but his attentions never become more than fitful. In the leisurely August atmosphere at the office, Lindau and Fulkerson argue politics; Lindau holds that all fortunes are tainted and all self-made men corrupt. He and Fulkerson quarrel but make up.

In October Dryfoos proposes a little dinner at his home to talk over the projected banquet. Dryfoos himself invites Lindau, along with Kendricks, Col. Woodburn, and the others. March is afraid that Lindau and Dryfoos will quarrel, but Lindau has already accepted the invitation. Fulkerson shepherds Dryfoos through the arrangements, and manages to make Col. Woodburn accept an invitation

even though he doesn't know the source of Dryfoos's money and
suspects that he is not a gentleman. At the dinner Dryfoos and Conrad awkwardly play host, in the enforced absence of the Dryfoos
women, to Fulkerson, March, Beaton, Kendricks, Lindau, and the
colonel. The dinner is fairly convivial at first. Everyone drinks to
Lindau's war record. Then the colonel takes the floor and denounces
business. A gas well made of white sugar provides a brief diversion,
but Fulkerson's approving account of Dryfoos's union-breaking activities infuriates Lindau, Lindau and the colonel differ passionately on the idea of the perfect society, and the dinner ends coldly,
after Lindau has made some angry personal remarks about Dryfoos
to March in German.

Next morning Dryfoos, in a cold rage, demands that March fire
Lindau, whom he sees as a foul alien agitator. March defends him,
and refuses to take orders about Lindau from anyone except Fulkerson. After Dryfoos stomps out, March is sure that he himself will be
fired. Conrad nervously apologizes for his father's behavior, and to
March's astonishment declares himself more radical, in Christian-
socialist terms, than Lindau. When March talks to Fulkerson about
the quarrel with Dryfoos, Fulkerson says that March should let Lindau go and not make a fuss. March angrily says that he will resign if
Fulkerson fails to back him up, and stalks out, leaving Fulkerson
dazed. March quails at the thought of losing his work, which he has
come to love, and must force himself not to go back and give in. Isabel blames Lindau for the trouble, and takes a purely selfish view, to
March's dismay. He wanders about the city all day and returns to
find Isabel calm, approving, and helpful. They plan a future based
on her private income of $2,000 a year. Fulkerson arrives to say that
he and Dryfoos have arranged to have Lindau simply ignored, or
dropped by Fulkerson. March still can't accept the idea of punishing
Lindau for his opinions, especially because the magazine has never
used them. Fulkerson now realizes that he must choose between
March or Dryfoos. Later Lindau, who knows nothing of the day's
events, appears, and hands back to March the money he has earned
from Dryfoos, with reproaches to March for working for such a man.

Deeply troubled, Fulkerson tells Beaton about the affair. Beaton's
reaction, personal as always, is to suggest facetiously that Fulkerson
fire Dryfoos or March, or get Col. Woodburn to act as intermediary.
Grasping at the latter idea, Fulkerson lays the entire affair before the

Woodburns. Deeply interested in this affair of honor, the colonel says that first Lindau must tell Dryfoos that he means nothing personal in his opinions. Fulkerson suggests that Woodburn see Dryfoos. The colonel agrees, after making Fulkerson commit himself to March. After Woodburn leaves Fulkerson and Madison stumble into acknowledging their love. Woodburn's mission fails. Next day Fulkerson and March agree that Lindau's action has brought the matter to an end, however unsatisfactory and impermanent.

Part V. Superficially, life at the magazine office goes on as before. March is full of guilt toward Lindau, though he disagrees with his economic opinions, and can't get back on the old easy basis with Fulkerson and Conrad. The colonel consents reluctantly to Madison's marriage. The news of that makes Beaton more self-pitying than ever; he is even more miserable, yet oddly relieved, when Alma Leighton firmly says that she doesn't care for him.

The Dryfoos girls continue to live in fretful social isolation. Kendricks ignores Mela, though he respects her simple good nature. Beaton continues to trifle occasionally with Christine, though he feels he has lost interest in everything. He can't share Margaret Vance's interest in the poor and in Conrad, and he is irritated when Mrs. Horn hints that he should help Margaret regain her interest in social affairs. Turning to Christine for amusement, he is staggered to be confronted by Mrs. Mandel's request that he either take a serious interest in Christine or stay away entirely. Leaving, he takes it as a personal affront that the street car workers are on strike and he must walk to the Elevated.

March and Fulkerson follow the strike closely. Rambling and riding around the city to observe the strike, March is aboard a car that stops suddenly.

Earlier that morning Christine berates Dryfoos for having Mrs. Mandel talk to Beaton. She hurls at him all the jewelry he has given her, and the intaglio ring associated with Beaton. Dryfoos absent-mindedly puts on the ring and goes off to Wall Street. When the stock market closes he goes to the magazine office to talk to Fulkerson about Beaton, but finds only Conrad. Dryfoos takes out on Conrad his fury at Christine and eventually strikes him, wounding him with Christine's ring. Dryfoos rushes home, and Conrad wanders the streets until he meets Margaret Vance. He thinks that Margaret appeals to him to help the strikers. In an ecstasy of love for her and pity for Dryfoos, Conrad wanders along until he encounters strikers and police scuffling around a halted streetcar, with Lindau shouting at the police. When a policeman turns to strike the stump of Lindau's wrist, Conrad leaps forward to interfere. A shot from the car fells him. March comes up from the car to find Conrad dead.

Fulkerson and the Marches help the bewildered Dryfoos family through their misery. Fulkerson tells March privately that Lindau's arm had to be completely amputated after the policeman hit it. Dryfoos stays up to look at Conrad in his coffin. Mrs. Dryfoos comes in, weeps over Conrad, and asks Dryfoos what the mark is by Conrad's eye. Recalling the blow he struck, Dryfoos cries out in anguish.

The Marches, especially Isabel, now often visit the Dryfooses, who are humbled, except for Christine, who keeps to herself. Fulkerson and March begin to worry about the future of *Every Other Week*. Dryfoos seems to have lost interest in it, and Fulkerson and March would like to buy it. March feels that the world is chaotic, that someone always has him by the throat, and that at fifty he is no farther from the poorhouse than he ever was. He sees people as creatures blindly controlled by their conditions.

March finds Lindau dying in a hospital with Margaret Vance at his side. Leaving Lindau's deathbed, March meets Dryfoos on the street. Dryfoos says that his understanding of Lindau's angry personal remarks in German at the dinner was what made him want to fire the man. He wants to say that to Lindau. March can't get a chance to say that Lindau is dead. Dryfoos nearly breaks down in saying that he wants to atone to Lindau for Conrad's sake. Finally March tells Dryfoos, as gently as he can, that Lindau is dead. March tells his children that the moral of this incident is that people must be good to each other in life and not wait until it is too late. He feels that Conrad suffered for the sins of others. Lindau's funeral is at Dryfoos's house, as part of Dryfoos's vain attempt to atone to Conrad. Christine continues to wait sullenly, in her room, for Beaton, who never comes.

Since his encounter with Mrs. Mandel, Beaton has remained broodingly aloof from the Dryfoos house. One day Dryfoos comes to Beaton's studio and after half-apologizing for setting Mrs. Mandel on him, asks him to paint a picture of Conrad. Though Dryfoos actually is sincere in trying to atone further to Conrad through this gesture, Beaton feels that he is being gotten at, and refuses. Brooding, Beaton concludes that Dryfoos's behavior implies that he can now visit Christine when and as he pleases. Subconsciously he desires Christine, her person and her money, but he still feels drawn, however vaguely, to Alma and Margaret; he can't believe that they really don't care for him anymore. Beaton visits Margaret, and offends and distances her with his egotism. He decides to turn to Alma. Complacently sure that Alma must still love him, Beaton calls on her and is staggered to find her finally and emphatically rejecting him. After he leaves, Mrs. Leighton is worried that Alma may be an old maid, but Alma replies that she will pick and choose the way men do.

Fulkerson and Isabel surprise March by saying that Alma should have accepted Beaton. March defends non-marriage as just as laudable as marriage. One day Dryfoos, saying the family is going abroad, offers to let March and Fulkerson buy *Every Other Week;* they can pay interest on the capital he has invested in it. Fulkerson says that Dryfoos has secretly admired March ever since March stood up to him about Lindau, but March can't believe that Dryfoos has really changed in any essential way.

After being turned down by Alma, Beaton is woozy with self-pity, and almost in spite goes to see Christine. Having waited in vain for him for a long time, she sits tensely through his call. When he calmly starts to leave, having failed to show any great interest in her, she leaps at him in a frenzy of loss and tries to claw his face. Shaken to his depths at last, Beaton thinks of shooting himself. He drops the gun and it goes off, scoring his cheek as Christine might have done.

After making *Every Other Week* over to March and Fulkerson, Dryfoos sails with his family for Europe. The new owners keep Beaton on, to his secret satisfaction. Fulkerson marries Madison Woodburn and with her retraces the route of the Marches' wedding journey to Niagara and Quebec. News comes that Christine has married a penniless French nobleman. And one day the Marches encounter a serene Margaret Vance wearing the uniform of a Protestant sisterhood.

Angus Beaton, Christine Dryfoos, Conrad Dryfoos, Mrs. Elizabeth Dryfoos, Jacob Dryfoos, Mela Dryfoos, Fulkerson, Mrs. Grosvenor Green, Mrs. Horn, Hubbell, janitor, janitor, Kendricks, Alma Leighton, Mrs. Leighton, Berthold Lindau, Mrs. Mandel, Basil March, Bella March, Isabel March, Tom March, Margaret Vance, Watkins, Wetmore, Madison Woodburn, Colonel Woodburn.

"His Apparition," 1902 (in *Questionable Shapes*, 1903).

In the half-real light of dawn, Arthur Hewson ponders the apparition he has just seen in his bedroom at the Berkshires house of his wealthy friend St. John. In order to stay awake until breakfast, Hewson jumps out a window, knocking down a trellis, and has coffee at a nearby hotel. Returning, Hewson tells St. John that he damaged the trellis, and realizes that he would ruin the reputation and value of St. Johnswort, the estate, if he talked about seeing a ghost there. The guests tease Hewson about his nocturnal activities. He meets Miss Rosalie Hernshaw, an intense, unconventional girl. Later, back in the city, Hewson tells his story to many people, too many, he feels, for the story soon becomes boring and people tease him about it. He feels responsible to the apparition and yearns to define its meaning. At a party in New York, Hewson takes Miss Hernshaw in to dinner. She defends her originality and candor. At table Miss Hernshaw snubs him and then asks him what he thinks of Ibsen's *Ghosts*, which gives him a turn. She supports frankness, in Ibsen and in real life. When Wanhope the psychologist says that he has never seen a man who has seen a ghost, Hewson tells the guests his story, briefly. Hewson's account puzzles the guests and annoys Wanhope. Hewson learns that Miss Hernshaw's father is very rich.

Hewson feels he has let the apparition down by discussing it before unsympathetic people. He pays for his error by having the apparition written up in a newspaper, evidently through the indiscretion of Miss Hernshaw. St. John demands that Hewson label the story a fake, but all he can reply is that it did happen. St. John says that people are declining invitations, the servants are leaving St. Johnswort, and the value of the estate is nil. Hewson can't divulge the identity of the person who said it happened at St. Johnswort, but he does say it's an excessively honest woman who is now abroad; finally he offers to buy the house at St. John's evaluation, and St. John is unable to resist. Back from London because of that newspaper story, Miss Hernshaw confesses to telling the reporter, who she thought was merely an inquisitive acquaintance. After hearing the story of Hewson's talk with St. John, all but the end, Miss Hernshaw says that she will buy the estate. Embarrassed by not having told Miss Hernshaw all the truth, Hewson returns and does so, but she has already written St. John. She agrees, to his dismay, with his proposal that the penalty should fall on him. St. John offers to release Hewson, but can't in good conscience say that the other offer is higher—through clearly it is—and therefore is stuck with Hewson's lower offer. Hewson and Miss Hernshaw get the matter of the purchase cleared up. Then he asks her to come to the estate as his wife. She says she likes and admires him, but doesn't know if she loves him, so she goes to Colorado to try living without him.

Taking over St. Johnswort, Hewson lives there six weeks in great suspense, admiring Miss Hernshaw and her truthfulness more and more, and his previous New York life as a man of leisure less and less. Finally she writes that she loves him. He rushes out to Colorado and meets her affable father. After marriage the Hewsons reside a year at St. Johnswort and live down its reputation. They conclude that the apparition (which is never described) was sent to portend their meeting; if not that, then it would appear again, to portend some future happiness (children, perhaps?).

Gardener, Rosalie Hernshaw, Hernshaw, Arthur Hewson, Mrs. Rock, St. John, waitresses, Wanhope.

"Hot," 1859.
"We," the narrator, a newspaperman, comments on the broiling street scene outside the office until he is interrupted by his editor calling for copy.

Editor, "we" (the narrator, a newspaperman).

"How I Lost a Wife. An Episode in the Life of a Batchelor," 1854.
"I," the protagonist-narrator, explains his hatred of dogs. Years before, he overcame his bashfulness enough to court Mary, sister of his friend Charley. During a visit to their country home, he went swimming by himself and looked up to see Charley's big dog Ponto

ripping up his clothes. When the others came looking for him, he hid in a tree, and listened to them lamenting his apparent drowning, but suddenly the limb broke, dropping him squarely among the girls. They screamed and ran; "I" left in shame, never came back, and is still a bachelor.

Charley, girls, "I" (the narrator-protagonist), Mary, Ponto.

An Imperative Duty, 1891 (dated 1892).

Dr. Edward Olney, a thirty-year-old nerve specialist, returns to Boston after five years in Florence. When he went abroad to study he had a good income from Union Pacific stock, but now, after the panic of 1873, he has nothing. A medical friend urged him to stay on in Italy, but he has returned to Boston to try to earn some money. Since it is midsummer, all his friends are at the seashore. Depressed, he finds Boston alien and inhabited only by Irish and blacks. He would prefer black waiters to the Irish waiters in his hotel. After living in Europe he has forgotten how black and white people segregate themselves even in public places. The black dandies look much more refined in their courtship than the white ones, and some of the black girls actually have creamy white complexions.

An Irish porter comes to Olney's room to ask whether he is a physician. When Olney identifies himself, the man brings him a note from Rhoda Aldgate, a young girl whom Olney met in Italy; she asks him to attend her aunt, Mrs. Meredith. On his way to their room, he remembers Rhoda: her rich olive complexion, crinkly black hair, inky black eyes, and a face like a tragic family mask. He also remembers her aunt, with whom he had analyzed a novel.

Rhoda tells Olney that they noticed his name in a list of arrivals in the hotel. Mrs. Meredith complains of insomnia. When she asks him whether anyone can live a lie, he wonders idly whether she is worrying about her niece. The denseness of the Irish porter, sent to get a prescription filled, leads to a discussion of racial differences. When Olney attacks the social rejection of blacks, Mrs. Meredith asks him if he is advocating intermarriage. Although he is not, he criticizes segregated churches. Mrs. Meredith asks Olney whether the prescribed sedative contains chloral. He says it does not, and insists that as a doctor he always tells his patients the truth. Mrs. Meredith agrees that the truth is the only thing, but Rhoda feels that sometimes the truth is cruel.

Next day, while Rhoda is out, her aunt tells Olney that she has something on her mind, but he doesn't want to know what it is because he remembers her as a novel reader who bases her judgments of real people on fictional characters. He wonders if her problem concerns Rhoda's interest in Rev. Bloomingdale, the young clergyman she spent an evening with in Florence. Mrs. Meredith suddenly asks him if he believes in heredity or atavism. He answers that in a person of mixed racial heritage the natural tendency is the permanent effacement of the inferior race, not reversion to it. So he is confident that whites must absorb blacks. After deciding to speak and then not to speak, Mrs. Meredith begins to talk about Bloomingdale. Rhoda turned him down once, but the second time she would have accepted him if her aunt hadn't insisted on her considering it for a week. Although he is still in Europe, his widowed mother and his sisters, who are in Boston, are entertaining Rhoda, and she seems to have her heart set on marrying him. But the marriage cannot take place, Mrs. Meredith says, until the truth about Rhoda's ancestry is revealed. Olney assumes that Rhoda must come from a family of criminals, but this assumption does not alter his opinion of her.

Mrs. Meredith says that Rhoda is of Negro descent. Olney is at first disgusted, then resentful at being forced to face the cruel question of Rhoda's future. Mrs. Meredith tells him that Rhoda is the daughter of her brother, a physician, and a beautiful illegitimate octoroon whose Creole father had her educated in a Northern convent. Dr. Aldgate married the girl, but lost his Southern practice as a result. Both parents died, and the Merediths brought up the Aldgates' little girl without telling her the whole truth about her background. When she grew up, they took her to live in Italy in the vague hope that she would find an unprejudiced Italian husband. But Rhoda always insisted that she would marry only an American. After Mr. Meredith's death Rhoda met Rev. Bloomingdale, who is coming to Boston for his answer. Mrs. Meredith is determined to tell Bloomingdale about Rhoda's ancestry and then to leave it up to him to decide whether to tell Rhoda. Olney insists that she must not tell Bloomingdale first, that the secret is Rhoda's, to tell or not, as she chooses. Neither of them can face the discussion of a possible baby, but Mrs. Meredith feels that the truth could be revealed in many other ways, that Rhoda would never tell Bloomingdale, and that it is better to die or to kill than to live a lie. She decides to tell Rhoda and then, if she won't tell Bloomingdale, to tell him herself. At this moment Rhoda whirls into the room and gaily tells Olney and her aunt that she would like to be able to buy a lovable black hotel waiter. After she has left, Mrs. Meredith repeats her determination not to live a lie any longer.

When Rhoda returns, she discusses the Bloomingdale family with her aunt. She tells her that they are formal, conventional people who would dread being different. She wonders whether Bloomingdale is like Mrs. Bloomingdale and his sisters and whether she really cares for him. She has been impressed by Olney's criticism of segregation and has repeated his opinions to the Bloomingdales, whom she found very narrow-minded on this topic. All these innocent comments only increase the distress of Mrs. Meredith and drive her to reveal the secret. First she tells Rhoda that her maternal grandmother was not her grandfather's wife. Then she blurts out that her grandmother was her grandfather's slave. Rhoda's first reaction is to ask her aunt if she has gone crazy. Unable to accept the truth, she weeps and repeatedly begs her aunt to deny it. Then she asks if her mother was her father's slave, too. When she is told that her parents were married but that the marriage ruined her father, she instantly imagines and understands the whole situation. Mrs. Meredith is relieved to have her confession behind her. When Rhoda asks her aunt whether anyone else knows about her background, Mrs. Meredith answers that no one does. For a moment she has actually forgotten about telling Dr. Olney, and then, because Rhoda is frantically demanding the truth, she cannot make herself correct her error. Rhoda writes to Bloomingdale telling him that she cannot marry him and that he must never try to see her again. When Rhoda gives her aunt a forgiving kiss and goes out to mail her letter, Mrs. Meredith is so exhausted and so overcome by what she has done that she takes an overdose of the sedative without realizing it.

Without mailing her letter, Rhoda walks aimlessly through the streets and begins to meet more and more black people. In her hysteria she finds them all hideous and loathsome and tortures herself by imagining her great-great-grandmother as a naked black cannibal. For a moment she wonders if she is insane; she feels that her aunt has killed her. She stops a kindly old black woman going to church and asks whether she can go with her. When Rhoda asks her if God can make black white, she answers submissively that someone's got to be black. As they reach the church Rhoda feels that perhaps she can reconcile herself to her situation by surrounding herself with her people, but during the service she is again overcome by her hysterical loathing. Closing her eyes, she hears the preacher say that love is the answer to racial hate, but as she rushes back to the hotel to see her aunt, she feels full of hate and accusation. She finds Mrs. Meredith unconscious, the empty bottle beside her.

Olney, meanwhile, realizes that he is in love with Rhoda. After analyzing his feelings, he decides to ask Mrs. Meredith to let him talk to Bloomingdale and sound him out before she tells Rhoda anything. He goes to Mrs. Meredith's room twice, but receives no response to his knock. The third time he finds Rhoda standing over her unconscious aunt. He tries to save Mrs. Meredith, but he can't. After it is all over, he is anxious to know whether Mrs. Meredith has spoken to her niece, but he cannot bring himself to ask her directly, and Rhoda's dazed behavior does not give him any positive clue. He telegraphs to Mrs. Meredith's in-laws in St. Louis. Clara Kingsbury Atherton, an old friend of Olney's, takes Rhoda to stay with her in Beverly. When the St. Louis relatives telegraph that they can't come, Olney begins to suspect that they know Rhoda's secret. Mrs. Bloomingdale arrives at the hotel and questions Olney about Mrs. Meredith's death. He assures her that it wasn't suicide and that Rhoda did not want the Bloomingdales notified. Mrs. Bloomingdale is confused and faintly hostile; she emphasizes her family's willingness to accept Rhoda although she has lost all her money. After the Bloomingdales have left, Olney decides that he wants to ask Rhoda to marry him, but he doesn't know how he will go about it.

The day of Mrs. Meredith's funeral Bloomingdale arrives and asks Olney to ask Rhoda whether she is willing to see him. After Olney convinces him that Mrs. Meredith did not commit suicide in a fit of insanity, Bloomingdale insists that no matter how disgraced Rhoda might be, nothing would ever make any difference in his love for her. Olney recognizes this avowal as an expression of his own feelings about Rhoda. So, in an effort to be scrupulously fair to

Bloomingdale, he tells him that Rhoda is staying with Mrs. Atherton. But when Bloomingdale says that he won't be able to go to Beverly until the next morning, Olney decides to go that night. Once there, Olney finds it impossible to do more than hint at his own hopes to Mrs. Atherton. He merely tells her who Bloomingdale is and why he is coming the next morning. Then he returns to Boston, where Mrs. Atherton writes him that Rhoda refused to see Bloomingdale, who accepted her refusal.

The Bloomingdales all leave Boston. As Olney becomes a frequent visitor in Beverly, he finds Rhoda increasingly attractive in her mourning clothes and falls even more passionately in love with her. When the St. Louis relatives do not question Rhoda's inheritance of Mrs. Meredith's property, Olney is sure he knows why. His intuition also tells him that Rhoda knows Mrs. Meredith's secret but she does not know that her aunt confided in him. Although he believes that Rhoda is in love with him, he is puzzled by her passivity. When she announces that she wants to go to New Orleans to find her mother's family, he proposes. She rejects him immediately by confessing that she is "a Negress," but he tells her that he already knows the whole story from her aunt. When Rhoda tells him how she virtually forced her aunt to deny Olney's knowledge, he succeeds in making her see the psychological effect of this new lie on her aunt; then he has to convince her that she is not responsible for her aunt's accidental death. Gradually he also persuades her that the reason for her self-hatred is that she is the descendant of slaveholders as well as slaves. She tells him then that she never mailed the letter to Bloomingdale and she never cared for him. In the end she makes Olney promise that he will never share her secret with anyone, and he consents as long as she believes that he is neither ashamed nor afraid to do so. They marry and settle in Rome, where many people take her for an Italian. Sometimes she is confused and despondent, but her husband attributes these feelings not to her black ancestors but to her puritan hypochondria of the soul.

> Rhoda Aldgate, Clara Kingsbury Atherton, Atherton, Josie Bloomingdale, Roberta Bloomingdale, Rev. Bloomingdale, Mrs. Bloomingdale, Miss Bloomingdale, Professor Garofalo, Meredith, Mrs. Caroline Meredith, Dr. Edward Olney, Irish porter, black divinity student, Dr. Wingate, old black woman.

"Incident," 1872.

At a country station, during a tedious train ride, a young lady and a young gentleman idly spin pleasant fantasies about a house painter who bids farewell to his small son Willy and with his paint boards the car to ride to a job nearby. Discomfited by the conductor's unspoken objections to the paint smell, the painter moves out to the steps of the car. He falls off and is run over by the train. Though the young lady is unaware of this brush with death, the young man (along with the narrator) is sobered by it.

Train conductor, young gentleman, young lady, house painter, Willy.

"The Independent Candidate. A Story of Today," 1854.

Writing to his friend George Berson, a politician, Wat (Walter Larrie) describes his trip to Beauville, a sleepy village (evidently in Ohio). Wat delivers to John Trooze, the tavern landlord, a letter from Berson saying that he is declaring himself an independent candidate against Cuffins, the regular Whig candidate, and wants Wat to make a speech for him in Beauville. Trooze is agreeable to helping Wat, but a group of Cuffins' supporters, led by the wily Sliprie, easily persuade Wat to put off his speech for a week. Wat, we are told, is happy to stay in Beauville so he can see Merla Cuffins, whom he has loved since he first saw her, and who loves him too, as she told her friend Harry (a girl). Now Wat goes to nearby Errington to see Merla.

At twilight in the somewhat larger village of Oldbury, Berson recruits Moro Gilky, a shallow weakling, to stump for him, and then goes to his law office, where he is disturbed by a drunk. "I," the narrator, now intervenes to argue about the story with Old Smith. Next, Cuffins tells Doan, editor of the Oldbury Herald, that Berson should abide by the convention's nomination of Cuffins. Worried by the possibility of a Locofoco candidate draining off even more votes, Cuffins decides to spread the rumor that Berson is liable to go insane at any moment, as his grandfather did. Doan angrily refuses to print this.

The drunk in Berson's office is Robert Wate, husband of Berson's sister, whose death Wate's drinking caused. Berson sends him away, but he keeps coming back, trying to see his daughter Clara, now Berson's ward. Berson gives him money and finally sends him off.

Arriving at Doan's print shop, Wat chats with his friends, the printers Strawberry and Elfred Larker, but fails to get Doan's backing for Berson. After dinner at Larker's lodgings, Wat and Larker spend the evening with Merla Cuffins and a Miss Rueford, Larker's beloved. Later Wat writes Frank that he and Merla became engaged that night.

To Cuffins' dismay, the opposition parties unite against him. In Beauville Wat regrets attacks in the *Herald* on Cuffins, and watches Sary Ann Trooze browbeat her husband. Gilky arrives, and Wat introduces him to Sliprie. Wat kills time with the general storekeeper Hasker and the school-master Witheron. At the meeting that night, Wat angers a Whig, a big butcher, who beats him up. Wat flees the town. Berson's campaign flourishes, however. As election day approaches, his niece Clara is ill, only slightly, it appears, and we learn about his devoted old-maid sister Annie.

On election day, as Cuffins enters the *Herald* office carrying an umbrella, we are told an anecdote about Stub, whose umbrella carried him away in the wind, never to be seen again. Cuffins goes off with some blank ballots, evidently to no purpose (unless the narrator forgot about them). As night comes Annie waits patiently for Berson beside the ailing Clara. Very late Berson returns, excited and incoherent. Later, Berson's supporters, led by Wat, sneak into the house and surprise him with news of his victory. Clara, startled, faints. Thinking her dead, Berson attacks Wat and has to be shut up as a madman. Two years later Robert Wate is dead, Clara is healthy, Wat is about to be married, and Berson, though no longer violent, is still in an amnesiac daze.

> Annie Berson, George Berson, a butcher, Merla Cuffins, Cuffins, Doan, Angelica Gilky, Moro Gilky, Harry, Hasker, "I" (the narrator), Elfred Larker, Walter (Wat) Larrie, Lizzy, Mrs. Rueford, Miss Rueford, Sliprie, Old Smith, Strawberry, Stub, John Trooze, Marquis de Lafayette Trooze, Sary Ann Trooze, Clara Wate, Robert Wate, Dr. Wetherbee, Witheron.

Indian Summer, 1886.

On a dull January day in Florence, Theodore Colville, an American of forty-one, stands on the Ponte Vecchio, gazes at the Arno and the town, and reflects on his recent departure from Prairie des Vaches, Indiana. For seventeen years he had published a newspaper there until after a sordid political squabble he sold out in disgust and returned to Italy, where at twenty-four he had studied architecture and broken his heart over an American girl. He plans to resume his youthful studies. He finds the people of Florence lively, but somehow the city has lost the charm it once had. Colville's reveries are interrupted by the appearance of a Mrs. Bowen, a charming widow, with her ladylike little daughter Effie. In the earlier time Mrs. Bowen was Evalina Ridgely, the companion of the girl who spurned Colville, and, as Colville recalls, liked him. Now very stylish, she is living in Florence after the death of her well-to-do husband.

At his pension Colville dines agreeably with an international group. Later, at Mrs. Bowen's reception, he meets Imogene Graham, a strikingly lovely girl of twenty, who is with Mrs. Bowen for the winter. Colville finds Imogene charming and approachable, but both are conscious of their age difference. After he leaves, Mrs. Bowen recalls Colville's sad affair of the past, and Imogene remarks how old he looks. Colville is pleased at the good impression he made on the ladies. At Mrs. Bowen's again, he talks enthusiastically about Florence to Imogene. Mrs. Bowen tells Imogene that Colville is much improved over the shy, priggish, slovenly youth of the earlier time. Imogene finds him more interesting than the young men she knows, but old and plain.

Through Mrs. Bowen, Colville meets many people. At a party he watches Imogene dancing and is awed and saddened by her youthful intensity of pleasure. He joins in the Lancers, makes a fool of himself, and quits. Mrs. Bowen consoles him. Imogene unfeelingly keeps Colville and Mrs. Bowen there until 3 A.M. Colville goes home feeling disgusted at Italy, the ladies, and himself. Next morning Colville returns with relief to his old plan of a book showing how the Florentine spirit informs its architecture. He looks for books at Vieusseux's reading room and enjoys a serious discussion of Savonarola with Rev. Waters, an elderly American divine whose scholarly zeal Colville finds particularly attractive, for Colville realizes that he still wants to live some of the time in his own world, that of maturity. Strolling by the Arno, he meets Mrs. Bowen and Imogene, who charms him more and more, though he realizes he has more in common with Mrs. Bowen and Effie. He finds Imogene's naïve, gushing comments on literature tiresome, and she finds his ironic comments puzzling. Dining at a *trattoria*, Colville sees a gay group of painters, the so-called Inglehart boys, who have come to Florence from Munich. They know Imogene and are dazzled by her brilliance. Meanwhile Imogene tells Mrs. Bowen that she finds Colville cynical but charming; Mrs. Bowen, oddly, is distressed.

Time passes. Colville studies Florentine architecture and goes little to Mrs. Bowen's, where he feels he is received coolly. He finds a little too much Americanization in the city as a side effect of the large American colony, which he frequents along with the artists' studios. During the Carnival Colville visits Mrs. Bowen, is received cordially, and goes there constantly thereafter. He squires the ladies around the town to see the Carnival. Colville escorts Mrs. Bowen and Imogene to a *veglione*, a masked ball at a theater. Colville waltzes with Imogene, and identifies her with the girl he loved and danced with there seventeen years before. He realizes that Imogene feels she has a mission to make him less cynical and morbid. After a waltz Colville finds that Mrs. Bowen and Effie are gone; he and Imogene wait and finally learn that Effie is ill and Mrs. Bowen has taken her home. Mrs. Bowen seems irritated with Colville for going off with Imogene for so long. Next day he apologizes to Mrs. Bowen, who is coolly ironical to him. He tells stories of old Florence to Effie, who worships him. When Colville leaves, Mrs. Bowen tells Imogene that it is her duty to warn her against any man who might make her unhappy, and then nervously says that Imogene can do anything she likes. Colville's name is not mentioned.

As he leaves Mrs. Bowen's, Colville realizes that he has rejected her attempt to forgive him. Later Rev. Waters tells him that forty-one is an excellent age and that he should be married—perhaps, he hints, to Mrs. Bowen. At a painter's tea Colville finds Imogene rather cold and is hurt when she implies that he has been trifling with her; it's clear that the idea is not hers. Next day she writes him her apologies; he takes the letter to Mrs. Bowen, who admits that the idea of Colville's trifling is her own. After an argument he tells her stiffly that he will leave Florence. They part coldly, but she is at once regretful. She and Imogene mull over and condemn their behavior throughout the Colville affair.

As Colville packs, he notes that he has cooled down more quickly than he would have in his youth. He finds that because he lacks cash to pay his hotel bill, he must stay on over Sunday. Meanwhile Imogene regrets Colville's departure and feels responsible for forcing Colville into his loss of a second woman. She decides to write to Colville asking him to stay, even though Mrs. Bowen says that that will be the same as offering herself to him. Imogene agrees to let Mrs. Bowen write to him; she invites him to lunch. In the morning Colville receives and declines the invitation, but later his will reasserts itself and he decides to stay on in Florence.

Walking that day in the Boboli Gardens, Colville smiles grimly at the sight of the spot where he was rejected seventeen years earlier. As he mopes on a bench, Effie and Imogene walk past with Mrs. Amsden, an American living in Florence. Colville tries to avoid Imogene, but she insists on asking him why he is leaving, and when he asks her if she wants him to stay, she says yes and says she will show him how mature she is. Mrs. Amsden says that the four of them are a dramatic group. Colville suggests that they are from a James novel; Mrs. Amsden, a Howells novel.

When Colville tells Mrs. Bowen that Imogene has allowed him to stay, Mrs. Bowen is upset. In turn Colville is upset when she asks him if he and Imogene are engaged. Imogene tells Colville she hates Mrs. Bowen, proving, Colville thinks, that she must have done Mrs. Bowen a great wrong. Later Effie tells Imogene that Mrs. Bowen has been acting strange. Mrs. Bowen writes to Imogene's mother discussing Colville and his engagement to Imogene; Mrs. Graham finds the letter hostile to Colville. Imogene writes briefly to her mother, and at length to a school friend, saying that by marrying Colville she will make up for the cruelty of Colville's beloved of seventeen years earlier. Next morning Colville asks Mrs. Bowen what he should do about Imogene; Mrs. Bowen refuses to help him. At Mrs. Bowen's request Imogene sulkily agrees to have the engagement kept quiet for the time being. She tells Colville that she is sure Mrs. Bowen detests her; Colville defends Mrs. Bowen. Later Mrs. Bowen asks him not to defend her; he answers angrily, and they are estranged. He is upset to hear Imogene's concept of her sacrifice for him, and feels as if she is his child rather than his fiancée. She wants to go to a fancy-dress ball, and he says that he will go to please her. As they talk he realizes that they are making a mistake in their engagement, but she won't listen to any objections.

Colville goes with Imogene to many affairs, where he is treated as a middle-aged man and tries to act like a young one. He finds this life exhausting. Meanwhile Mrs. Bowen is in poor health, and when Colville proposes to divert her, Imogene is first sulky, then tearfully apologetic. Nobly, but bewildering herself, Imogene vows to act more like a person of Colville's age and not drag him to any more late parties. Now Rev. Morton, a young American clergyman, returns to Florence after an absence. Colville dislikes his suave manner with Imogene. Mr. Waters says that Imogene and Colville will get along in married life if Colville loves her; he can't admit that he doesn't. While Colville and Mrs. Bowen, partly reconciled, have a talk, he notes how well Morton and Imogene look together.

Colville is rejuvenated by not going to parties, and is happy finally to find Mrs. Bowen his friend again, though Imogene now seems a little distant. Morton earnestly wants Imogene to study books; in contrast, Colville disappoints her with his frivolous remarks. Colville begins to like Morton better. Mrs. Bowen points out that Morton has a right to court Imogene, because her mother hasn't written yet. Colville suggests that he leave until the letter comes and thus give Morton a chance. When he asks Mrs. Bowen to try to understand him, she runs from the room. Later Mrs. Bowen points out to Imogene that Morton loves her and she must tell him about Colville. Imogene is in a quandary. Mrs. Bowen finally decides to speak to Morton herself. Imogene objects and says that she will sacrifice herself; no one but Colville can say anything. But then she wonders if Colville really loves her and isn't perhaps sacrificing himself to her. Both women agonize.

Mrs. Bowen now learns that Mrs. Graham has sailed for Europe. That night Imogene goes to the opera without Colville, and the next day cultivates Morton and snubs Colville during a trip to Fiesole. Colville finds himself more and more at ease with Mrs. Bowen. Imogene's intense gaze at a pair of rapturous young lovers in Fiesole makes Colville realize that she wishes her own engagement were like that. Imogene tells Colville that her mother is coming, and asks what he will do if her mother refuses her consent. Colville says all that matters is how Imogene feels, but she can't make herself say that she is worried about her feelings. When later he says that he thinks she should tell Morton about the engagement, she tells him angrily that he is saying that for Mrs. Bowen. On the way back from Fiesole the horses rear, Colville saves Mrs. Bowen and Effie, Imogene impulsively refuses to let Colville save her, Morton does save her, and Colville, entangled with the harness, is pulled down over a wall in the wreckage of the carriage. Colville revives in bed at Mrs. Bowen's palazzo. Effie and Mrs. Bowen visit him; Imogene doesn't. Mrs. Bowen tells him that Mrs. Graham and Imogene will see him when he is stronger. Mrs. Graham, a brisk, sensible woman, eventually tells Colville that she is taking Imogene home because Imogene has discovered that she doesn't love Colville. He releases Imogene from her engagement, and says she needn't see him; she rushes in, however, and delivers a passionate farewell. Colville subsides into a torpor, with Mrs. Bowen and Effie watching over him.

In late May Colville is well and ready to leave Mrs. Bowen's house, though he is still rather vague-minded from a concussion. He feels close to Mrs. Bowen and Effie now. Talking with Waters, Colville resents the old man's comparison of Colville's relation to Imogene to Faust's trying to recover his youth with Marguerite. Colville does realize that he loves Mrs. Bowen, but he is convinced that she dislikes him. That evening Colville, made confident by a new suit, visits Mrs. Bowen and tells her that he loves her. She says that she loves him but will not marry him, because she is still indignant at the way he has treated her in the last months and forced her to be an adversary to Imogene. He submits to her will and rises to go, but Effie wants him to stay and Mrs. Bowen calls him back, for good. Colville and Mrs. Bowen are married at once, and now live in Rome, where they hear that Imogene is back home in Buffalo, where Morton may visit her.

Mrs. Amsden, Effie Bowen, Mrs. Evalina Bowen, Theodore Colville, carriage drivers, young Englishman, Italian gentlemen, Imogene Graham, Mrs. Graham, maskers, Rev. Morton, Paolo, servants, Madame Uccelli, Rev. Waters.

"Jim Leonard's Hair-Breadth Escape." See The Flight of Pony Baker.

"The Journeyman's Secret. Stray Leaves from the Diary of a Journman Printer," 1853.

"I," the narrator, a printer, is puzzled by the behavior of another printer, a pale, silent, hard-working man who lives in the shop. Despising him for his miserliness, the other printers eventually force him into a fight. Stopping it, the narrator makes the man explain himself. He says that he is supporting his mother and five siblings, including a blind sister who can perhaps be cured, at great expense. The other printers, repentant, now insist on his taking their wages. Shortly after, he leaves, and they hear later that his sister was cured.

Foreman, "I" (the narrator), a silent printer, printers, Zeke.

The Kentons, 1902.

Judge Rufus Kenton and his wife, Sarah, an elderly, well-to-do couple, live in a large house in Tuskingum, Ohio, a pleasant county seat. They have four children: Richard, a lawyer, who lives next door with his wife and son; Ellen, a sensitive, literary girl; Lottie, a pretty, pert sixteen-year-old; and Boyne, their fourteen-year-old son. The Judge was a colonel in the Civil War, and in his retirement from the bar and the bench he is writing a history of his regiment. Lottie is very popular, but Ellen is too serious to be. Then Bittridge, a young reporter on the Tuskingum *Intelligencer*, interviews the Judge about his projected history and thus meets Ellen, who falls in love with him. But Bittridge simply uses the Kenton house as a base for flirtations with other girls, including a young wife, Mrs. Uphill. The Judge and his wife discuss ways to break up this situation, and finally accept Ellen's shy suggestion that they go to New York for the winter.

In New York the Kentons settle into an apartment hotel. After an initial period of homesickness, Lottie and Boyne begin to make friends and enjoy themselves in New York. Mrs. Kenton also enjoys her new freedom and the city opportunities, but the Judge becomes depressed in an alien environment where nobody knows who he is, and finally takes to his bed for six weeks. When he recovers, his doctor prescribes a trip to Europe. Though the Judge feels that Tuskingum would be much better medicine, he changes his mind when Ellen receives a letter from Bittridge asking her for a meeting when she returns home. Ellen can't decide whether she will see Bittridge or go to Europe. She admits that he hasn't said he loves her, but she blames her family's opposition for that. When she bursts into tears at the imminent prospect of going abroad, the Judge tries to return their tickets, but then, despising herself for her weak feelings, she agrees to sail at a later date. The Judge now invents an excuse for a short trip back to his beloved Tuskingum.

The Judge goes sadly through his empty house and finally sits down in his library, where he tries to understand why he should be punished by exile in his old age. Unconsciously weeping, he looks up to see Bittridge lounging in the door. The Judge orders him out of the house, but Bittridge blandly insists on explaining himself and assuring the Judge that there was nothing between him and Mrs. Uphill. Even his mother, Bittridge complains, is after him to apologize to the Kentons. And he says he wrote to Ellen because he feels that she is something sacred. The Judge doesn't believe all this, but Bittridge is so persistently ingratiating that the Judge just doesn't know how to get rid of him. The next afternoon Bittridge insists on seeing the Judge off at the depot and thus publicly demonstrates his friendliness with the Kentons, but he upsets Richard Kenton and his wife, Mary. Back in New York, the Judge tells his wife what has happened, and she tells Ellen, who says that she won't write to Bittridge, because nothing has changed. But a week later Bittridge suddenly arrives at their hotel with his mother, a fatuous, vulgar little woman with bleached hair. They insist on calling on the Kentons. Bittridge behaves like Ellen's suitor and dominates the conversation except when his mother is singing his praises. After this bewildering episode, the Judge retires to the hotel reading room, only to find Bittridge already there. He confides to the Judge that he has been offered a position in the advertising department of a New York newspaper and has brought his mother along to look the place over because she has been the guiding-star of his life. He asks the Judge's advice in selecting a theater to take his mother to.

The Judge and his wife decide that they must let Ellen give Bittridge another trial so she will see him for what he is. In the evening Bittridge says that his mother has a headache and asks Mrs. Kenton's permission to take Ellen to the theater instead. After Ellen has gone, Lottie and Boyne are indignant that Mrs. Kenton has allowed her to go without a chaperon. Waiting up for her, her parents hear Bittridge and Ellen outside the door. He kisses her by force and runs downstairs. Ellen is hysterical. Her mother is sure that Ellen hates Bittridge now. The Judge is ready to kill Bittridge, but his wife makes him promise that he won't touch him. The next morning, when Bittridge genially greets the Judge as if nothing had happened, the old man refuses to speak to him. But Bittridge insists that he must talk to him about Ellen. When the Judge refuses again and orders him to go away, Bittridge, sneering, rubs the back of his hand into the Judge's face. As Boyne springs to his father's defense, Bittridge knocks the boy to his knees. A porter offers to send for the police. After the Judge refuses to have the police sent for, the manager has Bittridge and his mother thrown out of the hotel.

Lottie and Boyne report the incident to Richard. Shortly thereafter, when Bittridge gets off the train in Tuskingum, Richard whips him with a cowhide. The two men part in absolute silence. Just before the Kentons sail for Europe, Mrs. Kenton receives a letter from Mary Kenton telling her what Richard has done.

On board, the Kentons meet Rev. Hugh Breckon, of New York, Boyne's roommate. The friendly young minister chats with Lottie, who dismisses him as trivial. Everybody except the Judge and Ellen gets seasick. When these two have breakfast with Breckon, he senses that all the Kentons are concerned about Ellen and that her suffering is psychological rather than physical. Breckon and Ellen go up on the heaving deck to watch the waves, and he catches her in his arms to prevent her falling overboard. Boyne is scandalized by this incident. By lunch time only Breckon and Ellen are able to eat. At first they get along well, but then a teasing remark from him sends Ellen indignantly from the table and to her stateroom, where Lottie says tartly that Ellen and Breckon will be a repetition of Ellen and Bittridge. Ellen flees, only to meet the young minister again. He apologizes. Ellen tries to initiate a conversation about the justice of avenging an injury, but Breckon, sensing how serious and personal this question is for her, backs off. Diasppointed, Ellen leaves him again.

The Kentons discuss their daughter and Breckon. Mrs. Kenton worries that Ellen is too countrified and moody to attract the fashionable Breckon; the indignant Judge is sure that Ellen looks pretty and stylish enough for anybody. Lottie and Boyne have one of their typical spats. Then Mr. Pogis, a very young Englishman, manages to get himself introduced to Lottie. As he goes off for a stroll with Lottie, Boyne tells Ellen that Lottie is annoyed because Breckon has met a young lady and her mother, people he already knows. Breckon broods about Ellen; although he considers both her diction and her clothes provincial, he finds her fragility beautiful and continues to wonder about her mysterious unhappiness. Ellen tells her mother that she would like to confide her story to Breckon to see what his reaction would be. She says that she can forget Bittridge now because the Kentons haven't done anything to revenge themselves upon him. Mrs. Kenton makes Lottie and Boyne promise not to tell Ellen about Richard's whipping Bittridge. She sings Breckon's praises to her husband; the Judge is less eager to have him for Ellen.

Miss Rasmith, Breckon's young lady, takes pains to ingratiate herself with the innocent and trusting Boyne; they discuss a romance he has been reading about a European princess in love with a young American. Meanwhile, Lottie and Pogis continue their flirtation, and she teases her brother about Miss Rasmith's being old enough to be his grandmother. We learn that Mrs. Rasmith, a wealthy widowed member of Breckon's congregation, and her thirty-year-old daughter, Julia, are on board trying to attract the minister. Julia tries to get Breckon to say he will visit her in Europe. He evades her attempts to talk about Ellen. Julia makes friends with Ellen and tells her that although girls are said to be dying for Breckon, she thinks he has made up his mind to remain unmarried. She adds that she and Breckon have always been very good friends. Breckon confides to Ellen that he is trying to decide whether he should accept a call from London or return to his New York congregation, some of whom would prefer an older minister. Feeling unqualified to help him in reaching his decision, she urges him to consult her father.

Ellen tells the Judge that there is something Breckon wants to talk to him about, and her father immediately leaps to the conclusion that Breckon is coming to ask for Ellen's hand. He and his wife talk each other into a state of joyous excitement. At lunch Breckon jokes with Lottie, and the Judge is furious with the minister's failure to pay enough attention to Ellen, but when Breckon spends the entire afternoon with her, the Judge is appeased. When Mrs. Kenton finally discovers what Breckon wanted to speak to the Judge about, she cannot help giving away their mistake, and Ellen bursts into tears of shame. When Mrs. Kenton succeeds in convincing her husband of how wrong they were, his reaction is to treat Breckon with great haughtiness. Breckon in turn is completely confused, espe-

cially when Ellen stops coming to meals. When the Rasmiths get
ready to leave at Boulogne, they are astonished by Breckon's an-
nouncement (which astonishes himself) that he is continuing on to
Rotterdam. Since that is the Kentons' destination, Mrs. Kenton
takes this as a hopeful sign and consults first with her husband and
then with Ellen about how they should behave now. Ellen's answer
is to go up on deck and thank Breckon for his decision. Then they
walk and talk for hours.

The next day the ship arrives in Rotterdam, and Breckon and the
Kentons take a train to the Hague. They finally settle into the Kurhaus in Scheveningen, where Ellen and Breckon enjoy themselves
strolling on the beach. She happily confides to her mother that she
would like to live in the present. The Kentons are concerned for ap-
pearances because a Dutchwoman takes Ellen and Breckon for a
newly married couple. When the young Queen of Holland attends a
concert at the hotel, Boyne fantasizes about her; Mr. Trannel, a conceited medical student who hangs around Lottie, sarcastically urges
him on. Boyne awkwardly asks his mother if it is possible for a person to control his fantasies about falling in love, but when she
thinks that he is referring to Julia Rasmith, he refuses to confide
anymore. As Boyne's fantasies about the young Queen increase in
intensity, he buys her miniature, sees her twice, and imagines dying to save her from an anarchist. Trannel continues to tease him
about his infatuation. Boyne almost confides the whole story to Ellen, but although he gives her the miniature for safekeeping, she
doesn't guess that he is dreaming about the Queen.

The Kentons plan an excursion including Breckon and Trannel.
When Lottie refuses to go because she scorns Trannel as a Cook's
tourist, Mrs. Kenton also decides to stay behind. Arriving in Leyden, the group find it decorated for a visit from the Queen. With
Trannel as their guide, they set off in two carriages, the Judge, Ellen,
and Breckon in one, and Trannel and Boyne in the other. Trannel
regales Boyne with a preposterous story about himself which he insists is the true story behind a romance that Boyne has been reading
about a fifteen-year-old princess and a young American. Boyne believes that Trannel gave up marrying the princess only because he
would have lost his American citizenship by doing so. Just then the
young Queen's carriage appears, and Trannel pretends that he sees
her beckoning to Boyne. Convinced, Boyne starts toward his idol.
He is instantly seized by the Queen's detectives and marched off to

a magistrate. Fortunately, Breckon speaks Dutch, and with him as their interpreter the magistrate and Judge Kenton soon understand each other. Boyne is merely given a fatherly warning. At the family conclave that evening, when Boyne is forced to describe Trannel's role in the affair, Lottie says that it justifies her earlier rejection of Trannel and loudly adds that if her brother Richard were there he would cowhide Trannel just as he had Bittridge. Horrified by the disclosure of the secret, Ellen's parents find out that she has known all along because Mrs. Bittridge wrote to her about it. She tells them that she answered Mrs. Bittridge's letter simply by saying that she was sorry. The elder Kentons, who expected her feelings for Bittridge to revive in sympathy, are bewildered but hopeful.

When Breckon finally asks the Judge's permission to propose to Ellen, the older man at first believes that the minister wants to ask him whether he should return to his New York congregation. Informed of Breckon's request, Ellen insists that her mother must tell him all about Bittridge before she will let him propose to her. Mrs. Kenton persuades the Judge to perform this embarrassing task for her, and he does it beautifully. Ellen asks Breckon whether he cares about what Bittridge has done. When he says yes, she accepts him.

The Kentons return to Tuskingum, and Ellen and Breckon are married. Lottie marries Mr. Elroy, a rising lawyer, and they build a house on the Kentons' lot. Boyne begins to read law in his brother Richard's office. The Kentons visit the Breckons in New York every winter. Breckon and Ellen discuss the Bittridge affair in full detail. Although Bittridge works on a New York newspaper, the two men never meet each other.

> Clarence Bittridge, Mrs. Bittridge, Rev. Hugh Breckon, Dutch detectives, Elroy, Boyne Kenton, Ellen Kenton, Lottie Kenton, Mary Kenton, Richard Kenton, Judge (or Colonel) Rufus Kenton, Sarah Kenton, Dutch magistrate, Jim Plumpton, Rita Plumpton, Pogis, porters, Miss Julia Rasmith, Mrs. Rasmith, Trannel, Mrs. Uphill.

The Lady of the Aroostook, 1879.

In a parlor in South Bradfield, a Massachusetts hill town, three people wait for the stage to stop outside. They are Lydia Blood, a charming New England girl, well-dressed and self-possessed, but naïve; her rustic aunt, Miss Maria Latham; and her even more rustic grandfather, Miss Latham's father. Orphaned years ago, Lydia has lived with the old people, and recently has been teaching school. The hens scratch and cluck outside as the three discuss Lydia's forthcoming trip to see her father's sister, Mrs. Erwin, in Venice. Lydia will go to Trieste on the sailing ship *Aroostook* from Boston.

After a confusing trip to and across Boston, Lydia and her grandfather rest on the wharf at East Boston. Two handsome young men passing by ask if she is ill, to her embarrassment. Accidentally encountering Captain Jenness of the *Aroostook*, Lydia and the old man row out to the ship with him. The captain takes Mr. Latham back to his train, leaving Lydia alone on the ship. She meets the friendly cabin boy, Thomas, age fourteen. We learn of Lydia's vocal gifts which so impressed Lydia's aunt on a visit to America that she invited Lydia out to Venice for training. The next morning, the young men Lydia saw on the wharf board from a tug as the ship is leaving the harbor.

At home, Miss Latham and her father discuss the double problem of Lydia's being the only woman on board the *Aroostook*, and the presence of the two young men. Later the minister tells Miss Latham he thinks it will be all right, because Lydia has self-reliance and native good sense. On the *Aroostook*, meanwhile, Captain Jenness introduces Lydia to the young men, Mr. Dunham and Mr. Staniford, and to another passenger, Mr. Hicks, a weak young man, who, we learn later, is being sent on a voyage by his father in an attempt to conquer his alcoholism. Dunham and Staniford show their contempt for Lydia and their boredom in her presence, but decide not to let her realize the anomaly of her position as the only woman on board. The two young Brahmins snub Hicks. As for Lydia, they are sure that she is named Lurella. Staniford especially feels of a different race from her kind of raw, rural Yankees. Staniford is traveling to Europe for six months to indulge his artistic tastes before going West somewhere to ranch and eke out his small inherited income. As time passes, he continues to jeer at the life he imagines "Lurella" has led, but he is clearly becoming attracted to her. Dunham, a kindlier, softer person, is pained at Staniford's jesting. Dunham is en route to Dresden to join his fiancée, a demanding, neurasthenic woman. Talking to Lydia, he feels her freshness and seriousness. He lets a hen escape from its pen and over the side.

Lydia soothes his chagrin dexterously, to the later amusement of Staniford, who is obsessed with Lydia, though he avoids her company.

The passengers amuse themselves while Staniford stands aloof, tries to analyze Lydia's self-possession and her lack of open interest in books, and ridicules Dunham's High Church Anglicanism. Staniford is convinced that Lydia dislikes him for his indifference to her and to women in general. He and Lydia discuss Venice in their first long talk. He learns that her initial is L. and is much confused to hear that it stands for Lydia. They learn a good deal about each other; we learn that Staniford is twenty-eight. On Sunday Lydia impresses everyone with her beauty in her best dress (her aunt is an expert dressmaker) and with her singing at the church service organized by Dunham. Staniford is now much impressed with Lydia, but conceals his feelings and annoys everyone by appearing to scoff at religion. Staniford and Lydia walk on deck in the moonlight, and become more intimate. Now he is really smitten and barely keeps himself from kissing her hand. Later Staniford feels ashamed for what he thinks is his flirting and trifling with Lydia. He and Lydia blush when they meet. Dunham thinks that he has misled Lydia into caring for himself. Staniford is sardonic at this, and bitter at himself, and is furious when he sees Lydia laughing with the cad Hicks. Staniford and Dunham draw off as Hicks and Lydia practice music together. Later Staniford is reconciled with Lydia and learns that she doesn't care for Dunham, but again Lydia goes off to practice with Hicks, and again Staniford is angry.

The second mate expresses his contempt for Hicks to Staniford, who feels it is up to him to separate Lydia from the cad. After a brief spat Staniford and Lydia are closer than ever. The weather turns bad, and Staniford sulky, to his own and Lydia's dismay. A great storm comes. Staniford collapses completely, but Lydia is a fine sailor. Finally, in good weather, the ship arrives at Gibraltar, where Hicks and Lydia go sightseeing while Staniford sulks on board. Hicks pawns his watch ashore, smuggles some liquor on board, and appears drunk at the dinner table. All are disgusted, especially Lydia. Hicks annoys everyone, and especially baits Staniford. Hicks tries to punch Staniford, slips, and falls overboard. Staniford plunges in and holds Hicks up until the ship's boat can get to them. Staniford is typically sardonic about his heroism. Hicks is abjectly apologetic. As the days pass, Lydia, rather disgusted with the whole situation, avoids all the men. Hicks (and Howells) regret Hicks's inevitable alcoholic doom. Hicks leaves the ship at Messina.

During four days at Messina, Staniford is puzzled at Lydia's continued coolness, but he is forced to contrast her favorably with Mrs. Rivers, a silly American society woman who pursues him. After the ship sails again, Lydia is friendly, and both happy and nervous about the prospect of reaching Trieste and leaving the ship. Staniford finds her unsympathetic to Hicks, but not as impressed by his rescue of Hicks as he thinks she should be. Struck by Lydia's high level of ideals, Staniford wonders how she will fare amid the crudities of European behavior. He admits to Dunham that he is in love. Once Staniford and Lydia almost tell each other their feelings, but draw back. Dunham thinks that Staniford is in love with a married woman, but is glad when he realizes that Staniford loves Lydia, although he considers her Staniford's social inferior. Staniford and Lydia are very close as the ship approaches Trieste. Finally he seizes her hand and she lets him hold it. After arrival in Trieste, Lydia leaves for Venice, expecting Staniford there shortly, though no explicit words of love have passed between them. Suddenly Staniford feels ashamed of letting Lydia go without an open declaration; he was silent because of his and Dunham's opinion that he should not speak until Lydia was under her aunt's wing. While they are looking frantically for Lydia at the Trieste docks, Dunham falls and has a concussion. Staniford must stay with him in Trieste.

Lydia is escorted from Trieste to Venice by her uncle, Mr. Erwin, a genial Englishman of sixty, much interested in American slang. Arriving with him in Venice at dawn, Lydia is amazed and bewildered by the city. Unimpressed by her aunt's splendid palazzo, she feels homesick for the *Aroostook*. Her aunt greets her with warm volubility, and after breakfast takes her in a gondola to the English church, explaining European mores en route. Lydia's singing at church makes her an instant celebrity with the English colony, especially Lady Fenleigh, its leader. Lydia, however, has much trouble adapting to Mrs. Erwin's European ways and her total submission to English demands on Americans. Mrs. Erwin wants to subordinate Lydia's voice training to her social progress. Lydia meets a Miss Landini, who scandalizes Lydia with her swearing and dubious parentage. Put off further by the many other Italian and English people she meets at her aunt's house, Lydia refuses to sing to them, and to go to the opera on Sunday night. Mrs. Erwin admits to Lydia that it is hard to absorb European ways. She has deliberately confined herself to the English, whom she detests, because she wants to beat them on their own ground. She lectures Lydia on proprieties, and is horrified to hear that Lydia was the only woman on the *Aroostook*. Lydia defends her shipboard friends and attacks European corruption, but is forced to conclude that Staniford, having been in Europe before, was merely taking advantage of her. Mrs. Erwin is optimistic about Staniford's intentions, but feels that he is socially too high to care for Lydia. The two women expect Staniford that day, and with Lydia hopeful again, they get ready for his arrival, but days drag by, he never comes, and Lydia is in despair.

Meanwhile, after five days of delirium in Trieste, Dunham recovers. To his horror, Staniford finds that his letter to Lydia was never mailed. He rushes to Venice, where he finds Mrs. Erwin prostrated and Lydia bitter. Staniford now woos Lydia ardently, but he is hamstrung by his previous failure ever to say that he loved her. Slowly he beats down her suspicions about the recent events and the voyage. Finally, she accepts him. Six weeks later, they are married, in Europe. Staniford, because of his tendency to sea-sickness, declines the captain's invitation to return home in the *Aroostook*. The Stanifords, with the Erwins, return to America via England. The young couple settle on a ranch in California; the Erwins are very content in Santa Barbara. Dunham marries his fiancée Miss Hibbard (who has utter contempt for Lydia) and returns to Boston. Eventually the Stanifords visit South Bradfield, which depresses Staniford. Lydia's aunt and grandfather are not one bit impressed with Lydia's Boston husband.

> Lydia Blood, Charles Dunham, Mrs. Dunham (*née* Hibbard), Henshaw Erwin, Mrs. Josephine Erwin, Lady Fenleigh, gondoliers, Hicks, Captain Jenness, Miss Landini, Miss Maria Latham, Deacon Latham, Mason, Colonel Pazzelli, Ezra Perkins, Mrs. Rivers, Rose-Black, sailors, James Staniford, Thomas, Veronica, Watterson.

The Landlord at Lion's Head, 1897.

Lion's Head, a large mountain in northern New England, resembles a recumbent lion, especially when viewed from a shelf across the valley on which sits an old farmhouse. Summer people come to admire the view while the farm wife sells them refreshments. She has a tubercular husband, several tubercular children, and, when the story begins, a vigorous three-year-old son. Ten years pass. Two of the three older sons go West, and the two little girls die, leaving the parents and two sons.

One August day, when the farmer is ready to give up, a stranger, carrying an easel, walks up to the farm. He is Jere Westover, a painter living in Boston. Checking the impudence of the youngest son, now a sturdy thirteen, Westover asks for dinner, and after enjoying it arranges for board with the nervous farm wife, Mrs. Durgin. Westover paints a picture of Lion's Head while the boy, Jeff, watches skeptically. Later Westover stops Jeff's bullying of a little girl and a small boy. Unabashed and unrepentant, Jeff identifies them as Cynthia and Frank Whitwell, who live nearby with their father, a widower. For a few days Westover works on his picture at sunset, tramps around with Jeff, and sleeps well at night. He meets Whitwell, a shabby, garrulous man who says that Jeff got his devilment from his grandfather, a cantankerous Copperhead who died in the flames of his tavern. When the picture is finished, Jeff brings all the neighbors to see it. Mrs. Durgin can't afford to buy it, so Westover promises to send her a photograph of it. Though she dislikes hotel guests as a species, she plans to have boarders and advertise for them in Boston. Next day, when Westover leaves, Jeff, concealed in the family graveyard, rains apples on him.

The following spring Westover puts in the Boston papers an advertisement that Mrs. Durgin sends with the news that Mr. Durgin is dead. Westover goes to France to study. Five years later he returns, in a heat wave, and goes at once to Lion's Head, where the house is now a small hotel, and Jeff a stocky, coolly confident youth of eighteen. Westover has his old room, and finds his dinner good and the hotel simple but comfortable. Mrs. Durgin says that the hotel is a success and gives Westover much of the credit. She wants Jeff to go to Harvard and become a lawyer, not a hotel keeper. Reluctantly Westover agrees to help Jeff. Westover meets Cynthia, now a shy, pretty young lady who reminds him of a hermit thrush. Whitwell, equipped with new teeth, is now the guide and rustic philosopher for the lady hotel guests. These ladies make much of Westover, who finds the American summer-hotel world simple and wholesome. One day a Mrs. Marven snubs Jeff at a picnic by giving him the first plate and suggesting that he go eat with the horses; he stalks off, and so does Whitwell. Next day Mrs. Durgin throws the woman out. Westover is a little disgusted that Jeff's mother fights his battles for him, but Mrs. Durgin feels justified.

At Harvard that fall, Jeff is soon at home in Boston night life but not in the Yard, where he remains a "jay," an outsider. When Jeff treats with indifference an invitation Westover gets him, the artist drops him, but Jeff comes to see him now and then. In the spring Jeff is suspended for drinking. During the summer he works his way to Europe and studies hotel keeping there, as Westover learns at Lion's Head. With the ailing Jackson Durgin, the older son, Jombateeste, the French-Canadian handyman, and Whitwell, Westover watches one evening as a planchette seems to draw the words "broken shaft" and "Thomas Jefferson Durgin," suggesting a fault in Jeff's ship. Then Jeff himself walks in, with vivid impressions of Europe and its hotels. Later, Westover, to his distress, sees Jeff strolling with his arm around Cynthia.

Two wealthy ladies, Mrs. Vostrand and her daughter Genevieve, newly back from Europe and arrived at Lion's Head, talk to Jeff and Whitwell in a condescending way. Westover had known the Vostrands in Italy and found them shallow. Remembering Mrs. Marven, Mrs. Durgin won't let Jeff squire these ladies about. Jeff goes off to Cambridge early, leaving Cynthia to do all the work. Westover parts with Jeff coldly. In the fall, when the Vostrands take an apartment in Boston, Westover tries to help them socially, but they are not accepted, and are happy to be taken about by Jeff, who now dresses fashionably, though he looks too powerful and primitive for his clothes. Mrs. Vostrand questions Westover closely about Jeff's prospects, and tells him about Genevieve's broken-off affair with an Italian count. One day, from Mrs. Vostrand's window Westover apparently sees Jeff propose to Genevieve and be refused as they sit on a park bench. That evening Jeff confirms Westover's supposition, and adds that Genevieve is already engaged. The Vostrands then leave Boston.

After two summers Westover returns to Lion's Head to find the hotel greatly enlarged, under Jackson's supervision, but still simple. Jeff finds it very unsophisticated and wants to run it his own way; he wants to be a hotel keeper, not a lawyer, and have a Southern

hotel, for the winter, to balance Lion's Head. When Jeff asks Westover to convince his mother of the need for this policy, Westover
notes again how willing Jeff is to use his friends. The two men discuss Genevieve's recent marriage to the count, whom Mrs. Vostrand
supports.

One day Jeff tells Cynthia that Jackson is worsening and must be
sent away, that he plans to keep a hotel, Lion's Head or some other,
and that he wants to quit Harvard and go to work. Suddenly he proposes. Cynthia points out that she has always cared for him, but he
hasn't always cared for her; however, she tacitly accepts him on the
basis of his finishing Harvard. Whitwell is still suspicious of Jeff,
but approves of his plan to take over and improve Lion's Head with
Cynthia's help. Mrs. Durgin jealously thinks that the plan to send
Jackson away is Cynthia's, and when Jeff tells her that he and
Cynthia are engaged, she thinks that the engagement is Cynthia's
scheme too. Jeff points out that he can never marry a Boston girl (as
his mother wishes) because to Boston he is a jay. Jackson finds
Cynthia good enough for Jeff, to Mrs. Durgin's irritation. Finally she
accepts Cynthia, and, even more reluctantly, Jeff's decision to run
Lion's Head rather than pursue a city career. Irrationally, Westover
resents the engagement, but congratulates Jeff. Jackson leaves for
Egypt. At Lion's Head during the harsh winter Mrs. Durgin eagerly
reads Jackson's letters, and Cynthia, Jeff's. He wants to quit Harvard, but Cynthia persuades him to finish.

At a tea Jeff is asked to by a charitable student, his barbaric vigor
attracts Bessie Lynde, a vivacious, bored post-debutante. She is impressed by his self-assurance but disdainful of his jayhood; he admires her audacity and sexual attractiveness. Later, Jeff goes to a
Mrs. Bevidge's charity tea to see her and walks her home. At her
door he meets Alan Lynde, her alcoholic brother. Later Lynde
chides Bessie for being seen with a notorious jay and cad. Bessie
jeers at a drunkard's assuming such a pose of virtue. Secretly Bessie
likes Jeff, who isn't afraid of her the way most of the acceptable men
are. The Lyndes are a wealthy old family, reduced to the orphaned
Lynde children and Miss Louisa Lynde, their deaf, ineffectual aunt.
Lynde and Bessie regret to each other their aimlessness and their
weakness for excitement—jays for her, jags for him—and half-
seriously promise each other to reform.

At a ball Jeff dances with Bessie and gets Lynde so drunk that

Westover must take him home, but Lynde won't leave the carriage unless Jeff is there. While Westover fetches him, Lynde disappears. Back from the ball, Bessie broods about her flirtation with Jeff. Then Lynde, dragging Jeff forcibly, staggers in and passes out. With amusement Jeff tells Bessie about the evening, and leaves. Bessie feels compromised. Later her friend Mary Enderby gives her the harsh Boston opinion of Jeff. Dr. Lacy then tells her that Lynde must go off again to take the cure. Bessie wishes she could confide in the doctor but finds him too pompous, and she can't get Lynde sober enough to discuss the case.

With Westover, Jeff refuses to feel or act ashamed or guilty for these goings-on. He argues that evil just happens. Westover is angry, but finds Jeff's easy moral relativism unpleasantly attractive. Depressed, Westover goes up to Lion's Head, austerely beautiful in the winter. He is charmed again by Cynthia. Mrs. Durgin and Whitwell both question Westover about Jeff, whom Westover tries awkwardly to defend. The winter hills revive Westover and remind him of his boyhood in Wisconsin, where he lived, in a lumber camp, until he was sixteen and some visitors noted his talent and helped him get out into the world. At sunset every day Westover paints Lion's Head. He joins Mrs. Durgin and Cynthia in airing out the empty hotel. Cynthia avoids speaking of Jeff. Westover tells her that she is better than Boston society people, and she is pleasantly confused.

Back in Boston, Westover finds Jeff more self-possessed and less attractive than ever. Meanwhile Jeff has renewed his acquaintance with Bessie. Mary Enderby fails to get Bessie to give Jeff up. In April she horrifies Mary by saying that she might spend a jay Class Day with Jeff. That night Jeff walks over from Cambridge and calmly makes himself at home. After they flirt, she stands in the door and refuses to let him pass unless he explains a remark. He seizes and kisses her, which she finds insulting but unpleasantly enjoyable. Jeff later tells Westover that it was only a game, which he thinks he won. He asks Westover what he should say to Cynthia about it. Disgusted, Westover says that Jeff should stick to Bessie, but Jeff can't see any advantage in that. Westover is deeply upset by Jeff's calm egotism and his philosophy of strength and amoral self-interest.

At Lion's Head Cynthia also tells Jeff to go back to Bessie. Whitwell is furious with him. Cynthia won't tell Mrs. Durgin what is wrong, but Jeff does tell her. She sympathizes with Cynthia and visualizes Bessie as a hussy. Later, during a stroll Jeff instinctively flirts with a young girl he meets on the road. That night, after Jeff prods Cynthia, she tells him that he should offer himself to Bessie. He doesn't want to, but Cynthia says that she can't go on with him as before. Later Cynthia tells her father that they must leave when Jackson returns.

Back in Cambridge Jeff finally accepts the loss of Cynthia, gives up trying to get his degree, and begins to think of Bessie again. At a jay spread on Class Day he meets Bessie, and at the Tree he seizes some flowers for her, but when he takes them to her, she is gone. While walking on a lonely road that evening, he is horsewhipped from a passing carriage by Alan Lynde. A few days later, after Jeff has recovered from his wounds, he refuses Westover's request to help Jackson, who has just landed in Boston and is very ill. Westover himself takes Jackson to Lion's Head. With Jackson dying, Jeff does come up, and tells Jackson that he will leave Cynthia alone now. When Jackson dies and Jeff takes over the hotel, the Whitwells and Jombateeste plan to leave, but Mrs. Durgin has a stroke, and they agree to stay on. She tries to get Cynthia and Jeff to make up, but Jeff can't do that for Cynthia's sake alone, and she refuses on any other basis. In September Mrs. Durgin dies. Jeff, who is going to Europe, renews the insurance and gets the Whitwells to look after the hotel during the winter. Just before leaving, Jeff meets Lynde (who is taking the cure nearby) in the woods, attacks him, and nearly kills him, but lets him go, either out of mercy or because Jombateeste appears—Jeff himself is never sure.

After Thanksgiving Whitwell appears in Boston and tells Westover that the hotel has just burned and everyone assumes that Jeff had him do it. Westover's lawyer reassures him. Whitwell tells Westover about the fight with Lynde. Westover can't figure out why Jeff let him go. Whitwell also says that Jeff is in Florence, which reminds Westover of the Vostrands. When Jeff hears of the fire, he cables Westover, rather than Whitwell, thus saving himself money and involving Westover, but the latter, vastly irritated, simply hands Jeff's affairs over to an expensive lawyer. Wondering why Jeff doesn't return, Westover receives a letter from Mrs. Vostrand. She says that Genevieve with her small daughter was separated from the count, who is now dead. The Vostrands met Jeff in Florence; he renewed his suit, saying that he had always loved only Genevieve, and she has accepted him. Mrs. Vostrand asks, with Jeff's consent, for any comments that Westover may have about Jeff. Disgusted, Westover sends his reply to Jeff and tells him to show it to Mrs. Vostrand if he wishes. In the letter he points out what he knows of Jeff's sins, and asks him to evaluate them himself. After mailing the letter Westover realizes that he should have written directly to Mrs. Vostrand. He sends her letter to Cynthia for an opinion. Shortly after, Mrs. Vostrand cables that Jeff and Genevieve are married. Later she writes that Jeff showed them the letter and they considered it favorable.

Westover now corresponds frequently with Cynthia. In the spring the Whitwells move to Cambridge with Jombateeste. Frank Whitwell stays behind to study for the ministry. Jeff is rebuilding Lion's Head House and staying in the Whitwell house. Westover visits Cynthia, gets on better terms with her, and has her pose for him. After a stay in Paris, Westover returns to find the Whitwells in Cambridge again. Cynthia is teaching school. Jeff, Whitwell says, has built a pretentiously elegant new hotel. Speculating about the phrase "broken shaft," Whitwell figures it means that Jeff has changed; Westover thinks it means that Jeff's evil destiny remains unfulfilled, but surely must be evil. Westover concludes that in this world all men, perhaps, are broken shafts. Realizing finally that he has loved Cynthia for a long time, Westover proposes. She says that she cares for him but must wait to be sure that her feeling is real.

> Andrew, Mrs. Bevidge, Andrew Jackson Durgin, James Monroe Durgin, Mrs. Durgin, Thomas Jefferson (Jeff) Durgin, Durgin daughters, Durgin sons, Mary (Molly) Enderby, girl, Captain Count Grassi (Gigi), Jombateeste, Dr. Lacy, Freddy Lancaster, Alan Lynde, Bessie Lynde, Louisa Lynde, Mrs. Marven, Willie Morland, Genevieve Vostrand, Mrs. Vostrand, Jere Westover, Cynthia Whitwell, Frank Whitwell, Whitwell.

The Leatherwood God, 1916.

In the 1820's the early settlers in the valley of Leatherwood Creek, in southern Ohio, are fairly well off, but not so well off that they have lost their profound interest in religion, which draws the

classes and sects of the community together in a large log building
called the Temple. One August morning Abel Reverdy, a gawky
young farmer, tells his neighbor, Matthew Braile, the local Squire or
Justice of the Peace, that a shouting, snorting stranger electrified the
crowd at the camp meeting the night before. With David Gillespie
and his beautiful red-haired daughter Jane, the stranger, a city-
dressed, long-haired man who calls himself Dylks, comes to the
Temple on Sunday night and preaches with great effect, though
Braile, an ironic skeptic and atheist, concludes at once that he is a
rascal. Talking with Gillespie, Dylks reveals that he is the first husband of Gillespie's sister Nancy, who remarried after Dylks disappeared years before. He has been East, largely in Philadelphia;
the stylish clothes, long mane, and confident manner he acquired
there disguise him with the local folk. Dylks has the Gillespies in
his power, because of Nancy's bigamy, and plans to use them as a
base to dominate the community. Nancy begs Gillespie not to reveal
Dylks's identity and the fact of her bigamy, but Gillespie
remorselessly insists that she is living in sin, and demands that she
leave her second husband, Laban Billings. Nancy tells Laban that
they must part; he lets her go to Gillespie's house with their baby
daughter and with Joey, Nancy's son by Dylks. Joey, a lively boy
who is apprenticed to the miller Hingston, insists on hearing the
new preacher, to whom he is mysteriously attracted.

In his preaching Dylks begins to hint that God has sent him.
Dylks has now managed to get himself sponsored by Hingston, a
man of greater wealth and standing than Gillespie. After the meeting Sally Reverdy, Abel's silly wife, is ecstatic over Dylks, and Jane
Gillespie quietly agrees that he has been sent by God, to her father's
and Nancy's irritation. Gillespie and Nancy agree to oppose Dylks.

The well-to-do people now believe that Dylks is sent by God; the
lowly are less susceptible but are puzzled and turn to the sardonic
Braile for explanations and support. The Hounds, a group of wild
irreligious young men, jeer at Dylks. Wild rumors circulate of his
powers and "doin's." Eventually Dylks proclaims himself God and
is worshipped by most of the people, including Jane Gillespie.
Braile is still scornful, but fears that Dylks will harm some foolish
woman. Gillespie is horrified by Jane's infatuation with Dylks.
Nancy can't help Gillespie, but agrees to try to reason with Jane.
Dylks visits Nancy. She treats him with cold contempt, but that

doesn't faze him. He coolly tries to convince her that he is God and that she should join him to take his message to the world. She stands up against his argument that anything that he, God, wills is right because God, he, wills it. Later Laban visits Nancy but refuses to stay because he feels that Dylks is her true husband. Nancy discusses her problems with Braile, who comforts her even though he can't be certain either way about the theology involved. In the evening Nancy watches the local people go to Hingston's mill to worship Dylks and see him perform a miracle. Again she lets her son Joey go.

At the mill the believers, the Little Flock, wait for Dylks while the unbelievers watch and the Hounds jeer. Jim Redfield, a powerful youth and leading Hound, makes his friends stop teasing Jane. The crowd goes into the mill to see a bolt of linsey-woolsey turned into a seamless raiment. After two hours Dylks has not appeared and Redfield is about to fetch him when he speaks from the darkness and says the miracle has occurred. The Hounds grab the cloth and tear it to bits. In the days after this "miracle," believers and unbelievers continue to spar. Jane angrily tells her father that she will deny Dylks only if Gillespie succeeds in bringing her a hair of Dylks's head. When the regular minister denounces Dylks in the Temple, the Little Flock rush out and go to the house of Enraghty, a well-to-do supporter of Dylks. Certain Dylks is hiding there, the unbelievers and Hounds storm the house; they glimpse him, but he vanishes. Finally he is found hiding in the chimney. Redfield tears out a strand of Dylks's hair, and Gillespie gives it to his wretched daughter. During the night the unbelievers keep Dylks captive in the Temple and abuse him despite Redfield's protection. In the morning Dylks is taken to Braile, who hears testimony and concludes that Dylks must be released because there is no Ohio law against a man's claiming to be God. Braile then escorts Dylks to the edge of the village and lets him run off.

Dylks takes refuge in a swamp, where he suffers acutely from hunger, pain, and self-pity. After a few days he creeps out past a sleeping guardian Hound and staggers to Nancy's house. She scorns him and his whining, but gives him food and shelter. She advises him to repudiate his pretensions and go to Braile for help. Dylks tells Braile that he was led on by his own hunger for immortality and even more by the spiritual hunger and the frantic re-

sponses of his Little Flock; their belief in him strengthened his belief in himself and vice versa in an uncontrollable spiral. Now he is
afraid to tell them that he was a fraud, because he has made Enraghty and Hingston "saints" and they will be angry at losing their
status and along with the rest may turn on him. He does promise to
leave without making more trouble. Braile puts Dylks under the
grudging protection of Redfield until Dylks can get away.

A chastened Dylks and a still zealous Flock gather with the unbelievers and the Hounds at the Temple. Dylks's silence under Enraghty's frantic praise is taken as approval of it. In his murky rheto-
ric Dylks tells the Flock that he will go "Over the Mountains" (to
Philadelphia) and create the New Jerusalem there. Many of the
Flock plan to follow him. Braile is disgusted by Dylks's unwillingness to be frank, but decides to let him try to sidle out of Leatherwood and his quandary in this way. Nancy lets Joey go with the
Hingstons on the march to Philadelphia, but only after she has convinced Joey that Dylks is bad. Dylks finally leaves, with the hard
core of the Flock.

A month later, in October, Redfield and Jane are courting. Jane
now spurns Hughey Blake, her awkward former swain. Nancy tells
Hughey not to worry about it, because Jane is a hard, headstrong
girl who needs a hard man. Joey suddenly returns, saying that Dylks
was drowned in Philadelphia.

According to Joey, as the group neared Philadelphia, many of the
Flock were beginning to doubt and to grumble at Dylks, and during
an argument Dylks somehow fell into a river by the road. Joey
leaped in and tried to save him, in vain. Before Dylks went down he
called Joey "son." Nancy now tells Joey that Dylks was his real father, and then asks him to go and bring back his true father, Laban.

Some thirty years later, in the early 1850's, T. J. Mandeville, a
scholar from Cambridge, Massachusetts, visits the now-aged Squire
to ask him about the legendary Leatherwood God. Braile says that
some of the Flock are still faithful. He thinks that Dylks appealed to
the longings of worn, anxious people for certainty and salvation,
and failed because he was timid and had a narrow field to work in.
Braile says that Nancy, Laban, and their daughter all died of fever
years ago, but Joey survived and is now running the Hingston Mill.
Redfield and Jane Gillespie are married, have many children, and
are reasonably happy together. Braile compares Dylks to Joseph

Smith, the Mormon leader, a similar phenomenon, who succeeded because he claimed to be only a prophet, not God.

Baby Girl Billings, Joey Billings, Laban Billings, Nancy Gillespie Dylks Billings, Hughey Blake, Matthew Braile, Mrs. Braile, Briggs, Joseph Dylks, Richard Enraghty, David Gillespie, Jane Gillespie, Elder Grove, Benny Hingston, Peter Hingston, T. J. Mandeville, David Mason, Jim Redfield, Abel Reverdy, Sally Reverdy.

Letters Home, 1903.

An epistolary novel. All letters are headed New York.

I. Otis Binning to Mrs. Walter Binning, Boston; Dec. 12, 1901. Mr. Binning, an elderly and prim Boston bachelor, tells his sister-in-law that he is provisionally settled in New York, which he finds noisy and dirty but intriguing.

II. Wallace Ardith to A. Lincoln Wibbert, Wottoma, Iowa; Dec. 15, 1901. Just arrived from Wottoma, Ardith, a young journalist with vague literary aspirations, is enraptured by the huge city and has already gotten over being jilted by a Wottoma girl, Caroline Deschenes. He has a chat with a literary gentleman in Central Park.

III. Abner J. Baysley to Rev. William Baysley, Timber Creek, Iowa; Dec. 19, 1901. Baysley has just been transferred to New York from Timber Creek, a village close to Wottoma, by Ralson, head of the Cheese and Churn Trust. The Baysleys have settled down in a flat. He misses Iowa and finds New York business very competitive. He runs into Ardith, a fellow native of Timber Creek.

IV. Miss America Ralson to Miss Caroline Deschenes, Wottoma; Dec. 18, 1901. After forming the Trust, the Ralsons have moved to New York and are beginning to make progress in the New York social whirl. They live in a luxury hotel, the Walhondia, and plan to build uptown. America has seen Ardith, who is nice but too literary and serious for her, she says. She invites Caroline to come to New York.

V. Miss Frances Dennam to Mrs. Ansel G. Dennam, Lake Ridge, New York; Dec. 19, 1901. To make money to help her widowed mother, Frances is job-hunting in New York and is rooming with Miss Holly, an energetic journalist from the South.

VI. Frances Dennam to Mrs. Dennam; Dec. 26, 1901. Frances doesn't have a job yet, but is confident.

VII. Wallace Ardith to A. L. Wibbert; Dec. 18, 1901. Ardith has encountered the Ralsons at their sumptuous hotel and is struck by their social isolation.

VIII. Ardith to Wibbert; Dec. 19, 1901. Ardith runs into Baysley and takes the spare room in their flat.

IX. Frances Dennam to Mrs. Dennam; Jan. 10, 1902. After many failures, Frances lands a job as secretary and companion to America Ralson.

X. Ardith to Wibbert; Jan. 10, 1902. Ardith is still overwhelmed by New York. He sees a good deal of the Ralsons, and rather looks down on Frances Dennam.

XI. Otis Binning to Mrs. Walter Binning; Jan. 11, 1902. Binning finds that New York atomizes him but piques him. He meets Ardith, America, and Mr. Ralson.

XII. Ardith to Wibbert; Jan. 17, 1902. Ardith meets Binning at a reception, and helps the Baysleys when Mr. Baysley is ill.

XIII. Frances Dennam to Mrs. Dennam; Jan. 17, 1902. The Ralsons keep Frances busy but are very nice to her. She also finds Ardith pleasant, but considers him a social climber. She meets Binning and finds him stuffy.

XIV. Otis Binning to Mrs. Walter Binning; Jan. 19, 1902. Binning analyzes the Ralsons as the type of the aggressive newly rich who flock to New York from the provinces in total ignorance of local social relations; and Ardith as the type of the young litterateur drawn nowadays to New York rather than Boston. It is clear to him that America wants Ardith.

XV. Ardith to Wibbert; Jan. 17, 1902. Ardith finds that New York's difference from Wottoma is essentially quantitative. At Miss Holly's suggestion he is writing a piece, "The Impressions of a Provincial," for the *Signal.*

XVI. America to Caroline; Jan. 19, 1902. America is glad that Caroline can come to New York sometime soon.

XVII. Ardith to Wibbert; Jan. 19, 1902. Ardith takes Essie Baysley, a naïve sixteen-year-old, to a French restaurant and to Keith's vaudeville.

XVIII. Frances Dennam to Mrs. Dennam; Jan. 19, 1902. A triangle is developing between Ardith, America (who wants Ardith), and

Caroline (who wants to renew the engagement she broke with Ardith). Frances likes the Ralsons.

XIX. Ardith to Wibbert; Jan. 20, 1902. Ardith describes a night at the opera with the Ralsons and Binning. He finds America more attractive than he did before.

XX. Otis Binning to Mrs. Walter Binning; Jan. 21, 1902. He comments on the opera evening, the crudeness of Ralson, and the mutual attraction of Ardith and America.

XXI. Frances Dennam to Mrs. Dennam; Jan. 21, 1902. Frances is amused by America's way of analyzing Ardith, her desire for him, and her jealousy of Caroline.

XXII. Ardith to Wibbert; Jan. 23, 1902. Ardith intercedes with Ralson on behalf of the ailing Baysley, who is afraid he might lose his job. In gratitude Essie kisses Ardith, and he feels bound to her, to his distress, but he can't hurt her by saying he doesn't love her.

XXIII. Ardith to Wibbert; Jan. 24, 1902. Ardith still doesn't know what to do about Essie.

XXIV. Binning to Mrs. Walter Binning; Jan. 24, 1902. He admires *The Second Mrs. Tanqueray*, which he saw when America was there with Ardith in a box.

XXV. Baysley to Rev. William Baysley; Jan. 25, 1902. He is better and has a raise; Ardith has been a great help.

XXVI. Ardith to Wibbert; Jan. 27, 1902. Ardith has been staying away from America, who concluded that he was ill and called on the Baysleys, to the embarrassment of Ardith and Essie.

XXVII. America to Caroline; Jan. 27, 1902. Being disillusioned with Ardith, America renews her invitation to Caroline.

XXVIII. Frances Dennam to Mrs. Dennam; Jan. 27, 1902. She wonders if she hasn't misjudged Ardith. America is staggered by Ardith's apparent engagement to Essie.

XXIX. Ardith to Wibbert; Jan. 28, 1902. Wibbert's good advice does not help Ardith, who is in a helpless muddle with Essie.

XXX. Binning to Mrs. Walter Binning; Feb. 6, 1902. In her attitudes toward Ardith and the Ralsons, Frances seems to be a remnant of New England morality. Binning wonders if Ardith will turn down the Ralson millions.

XXXI. Ardith to Wibbert; Feb. 6, 1902. Ardith told a grumpy America that he loved her, not Essie. Now he must explain himself to Essie.

XXXII. America to Caroline; Feb. 6, 1902. America triumphantly announces her engagement to Ardith, and repeats her invitation to Caroline to pay a visit.

XXXIII. Ardith to Wibbert; Feb. 7, 1902. Essie is ill, but Ardith, oddly enough, still finds himself able to write.

XXXIV. Binning to Mrs. Walter Binning; Feb. 14, 1902. He sees Ardith in Central Park looking grieved and despondent. They discuss love, and especially the man who is in love with more than one woman at a time. Ardith departs sneezing and very gloomy.

XXXV. Frances Dennam to Mrs. Dennam; Feb. 14, 1902. Frances can't believe that Ardith was never in love with Essie. Ardith comes to Frances, confesses that he did care somewhat for Essie, and says that he is going away. To her own surprise, Frances sympathizes with Ardith, but he won't accept her sympathy.

XXXVI. Ardith to Wibbert; Feb. 14, 1902. Coming down with the grippe, Ardith writes disjointedly about his love problems and breaks off in mid-sentence.

XXXVII. Frances to Mrs. Dennam; Feb. 15, 1902. America is furious that Frances talked to Ardith alone, and accuses Frances of betraying her. Frances walks out. Next day America, repentant, gets Frances to come with her to the Baysleys' to help take care of Ardith, who is delirious. Essie finds Ardith's unfinished letter and shows it to America, though it contains nothing incriminating. Frances is troubled that America and Essie hate each other. The doctor says not to notify Ardith's mother yet of his illness.

XXXVIII. America to Mrs. Rebecca Ardith; Feb. 15, 1902. America tells Mrs. Ardith that Ardith is ill but will recover, and should be moved because the Baysley place is too small and unhealthy.

XXXIX. Frances to Mrs. Dennam; Feb. 19, 1902. Ardith has been very ill and America is staying at the Baysleys', thus creating a good deal of friction. Frances persuades America to omit the conclusion of her letter to Mrs. Ardith in which she seems to blame the Baysleys for Ardith's illness.

XL. Frances to Mrs. Dennam; Feb. 20, 1902. Ardith is better and America is at home again. Rev. William Baysley read America's letter to Mrs. Ardith, who has bad eyesight, and cheered her up. America says that both she and Essie eavesdropped on Ardith's raving; she condemns Essie for this. When Frances accuses her of being hypocritical, America is angry but later repents.

XLI. Binning to Mrs. Walter Binning; Feb. 23, 1902. He writes whimsically of his many feminine fascinations, his current interest being Frances and her puritan nature.

XLII. Baysley to Rev. William Baysley; Feb. 23, 1902. Ardith is better. Baysley realizes now that Ardith has been involved with someone beside Essie. America has a spat with Essie.

XLIII. Mrs. Baysley to Mrs. William Baysley; Feb. 24, 1902. Baysley's letter is too gloomy, she thinks. Ardith may have been at fault, but not seriously so, and it was the Baysleys, after all, who persuaded him to stay there.

XLIV. Frances to Mrs. Dennam; March 4, 1902. America makes Frances listen to Ardith, weak and confused, say that he is ending his engagement to America because he must be good to Essie and marry her. America convinces herself that she must give Ardith up to Essie.

XLV. Ardith to Wibbert; March 4, 1902. Ardith has left the Baysley flat, but plans to go back there and propose to Essie, though he loves America.

XLVI. Frances to Mrs. Dennam; March 5, 1902. Binning is very nosy with Frances about the Ardith matter; she puts him off. She does explain the whole affair to Ralson, who has been away for some time. Baysley comes to complain about the way Ardith has been drawn away from Essie, but Ralson handles him smoothly and arranges to transfer him back to Timber Creek. Next morning Mrs. Baysley comes to see Ralson, but Frances and America come in first. Mrs. Baysley gives America back the check Ralson secretly gave Baysley, and says that the Baysleys want to stay in New York. Mrs. Baysley says that the Baysleys have seen Ardith and have released him. In fury America tells Ralson he can't buy Ardith for her.

XLVII. Frances to Mrs. Dennam; March 10, 1902. America tells Frances that she doesn't respect Ardith and is glad that she has lost him; this mood actually lasts for a day or two. Finally Ardith comes in with Ralson, and the lovers are reconciled.

XLVIII. Ardith to Wibbert; March 10, 1902. Mrs. Baysley's honesty overcame Ardith's complexities and scruples, and he had to confess to her that he loved America, not Essie. Ardith feels permanently embarrassed.

XLIX. Binning to Mrs. Walter Binning; March 12, 1902. He is irritated because he knows less and less of the affair, never did know much, and now finds it passing completely out of his ken.

> Wallace Ardith, Abner J. Baysley, Mrs. Abner J. Baysley,
> Miss Essie Baysley, Miss Jennie Baysley, Rev. William Bay-
> sley, Mrs. William Baysley, Otis Binning, Mrs. Walter Bi-
> nning, Casman, Mrs. Ansel G. Dennam, Frances Dennam,
> Caroline Deschenes, Miss Custis Holly, America Ralson,
> Ralson, Mrs. Ralson, Mrs. Van der Does, A. Lincoln Wib-
> bert.

"Letters of an Altrurian Traveller," 1893 (1968).

I. Aristides Homos writes from New York to his friend Cyril in Altruria. Having been in America for over a year, he finds that Americans are repeating in the nineteenth century the same mistakes the Altrurians made in the tenth. He tells Cyril that no Altrurian would consider America a civilized, democratic, or Christian country, although some Americans possess these virtues in spite of their country's conditions. As an illustration, he describes recent strikes. He is astonished by the attitude of most Americans toward these events; although a few of them understood the significance of these strikes as symptoms of a terrible internal disorder, most Americans felt only pride in their quick suppression by hired force or by the militia. Because their economics are pagan, Americans cannot understand that it is possible for people to live for instead of upon one another. Although there are no strikes at present, the depression going on is like the calm at the center of a cyclone. Tinkering with the monetary system has had no effect. Homos compares the position of the very rich and the very poor in America and Europe. Only the American middle class is still American in the old sense, and only they show an interest in Altrurianizing. He is convinced that conflict is imminent, but it will not effect any fundamental change. Americans will first have to give up their primitive ideas about money. All this, Homos tells Cyril, will seem strange to him in spite of his study of America. There is neither liberty nor equality in America. Class divisions are the sharpest in big cities like New York, which is why Homos is visiting New York City. He has found America disappointing and New York the ugliest city in the world, although there are a few beautiful buildings.

II. From Chicago, Homos writes enthusiastically about the

World's Fair. There he meets Mr. Bullion, the banker he met in New Hampshire the summer before. Bullion, a Bostonian, must admit that no city but Chicago could have built the Fair. Homos observes the quiet behavior of the country people at the Fair and is astonished by their apparent lack of resentment against the rich. Homos sees in the architecture of the Fair an Altrurian spiritual beauty because the capitalists who paid for it and the artists who created it made their contributions without any hope of material gain.

III. "A Bit of Altruria in New York." Back in New York City after an unpleasant train trip, Homos finds it even uglier than before. He enjoys Central Park, but is disturbed by the poverty he sees there. Homos also describes the procession of fashionable vehicles and cyclists. He finds the pleasure of the people in the natural beauty of the Park marred by the envy created by economic inequality.

IV. "Aspects and Impressions of a Plutocratic City." The Altrurian is appalled by the filth in the streets of New York. He describes Madison Avenue and Fifth Avenue and some of the business streets of the city. The poverty of the tenement district near the Hudson horrifies him, although he finds the area lively. Industry spoils the river's beauty, but near the docks there are fishermen and people enjoying the animated river scene. He finds himself ignoring and forgetting American poverty, like the well-to-do Americans who feel helpless to do anything about it; so he begs Cyril to remind him of the reality of Altruria, where things are very different.

V. "Plutocratic Contrasts and Contradictions." Homos describes vividly and at length the constant hurry and uproar of New York. He describes a typical New York street with its "savage anarchy" of ill-assorted buildings and vacant lots. He deplores the miles of saloons and the election frauds which are organized in them. He is also depressed by the contrast between the Parisian fashions of the rich and the ragged cast-offs of the poor. Many well-to-do American men he finds slovenly; but the women of all classes dress as well as they can. He pities the poor Italians who live in Greenwich Village. An ugly, barren field seems to symbolize the life of the urban poor to Homos. But he concludes that New Yorkers do not seem to be bothered by their city's ugliness.

Bullion, Cyril, Aristides Homos.

"Life and Letters," *Harper's Weekly*, 1895-1898.

Only those "Life and Letters" are summarized that are basically or preponderantly fictional.

Jl 6, 1895. "I" and a friend discuss household effects and their influence on women.

Jl 13, 1895. With his friend "I" continues the discussion of the effects of household possessions on women.

Ag 10, 1895. At a Long Island summer resort Life and Letters, two characters, discuss women cyclists.

Ag 24, 1895. Life and Letters, two characters, discuss summer hotels and the effect on marriage of the separation of married couples during the summer.

D 14, 1895. "I" is visited by the Christmas Muse—a lady cyclist, smoking, and dressed in knickerbockers. She doesn't inspire him, because she doesn't bring any Christmas presents, but she protests that on a bicycle she can't. When she regrets the way he has imagined her, he re-imagines her in the traditional way. They agree that Christmas being for children, Christmas literature should reflect the hopefulness in children's hearts.

Ap 25, 1896. With a friend, "I" discusses popular theater.

My 9, 1896. With a friend "I" discusses advertising.

D 12, 1896. The Christmas Muse arrives in a "horseless cutter," which she says Santa Claus is also going to use, and tries to help "I," the narrator, write his Christmas essay. After they discuss the women's clothing styles of the season, she concludes that Christmas beauty should be "the beauty of holiness," which she defines as "beauty of conduct." Then she vanishes.

Ja 23, 1897. "He," a friend of "I," the narrator, observes from his carriage a bread line of the unemployed, and discusses it with the child he has with him; later he expresses to the narrator his embarrassment at his own comfort.

D 25, 1897. The Christmas Muse brings Santa Claus to visit "I," the narrator, because Santa hopes that the narrator will support him against his debunkers. Santa is disappointed to hear the narrator argue that he is a useless superstition. When the others suggest that he be modernized, Santa protests that he must be accepted as he is, a symbol of goodwill, or rejected. The Muse agrees, and she and Santa vanish up the chimney.

Child, a friend, "he," I, "Letters," "Life," the Christmas Muse, Santa Claus.

"The Lost Child—A Street Scene," 1859.

On the street (evidently in Columbus, Ohio) the narrator, "I," observes a small, lost German child being comforted by an adult German immigrant. The pair go off looking for the child's mother, and the narrator wishes them well.

Lost German immigrant child, "I" (the narrator), German immigrant.

"The Magic of a Voice," 1899 (in *A Pair of Patient Lovers*, 1901).

In a small-town New England hotel, Stephen M. Langbourne, worn out from disappointment in love, finds himself awakened and then fascinated by the beautiful contralto speaking voice of one of two young women talking in the next room. He pictures her as tall and lovely. Next morning he gets up late and in the hall has only a brief partial glimpse of a tall girl and a short girl. He finds a letter on the floor lost apparently by the tall girl; it is addressed to Miss Barbara F. Simpson, of Upper Ashton Falls, New Hampshire, a nearby town. The hotel clerk says that the girls are cousins and live at the Falls with an aunt. After learning from the register that the other girl is Juliet D. Bingham, Langbourne is about to go see them when he gets a telegram recalling him to New York at once.

By fall, a few months later, Langbourne is so obsessed with the memory of the girl's voice that he sends her the letter he found, with an explanatory note. After some time he receives a discreet thank-you note. He sends her some seed catalogues (her letter was from a seedsman). During the voluminous correspondence that follows, she sends him a picture. In May he goes to the Falls, though he doesn't know exactly where Miss Simpson lives. He hears her voice in a house and goes in, only to find that the voice he loves and the name of Simpson belong to the wrong girl, the short one; the tall one is Juliet Bingham, who is high-voiced and bossy. Langbourne now realizes that the picture Miss Simpson sent him was really Juliet's; she says that they sent him the picture and wrote the letters in a spirit of fun. Langbourne is crushed at the loss of his dream. Barbara can't help him, and the situation becomes painful, though she seems to be able to find some humor in it. Juliet returns and gets Langbourne out of the house. He would like to drop the whole mat-

ter, but at thirty-five he feels that he can't do that, and he is beginning to feel drawn to Barbara anyway.

Next day Juliet returns Langbourne's letters to him, says that she
put Barbara up to the whole thing, and adds that they had the
wrong idea of Langbourne—they thought he was young. Irritated,
especially by that last remark, Langbourne feels now that he is the
wronged one. Juliet introduces Langbourne to John Dickery, youthful owner of the local lumber mill, and evidently her beau. When
Langbourne hears Juliet's voice from the Simpson house that night,
he turns away and returns to New York, after mailing Barbara's old
letters to Juliet.

As the summer passes he comes to believe that last act a mistake.
In the fall he returns, talks at length to Barbara, and proposes. After
she refuses him he confesses his early fantasies about her and his
confusion of her with Juliet. At his suggestion she plays a song he
once sent her; she forgets that she has arranged with Juliet to play
that song if she accepts Langbourne. Gushing with joy, Juliet rushes
in; Barbara, tearful, rushes out. When Langbourne leaves, Barbara
meets him at the gate and apologizes. He realizes that she is really
saying that she loves him, and he embraces her.

> Juliet Bingham, hotel clerk, John Dickery, Stephen M.
> Langbourne, Barbara Simpson.

"A Memory that Worked Overtime," 1907 (in *Between the Dark and
the Daylight*, 1907).

Acton (the narrator), Minver, and his brother Joe (a painter), discuss a painting that Blakey, an artist, gave Joe ten years earlier when
Joe was engaged. Joe tells a story about the painting. Joe brought the
picture back on the train from Blakey's house in Lexington to Boston, but left it on a horsecar. Inquiries were futile, and he had to
confess the loss to his fiancée. Finally the picture turned up at a flor-
ist's shop at which he had stopped after leaving one car and before
getting on another. He had invented his memory of having the picture on the second car.

> Acton, Blakey, General Filbert, Joe Minver, Minver, Mrs.
> Minver, horsecar stationmaster.

The Minister's Charge, 1887.

During his summer vacation in Willoughby Pastures, a New England village, Rev. David Sewell, a Boston minister, overpraises the poetry of a local farm youth, Lemuel Barker, and to his wife admits that he did, but maintains that Barker was not greatly impressed by the praise; however, Barker was, and tells his mother so. In October Barker sends Sewell, in Boston, some more bad poetry and adds that he will come to Boston and look for a publisher if Sewell approves of the idea. Upset, Sewell is moved to preach of the wickedness that can be caused by carelessly saying kind things, but puts off writing to Barker and finally forgets him. A few days later Barker calls on Sewell unannounced. Sewell bluntly tells Barker that his poetry is worthless. Apparently unmoved, Barker dines, silently, with the Sewells. Mrs. Sewell dislikes him. When the Sewells' friend, Miss Vane, arrives, the Sewells ignore Barker, who suddenly gets up and leaves, to Sewell's embarrassment. Reviewing the case for Sybil, Miss Vane's niece, Sewell says that Barker should have stayed in his place, though that doctrine makes the minister uneasy.

Feeling betrayed by Sewell, and unwilling to go home, Barker wanders around Boston and sits in the Common. A young man there warns him against the "beats" (confidence men) and then swindles him neatly out of his last ten dollar bill. Bewildered and wretched, Barker eventually falls asleep on the Common and is robbed of his change and left penniless. After a day of staggering unfed around Boston, he sees one of the beats and chases him, but is himself taken for a criminal and caught by a policeman. At a police station a girl named Statira Dudley accuses him of helping to steal her satchel. Too late Barker says he never did it; Statira has already left. He is locked up overnight. Next day, after a hearing, his case is dismissed. Too proud to borrow from Sewell, he is unable to decide what to do next. In the evening the policeman who captured him sees him and sends him to the Wayfarers' Lodge, a house for tramps.

At the lodge Barker is put through the routine of the place, under the tutelage of a habitué. Next morning Sewell discovers Barker's name and case in the newspaper police report. The Sewells are embarrassed; they feel responsible for not helping Barker. Sewell traces Barker to the Lodge, and insists that Barker should go home, with Sewell if he wishes. Barker refuses to go home, or to tell Sewell what he will do, and stays at the Lodge temporarily. Sewell persuades Miss Vane to take him on as her handyman. Profiting from his day's experience, Sewell preaches on the need to accompany remorse and repentance with good works. Barker does well at Miss Vane's.

A month later, Miss Vane is satisfied with Barker, and Sewell appreciates his attentive manner in church. Meanwhile, Barker runs into Statira Dudley again, along with her bossy friend Amanda Grier. Barker likes Statira, and visits the girls' rooming house. When Amanda leaves for a moment, Statira stumbles against Barker, and he involuntarily kisses her, to their mutual consternation. He rushes back to Miss Vane's and broods over his sin. Then he and Sibyl, in Miss Vane's absence, have a long talk, in which his awkwardness and her nervousness put them at cross-purposes. When Miss Vane returns, Sibyl tells her Barker was insolent. In his angry pride Barker refuses to defend himself and Miss Vane fires him. After he leaves, the two women are stricken with guilt. Barker himself feels guilty, but not very guilty, for making Sybil angry. He stays the night at a residential hotel, the St. Albans. The next day he luckily gets a job as porter from Mrs. Harmon, the landlady, and is introduced to Mr. Evans, editor of *Saturday Afternoon* and a friend of Sewell.

The day after firing Barker, Miss Vane tells Sewell that she is sure that Barker was not at all to blame, though Sibyl won't or can't explain clearly what happened. Mrs. Sewell vetoes Sewell's suggestion to have Barker taken back. Unable to find Barker in Boston, Sewell is surprised and troubled to see him in his congregation every Sunday, looking prosperous in a new suit. At the hotel Barker becomes the general factotum, is popular with the residents (mostly ladies), and soon becomes citified. He sees Statira again and becomes closer to her. Evans visits Sewell and proposes that the latter write a sermon, which Evans will publish, on social complicity in evil. As an example of non-complicity Evans offers the headwaiter at his hotel who won't take tips. Sewell helplessly identifies the man as Lemuel Barker. They decide to leave Barker alone to work out his fate, but Sewell wants to see Barker in order to offer him Miss Vane's pay.

During the winter Barker learns much about Boston, the public not the social Boston. He now likes the city much better than the country, but is beginning to discover social distinctions and to feel self-conscious about being in service. Statira now considers herself

engaged to him. Through Berry, a bumptious law student living at
the St. Albans, Barker meets Miss Swan and Miss Carver, ladylike
art students living there, and comes to admire Miss Carver, who he
feels looks down on him. When Berry says that Barker is engaged,
the girls are cool to him. He has Statira and Amanda up to see the
two students, but the first two are truculent and the others frosty.

Evans tells Sewell of Barker's growing sense of his low social position. Evans and Sewell discuss the anomaly of social prejudice, especially against service occupations, in a Christian and democratic
society. When Barker visits his mother in early spring, he feels distant from her but still filially affectionate. She warns him against becoming too involved with girls. Depressed by rural squalor, he returns quickly to Boston. Berry assumes that Barker is in love with
Miss Carver, while Barker wonders if he really is engaged to Statira,
whom he compares unfavorably to Miss Carver. Visiting Sewell,
Barker discusses the questions of social distinction and prejudice.
Sewell thinks that a slight is not a slight if one does not think it is,
and that young people should be willing to take service jobs. Sewell
advises Barker to be friendly only with refined women and to avoid
casual entanglements. Barker takes all this to heart. When Barker
leaves, Mrs. Sewell chides Sewell for encouraging Barker to break
off with some poor girl. Sewell defends breaking off if either party is
tired of the other, and attacks the idea of useless self-sacrifice.

Barker has now advanced virtually to managing the hotel. The
summer and another winter pass quietly. One evening Barker has a
long and intimate talk with Miss Carver. Next day his former mate
at the Refuge, who calls himself Williams, comes in and pushes
himself into the job of elevator boy, though he is just out of jail,
while Barker stands by tongue-tied. Next day the mate works well,
but Barker is in despair about him. The next evening Barker asks the
advice of Sewell, who blames himself for the situation and says he
will do something about it in the morning. After Barker returns to
the hotel, Jerry, the drunken Irish porter, who dislikes Barker, calls
him and his friends guttersnipes. Barker stands silent, and Berry
throws Jerry out. Evans, who knows all about Barker, supports him
and tells him that people must live things down, not be killed by
them. About 11 PM. the hotel catches fire. Everyone rushes out.
Barker goes back in and helps Mr. and Mrs. Evans out, not a difficult
feat since the fire is not widespread. Berry and Barker find Williams

with Berry's valuables. Berry accuses Barker of being Williams' accomplice. Barker allows Williams to get away. Everyone praises Barker for saving the Evanses, and he feels wretched.

With Mrs. Sewell more hostile than ever, the Sewells discuss the newspaper reports of Barker's heroism. Some days later Barker tells Sewell all about the Williams affair. Now staying at Mrs. Nash's on Canary Place, Barker broods constantly about Miss Carver, whom he expects never to see again. He refuses to work as a waiter with Statira at a seaside hotel.

Sewell visits his friend Bromfield Corey, who is older than in *The Rise of Silas Lapham,* but much more prosperous, because of vast profits from the paint-company stock recommended by his son Tom. Sewell tells Corey and his cousin Charles Bellingham about Barker. Corey sees him as an "ancestor," the founder of a great family. Sewell asks Corey to take on Barker to read to him (Corey's eyes are now very bad). Bellingham tests Barker by having him read for two friends, Mr. Meredith and a Rev. Seyton. He does well and is invited to live at the Coreys and read to Corey. He does an acceptable job for Corey, who helps him improve his pronunciation. Barker is deeply impressed by the luxury and culture of the Corey house. Except for Bromfield, the Coreys are politely distant. Barker begins hesitantly to write again — didactic essays, not poems. Barker's growing polish both amuses and alarms Sewell as the summer passes.

Barker still sees Statira occasionally, but he loathes Amanda more and more. Statira has lung trouble. Amanda says that it's Barker's fault for making her stay in the city during the summer, and accuses Barker of being stuck-up, not loving Statira, and not having the courage to break with her. Barker knows she is largely right, but is furious and rushes off. He convinces himself that Statira got Amanda to say all that, and that he is therefore free. Next day he runs into Miss Carver. She is very pleasant. She tells him that Berry and Miss Swan are married. He tells her all about his troubles in Boston, and she is very sympathetic. Later Berry writes to Barker and apologizes for his suspicions at the hotel.

Receiving an illiterate, apologetic letter from Statira, Barker feels crushed by his responsibility for her, and rushes to Sewell for help. He is briefly at home from his summer place, and not eager to see Barker, so he eases Barker out. Feeling that Sewell has failed him,

Barker works things out for himself. He treats Statira tenderly again, but forgets her as soon as he leaves her; he sees Jessie Carver frequently, and grows close to her. He finds this double life wearing. Finally, in Statira's presence Amanda savagely attacks Barker for going with Jessie. Barker starts to leave in a fury. Statira pleads with him not to, has a paroxysm, and coughs up blood. She clings to Barker pathetically.

In the fall Barker comes to see Sewell. In his reluctance Sewell sends his wife down to talk to Barker, who leaves quickly. Mrs. Sewell feels contrite, he looks so haggard. Next day Sewell learns that Barker has disappeared from the Coreys' home. That evening a veiled young woman visits Sewell and asks him if she should relinquish a young man to a rival with an earlier claim. Using the reasoning he used on the elder Laphams in the case of the Lapham sisters and Tom Corey, Sewell advises against wasteful sacrifice. The young lady leaves in confusion.

A month passes. Barker has apparently vanished. One night he turns up at Sewell's, gaunt and shabby, to borrow money to start work as a horsecar conductor. Barker says he is getting married, his fiancée is ill, and his mother is in Boston caring for her. Sewell is full of distress and admiration for Barker. On his first day at work Barker breaks his leg. Sewell concludes that Barker should marry Statira and go back to the farm, even though he does not love her. Barker leaves the hospital and returns to Willoughby Pastures to make a home for Statira.

The Sewells discuss the case of the girl who called on Sewell; they hope she didn't force her beloved into marriage with a girl he didn't love. Sewell feels that the case of the girl and Barker are somehow entangled; Mrs. Sewell ridicules the idea. After ruminating about the whole Barker affair, Sewell writes his sermon "Complicity" on the text "Remember them that are in bonds as bound with them," and achieves a measure of national fame. In the sermon he advocates a life of responsibility and care for others. Eventually Sewell hears that Barker is teaching school near his home. Statira is more and more under Amanda's thumb, and Sewell happily concludes that Statira will never marry Barker. The author says that Barker never did marry Statira, but did marry someone whom he won't name, obviously Jessie Carver.

Lemuel Barker, "beats," Charles Bellingham, Alonzo W.

Berry, Jessie Carver, hotel clerk, horsecar conductor,
Bromfield Corey, Lily Corey, Nanny Corey, Statira Dudley,
Evans, Mrs. Evans, Amanda Grier, Mrs. Harmon, Mrs. Har-
mon's nephew, jailers, Jane, Jerry, judge, Meredith, police-
man, policemen, Alfred Sewell, Rev. David Sewell, Edith
Sewell, Mrs. Lucy Sewell, Rev. Seyton, Sibyl, Madeline
Swan, Miss Vane, "Williams."

Miss Bellard's Inspiration, 1905.

At their summer home in the White Mountains, Mr. and Mrs.
Crombie, a well-to-do elderly couple, agitatedly discuss a letter
from their niece Lillian Bellard. She is on her way from Kansas City
to see them. The Crombies resent having their peace disturbed. Lillian's mother has married a second time, and Lillian is being shoul-
dered off on the Crombies, Mrs. Crombie thinks, until the girl can
go to stay with other friends at the shore. Returning home after a
drive, the Crombies find that a Mr. Edmund Craybourne has been
there. They suspect that he may be pursuing Miss Bellard. That evening Lillian arrives, a day early. She is a poised, coolly lovely young
lady, on vacation from teaching oratory in a secondary school connected to a California university. Her training was in dramatics. She
says that Craybourne, a younger son of an English peer, has proposed to her, but that she is hesitant about marrying unless she is
quite sure, because of the discord in her parents' marriage. Next
morning Lillian admits that she wanted to come to the Crombies
and see Craybourne there, because if she is married she wants to be
married from the Crombies' house. Mrs. Crombie dislikes this idea.

Craybourne calls, talks to Mr. Crombie, and says casually that he
saw Lillian at the station the day before. Crombie is amazed that
Lillian concealed this fact. Punctiliously, Craybourne offers to leave
if Mrs. Crombie doesn't want him. Craybourne praises Lillian's
character and says wives should be financially independent; he is,
too, though his family's estate went to his brother. Craybourne and
Lillian stroll off. Mrs. Crombie evaluates both of them favorably.
When Lillian comes down to lunch, she is so beautiful that Craybourne impetuously proposes. She accepts, and all are happy. By
and by he mentions a couple at the local hotel who kept asking who
lived at a certain cottage (the Crombies'); this couple was quarreling
during the night in the room next to Craybourne's.

Arthur Mevison, the man at the hotel and a friend of Crombie's far-distant bachelor days, comes to call on him, and is received by Mrs. Crombie, who invites both the Mevisons to stay with the Crombies. After Mevison leaves, protesting but overridden, Crombie appears and says that Mrs. Mevison is a disagreeable fool. Lillian, however, backs up Mrs. Crombie about the invitation. Mrs. Crombie calls on Mrs. Mevison at the hotel and reiterates her invitation. Mevison is still unwilling, but Mrs. Mevison cattily insists on accepting. Mrs. Crombie returns home in dismay, with sympathy for Mevison. The Mevisons come to lunch and Mrs. Mevison is effusively on her best behavior, but later in the day the Crombies see Mrs. Mevison fly at her husband in a fury. The Crombies keep their knowledge of the Mevisons' behavior from the young couple. Mevison later bursts out to Crombie in private about his trouble with his wife, who is so possessive that she drove him from his painting, for which he had great talent, and into a kind of slavery. They have lived everywhere, on her money, but they are simply incompatible.

Next day Lillian tells Crombie that Mrs. Mevison woke Mevison up in the night and quarreled with him. The lovers conclude that love must be mixed with friendship and reason in order to succeed. Later, with Mevison gone, Mrs. Mevison bursts out at Lillian, accusing her of making a play for Mevison; then she begs the girl's pardon and says it's Mevison's fault; then she says that Lillian must convince Mevison that she does not care for him. Lillian stalks off in a rage. That afternoon Mevison tells Crombie that he and his wife have agreed to part in peace. At Crombie's request the Mevisons decide to separate at the Junction, not at the house; they will leave in the morning. That night, before going to bed, the Crombies discuss the Mevison affair and are glad it is ending peaceably. Later Crombie hears noises in the hall; after keeping watch for a while, he sees Mrs. Mevison tapping on her husband's door. She calmly wakes Mevison up and makes him have a long private talk with her. Next day Mevison tells Crombie that he and his wife are going to try to get along again. Mrs. Mevison bids a vivacious farewell to all. Neither Lillian nor Mrs. Crombie believes Mrs. Mevison's pledges. Lillian then tells Craybourne that they must part because she is too much like Mrs. Mevison and would make them both miserable. He disagrees, and they argue at great length, make up, and part again, to his surprise and chagrin.

When Lillian tells her aunt that her engagement is broken and she wants to leave, Mrs. Crombie says that it is a mistake to give up a man of Craybourne's virtues and background, but Lillian decides to go at once to California. Next day all the guests have left and Crombie is having a nap in peace when Craybourne appears to ask if he should follow Lillian. Crombie encourages him, saying that Lillian will soon forget Mrs. Mevison. Eventually Lillian writes from California: she and Craybourne decided to remain separated until she heard that Mrs. Mevison was nearby and planning a divorce; then they reopened the question of marriage, with Craybourne insisting that with the Mevison couple broken up they had their chance; eventually her inspiration was to leave the question to Craybourne; and he of course insisted on marriage. The Crombies are happy too, although they continue to argue about the precise overtones of Miss Bellard's inspiration.

Lillian Bellard, Edmund Craybourne, Archibald Crombie, Mrs. Hester Crombie, Crombie's maid, Arthur Mevison, Mrs. Clarice Mevison.

A Modern Instance, 1882.

On a cold February evening in Equity, Maine, Bartley Hubbard and Marcia Gaylord return to her home from a church sociable. She is the dark, beautiful daughter of Squire Gaylord, the principal lawyer and first citizen of the town. Bartley, a handsome, smooth-mannered young man, edits the Equity *Free Press*. Alone together in the parlor at midnight, they discuss the town and themselves, he playfully, she earnestly. Bartley uses her stationery to write her an invitation to go sleigh riding the next day, and, with his hand guiding hers, forces her to write him a note of acceptance. Turning earnest (apparently), he tells her that her influence on his character has been the most powerful and the best of anyone's. He kisses her goodnight and leaves. She kisses the doorknob he has touched—a gesture witnessed by the Squire as he comes downstairs. The old lawyer and his daughter resemble each other in their proud aquiline profiles and strong feelings. He bluntly asks whether she is engaged to Bartley Hubbard. Deeply embarrassed, Marcia does not answer.

Back at his hotel, Bartley wakes the young hostler, Andy Morrison, to make him a snack, and muses on Marcia's obvious passion for him. He himself still feels free as air. He recalls his arrival in Equity where he got his position because he was recommended by his college as a hard-working orphan who had come by everything through his own unaided smartness. Before he met Marcia, he ambitiously asked Squire Gaylord whether he could study law with him and thus rise further in the world. Next morning Bartley, self-pityingly indisposed, declines invitations to church and stays in his room, mentally comparing girls in his college town to the superior girls he met in Boston during a vacation spent with a rich college friend, Ben Halleck. The narrator summarizes Bartley's experiences as a young orphan, as a college student, and as an editor in Equity, and describes his somewhat cynical promotion of the *Free Press* to advance his own career. Bartley concludes that Marcia is superior to all the other girls he has known, especially because she can't conceal her love for him.

Somewhat revived, Bartley calls at the Gaylord house and chats with Mrs. Gaylord, a mousy, beaten-down woman, until Marcia returns from church. Hurt by Marcia's unexpected refusal to let him embrace her, Bartley says he loves her, and she throws herself into his arms. She had resolved not to let him touch her again unless they became engaged. They announce their engagement to Mrs. Gaylord, who is dazed. After midday dinner the Squire tells his wife that he wants Bartley to take over his law practice; he realizes Bartley's egotism, but likes his smartness. Meanwhile, Bartley and Marcia go for a sleigh ride during which they run into and overturn another cutter. Bartley rescues the passengers, who are a Mrs. Morrison and her flirtatious redheaded daughter Hannah, who works in Bartley's office. Next day Mr. Morrison, Hannah's father, comes to Bartley's office in a drunken rage to accuse Bartley of turning his daughter's head and flirting with her. Furious, Bartley throws Morrison out and fires Hannah. Henry Bird, a young printer secretly in love with Hannah, defends her, repeats her father's accusations, and feebly hits Bartley. When Bartley returns the blow, Bird falls, hits his head, and loses consciousness. Bartley fetches Dr. Wills, who examines Bird and diagnoses a concussion. The doctor drily advises Bartley to seek the Squire's legal help. In Marcia's presence the Squire questions Bartley sharply about the affair. When Bartley doesn't deny kissing Hannah, Marcia returns his ring and breaks their engagement. The Squire promises to help him out of his difficulties with Bird, but he is contemptuously ironic about Bartley's protests against the broken engagement, and tells him that he plans to close down the paper, which he owns.

Marcia leaves town for a visit, and Bartley, now unpopular in the town, devotes himself to his work. One day Kinney, the garrulous cook at a nearby logging camp, drops in to invite Bartley to visit the camp. Bartley goes to see the Squire to tell him that he is giving up the paper and leaving for the camp. He tries unsuccessfully to pick a quarrel with Squire Gaylord. Later Marcia returns. The Squire is deeply disturbed by her irrational yearning for Bartley. When Mrs. Gaylord goes to bed, Marcia beseeches her father to go to Bartley and apologize to him for Marcia's breaking off the engagement. When the Squire repeatedly refuses, and insists that she ought to be ashamed, Marcia faints.

Bartley drives to the camp with Kinney, who entertains him with his naïve opinions. After the loggers' dinner, Bartley takes notes on Kinney's chatter about logging for an article he hopes to sell to a Boston magazine. Willett, the owner of the camp, arrives with a sleighful of city guests. Mrs. McAllister, a Canadian woman, flirts with Bartley, and he is gratified by her attentions, even though they make him miss an opportunity to talk to Witherby, the owner of the Boston *Events*. After dinner Mrs. McAllister urges the loggers to sing and dance, but when Bartley volunteers a college song, Mrs. McAllister snubs him, and the company leaves. Infuriated by this snub and Kinney's lack of sympathy, Bartley goes back to Equity that night. The next morning, after refusing to sell his colt and cutter to the hotel landlord at a loss, he leaves Equity. After failing to sell the rig to a farmer, Bartley drives to the Junction to take the train to Boston. Marcia, who has left home under the pretense of visiting a friend, arrives at the railroad station looking for Bartley. The lovers are instantly reconciled. They drive across the state line and are married by Rev. Jessup, a befuddled old minister. After Marcia has written a note to her father and Bartley has sold his rig for $150, they entrain for Boston together.

In Boston they dine at the Revere House and go to the theater. Marcia is very much impressed by all this, but doesn't understand the play. After a few days they rent an attic room and eat in a cheap restaurant. Bartley begins to write an article about the logging camp and Kinney's reminiscences. Marcia is jealous because he plans to include a description of Mrs. McAllister, so he promises to omit it. Bartley takes his article to Witherby, the owner of the *Events,* who rejects it. But the third editor he tries, Ricker of the *Chronicle-Abstract,* buys it for $25. During his absence Squire Gaylord arrives with Marcia's things, asks to see the Hubbards' marriage certificate, warns his daughter against jealousy, and leaves. Coming home with his happy news, Bartley hears that the Squire has just left and angrily asks his wife why she hadn't gone home with him. Marcia locks him out of their room. The Hubbards quickly make up their quarrel. Bartley's second article, on Boston boardinghouses, is also bought by Ricker, who invites Bartley to join his newspapermen's dinner club. Marcia is pleased by his success.

Bartley becomes a free-lance reporter for several Boston newspapers. His uncertain income and status worry Marcia, who is pregnant. At a charity concert Bartley is covering for a newspaper, the Hubbards meet the socialite in charge, Clara Kingsbury, a rich young woman Bartley met before at the Hallecks. Although she gives Bartley material for his article, Marcia is offended by her obvious condescension. By and by Ricker tells Bartley that Witherby is looking for a new managing editor for his newspaper because he is dissatisfied with the one he has. Bartley goes to see Witherby, agrees blandly with his money-oriented approach to journalism, and gets the job. Witherby is impressed by the fact that Bartley knows Miss Kingsbury and the Hallecks, especially since he wants Bartley to interview Ezra Halleck, a leather merchant, for a series of articles on leading Boston businessmen. Marcia is overjoyed that Bartley has a regular job, a basis.

Bartley interviews Ezra Halleck, who invites the Hubbards to tea. The Hallecks are devout, old-fashioned people who insisted on sending their crippled son, Ben, to a Down-East denominational college instead of Harvard. Now he, and his youngest sister, Olive, are outside everything in Boston. Ben fell in love once with a boarding-school girl he saw walking in his college town. He still has her photograph, for which he bribed the village photographer. At tea with the Hallecks, the Hubbards are re-introduced to Eustace Atherton, a Boston lawyer whom Bartley already met at the charity concert. Marcia tells Mrs. Halleck about her pregnancy, and the older woman promises to take her house hunting in her carriage. With his friend Atherton, Ben Halleck, returned from Europe, calls on the Hubbards at their new little house on Canary Place. Halleck is dazed by Marcia's beauty. Atherton, who manages Clara Kingsbury's fortune, tries to advise her in her somewhat whimsical charities. Her present whim is to invite some friends to tea to meet the Hubbards. Olive Halleck, her closest friend, accuses her of inviting only her second-class acquaintances. Though Miss Kingsbury denies this, the party is a failure. Marcia insists on leaving early because she grows jealous of Miss Kingsbury's reminiscences about Bartley's former stay in Boston.

The Hubbards' baby girl is born. At Bartley's suggestion they name her Flavia after the Squire, whose Christian name, never used, is Flavius. He comes to visit his grandchild, and Bartley takes him around Boston and to tea at the Hallecks. When the Squire leaves, he gives his daughter a $500 check.

Marcia visits the Hallecks with Flavia. Halleck is disgusted by her marriage to a man like Bartley, but Marcia is utterly oblivious to his feelings. Mrs. Halleck tells Marcia of the childhood injury that left her son with a limp. Marcia asks Mrs. Halleck to let Flavia be baptized in the Hallecks' church because of its status; Mrs. Halleck agrees, though she is shocked by Marcia's ignorant approach to religion. Bartley begins to drink a lot of beer and put on weight. When Marcia wants to go to Equity for a vacation, he grumbles and refuses to go; they quarrel bitterly, and once again Marcia locks him out. Bartley then goes to Ricker's office and invites him to an oyster house, where Ricker attacks Bartley's irresponsible approach to journalism. After Ricker leaves, Bartley goes to a bar and gets very drunk. The next morning he wakes up in the grip of a policeman in front of the Hallecks' house. Halleck takes him home to a distraught Marcia who in her naïveté at first doesn't realize that he is drunk. Bartley sends Halleck to the newspaper office to make his excuses. When Bartley tells Marcia that he has never been drunk before and promises never to get drunk again, she forgives him. Later Halleck tells Atherton that he is very upset by Marcia's acceptance of the incident. Realizing that Halleck is in love with Marcia, Atherton tries to warn him against it.

In the summer Bartley escorts Marcia to Equity and tries to impress everybody with his success in Boston. After Bartley has returned to Boston, Olive and Ben Halleck come to visit, and Marcia

plans a picnic for them; but Bartley, who has come back briefly to
Equity, spoils it by arriving late, bringing the McAllisters to share
the picnic, and flirting with Mrs. McAllister. When Marcia cries
from jealousy, Halleck feels sick with pity for her. Returning to Boston on the train, he tells Olive that he has burned the photograph of
the girl he was in love with because it was a photograph of Marcia.

That fall, when Bartley invites Ricker to dinner, he accepts, although he feels that Bartley is beginning to degenerate. A few days
before the dinner, Kinney unexpectedly arrives, penniless, on his
way to work in Illinois. At the dinner Kinney recounts some of his
adventures to Ricker and Bartley. Kinney confesses that he has always wanted to write them down and do something with them.
Ricker says that if Kinney could write he would publish his story in
his paper, but Bartley jokes that his paper has already bought the
material. To pay for a sacque for Marcia (without telling her how he
is doing it), Bartley offers Ricker an article about Kinney's adventures. Ricker feels that the material belongs to Kinney, but Bartley
convinces him that it's all right, and that Kinney would be pleased if
he saw the article. When Marcia sees the story in Ricker's paper, she
assumes that Ricker is the author and denounces him as a thief.
Bartley confesses that he has written the piece. When they quarrel
about this, Bartley sarcastically confesses another trick: he failed to
remind the old minister who married them that he should have re-
quested proof that they had declared their intention to get married.
The minister could have been fined for this omission. Marcia is
crushed.

When Witherby objects to Bartley's writing for a rival paper,
Bartley retorts brutally that Ricker would also be interested in an article about Witherby's financial secrets. Witherby backs down.
Then Bartley receives a letter from Kinney saying that he has read
the article, reprinted in an Illinois paper, and he no longer considers
Ricker a gentleman. When Bartley shows this letter to Ricker as a
joke, Ricker breaks off their friendship, puzzling and then angering
Bartley. Witherby offers Bartley stock in the newspaper, but he has
to take a cut in salary and to borrow $1500 from Ben Halleck to buy
it. Bartley toys with the idea of reforming himself, but it comes to
nothing. To his journalist friends (not the top journalists), he makes
fun of Ricker's indignation about the Kinney affair. Ricker no longer

speaks to him. When Marcia goes to Equity for the summer, Bartley thoroughly enjoys his freedom and amuses himself with reveries about what his life would be like if he weren't married.

Witherby confronts Bartley with his knowledge of the truth about the Kinney affair. Bartley accuses him of using it as an excuse to get rid of him but offers to go. Witherby repays Bartley the money he has paid for the stock. When Marcia returns, Bartley is surprised by her sadly docile acceptance of this new situation. She tells him that Hannah Morrison has vanished from Equity. Bartley begins to dabble in mining stocks with Halleck's money and then bets $700 on the outcome of the presidential election. Although Tilden, his candidate, loses, he manages to get his money back by arguing that he bet on the popular vote, not the electoral vote. When he gets home with the money, Marcia, returning from a visit, says that in the street she has just met Hannah, drunk. She told Marcia to ask Bartley how she had come to such a state. In his injured pride, Bartley not only refuses to deny the implied accusation but warns Marcia that if she leaves him he won't take her back. Though Marcia insists that she doesn't believe Hannah, she dresses the baby and leaves. Bartley takes a train to Chicago, gets off at Cleveland, and decides to return to Boston but discovers that all his money, including Ben Halleck's, has been stolen.

In a flashback chapter Ben Halleck announces to his family that he is thinking of going to Uruguay to teach. His parents are mystified, but Olive senses that something specific is driving her brother from Boston. She tells him about Bartley's losing his job, and Ben tells her about the loan. Olive urges him to talk to Bartley because Marcia is worried, but Ben refuses to interfere. His sister doesn't realize that his scruples are motivated by his hopeless love for Marcia. Halleck tells Atherton of his plan to leave. Atherton carefully restrains him from confessing the reason, but after they have walked past the Hubbards' house together, Atherton's decent pretense of ignorance disappears, and he repeatedly urges Halleck to go. On his last night home, Halleck returns to his house to find Marcia there. She has just run away from Bartley after their quarrel about Hannah Morrison. When Halleck escorts her home, she begs him to come in because she is afraid of her husband. He refuses, and runs wildly down the street.

At first Marcia tries to conceal the fact that Bartley has deserted her, but when a creditor threatens her with the law, she seeks Atherton's help. He has just been on the verge of resigning his charge of Clara Kingsbury's affairs because his client is so exasperating. Marcia confesses to Atherton that she doesn't know where her husband is, refuses his suggestions that she go home to her father or confide in the Hallecks, but finally agrees to let him tell Miss Kingsbury. As soon as she leaves, Atherton writes to Squire Gaylord, and consults detectives, who are sure that Bartley has gone to Europe. Atherton asks Clara to help Marcia. Then he tells her that he can continue as her lawyer only if she will marry him. She consents happily. Marcia thinks of suicide, but she feels better when Miss Strong, a music student sent by Clara, comes to board with her. Squire Gaylord comes to Boston, repays the Hallecks the money Bartley borrowed, and tries in vain to persuade his daughter to go home with him. Marcia begins to support herself by taking more boarders. When Mrs. Gaylord dies, the Squire comes to Boston to live, and begins to age rapidly.

Nearly two years after the Athertons' marriage, Ben Halleck, convinced of Bartley's death and determined to marry Marcia, returns, but Atherton argues that Bartley might be alive and insists that divorce would be wrong. The two old friends almost quarrel over the matter. But when Halleck goes to see Marcia, she persuades him to start writing letters to insane asylums to inquire whether Bartley is a patient. Olive's description of Marcia as narrow and complaining leaves Halleck more determined than ever to be faithful to her.

After months of illness Halleck meets Marcia, who tells him that she has given up hope and is returning to Equity. The same day Halleck receives a summons to a divorce hearing in Indiana, addressed to Marcia but accidentally delivered to him after many delays. The summons, an advertisement placed in an Indiana newspaper, represents Marcia as abandoning Bartley. Halleck, Olive, and Atherton take the paper to Marcia. At first she thinks that Bartley really believes that she has abandoned him and that she need only explain his mistake to him, but the Squire finally convinces her that Bartley wants to get rid of her. Then she says he may. But when the Squire adds that Bartley surely has his eye on some other woman, she instantly decides to go to Indiana and contest the divorce. Meanwhile, discussing Halleck and the Hubbards with Clara, Atherton opines that what untrained people like the Hubbards do "doesn't matter much, socially," but that Halleck must act well because he has been trained to be decent and unselfish.

Halleck and Olive join Marcia, Squire Gaylord, and Flavia for the journey to Tecumseh, Indiana. Halleck is sickened by the Squire's threats of vengeance against Bartley and wonders if Marcia feels vengeful, too, but Marcia doesn't seem to know what she wants from Bartley. When she wonders wearily why Bartley shouldn't divorce her and marry someone else, Halleck insists that she has a public duty to prevent this divorce because divorces break up society and destroy civilization. In the Indianapolis depot Marcia suddenly decides to go back East, but then she meets Kinney, who tells her that Bartley told him she was dead. This information hardens Marcia to continue her journey.

A minor railroad accident delays the party, but they enter the Tecumseh courthouse just in time to hear the divorce court clerk declare that, as the defendant has not appeared, Bartley Hubbard is granted his divorce. Bartley, now very fat, is appalled to see his father-in-law. The Squire is admitted to the local bar, the case is reopened, a lying witness discreetly vanishes, and the Squire delivers an impassioned oration in defense of his daughter. He asks the court to set aside its previous judgment against Marcia, to accept her cross petition for divorce, and to indict Bartley for perjury. When Marcia in horror protests that she doesn't want Bartley punished, the Squire collapses. In the resulting confusion Bartley disappears.

That night Bartley offers to repay Halleck $500 of the loan, but Halleck tells him that the Squire has already repaid it. Bartley says that if he hadn't been robbed he would have returned to Marcia, but then he became reconciled to the separation because he and Marcia were incompatible. He denies being in love with someone else, asks Halleck to tell Marcia that he has never had anything to do with Hannah, and then suggests that Halleck marry Marcia. Bartley then leaves town. Marcia returns to Equity with her father and child. After a few months the Squire dies and is buried by Halleck, who has become a minister in a backwoods church. A few months later Bartley is fatally shot in Whited Sepulchre, Arizona, by a citizen whose private life he criticized in his newspaper. A year after Bartley's death Halleck writes to Atherton to ask him whether he should marry Marcia. When Atherton discusses the letter with his wife, she feels that the way is clear now, but Atherton is still uncertain that Marcia is worthy of Halleck.

> Clara Kingsbury Atherton, Eustace Atherton, Henry Bird, Mrs. Bird, Clayton, Laura Dixmore, Squire Flavius Josephus Gaylord, Mrs. Miranda Gaylord, Anna Halleck, Ben Halleck, Ezra B. Halleck, Mrs. Halleck, Louisa Halleck, Olive Halleck, Hathaway, Bartley Hubbard, Flavia Hubbard, Marcia Gaylord Hubbard, Rev. Jessup, Kinney, Kitty, Mrs. McAllister, Miss McAllister, Marilla, Andy Morrison, Hannah Morrison, Morrison, Mrs. Morrison, Mrs. Nash, railroad men, Ricker, Lizzie Sawyer, Sheriff, Simpson, Miss Strong, Tommy, Willett, Dr. Wills, Witherby, Mrs. Witherby, Miss Witherby.

"The Mother-Bird," 1909 (in *The Daughter of the Storage*, 1916).

On a ship sailing to Europe, a faded, wistful woman, dressed much too youthfully, speaks so constantly of going to see her daughters in Dresden that she is christened "the Mother-Bird." When the other women passengers begin to snub her, she appears in the smoking room and gradually moves from the elderly men there to two loud "birds of prey." At first these men seem to laugh at her; later, even they desert her. The last night on board she falls asleep, alone, at a table outside the grill.

> "Birds of prey," "the Mother-Bird," men passengers, women passengers.

Mrs. Farrell, 1921 (as "Private Theatricals," 1875).

West Pekin is a dying New England rural township that comes alive in the summer with boarders because Mrs. Woodward keeps a clean house and a good table. Most of the boarders are ladies, some with husbands who come out on weekends. One day in July the ladies admire a charcoal drawing made by Rachel Woodward, a prim young schoolteacher and daughter of the landlady. In a meadow one of the boarders, Mrs. Farrell, a very beautiful and stylish widow, praises Rachel's talent, and invites Rachel to stay with her in Boston and study art during the winter. Rachel is shocked at the expense

and at the idea of nude models. The two women run off at the approach of two men, Wayne Easton and William Gilbert; Mrs. Farrell
returns briefly to get a book she left behind on purpose, in order to
look the men over.

Easton and Gilbert are staying at the hotel in the village. Calling
on his sister-in-law at the farm, Gilbert discusses Easton's restless
devotion to his projected book, "Contributions to the Annals of
Heroism," and to its subjects, whom he searches out in the back
streets of New York. Mrs. Gilbert, ten years older than Gilbert, has
made him her pet since he was a small boy; now, he is in his
thirties. She tells him that Mrs. Farrell is the charming but unconventional widow of an elderly Maine merchant, whom she married
very young. She is only twenty-four, but instead of looking deco-
rously for another husband, she lives a free, semi-bohemian life and
offends Boston society. She is the only boarder who knows the
Woodwards well. Later Gilbert and Easton discuss Mrs. Farrell;
Easton is already smitten.

Next day Easton goes to church in the village and admires Mrs.
Farrell in the choir. Then he strolls along the road toward the Woodward farm. Mrs. Farrell, Mrs. Woodward, and Rachel pass in a
wagon; the horse becomes unruly; Easton controls the horse and
thus meets the three women. After making Easton come along, Mrs.
Farrell teases and flirts with him. After the four arrive at the farm,
Mrs. Gilbert teases Easton and talks to him about Mrs. Farrell. After
midday Sunday dinner Gilbert and Easton go with the lady boarders to gather flowers in the woods and pastures. Easton tells Mrs.
Farrell that he was appointed colonel of his Civil War regiment over
Gilbert's head; Easton has always regretted accepting the promotion, although Gilbert said he should take it. Mrs. Farrell gets Easton
off to herself and flirts with him. He describes himself to her as a
modestly well-to-do man of leisure. In an emotional moment he
seizes her hand and kisses it. They part in agitation. That evening
Gilbert describes Mrs. Farrell to Easton as a congenial flirt, but
Easton is completely smitten and ignores his friend. Next morning
Easton goes to see Mrs. Farrell to propose to her, but she is sitting in
the back door and shelling peas and he can't very well propose to
her then and there, so he goes back to the hotel. Gilbert, happening
by shortly after, tells Mrs. Farrell of Easton's stiff principles. Mrs.
Farrell angers Gilbert by introducing the Civil War incident and

asking him why Easton was the colonel and he was the major. After
Gilbert leaves, Easton returns and apologizes to Mrs. Farrell for the
kiss. She regrets causing friction between Gilbert and him. Easton is
too much in love to believe that she can do wrong. She is kind to
him, and he goes off in ecstasy; but when he meets Gilbert, he feels
it wrong to tell him how or why he talked to Mrs. Farrell about the
army incident, and the two men feel estranged.

That evening Mrs. Gilbert tells Gilbert that Mrs. Farrell is deliberately driving Easton and himself apart and that Mrs. Farrell really
wants Gilbert, not Easton. Later, Mrs. Gilbert refuses to take back
part of what she paid Rachel for the picture and tells her to think of
art as hard work, not divine inspiration as people like Mrs. Farrell
say it is. Rachel listens calmly and leaves the money anyway.

The author tells us that love and marriage are fatal to male friend-
ships. Easton is now utterly infatuated with Mrs. Farrell, though the
trouble with Gilbert worries him. After a few days, Gilbert, disgusted, leaves to go camping. The boarders are awestruck by
Easton's devotion. Mrs. Farrell is largely satisfied, but sometimes
alarmed or amused by Easton, who finally confesses his love. Playing with Easton, Mrs. Farrell is noncommital about her feelings for
him, and gets him to tell her how Easton was promoted over Gilbert's head by a politician general who disliked Gilbert. She says
that she and Easton can't even be friends until Easton squares
things with Gilbert. Later, at the schoolhouse, Mrs. Farrell finds and
examines Rachel's caricatures of her, the two men, and an observant
cow. With Rachel Mrs. Farrell discusses and ridicules Easton and his
love; finally Rachel angrily accuses her of being selfish and always
tormenting people. That evening Rachel apologizes for her anger to
Mrs. Farrell, who takes it lightly.

Next day, a hot Sunday, Easton, while not ceasing to love Mrs.
Farrell, broods about her flirtatiousness and recklessness. While
dozing in the woods, he dreams of Gilbert and Mrs. Farrell tormenting him, and wakes up to find Gilbert there. Gilbert apologizes for
being offish, and they are reconciled; but the old argument, now
with Mrs. Farrell behind it, keeps coming up. Gilbert says that his
most charitable opinion of Mrs. Farrell is that she was malicious and
now is sorry. Easton is furious, and their quarrel breaks out again,
with Gilbert accusing Easton of rising in the army at his expense,
and Easton accusing Gilbert of urging him to take the colonelcy and

then holding it against him all those years. Gilbert stalks off and at once returns, repentant, to find Easton all bloody. Easton has fainted, fallen, and cut his head. The two are reconciled again. After helping Easton to the vicinity of the farmhouse, Gilbert leaves him to get a carriage. Easton is discovered by Mrs. Farrell, and faints again. She takes him to her room in the farmhouse and nurses him. She tells Gilbert that she never meant to make them quarrel. Easton is ill for weeks. The boarders enjoy the drama of it all. Mrs. Farrell acts devoted to him at first but eventually wearies; she lacks endurance. She admits to Rachel that she is always acting and doesn't know herself what she feels; she says that Easton's devotion scared her and made her act strange and demanding with him. Gilbert is still distant with Mrs. Farrell, though Mrs. Gilbert is now her admirer. Gilbert admires Rachel, though. Walking one day with Mrs. Farrell, Gilbert irritates her with his barbed remarks; after a quarrel they make peace, but Gilbert is troubled about her. Easton gradually grows better. One day while Gilbert holds yarn for Mrs. Farrell, she flirts with him and he responds; though they part in irritation, he is, like Easton, becoming obsessed with her. She and Mrs. Gilbert have a long frank talk, about love and women and men, and Mrs. Farrell hints that she loves Gilbert and doesn't love Easton, but is afraid to crush his faith in her. Mrs. Gilbert appeals to Gilbert to leave before the situation blows up. She feels that he loves Mrs. Farrell for her shallowness and expects it to detach her from Easton. He balks, but finally agrees to go. He and Mrs. Farrell have a tortured parting in which they come close to admitting love for each other.

Early fall comes, and many of the boarders leave. Mrs. Farrell is more miserable than ever, and afraid to tell Easton she doesn't love him; she tells all this to Mrs. Gilbert. When the latter leaves, Mrs. Farrell is driven to seek advice from Ben Woodward, Rachel's clumsy brother, who at least does not disagree that a person in Mrs. Farrell's position should be forgiven. Easton, well recovered, discusses Mrs. Farrell's faults with her, but finds it hard to be serious with her. After Easton says he thinks Gilbert loved Rachel, he playfully gives Mrs. Farrell a chance to be free of him. She is very upset, but he thinks it's for love of himself. With Mrs. Farrell present, Easton reads a letter from Gilbert in which he says that he is going to South America, and repeats that he was at fault in their quarrel; he says nothing about Mrs. Farrell and thus, as she realizes, leaves it to her to resolve her relationship with Easton. She says that Gilbert

loved her, but she loathed him. Easton asks her bluntly if she loves
him. She replies indirectly that she does not, but urges him not to
cast her off. Though stunned, he refuses her request, and she admires him so much that she almost loves him for a moment. Next
day Mrs. Farrell leaves. Rachel and Mrs. Woodward discuss Easton,
Gilbert, and Mrs. Farrell. Rachel sobs out her love for Gilbert, and
refuses to accept, at this time, Mrs. Farrell's offer to support her in
the study of art.

Two years later Mrs. Gilbert and her husband wait in a Boston
theater for the curtain to rise on Mrs. Farrell's dramatic debut, in
Romeo and Juliet. Mrs. Gilbert says that Mrs. Farrell always has been
an actress but respects her courage in giving up Easton and sending
Gilbert away. Mrs. Gilbert says that she recently saw Gilbert paying
attention to Rachel in New York. As Juliet Mrs. Farrell is beautiful,
but she can't sustain the part, and draws too much attention to herself. She is judged best suited to private theatricals. Mr. Gilbert is
lenient toward Mrs. Farrell's actions at the Woodward farm, but
Mrs. Gilbert is still unforgiving.

> Mrs. Alden, critic, Wayne Easton, Mrs. Rosabel Farrell,
> Mrs. Susan Gilbert, William Gilbert, Gilbert, Miss Jewett,
> Mrs. Stevenson, Ben Woodward, Nehemiah Woodward,
> Rachel Woodward, Mrs. Woodward.

"Mrs. Johnson," 1868 (in *Suburban Sketches*, 1871).

On a blustery spring day, "I," the narrator, arrives with his
family at their new house in Charlesbridge, a suburb of Boston.
They are happy with their quiet, semi-rural life and their Irish cook
Jenny. When she leaves, they take on a black cook, Mrs. Johnson, a
colorful person with a saucy small daughter, Naomi, and a loutish
adolescent son, Hippolyto Thucydides. Ultimately the narrator is
forced to exile the latter, whereupon Mrs. Johnson leaves.

> "I" (the narrator), Jenny, Hippolyto Thucydides Johnson,
> Naomi Johnson, Mrs. Johnson.

New Leaf Mills: A Chronicle, 1913.

In Tuskingum, Ohio, in 1853, live two brothers, Owen and Felix
Powell, the one an abolitionist and a Swedenborgian, the other a

well-to-do merchant. When Owen's book- and drugstore fails, he and Felix buy a gristmill and sawmill in the country, which they plan to convert into paper mills. When Owen's young sons overhear their father remark that he plans to turn over a new leaf at the mills, they start talking about new leaf mills, and the name sticks. Owen takes two of his sons to help him repair the log cabin in which they are going to live. They see the floury-faced miller at the gristmill, and during the night they spend in the cabin, one of the boys thinks he sees a white face peering in at him.

Jacob Overdale, the gristmiller, feels that the mills are a part of him and he cannot live without them; he has always assumed that the Larrabee brothers, owners of the mills, would eventually sell the property to him. When he discovers that they have sold it to the Powells, he tells Bellam, the sawmiller, and the two men get drunk together. Captain Bickler, a young lawyer, offers him free legal help. Increasingly depressed by his situation, Overdale begins to drink a great deal, and spies on the Powells in the log cabin.

In October the Powells move into the cabin. Ann Powell feels that the farmers who are their neighbors are boors, with the exception of a retired merchant named Bladen and his daughter, Lizzie. Owen has promised his wife to build a new house in the spring. Until then she keeps all her good things hidden away in her own room. Felix and his wife Jessamy visit Ann and Owen. When Jessamy says that Felix would never be willing to live beyond the sound of church bells, Ann feels they will never join her and Owen at New Leaf Mills. To cheer her up, Owen suggests choosing the site of their new house. Owen adds a circular saw to the sawmill, and Bellam nearly cuts off his thumb with it, but Owen bandages it so skillfully that even Dr. Jenner approves.

Owen feels that Overdale is crazy in some way, but he tells Overdale that he can stay until the paper machinery is put in. Mrs. Overdale blurts out to Ann that when he is drunk Overdale says that the purchase of the property by the Powells will kill him. Appalled, Ann tells her husband. He in turn tells her the story of Bellam. The insolvent debtor of Elder Griswell, Bellam had to work for years on the Elder's farm and could never get away. The miller advised him to leave, and when he did he put him to work in the sawmill. Later, Owen saves one of Overdale's children when the child falls into the millrace, but Mrs. Overdale doesn't even thank him.

As the winter wears on and Ann becomes increasingly dejected, Owen suggests a trip to see Felix in Tuskingum and another brother, Jim, in Middleville. Ann enjoys both visits and returns home refreshed. Felix and Jessamy come to visit. They have arranged to send a hired girl, Rosy Hefmyer, to help Ann. The brothers also discuss a secondhand paper machine they plan to buy. But the visit is marred by the news that Felix has had a pulmonary hemorrhage. Rosy arrives, young and pretty and willing to work. When Owen's horse runs away with his wagon, Overdale stops the horse and declares himself even with Owen for saving his child. Owen tries to find out from Overdale what the miller has against him, but although he offers to keep him on even when the paper machinery is installed, Overdale not only refuses to discuss anything but threatens to kill him.

The Powells plan the house-raising, to which they have invited all their neighbors. Ann tells her husband that Captain Bickler has been courting Rosy and has given her a brooch, which Ann thinks Owen ought to return to the Captain. When Owen meets Bickler, he forgets all about the brooch because, after ingratiating himself by listening to Owen expound his philosophical ideas, the Captain asks him whether Owen will support him if he sends Owen to the county convention as a delegate.

A summer epidemic breaks out, and Bellam and all but one of his children die. Richard Powell, the eldest Powell son, and Lizzie Bladen help with the sick and the dead, but the younger Powell boy is terrified. Owen performs the funeral service. The house-raising is postponed until September. At it the men work all day and then sit down to a liquorless supper. A stud in a gable is noticed dangling loose, and Overdale, his whiskey jug in hand, climbs a ladder, hammers the stud home with the jug, and falls, breaking some bones.

The doctor comes to fetch Owen the next morning: there is something Overdale wants to tell him. The miller accuses Owen of arranging his death to occur a year after the Powells had bought the mills. Owen tells him that they had bought the mills two months before the miller knew about it and therefore he has already outlived the appointed time. Overdale faints, but when he comes to, he is so relieved that he wants to get up and go to work. Jessamy writes that because Felix has had another hemorrhage they are going to New Orleans for the winter. Bickler tells Rosy he wants to marry her but can't until he is elected to the legislature. In the meantime, he suggests a different position for Rosy, as a parlor girl for a lady in town. Then he could take her out in the evenings when he became a legislator. Suspecting that this is not an honorable proposal, Rosy slaps him and runs home to confide in Ann. She tells Owen, who still hasn't returned the brooch to Bickler.

Though the new house isn't completely finished, the family moves in. Jessamy writes that they want to come to New Leaf Mills in the spring. Owen returns the brooch, and Bickler tells him that he considers Rosy a child. Dreaming of Felix's death, Ann awakens to hear Rosy crying and arguing with her drunken old mother in the kitchen. She chases Mrs. Hefmyer out of the house and goes looking for Rosy, who has run away. Bickler is defeated in the election. Three days after Rosy's disappearance, he comes weeping to the Powells to ask them where she is. He confesses that he told Mrs. Hefmyer where her daughter was, but he hasn't harmed Rosy otherwise. It is believed that Rosy has drowned herself, and Bickler begs to be allowed to help a search party drag the dam and the millrace. Nothing is found, but Overdale leaps at Bickler's throat and Owen has to rescue him from the miller and the rest of the men, who all seem to believe the worst. When Ann finds the brooch in Rosy's drawer, Bickler confesses that he made her take it back again. He comes to the Powells every night for news of Rosy, and repeats his story, agonizing over his treatment of the girl. Ann tells him he must look for Mrs. Hefmyer and Rosy's cousin Polly, a cook on a canalboat, to see if they know where she is. Bickler finds Polly, who tells him that Rosy has gone off with her mother.

The Powells receive a telegram that Felix has died. After the funeral Owen decides that he can't stay on at New Leaf Mills without Felix, especially since Jim, his other brother, isn't going to join the project either. He asks Overdale to stay, but the miller refuses. Richard is sent off to the city to find some kind of business for his father to take up. The Overdales leave for the West. Richard first writes that he has a temporary job in a New Church bookstore, and then that the owners are willing to sell it to Owen because they are moving to Chicago. Ann is sad that her gentle husband must give up his dream of a rural utopia and return to city life. When Owen takes over the bookstore he turns its basement into a station on the Underground Railroad.

Jimmy Bellam, Bellam, Mrs. Bellam, Captain Harrison Bickler, Lizzie Bladen, Bladen, Blakely, "the Dreamer," Elder Griswell, Rosy Hefmyer, Mrs. Hefmyer, Dr. Jenner, the Larrabee brothers, a Pennsylvania-German miller, Jacob Overdale, Mrs. Overdale, Overdale boy, Cousin Polly, Ann Powell, David Powell, Felix Powell, Grandmother and Grandfather Powell, Jessamy Powell, Jim Powell, Owen Powell, Richard Powell, Sally Powell, Powell children, Walters, the Wilsons.

"Niagara Revisited," 1883 (1884; in *Their Wedding Journey*, 1887).

Basil March is now forty-two and fat; his wife Isabel, thirty-nine. They have two children, a boy of eleven and a girl of nine. Basil's insurance business has been only moderately profitable, so their family vacations have been spent near Boston, but eventually they are able to set out for Niagara one fine June day to relive their wedding journey and show it to their children. They take the new Hoosac Tunnel route west to Albany. Fellow travelers now seem less interesting to the Marches, but their children's interest and the beauty of the day make up for that. The Marches still have their old willingness to find poetry in things around them. Passing through Rochester, Basil wonders about the snooty hotel clerk of the first trip, while Isabel worries about marring their memories by trying to relive them. The Marches find that the Falls are more commercialized and the hotels more nearly empty than ever, but the children enjoy everything, for itself and because their parents were once there. Isabel recalls Kitty Ellison and her unhappy love affair and is sure that she sees Kitty on a passing train. As the Marches leave, their train crosses the Suspension Bridge high over the river, and Isabel refuses to look.

Basil March, Bella March, Isabel March, Tom March, hotel people, ticket sellers.

No Love Lost: A Romance of Travel, 1869.

An epistolary novel in verse (unrhymed dactylic hexameter).

Bertha, writing from Venice: After asking her father for sympathy, she says that she never loved the young man (Philip) to whom she became engaged just before he left for the war, and feels guilty for sending him off to die. In Rome she met another man, and, when he proposed, told him all, with a perverse pleasure in seeming to put him off while actually intriguing him. He followed her to Venice, where they have been wandering about dreamily. She describes Venice romantically and at length.

Philip, to Bertha: He releases Bertha from her vow. He feels as much to blame as she for their misunderstanding. He is alive. He was reported killed, but actually he was badly wounded and captured; he recovered in prison and escaped.

Fanny, to Clara: She has just reached Venice from Naples, along with Annie (her sister?), her brother Fred, and his male friend. Fanny finds Venice both glamorous and smelly. Fanny has known Fred's friend before, in America, and silently loves him. He is Philip, who came to Europe to recover completely from his wounds after his escape. Fanny and Philip watch the passing throng in the piazza and then ride in a gondola in the moonlight. They see a man and a girl, obviously lovers, in a gondola, and from Philip's expression Fanny can tell that he loves or loved the girl. Next day Philip tells Fanny that the girl was Bertha, whom he had followed to Europe out of a sense of duty, though he no longer loved her, and now he feels freed from Bertha and able to speak to Fanny. Philip writes Bertha, forgiving her; Fanny thinks this act heroic.

L'Envoy: Clara writes that she is glad that Philip and Fanny are happy, but she can't see anything heroic in Philip's giving up a girl who never loved him and who, as far as she knows, thinks he is dead anyway.

> Annie, Bertha, Clara, Fanny, father of Bertha, father of
> Fanny, Fred, young man, Aunt May, Philip.

"Not a Love Story," 1859.

On Fanny's porch in a small town Arthur steals a kiss from her, but goes no farther at the time. Later, at lunch, her mother and Arthur's uncle tease her and him about Job Green, a dull and prosperous young grocer; Arthur doesn't seem jealous. That evening, the plants in the garden watch as Arthur and Fanny spar about Green; finally Arthur is about to propose when Fanny's mother calls her in to catch a train. Later she marries Green. Arthur remains a lifelong bachelor.

Arthur, Charley, Fanny, Fanny's mother, Arthur's uncle.

"An Old-Time Love Affair," 1854.

Unsigned. "I" speculates about the fifteenth-century love affair of Margery Brews and John Paston as suggested in her love letters to him.

Margery Brews, Brews, "I" (the narrator), John Paston.

An Open-Eyed Conspiracy. A Saratoga Idyl, 1897.

On a hot summer day in Saratoga Springs, Basil March, the narrator, a fifty-two-year-old editor and part owner of the New York magazine *Every Other Week,* leaves his wife Isabel on the verandah of their modest hotel and goes to the park to take the air. In a pavilion there he notices a beautiful girl sitting wrapped in gloom; she is joined by a middle-aged provincial man and his much younger (evidently second) wife, who seems to be an old friend of the girl. The man, who is called Rufus, asks March a few questions, and he hears the girl speak; she has a melodious voice, and March feels an aesthetic interest in her as the varied crowd gathers for the concert in the park. Rufus draws March out about the hotels, and March praises his own. The girl seems hungry for excitement. Later he tells Isabel about his little adventure, and she says he has had girls on the brain ever since their little adventure with Kitty Ellison long ago (see *A Chance Acquaintance*).

Next day Isabel insists on March's asking the three strangers to sit with them at the band concert. Isabel takes to Mrs. Deering and Miss Julia Gage, as they are called, while March and Deering find seats in the back of the crowd. Deering turns out to be a tree grower and lumber dealer. The women have been having a dismal time at Saratoga: literally all dressed up and no place to go. Isabel tells March she likes and sympathizes with Julia, but can't do anything for her except ask the three to go to listen to the music at the big hotels. The Marches run into their friend Miss Dale, who has a summer place nearby. That evening the Marches stroll on Broadway past the big hotels, with their elegant crowds which promise an exciting social life that doesn't exist. Joining the other three, they go to hear the music at the Grand Union Hotel. March finds Julia charming. Later, March is unable to give Isabel a satisfactory analysis of Julia. The next day Isabel shops with Julia and finds her too direct in manner. Deering returns home, leaving the ladies.

Next day Isabel learns that Julia is very well off, and has been kept out of society by her possessive, provincial father, a banker. On his way at Isabel's request to get rooms for the ladies at the Grand Union Hotel, March meets Kendricks, who is a young writer, former contributor to *Every Other Week*, and fashionable New Yorker. He has just arrived and is enthusiastic about the Springs. March points out the social deadness of the place, compared to the old days, and engages Kendricks' sympathy for eager, forlorn girls like Julia. Returning to Isabel without getting the rooms he was sent for, March discusses Kendricks' arrival with her; she already sees the matter in terms of a courtship of Julia. Isabel promises Kendricks to introduce Julia to him; she does, and both are charmed. Mrs. Deering must go home, and the Marches agree to chaperon Julia. Isabel defends to March her ruthless policy of doing anything to give a girl a good time. In the evening the Marches, Julia, and Kendricks go off to hear the music at the Grand Union Hotel.

Julia settles comfortably into the Marches' hotel. The Marches tag after the two young people as they see the sights of Saratoga, and comment on the narrowness of Julia and her background. March regrets taking up Kendricks' time with Julia, but finds to his surprise that Kendricks likes her. Isabel, mothering Julia, opens up a wider social world for her. At a performance of *East Lynne* by black actors and actresses, March comments on their shortcomings and on the charm of the black race; the young people simply enjoy the show. After leaving the play and losing the others in the dark, March comes up undiscovered on Kendricks and Julia, eavesdrops on them, and finds in Julia an unexpected vein of poetry. At the hotel March confesses he followed the young people, and all three laugh.

Isabel now regrets bringing Kendricks and Julia together. March suggests telling Julia that Kendricks is not really interested in her. March worries about his conscience in the affair, about Julia's evident liking for Kendricks, and about ways to get Kendricks to reveal his intentions. At the races Kendricks shows interest in Julia but not enough for the Marches to be sure that he loves her. March chaperons Kendricks and Julia to a hotel hop. To conceal that they danced together all night, the young people add false names to fill up Julia's dancing card. Isabel is not deceived by the card, and is sure that Julia loves Kendricks, but can't bring herself to question Julia openly. March, with Isabel's assistance, decides to speak to Kendricks bluntly. When he starts to talk to Kendricks, March realizes that he feels no need to hurry Kendricks' affair with Julia, because Kendricks is so much younger than he is. After a confused conversation, Kendricks tells a startled March that he has proposed to Julia and she has accepted him, pending the permission of her father.

March finds that Julia has already told Isabel about her engagement. As March watches the young people bill and coo, he feels withdrawn and waits impatiently for the arrival of Mr. Gage, who appears next day, small, dry, and neat. After waiting for Gage to raise the question of Kendricks, March finally does so himself. Gage questions him sharply about the financial prospects of Kendricks, which Gage thinks inadequate. Gage maintains that he himself is not rich and grumpily says that Kendricks has been taking advantage of him. When March says that he will not tell this to Kendricks, Gage says that he will take Julia away. March realizes that Gage is not poor but miserly. When Julia comes in, Gage tells her that he is taking her home; Julia clouds up, and Gage begins to melt, as March discreetly leaves. The Marches ponder the power of Julia's will, and speculate on Kendricks' future with Julia and that will, once her bloom has worn off.

Miss Dale, Rufus Deering, Mrs. Deering, Julia Gage, Gage, Kendricks, Basil March, Isabel March.

"A Pair of Patient Lovers," 1897 (in *A Pair of Patient Lovers*, 1901).

On the boat down the St. Lawrence from Kingston to Montreal, Basil and Isabel March, repeating their trip in *Their Wedding Journey*, meet Rev. Glendenning. (March, the narrator, says that the year is 1870, but he refers to his children and says that he and Mrs. March are repeating the trip, so it must be some years after 1870.) Isabel March is sure that the minister is following a beautiful girl who is aboard with her mother. At dinner these ladies take March's and

Glendenning's places, and the mother, an arrogant Bostonian, quizzes March about Glendenning. Later the daughter, who is more agreeable than her mother, watches the rapids with Glendenning and the Marches. The ladies are named Bentley, March discovers. At Montreal the Bentleys go off with Glendenning while the Marches, anxious about their children, take the train to Boston.

Two years later Glendenning has a call to Gormanville, a New England mountain resort, and with his help the Marches rent a summer place there. The Bentleys have their ancestral home there. Isabel is sure that Miss Bentley got Glendenning to come. The young people are engaged and are obviously very much in love, but Mrs. Bentley doesn't want them to marry, though she has unbent toward the Marches. Glendenning says that Mrs. Bentley has asthma and depends on her daughter to care for her, so the marriage must be put off indefinitely. Isabel thinks that the young people are fools not to marry, especially after she sees Mrs. Bentley cruelly accusing her daughter of wanting to abandon her. Glendenning tells March that he feels guilty for wanting to marry Miss Bentley and take her away from her mother. March says that he should run off with the girl, and the lovers begin to agree.

Time passes. The situation remains unchanged, and the lovers grow older. On a visit to Gormanville March urges Glendenning to marry Miss Bentley, but he is reluctant. March finds Mrs. Bentley harsher than ever. That afternoon the girl, worn out, has a heart attack, and the doctor says that she is more ill than her mother. A few days later Mrs. Bentley has the Marches come to Gormanville and asks them what they think of letting the marriage take place, because the girl seems doomed to die soon. The Marches agree, and help to convince the lovers. After the marriage the girl recovers her health, to everyone's surprise, while Mrs. Bentley goes on much as before. The Marches wonder if Mrs. Bentley feels defrauded by this outcome.

Mrs. Bentley, Miss Bentley, doctor, Rev. Glendenning, Basil March, Isabel March.

A Parting and a Meeting. Story, 1896.

On a lovely June day in New England in the 1820's, a handsome young man and a pretty girl are driving down a country road. The man, Roger Burton, aged twenty-seven, is the teacher at the

Birchfield Academy; the girl, Chloe Mason, about twenty, is the daughter of the Birchfield doctor. They fell in love as soon as Burton came to Birchfield the previous fall. At the end of his first year she ran off to her grandfather's nearby to think things over; he followed, and now they are idling rapturously together. They hope that their love will never die away, as it does with other couples.

They drive to a Shaker village which Chloe visited frequently as a child. At the quiet village they go to the office and talk to Sister Candace. Elder Lindsley discusses with them the "angelic life" of the Shakers. They eat a simple but hearty meal, watched by the curious Shaker sisters. Escorted by the sisters, they go through the living quarters and discuss the Shaker doctrine with Elder Lindsley. He warns them against selfish love, but points out that to the Shakers worldly love is second only to unworldly love. Roger talks to Lindsley alone for a long time, and returns to Chloe distracted. As they are driving home, he bursts out that the Shaker doctrine and life are right, and that he should join the Shakers and thus keep their love pure and permanent. Crazed with grief, she leaves him on the road and drives home.

One Sunday sixty years later, in the same village, the drably dressed Shakers gather silently for their service. They sing, speak, and march in circles together, led by a handsome old man. He is Roger Burton, now almost ninety. A well-dressed old lady, with her granddaughter, asks to speak to him, and Elder Alfred reluctantly fetches him. At first Roger, who is almost senile, doesn't know Chloe, who is still hearty and chatty; he isn't very interested in her or her story of her marriage to Ira Dickerman of Birchfield and her prosperous life out West. She recalls her terrible grief years before when she and Roger parted, and her recovery of vitality later. Finally he recognizes her for a moment, and mixes regret for his loss of her with satisfaction in his Shaker years. Then he relapses into querulous senility. Now fully accepting the loss of Roger, Chloe leaves quietly.

> Elder Alfred, Roger Burton, Candace, Chloe Mason Dickerman, Ira Dickerman, granddaughter of Chloe Mason Dickerman, Elder Lindsley, Shakers.

"The Pearl," 1916.

In the spring of 1856 three young men, who are cousins, are traveling from Pittsburgh to St. Louis on their uncle's steamboat. When they are changing into their summer clothes, Dan misses his jeweled scarfpin. He asks Jim, the black cabin boy, if he has seen the pin. Jim at once concludes that Dan is accusing him of theft. Stephen West, who has been envying his cousins' fashionable city clothes, does not believe that Jim is guilty, but when he opens the bag containing his own clothes he finds his cousin's tie and pin on top. He agrees with Dan that Jim hid the things in there. But Stephen continues to doubt Jim's guilt. When he asks Jim again, Jim denies it vehemently, and Stephen believes him. Many years later Stephen tells Dan that the evidence was all against Stephen himself. If he had been among strangers, he would have been publicly accused of stealing Dan's pin. Dan says that Stephen is like an oyster, and his obsession with the long-past incident is like the grain of sand that turns into a pearl.

Dan, Jim, Lorry, Stephen West.

"A Pedestrian Tour," 1869 (in *Suburban Sketches,* 1871).

The narrator strolls through Charlesbridge, a Boston suburb. He observes the poor Irish neighborhoods from a strongly anti-Irish point of view, and comments on many other local sights and phenomena, such as horsecars and the life in the Square.

"I" (the narrator-observer), loafers, Irish mourners, Irish buttermilk peddler, woman storekeeper.

"A Perfect Goose," 1859.

Signed Chispa. Asked to define the feminine phrase "a perfect goose," Chispa cites examples to illustrate its range of meanings, from "darling" to "wretch"—examples involving Charles and Arabella (angry pride), Clementine and young Clumsie (contempt), and Clara and young Frederick (fondness).

Arabella, Charles, Chispa, Clara, Clementine, Clumsie, Frederick.

"A Pocketful of Money." See *The Flight of Pony Baker.*

"The Pony Engine and the Pacific Express," in *Christmas Every Day
and Other Stories Told for Children* (1893).

On Christmas Eve the papa of a small boy and girl tells them
about a bumptious Pony Engine that lived with its papa and mama
engines at the Fitchburg Depot in Boston. The Pony Engine wanted
to grow up to pull the Pacific Express. Finally, ignoring its mother's
warning, it sneaked out of the roundhouse, raced the Express all the
way across the country, kept going into the Pacific, and drowned.
The moral, says the papa, is, "Children, obey your parents."

> Little boy, mother engine, papa engine, Pony Engine, little
> girl, papa.

"A Presentiment" (originally "Talking of Presentiments," 1907, in a
slightly different form), in *A Daughter of the Storage* (1916).

At their club Minver, Rulledge, Acton, and Wanhope discuss presentiments. Minver, a painter, recalls that in his childhood his family used to talk a great deal about them. His Uncle Felix, a delicate,
flute-playing merchant, had such a foreboding about a long trip he
was planning to take to New York that he almost didn't go. All
through the trip on the Erie Canal packet and the Hudson River
steamboat he felt depressed but didn't know why. When the steamboat caught fire and he helped to rescue a woman passenger, she
said that God would reward him by sending him safely back to his
wife. Uncle Felix suddenly knew that he would never see his wife
again. In New York he got several letters from his wife, but when he
returned home he saw a group of neighbors gathered in front of his
house, and he knew that his wife had died.

> Acton, Minver's aunt, Minver's girl cousin, Uncle Felix,
> Richard Minver, Mrs. Minver, Minver, a woman passen-
> ger, Rulledge, Wanhope.

"The Pumpkin-Glory," in *Christmas Every Day and Other Stories
Told for Children*, 1893.

A papa tells his small son and daughter about two pumpkinseeds.
The good little pumpkinseed wanted to grow up to be a big pumpkin and be made into delicious pies, and it did. The bad seed
wanted, perversely, to be a pumpkinglory. After great effort it man-

aged to climb a fence and produce one pear-shaped pumpkin. The farmer's boy made it into a jack-o'-lantern which amazed everybody at the big family Thanksgiving, but eventually it fell down and was ignominiously eaten by a pig.

> Little boy, farmer, little girl, farmer's grandmother, papa, bad pumpkinseed, good pumpkinseed, farmer's relatives, farmer's son.

"The Pursuit of the Piano," 1900 (in *A Pair of Patient Lovers*, 1901).

While breakfasting in downtown Boston, Hamilton Gaites, a Harvard-trained lawyer now working in New York, sees a wagon pass carrying a piano box addressed to Miss Phyllis Desmond, Lower Merritt, New Hampshire. Gaites knows the town, and speculates that the piano is going to the now-grown daughter of wealthy summer people he used to see there. Gaites imagines each step of the piano's journey. Before taking the train to see Birkwall, a college friend, in Burymouth, N.H., he goes to the freight depot to see the piano unloaded. There he sees a wistful, charming young lady who later appears in his railroad car and refuses his offer of a better seat.

After visiting Birkwall, Gaites sees at the Burymouth station the same freight car, now disabled, with the piano still in it. Gaites goes on to Kent Harbor; Birkwall promises to keep an eye on the piano. At Kent Harbor, Gaites plays golf, socializes, and forgets about the piano. Mrs. Birkwall writes that the piano has continued on its way, but one day Gaites finds it in its car at the Kent Harbor depot, far off its proper route. At Gaites's request Elaine Maze, a local friend, telegraphs the situation to Miss Desmond. After flirting with the lovely Jane Albers for a few days, Gaites goes to Craybrook in the mountains, where he overhears an old gossip saying that the Desmonds have lost their money, now live in the mountains all the time, and have a daughter studying to teach piano. Gaites is now sure that the girl he saw in Boston is this Miss Desmond. Full of sentimental pity for her, he starts for Lower Merritt but stops at Middlemount, where he sees the piano in a freight car, so he continues at once to Lower Merritt in the caboose of the freight train.

At the hotel Gaites learns from the headwaiter that Miss Desmond plays in the little hotel orchestra. He sees her piano taken to her house and installed there. Later he is startled to find that Miss

Desmond is not the girl he saw in Boston, who turns out to be Millicent Arkwright, a violinist. He scrapes an acquaintance with her and courts her while Charles Ellett, a local youth, courts Miss Desmond. Gaites evades telling Millicent the truth about the piano until they have fallen in love and she asks him about it. The story ends on her question.

Freight agent, Jane Albers, Millicent Arkwright, Birkwall, Mrs. Birkwall, conductor, Phyllis Desmond, Charles Ellett, Hamilton Gaites, headwaiter, old ladies, Elaine W. Maze.

The Quality of Mercy, 1892.

Part First. On a cold winter evening, J. Milton Northwick, treasurer of the Ponkwasset Mills Corporation, gets off the train from Boston at Hatboro', a semi-suburban town, and is driven home by his handyman Elbridge Newton. On the way they almost run over Ralph Putney, a local lawyer, out on one of his periodic benders. At his large, ugly house, built for his long-dead wife, Northwick wishes he could talk to her, for he has been revealed, before the directors of the Mills, as an embezzler. For the sake of his daughters the president has given him a few days' grace before exposure. Outwardly respectable, Northwick worked his way up from shabby gentility to apparent solid respectability, but for years he has been speculating with the firm's money, until he has come to see it as his own. Now he can kill himself, or pay back the money, or stand trial, or flee to Canada. He convinces himself that he should go to Canada, increase the $43,000 profit from his illegal speculations, and then return the amount stolen. He tells his daughters, Adeline and Suzette, that he will be going up to the Mills early in the morning. He has believed that wrong is wrong only if found out, but now he is suffering, especially for Suzette (Sue), his pretty younger daughter. Before leaving he visits Newton's sick child, who dies of croup as he watches. Later, at the station, Putney tells Northwick, apropos of the near accident earlier, that he can't drive over the law.

The same night, Eben Hilary, president of the Mills, worries about giving Northwick a chance to escape, and plans to consult with his son Matt, despite Matt's radical economic ideas. Matt and Hilary discuss Sue, whom Hilary dislikes for her pride, and Northwick, whom Matt disapproves of shadowing before the three days are over. Sue, meanwhile, is looking forward to having a dance at the house. With Adeline, a homely old maid, she discusses Jack Wilmington, a young Hatboro' man with whom Sue has been in and out of love. Next morning Adeline commiserates with Mrs. Newton and shows Newton a newspaper in which appears the name "T. W. Northwick" on the passenger list of a train that was wrecked and burned near the Canadian line. They telegraph to the Mills to see if Northwick is there. Upset by the funeral of the Newtons' child, Adeline faints when Newton tells her that Northwick is not and has not been at the Mills. Sue ridicules the whole business, and goes off to telegraph to Hilary. Rev. Caryl Wade, a Hatboro' minister, goes to the Northwick house with Adeline to calm her. Leaving, Wade encounters Sue and her friend Louise Hilary returning. Matt Hilary has gone into town to send the telegram; Wade meets him there. Matt reluctantly agrees that Northwick is an embezzler and says that Hilary feels responsible for his flight and possible death. Wade and Matt learn that the bodies of the passengers can't be identified. Returning to the Northwick house, Matt tells Sue of the embezzlement and agrees to go in her place to the scene of the wreck.

As Matt waits for his train, a brash Boston *Events* reporter, Lorenzo Pinney, acquires Hatboro' gossip about Northwick and Putney and chats with Brice Maxwell, a reporter for the *Daily Abstract*. Embarrassed by his own intrusiveness, Pinney interviews Adeline, who tells him little. Certain that Northwick has run off, Pinney returns to Boston and tells his wife that he has a big scoop but must hold it until Manton, the detective on the case, approves publication. To his mother, meanwhile, Maxwell regrets his lack of Pinney's amoral drive; sickly and cynical, Maxwell works only to earn leisure for writing plays. Maxwell visits Hilary to interview him, meets Louise, and has an awkward talk with her. Hilary refuses to talk to Maxwell, and Louise chides him for his harshness. Later Hilary relents to the extent of telling him why he can't talk.

With detectives sent by Hilary, Matt examines the train wreck and finds nothing new. Sue is sure now that Northwick is dead. Two days later the news of Northwick's crime is released to the public and causes a great uproar. Pinney's distorted account, written in the tradition that Bartley Hubbard gave the *Events*, makes a great sensation. Maxwell's sober account impresses the Hilarys. Hilary, still angry at Northwick, vows to jail him. When Sue asks

Hilary if the stories are true, he denies them at first but finally gives
a guarded yes. She and Adeline refuse to believe him. Reluctantly
Hilary moves to indict Northwick. Louise tries to smooth relations
between the two families by visiting Sue and Adeline. Matt urges
Sue to see a lawyer to protect herself and Adeline; she refuses, but
when the Northwick property is attached, Adeline sneaks off to Putney, who assures her that the house, deeded long ago to the girls,
cannot be taken, and advises her not to fight the case. The girls
move into the porter's lodge, everything movable is sold, the house
is rented, and some of the land is sold as lots. With his usual cynical
air Putney handles all this well. Out of pride Sue breaks off with the
Hilarys, but Louise secretly buys some of the girls' things and returns them.

Part Second. On the train on the day of his flight, Northwick,
deeply dejected, evades the friendly inquiries of the conductor, and
at a junction decides to go direct to Montreal instead of to Quebec
first. Absentmindedly he signs with his own name a telegram re-
serving a seat on the Montreal train, the one that crashes. At another
junction he changes from the Montreal train to a Quebec train. He
overhears some Canadian businessmen talking about rich lands
near Chicoutimi and the route thence from Quebec. Soon after
reaching Quebec Northwick, worried and confused, starts by sleigh
for Chicoutimi. As the tiring journey goes on, he finds that the word
"money" is beginning to lose its meaning. Exhausted, he arrives at
Haha Bay, where he stops with a Mr. Bird (M. Oiseau). Next morning he comes down with a fever that keeps him in bed there until
spring. To Père Étienne, the young local priest to whom he talks
during his recovery, Northwick is a limited man who sees everything in terms of money. Dull and withdrawn, Northwick can't
nerve himself to confess to the priest, and eventually his dull in-
activity so upsets Bird that he orders Northwick to leave when the
first steamboat arrives.

Through Père Etienne, Northwick sends a public letter to the
Events. It fails to make a sensation; there have been too many em-
bezzlements in the meantime. At a dinner, Hilary, an Englishman,
Charles Bellingham, Bromfield Corey, and Rev. Sewell discuss
Northwick and his letter. Adeline and Sue are puzzled and resentful
at the letter. Sue thinks that they should now give up the property
and think of Northwick as dead. Sue insists that Putney see Hilary

and offer her half to the Mills corporation, even though that means selling the whole place. Next day Adeline, confused, asks for more time to decide whether or not to sell the house. Matt tells Wade that he loves Sue and wants to help her, but thinks he should wait, for her sake and his father's. Adeline says to Matt that the company should drop the suit against Northwick if he gives up his money and the girls give up the farm. Hilary finds this plan impossible, but admits that the corporation, being soulless, would accept the girls' property even though it had no legal or moral right to it. Putney thinks little of Adeline's scheme, but takes it to the state's attorney, who can say nothing about the matter, until the actual return of Northwick with the money. Sue decides to go ahead and give everything to the company, and Putney tells a bewildered Matt that nothing can be done to stop her. The Hilarys bemoan the fate of Adeline and Sue, but Mrs. Hilary criticizes Sue's pride, upsetting Matt.

In June, Maxwell is staying at the Hilary farm for his health and beginning slowly to get on with Louise. She and Matt regret the artist's hardness in Maxwell. The latter receives a letter from Pinney, who hopes to track Northwick down in the province of Quebec, and wants Maxwell to go with him. Uninterested, Maxwell shows the letter to Matt, who plans to mention it to Putney and the Northwick girls. Putney refuses to talk to Matt about it on the grounds of his client's confidence. Talking to Sue, Matt blurts out his love for her; she miserably replies that she loves him but can't marry him. Agreeing to keep their love a secret, they discuss Northwick. Sue has withdrawn her plan to give the farm to the company. The doctor treats Adeline for nervous exhaustion, for which Sue feels responsible, and then discusses Putney and Northwick with Matt. Matt, as Sue's agent, and Putney discuss Pinney's scheme and decide to wait for Northwick to write again, but he doesn't. Putney thinks that Northwick could be shown in court to be insane.

The elder Hilarys worry about their children's love affairs. Hilary says that he must resign from the board if Matt marries Sue. Mrs. Hilary tells Louise that she is packing her off to the seashore to get her away from Maxwell, who, as a mere literary man, is beneath her. Louise says angrily that it is unfair to oppose Maxwell and accept Sue. Next day Louise asks Maxwell if he wouldn't like to live out of the world always, and when he says that he accepts the world, she is irritated and leaves him. Ironically, he now loves her.

Part Third. With Hilary's agreement, Matt hires Pinney to find Northwick. Tracing him from Quebec and Rimouski to Malbaie with the reluctant help of Père Étienne, Pinney tracks him down. Not bothering to conceal himself, Northwick asks if all is well at home, and then reads a letter from Sue brought by Pinney. Northwick evidently grasps the situation at home, though he doesn't know about the railroad accident. Pinney tells him that if he comes home and returns the money he has, someone else (unnamed) will make up the difference. Northwick's account of his adventures arouses Pinney's newspaper instincts, which he restrains forcibly. After getting Northwick onto the Quebec boat, Pinney tries to persuade him to return to Boston, where he is sure Northwick will get off easy.

Though Northwick seems ill and weak, he sneaks off the boat at Quebec and goes home. Only after entering his house through a window does he realize that the house is empty. Thinking Northwick is a burglar, Newton grabs him, and then takes him to his daughters. After an agonizing reunion, in which Northwick realizes that he must leave or surrender and stand trial, he goes off to get a train back to Quebec.

Worried about helping Northwick return to Canada, Newton tells all to Putney, who is incensed. Later Sue tells Matt all about her father's visit. Adeline collapses, and orders Matt to get Northwick safely back. Respecting Northwick's love for his daughters, Matt first consults Wade, who thinks Northwick's return and conviction might be a blessing, and then talks to Putney, who thinks that Northwick would be acquitted on grounds of insanity. Matt reports Putney's theory to Adeline and Sue, who resolve to get Northwick back.

Four days after Northwick leaves Quebec, Pinney finds him at the hotel there. Sue writes, first that Adeline is ill, and then that she is dead. Now more collected in mind and spirit, Northwick writes Sue that she should stay home and marry Matt. After failing to persuade Northwick to return with him, Pinney goes back to Boston, leaving Northwick alone. He relapses into apathy, and begins to feel dimly that he must expiate his crime, even though he can't yet face the fact that it is a crime. Finally he sends for Pinney, who escorts him back, this time with a warrant. Northwick gives Pinney the remaining money and demands that Pinney handcuff him when they reach the

U.S. line. Embarrassed, Pinney does so, but refuses to lock the handcuffs. After leaving his seat briefly, Pinney returns to find Northwick apparently asleep. Actually he is dead.

Married, Matt and Sue turn seriously to farming. She gives the rest of her estate to Hilary's company, which accepts it with an air of unctuous virtue. Hilary makes up the rest of Northwick's debts and then resigns from the board. Reviewing the case, Putney thinks ruefully that nothing has turned out as expected; that no one, not even Northwick himself, got what he wanted from the embezzlement; and that Northwick was a victim of circumstances and in a way *was* his circumstances. The controlling factor, Putney believes, was Life in the sense of Mercy, the halfway point between Law and Fate.

> Baptiste, Charles Bellingham, Bird (Oiseau), train conductors, Bromfield Corey, Englishman, Père Étienne, Gates, Gerrish, Mrs. Gerrish, Eben Hilary, Mrs. Hilary, Louise Hilary, Matt Hilary, James, Manton, Markham, Brice Maxwell, Mrs. Maxwell, Dr. Morrell, Mrs. Morrell, Mrs. Munger, Elbridge Newton, Mrs. Ellen Newton, Adeline Northwick, J. Milton Northwick, Suzette Northwick, Mrs. Hattie Pinney, Lorenzo Pinney, Mrs. Ellen Putney, Ralph Putney, Ricker, Mrs. Saunders, Rev. Sewell, Simpson, Canadian bank teller, Rev. Caryl Wade, Watkins, Jack Wilmington, Mrs. Wilmington.

Ragged Lady, 1899.

Lost on New England country roads near Middlemount, Vt. (?), the Landers, an elderly couple, ask directions at a farmhouse of a beautiful barefoot girl named Clementina Claxon. Mrs. Lander finds that the large Claxon family has moved there from Portland for the father's health. Mrs. Lander is fascinated with Clementina. Lander is a retired self-made man. Lonely childless people of small-town origin, he and his wife live in hotels the year around. She believes herself to be delicate, but waxes fat as Lander grows thin and tags around after her.

One day Lander goes off driving from the Middlemount hotel by himself. He returns after talking to the Claxons and bringing back Clementina, much to Mrs. Lander's alarm. Mrs. Atwell, who runs the hotel, says that she will hire Clementina if Mrs. Lander doesn't.

Clementina charms Mrs. Lander, but her scheme for having Clementina's mother do sewing falls through, and Clementina won't take money from her for her trouble until Mrs. Lander says she can give it back if her mother doesn't like it. Mrs. Lander chides Lander for bringing Clementina to her because, she says, she likes Clementina too much and would always be worrying about her if she stayed. Clementina rushes back and leaves the money, saying she just couldn't keep it.

A week after the Landers leave the hotel, Clementina arrives to work for Mrs. Atwell. Clementina snubs Fane, the clerk, who praises her to moody Gregory, the student headwaiter. Gregory is brusque with the waitresses, but they respect him. He corrects Clementina's speech and makes her feel he despises her. One day an itinerant shoe peddler hawks his wares to the help, and after much chaff gets Clementina to try on a handsome slipper. Gregory seems to disapprove, so Clementina takes it off. Later Gregory stops the salesman on the road and buys the slippers.

With many young men at the hotel, there is much gaiety. Clementina reads to a nearly blind man, Milray, while his young wife chaperons the hotel fun. Clementina pleases Milray, who decides to employ her full time. Mrs. Milray helps arrange the hotel's entry in a coaching parade. Impressed to act as The Spirit of Summer, on top of the coach, Clementina helps the hotel win the first prize. Clementina, as a servant, is excluded from the supper following the parade, but she is invited to the dance being planned; however, she has no dancing slippers. Then Fane gives her a package, from an unknown person, containing the shoeman's slippers. The ladies all wonder who sent them. The chef suggests that Fane got them, and Clementina is distressed, because she dislikes Fane. She decides not to go to the dance. After the dance, which Clementina watches from afar, she gives the slippers back to Fane. Gregory tells Fane he sent them. Later, he tells Clementina, and adds that he loves her. She is bewildered. Gregory says that he must leave, and throws the slippers into the river.

Mrs. Claxon needs Clementina, and she goes home. Gregory goes back to college. Two years pass. Clementina, now nineteen, learns from Mrs. Atwell that Lander is dead. In October Mrs. Lander calls on Clementina, pours out her miseries, and asks Clementina to spend the winter with her in Boston. The Claxons talk the matter over with the minister, Rev. Richling, and have him evaluate Mrs.

Lander; he approves of her, but hopes that she won't spoil Clementina, and assures his wife that Clementina has no chance in society because of Mrs. Lander's vulgarity.

At Mrs. Lander's hotel in a Boston suburb Clementina acts as her companion. When the guests think that she is Mrs. Lander's maid, the latter hires a maid and gets Clementina a lot of fine clothes. The maid, Ellida, a Swede trained in England, soon has Clementina and Mrs. Lander in hand, but after a month she leaves, and they get along without a maid. Fane, who works at the hotel, tells Clementina that Gregory is now in divinity school. She realizes that she is still interested in Gregory. Studying French and dancing, Clementina begins to lose her gaucherie. When Fane proposes, by mail, Clementina wants to go home, but Mrs. Lander persuades her to go to New York.

At the hotel in New York they meet Mrs. Milray, who wants to spirit Clementina off to Europe. Clementina doesn't trust the constancy of Mrs. Milray's intentions, but Mrs. Lander offers to take her to Europe herself. The Claxons and Richlings approve a trip, Mrs. Milray remains interested, and the three women sail together, with Milray, who advises Clementina to see his sister in Florence and get into society there. On the ship Mrs. Milray introduces Clementina to Lord Lioncourt, who asks her to help in the ship's benefit concert. She decides to do a skirt dance which she has just learned. Clementina likes Lord Lioncourt, who has a spat about running the concert with the bossy Mrs. Milray. At the concert Clementina's dance is a great success, but she irritates Mrs. Milray by repeating it as an encore at Lord Lioncourt's request. Mrs. Milray chides Clementina for being too forward with gentlemen, but eventually regrets her meddling. Clementina is stony toward her.

At the pier in Liverpool Mrs. Lander and Clementina are helped by an English clergyman and his wife from the ship. Later Lord Lioncourt tells them how to get to Florence, and says that the Milrays are going to Egypt. Mrs. Lander and Clementina go straight to Florence, where Clementina sees nothing of the town until Milray's maiden sister gets in touch with her and invites her to a dance. Miss Milray gets Mrs. Lander to hire a maid, Maddalena, thus freeing Clementina, whom Miss Milray sees as a simple, natural force. At the dance, where Lord Lioncourt and others help her to have a triumph, she meets a young Ohio inventor, George W. Hinkle. A Russian, Baron Belsky, tells her of an earnest American divine whom he met in Naples and who is coming to Florence. Clementina returns at dawn to find Mrs. Lander sick and cross.

Later Clementina is visited by many of the men who were at the dance, including the Baron, who sees her as a sylvan deity, and talks often of his severe clerical friend. Clementina is now more worldly, but still natural. Mrs. Lander grows peevishly jealous of Clementina's popularity, but is calmer when the doctor begins to give her morphine for her digestive pains. Miss Milray considers Mrs. Lander predatory and suggests that Clementina live with her. Baron Belsky tells Clementina the story of Gregory and herself, which Gregory once told him without naming Clementina; the Baron says that Gregory still feels bound to the unnamed girl. When Gregory arrives, and the Baron tells him that Clementina is in Florence and that he has talked to her as he did, Gregory is horrified. Remorseful, the Baron plans to jump into the Arno, but his hat is blown in and his mood changes.

Gregory visits Clementina, and, learning that the Baron has apparently drowned himself (his hat has been found), is crushed. The Baron turns up in Rome. Gregory tells Clementina that he still loves her; she says that she likes him but must think it over. She feels that his presence takes her out of her present sophisticated life into her old simplicity and subjection to him. He says that he is going to be a missionary in China and asks her to join him. He is bewildered by her lack of formal religion and dependence on inspiration rather than prayer for doing right. He is sure that divine intervention led to their reunion. Next day Clementina writes to Gregory reaffirming her stand that she would go to China for him but not for her religion. They haven't settled their differences when Mrs. Lander has to go to Venice for her health, but by letter they agree to disagree. Miss Milray thinks that Gregory is bigoted and hardhearted.

In Venice Dr. Welwright indirectly tells Clementina that Mrs. Lander is dying; later he proposes and she has to say she isn't free. Hinkle shows up. Mrs. Lander is content, having both Clementina and Hinkle to herself, but is still difficult. In a good mood she tells Clementina that she will leave almost all of her money to her, but Mrs. Lander thinks that Clementina is leading Hinkle on, and advises her, as an heiress, to be careful with men. Clementina's easy relationship with Hinkle is destroyed when he says that Gregory is a tiresome fanatic, and Clementina must let him see that she and Gregory are more or less engaged.

Mr. and Mrs. Milray, and Miss Milray, arrive, separately, in Venice. Mrs. Milray is impressed with Clementina, but rather resentful of her hold on Miss Milray. Mrs. Milray plays up to Mrs. Lander, who then attacks Clementina for disliking Mrs. Milray. Miss Milray, in return, can't understand why Clementina doesn't coolly use her position to make a brilliant marriage. Clementina just wants to go home and give dancing lessons. Hinkle writes that he still loves Clementina, who is torn between him—she finds him restful—and Gregory. Miss Milray advises her to take Hinkle, but to follow her wishes in any case. Mrs. Milray, for whatever reason, encourages Gregory, through the Baron, to see Clementina again. She tells him she wishes to be free, and writes encouragingly to Hinkle. The other Americans leave, and Mrs. Lander is happy to have Clementina to herself, but still is of two minds about leaving her her money. Mrs. Lander wearies the American vice-consul, Bennam, with her troubles. Meanwhile Clementina waits for a letter from Hinkle. Eventually Mrs. Lander, very fretful, wants to leave but stays on rather than pay her exorbitant bill. Reconciled, the landlord brings Mrs. Lander an elaborate dish which she devours; that night she dies in her sleep.

After Mrs. Lander's funeral, Clementina and Bennam fail to find the will. Without a will, Mrs. Lander's Michigan relatives are the only heirs, but Clementina doesn't have their address. She turns over Mrs. Lander's ready cash to Bennam and waits patiently for Hinkle. Time passes, and no word from Hinkle. Finally arrives Rev. James B. Orson, a shy elderly rustic, one of the Michigan relatives. He has the will leaving almost all of Mrs. Lander's money to Clementina, but he says that Mrs. Lander spent her money so lavishly that there is nothing left for Clementina. Time passes. Rev. Orson has to borrow money from Clementina to keep going. Just as she is ready to go home, she gets a letter from Hinkle's sister saying he's suffering from the aftereffects of injury in a train wreck in America and is at home in Ohio. Bennam cables Hinkle for her; Hinkle's father cables that he will meet her ship. On the trip Clementina cares for the ailing Rev. Orson. Clementina is met in Hoboken by Hinkle's father and sister and her own father. Her reunion with

Hinkle is at first awkward, but soon they become close. Clementina takes charge and rather than tire Hinkle by going home, has Rev. Orson marry them in New York, after which they live on the Hinkle farm in Ohio while he tries to regain his health. She reads one day of Gregory's marriage and his departure for China. After a year Clementina has a child; Hinkle is still ailing. After a further couple of years they spend the winter in Florida, where Hinkle dies suddenly of a fever.

Several years later Miss Milray comes to Middlemount and sees Clementina, who is living with her family and teaching dancing at the hotel. In the meantime Milray has divorced Mrs. Milray. Clementina tells Miss Milray that her life has seemed strange and unreal to her. She tells Miss Milray further that Gregory's wife is dead and Gregory is living nearby and courting her. Gregory now believes not in preaching Christian doctrine but in living a Christian life. Clementina wonders if she should marry him. Gregory says that he wants Clementina for herself alone. She blames him for his past errors, but then says that they must forget the past and begin anew. He says that one can't simply ignore the past. As they approach the Claxon house, Claxon and his wife, looking on, say it looks as if she were saying yes.

> Atwell, Mrs. Atwell, Baron Belsky, Bennam, chef, Clementina Claxon, Jim Claxon, Claxon, Mrs. Claxon, Ellida, Ewins, Fane, farmer, Frank Gregory, George W. Hinkle, Hinkle, Albert Gallatin Lander, Mrs. Lander, Lord Lioncourt, Maddalena, Milray, Mrs. Milray, Miss Milray, Rev. James B. Orson, Rev. Richling, Mrs. Richling, shoeman, Dr. Tradonico, Dr. Welwright.

"Reading for a Grandfather," 1903.

A young girl of seventeen or so wants to give her grandfather a nice Christmas present and settles on the idea of a book. She quizzes him at length about his reading past and present, displays her own vast ignorance, lectures him on the stodginess of his tastes, and finally decides to get him some recent bestsellers, tastefully bound.

> Young girl, grandfather.

"The Return to Favor," 1915 (in *The Daughter of the Storage,* 1916). Morrison, an excellent tailor, never finishes on time the garments he always politely promises to deliver soon. The narrator, a male "favorite customer," often overhears Morrison's lady customers complaining about their unfinished clothes. Finally Morrison can't stand their complaints any longer. He sells his business to his journeyman and leaves. The new owner never promises anything that he can't do, but the ladies find his severe truthfulness disappointing. Morrison is asked to return to work as the new owner's assistant, because with his ingratiating promises he "gets along better with ladies."

Favorite customer, lady customers, tailor's journeyman, Morrison.

The Rise of Silas Lapham, 1885.

In Boston in the summer of 1875 Bartley Hubbard, a young reporter for the *Events,* interviews Silas Lapham, the paint millionaire. Lapham tells him of his hard early life on a Vermont farm, where his father discovered a mineral paint mine. After marrying a schoolteacher and running a small hotel, Lapham developed the paint business with his wife's help. Lapham proudly shows Hubbard his warehouse and his fancy brand, named "The Persis Brand" after his wife. He tells Hubbard modestly of his rise to a colonelcy in the Civil War, and hints at a residue of bitterness toward his former partner. Bragging about his horse, Lapham drives Hubbard to the *Events* office, where Hubbard writes up the interview with many flourishes. Later Lapham sends Marcia, Hubbard's wife, a large package of "The Persis Brand."

After dropping Hubbard off, Lapham takes his wife to look at the house they are building on Beacon Street. For years the Laphams have been living in the now-unfashionable South End of Boston and have had no social life because they don't know how to have one, even though they are now rich. Penelope and Irene, the two Lapham daughters, have had little schooling and no social contacts. Penelope, a dark girl generally considered plain, reads widely but, far from being serious, loves to make fun of everything. Irene, three years younger, is a stunning, blue-eyed redhead, ignorant and naïve, just ripening into maturity. The summer before, during a trip to

Canada, Mrs. Lapham and her daughters met the Coreys from Boston and cared for Mrs. Corey when she became violently ill. Tom, Mrs. Corey's son, was politely attentive to Irene. When Mrs. Corey and her daughters came to call in the winter, they remarked casually that none of their friends lived in the South End. This comment started Lapham thinking about building a house on a lot he owned on Beacon Street. During a long sleigh drive he won his wife's consent. When Irene received a Texas newspaper describing the ranch of the Hon. Loring G. Stanton of Boston, she was sure that the paper was sent by Tom Corey, who was then at Stanton's ranch. Meanwhile, the Laphams' young architect replaced their conventional ideas for their house with his own modern and elaborate ones.

At the new house after Hubbard's interview, Lapham and his wife meet Milton K. Rogers, Lapham's ex-partner, a cold, dry man. After he has left, Mrs. Lapham accuses Lapham of using Rogers' money to make the business a success and then crowding Rogers out of it. Lapham secretly feels guilty, but acts belligerently innocent. The next day, when all four Laphams visit the new house, Tom Corey happens by and Lapham proudly shows him around. That night the girls make fun of their father's bragging, and Penelope teases Irene about Corey.

The same night, Tom Corey and his father, Bromfield Corey, chat in their library. Bromfield jokingly suggests that Tom marry a rich girl. Tom mentions meeting the Laphams, describes Colonel Lapham, and confesses that he has been thinking of going into the paint business. His father is somewhat taken aback, but agrees that it is a practical idea. The elder Corey inherited plenty of money, but now, during the depression of the '70's, there is much less. After a youthful fling with Garibaldi, Corey became a dilettantish portrait painter, a passive man with modest tastes; he realizes that Tom has his grandfather's vitality and must live in the world. Later, at Bar Harbor, Mrs. Corey pronounces Tom's plans distasteful but doesn't try to stop him. Back in Boston, Tom asks Lapham for a job. Lapham is dumbfounded, but when Corey insists that he believes in Lapham's paint, the Colonel, deeply moved, tells him the whole paint story, and finally takes him to Nantasket, where his family are summering. Penelope meets her father at the pier, and is demurely polite to Corey. At the cottage Lapham brags to Persis about Corey's action; she concludes that he really wants Irene, but Lapham is gratified, regardless, that this aristocrat, whose family he has always resented, is interested in his business and his daughter.

A few days later Mrs. Corey tells Bromfield that Tom is throwing himself away, that he really doesn't have to work if they all economize; she worries that if Tom works for Lapham he will marry Irene, whom she considers insipid. Corey says they must leave Tom alone. When Tom comes home, Mrs. Corey questions him about his new position and his visit to Nantasket. Tom says that her brother, James Bellingham, an experienced businessman, supports him. He praises Irene's beauty and Penelope's sense of humor, and adds that he is starting work immediately. Defeated, Mrs. Corey returns to Bar Harbor.

Corey works hard and enjoys his new job. Walker, Lapham's head bookkeeper, tells Tom the office gossip about Miss Dewey, Lapham's pretty typist. The day before, Corey overheard Lapham telling Miss Dewey that she had better get a divorce. Outside Lapham's office Walker and Corey witness a struggle between a woman and a drunken sailor.

Though Mrs. Lapham won't let Lapham bring Corey and Irene together at the cottage, the two young people meet by accident at the Beacon Street house, and Irene chatters naïvely about books. They joke with each other over the woodshavings Irene is playing with. That evening Tom and Bromfield agree that the Laphams are uncultivated, but even so Bromfield feels that he ought to invite Lapham to dinner. Meanwhile, Mrs. Lapham reminds her husband that because the Coreys are their social superiors, they must wait for the Coreys to make the advances. Penelope notices a woodshaving Irene has brought home and teases her about it. Later, Penelope's comments make Mrs. Lapham conclude that Corey is not in love with Irene and that she must forget him.

Though Persis is nervous, Lapham spends his stock market gains on the new house, and to her satisfaction lends Rogers $20,000 on the security of $5,000 worth of stock. Now Lapham feels free to bring Tom Corey home for dinner. After an evening on the porch listening to Penelope's amusing conversation, Tom is convinced that she is charming.

When Tom gets home he and his father discuss the Laphams, and Bromfield, though unready to accept Lapham socially, pleases Tom by calling on Lapham at his office the next morning. Lapham lavishly praises Tom to Corey, and that evening exults to Persis about the visit. She still insists that the Coreys have to invite them first. They come close to quarreling about this, and the next day Lapham, feeling unwell, stays home. When Tom arrives in the evening to see how he is, Penelope stays in her room to let Irene entertain Tom alone. When he's gone Irene tells her sister that Tom talked the whole time about Penelope. When Mrs. Lapham worries about Tom's failure to declare his intentions, Lapham's pride is hurt, and he threatens to talk to Tom, but Persis calms him down again.

When Mrs. Corey returns to Boston with her daughters, Lily and Nanny, they talk over their brother's interest in Irene. Tom praises both Lapham girls to his mother. Corey again tells his wife that they can't do anything. Frustrated by both men, Mrs. Corey decides to call on the Laphams, who have also returned to Boston. Irene is not at home. Irritated at Mrs. Corey's condescension, Penelope makes flippant remarks, which in turn irritate Mrs. Corey. After she has left and Irene has returned, Penelope makes fun of Mrs. Corey's and her own behavior, and then suddenly begins to cry and runs upstairs, to the others' amazement. Mrs. Corey criticizes Penelope to Bromfield but reluctantly agrees with him that they must recognize Tom's intimacy with the family.

After Mrs. Corey has invited a number of relatives and friends along with the Laphams, Tom startles and secretly delights her by asking her not to give the dinner because he doesn't want a closer relationship with the Laphams; but it is too late. Although Penelope says that she won't go, Mrs. Lapham accepts the invitation, without mentioning Penelope. The Laphams are thrown into an agony of anxiety about the proper clothes for the affair, but finally get ready and go, leaving Penelope behind crying.

At the Coreys' quietly elegant house, Lapham puts on his new gloves and then takes them off again when he sees that Tom isn't wearing any. Everybody thinks that Irene is beautiful. Mrs. Corey is coldly astonished when Mrs. Lapham reveals that Penelope hasn't come. Lapham is embarrassed going into dinner and at the dinner table. He doesn't know the people the other guests talk about and hasn't read the sentimental novel they discuss, *Tears, Idle Tears,* which celebrates self-sacrifice. After the ladies have retired, he tells a long Civil-War anecdote about a Corporal Jim Millon who died as a result of trying to warn him against a sharpshooter, and who left behind a wife named Molly and a little girl called Zerrilla. After he drinks more, they join the ladies, some of the men urge him into the library, and he seizes the floor and brags about his wealth. When he finally leaves, he forgets to thank his hostess.

Next day, hung over and wretched, Lapham asks Tom Corey if he was drunk the night before, and offers to let Corey go if he wishes. Though confused and disgusted, Corey pooh-poohs the matter. During a long walk later, he feels at first that the social gulf between him and the Laphams makes his love impossible of fulfillment, but he finally goes to the Laphams' to try to apologize for his earlier lack of sympathy. Only Penelope is home. She tells him that she has been reading *Tears, Idle Tears*. Its plot — a girl giving up the man she loves because another girl cared for him first — made her cry, she says. Corey abruptly tells her that he loves her. Penelope is utterly dismayed. When Corey asks her why, she is unable to tell him but makes him promise never to visit her again. Bewildered, Corey promises. Penelope embraces him and runs out of the room just as her father enters. Corey flees.

When Penelope confides in her mother, Mrs. Lapham admits that she hadn't really considered Corey might be in love with Penelope. They search for a way to break the news to Irene. Penelope feels guilty because she has loved Tom Corey from the beginning and is convinced that she must have tried to make him love her. She says that Irene must not give Tom up, but her mother insists that Irene must, so that only one person suffers. But Mrs. Lapham herself can't sustain this belief and makes Lapham take her for a buggy ride so she can confide in him. Interrupting his talk about Rogers and business, she tells him about Tom and Penelope. Now both are miserable, they quarrel, and Lapham crashes into another buggy. They calm down, and at Lapham's suggestion consult Sewell, the Coreys' minister, who suggests strongly what Mrs. Lapham originally felt, that it is better for one person to suffer instead of three.

As soon as they reach home, Mrs. Lapham tells Irene the truth. With stony coldness, Irene gives Penelope the souvenirs of her romance. Then she goes up to the town of Lapham in Vermont. At the office Corey tells Lapham that he is in love with Penelope and asks him what the obstacle is that Penelope wouldn't explain. When Lapham suggests that Corey was interested in another girl at the same time, Corey's denial is so convincing that Lapham finally gives him permission to call that evening. When Penelope tells him that they all supposed he was in love with Irene, Corey says he never thought of her and explains that it was Stanton who sent that newspaper clipping to Irene. Penelope still insists that they stay apart, but Tom says that he will never give her up. When he tells his mother that he has spoken to "Miss Lapham," she thinks he means Irene and there is an embarrassing moment as he sets her right.

Lapham tells Persis that Rogers unloaded some Iowa mills on him, knowing that a railroad would squeeze him out of the property. With Irene, whom he picks up in Vermont, Lapham goes to Iowa to see about the mills, and returns, leaving her there to visit relatives. When Walker tells Tom that Lapham may be ruined, Tom hopes that he can lend Lapham some money, save him, and thus persuade Penelope. When Rogers asks Lapham what he is going to do, Lapham accuses Rogers of tricking him and says that he is going to sell Roger's collaterals and let the mills go. But Rogers says that there are some Englishmen who want to buy the mills at a fair price. Unbelieving, Lapham gives him twenty-four hours to produce these buyers. Lapham and Persis reluctantly agree that he can't dicker with the Englishmen without telling them about the railroad's determination to buy the mills cheaply. When Mrs. Lapham asks Penelope to stop thinking of herself and try to cheer her father up, Penelope writes Tom a note asking him to stop calling. The English buyers do not appear, and the railroad does not make the expected offer for the mills either.

As Lapham's business fortunes fluctuate, he has periods of deep depression and irascibility. One day Persis finds a memorandum recording large sums paid to "Wm. M." She puts the paper in her workbasket and eventually forgets about it. Eventually Lapham tells his wife that business is so bad that they must give up the new house and he has shut down the Works. Seeing him working on his papers, she remembers the paper in her workbasket and brings it to him. She shows him the memorandum; he tears it up and throws it in the fire. Next morning she finds one scrap and sees that it reads "Mrs. M.," not "Wm. M." Lapham angrily evades her questions about Mrs. M. At the office Lapham tells Corey that he should quit, but Corey offers to put $30,000 into the firm. Corey says that his Uncle James approves of his offer, but although Lapham agrees to talk to Bellingham, he insists that he doesn't want to take Corey into his business.

When Zerrilla Dewey's disreputable mother comes to demand money from Lapham, he orders her out. Walker hints to Corey that Lapham is involved in something disgraceful, but Corey defends Lapham's character. That evening Lapham gives Zerrilla some money, and visits the apartment where she lives with her mother, Molly Millon, the widow of Jim Millon. Zerrilla is married to Hen Dewey, a drunken sailor whom she wants to divorce for a Mr. Wemmel. Out of gratitude to Millon, Lapham will help the two women, but not Hen. Near the Millons', he bumps into Rogers, but neither man speaks. At home Lapham insists on making a confession to his wife. She thinks he is going to tell her about "Mrs. M.," but he tells her that trying to recoup his losses with Rogers he lost a great deal playing the market. Relieved that there is nothing else on her husband's conscience, Mrs. Lapham gets him to tell her of Corey's offer. She realizes that he made it because of Penelope.

James Bellingham tells Tom that Lapham has asked his advice; a new paint company in West Virginia is threatening to undersell him. Bellingham realizes that Lapham's refusal of Tom's offer must have cost him a great effort. After Mrs. Lapham tells Penelope of Tom's offer, the girl writes to thank him for it, but insists that if her father loses his money all is over between them. Visiting by himself the new house that he cannot bear to sell, Lapham builds a small fire in a fireplace, fails to put it out, and comes by later to see it burning down. The insurance on it has just expired.

The West Virginia paint people agree on a merger if Lapham can contribute capital, but he cannot raise the money. Then Rogers says that those English parties are in town, ready to pay Lapham's price. Rogers has not told them of the railroad's maneuvers. Though Lapham balks, Rogers persuades him to see the parties. When he does so, Lapham soon realizes that the Englishmen are in collusion with Rogers to defraud an English philanthropic fund whose agents they are. Lapham is tempted, but says he can't reach a decision until morning. When he arrives at home he finds Rogers already there, playing on Mrs. Lapham's remorse for Lapham's earlier treatment of him. Then Rogers asks Lapham to sell the mills to him, after which Lapham will have no further responsibility. Persis hears Lapham walking up and down all night, wrestling with his conscience. He cannot reach a decision. The next morning the absurdly low offer from the railroad arrives. Rogers says that Lapham has ruined him.

On Bellingham's advice, Lapham asks the West Virginians for more time. When his wife comes to the office to reassure him about Rogers, she finds only a pretty girl there, typing at his desk. That evening she receives an unsigned note suggesting that she ask her husband about his lady clerk. When Lapham returns, Persis, half insane with jealousy, demands to know if the clerk is "Mrs. M." When Lapham refuses to answer, she faints. Recovering consciousness, she finds him gone again, and rushes to the office. This time she recognizes the girl as Jim Millon's daughter, who tells Persis her story. Persis recalls Lapham's obsession about Jim Millon's wife and daughter. Ever since Mrs. Lapham made him promise five or six years ago to stop helping them, he has kept his continuing help a secret. Mentally she forgives him and goes home. She doesn't know where Lapham has gone; finally she has Penelope send a note to Tom Corey to ask him. Tom, who knows that Lapham has gone to Vermont, seizes the opportunity to call again, and when Irene unexpectedly returns from Iowa, she finds him and her sister together. Irene is quite calm; her unhappiness has hardened her. The next day Corey happily asks his mother to call on Penelope, and his father announces that he will go, too. Penelope receives Tom's parents alone. Bromfield says that he likes her sense of humor; Mrs. Corey remains unconvinced.

Back from Vermont, Lapham tells his wife that he is finished. He lost a buyer for the works, because he had to tell the man about his financial situation. Now he is putting himself in the hands of the creditors. He is sure that Rogers sent that anonymous note. When the family has to move back to the old Lapham farm in Vermont, Silas feels like a dead man, but the others are content. Tom now goes to work for the West Virginians, who take over the Lapham interests, and when they decide to send him to Mexico, he finally succeeds in persuading Penelope to marry him, but she feels as distant from the Coreys as ever. Irene remains unmarried. Later, Silas tells Sewell that it was only luck, not his own virtue, that enabled him to act morally with the Englishmen.

Charles Bellingham, Mrs. Charles Bellingham, James Bellingham, real-estate broker, English businessmen, Anna

Bellingham Corey, Bromfield Corey, Lily Corey, Nanny Corey, Tom Corey, Dennis, Hen Dewey, Zerrilla Millon Dewey, Bartley Hubbard, Marcia Hubbard, Jerry, Clara Kingsbury, Irene Lapham, Penelope Lapham, Persis Lapham, Colonel Silas Lapham, West Virginia paint manufacturers, Corporal Jim Millon, Molly Millon, Milton K. Rogers, Rev. Sewell, Mrs. Sewell, Seymour, Walker, Wemmel, William, Witherby.

"A Romance of Real Life," 1870 (in *Suburban Sketches*, 1871).

Late one evening Jonathan Tinker appears on the Charlesbridge doorstep of a contributor to the magazines, and says that he is just back from the sea and is looking for his family, which he believes is in the vicinity. The event confirms the contributor in his belief that real life offers romance. The dark neighborhood seems different and exciting as he goes from house to house making inquiries with Tinker. The matter seems like farce, yet still fascinating, when the contributor learns, the next day, that Tinker is a fraud, a bigamist, just out of prison. The narrator, "I," is amused at the contributor, but sympathetic.

A contributor to the magazines, Mrs. Hapford, "I" (the narrator), Jonathan Tinker, Julia Tinker.

"Romance of the Crossing," 1859.

Signed Chispa. After a silly quarrel, Edwin and Angelina are reconciled when they meet on the stepping-stones of a muddy street crossing and he gallantly steps into the mud so she can stay on the stones.

Angelina, Chispa, Edwin.

"The Rotational Tenants: A Hallowe'en Mystery," 1916.

Fred and Margaret Erlcort, an elderly couple, stay on in their seaside cottage after all their neighbors have gone back to the city. They think about all the unemployed people who would be glad to rent the cottages at winter rates. On Hallowe'en they are awakened by party noises and a blaze of lights in all the shut-up cottages. A parade of people in Hallowe'en costumes comes to their cottage. Their leader asks the Erlcorts to stay on for the rest of the winter and keep on imagining them. He says that he is the representative of the Rotational Tenants, who include all kinds of creative and skilled workers. Paying only a nominal rent, they have promised to leave the houses in better shape than they found them. After dancing for the Erlcorts, they disappear, but then the Erlcorts find themselves serving tea to Old Sir, the oldest of the natives and the owner of most of the cottages.

Suddenly there is another Hallowe'en parade, this time of very poor people carrying skull lanterns. The Old Sir disappears, and the chief Rotational Tenant returns to argue with Erlcort about the problem of poverty. The first set of Rotational Tenants has moved to the Summer Palace Hotel, from which they watch the social experiment that Erlcort's idea has generated. The poor people live in the cottages now. Erlcort halfheartedly defends his belief in complete economic equality, but the Rotational Tenant defends the concept of waste. When he insists that "to those who have it shall be given," Erlcort accuses him of being a disguised capitalist, and his dream disappears. The next morning a native tells them that a Hallowe'en lantern was left behind in a cottage by some boys.

Fred Erlcort, Margaret Erlcort, native, Rotational Tenant, Rotational Tenants, the Old Sir.

"Scene," 1871 (in *Suburban Sketches*, 1871).

While strolling through the beautiful autumn streets of Charlesbridge, a Boston suburb, the contributor, a magazine writer, sees the corpse of a poor Irish girl brought back from the river in a cart after she has drowned herself. The harsh details of the human scene clash with the beauty of nature and with his romantic literary ruminations about the event.

Contributor, dead Irish girl, Irish women and boys.

The Seen and the Unseen at Stratford-on-Avon. A Fantasy, 1914.

The unnamed first-person narrator, a seventy-six-year-old Amer-

ican writer, and two unidentified companions are staying in Chel-
tenham at the beginning of August. At an open-air performance of
Shakespeare in Stratford, the narrator notes that two men sitting in
front of him seem to turn into Elizabethans. The stout one seems to
be Shakespeare himself. Then the narrator realizes that he has been
napping. Later, on the train, when he moves his party to Stratford,
he sees the two gentlemen again, this time in modern dress; as he
realizes that they must be Shakespeare and Sir Francis Bacon, they
disappear. Later he imagines he hears Shakespeare pounding on
the doors of the crowded town, demanding lodgings for himself and
his friend.

The narrator finds himself talking with the spirit of Shakespeare,
who discusses his happy marriage, and his inability to get lodgings
for Bacon now because the innkeeper rejected the theory that Bacon
had written Shakespeare's plays. When the narrator tries to find out
just where Bacon did spend the night, the spirit disappears. Then
the narrator realizes that a whole eventful day in Stratford has
passed.

Shakespeare materializes again and tells the narrator that perhaps
Bacon could have written one tragedy: the story of his own life.
Later the narrator, and Shakespeare rejoining him, watch the folk
singing and folk dancing exhibitions. Shakespeare takes the narrator for walks around Stratford. At the house of John Harvard, Shakespeare says that the spirit of Harvard refused Bacon and him lodgings there, because his Puritan mother would have objected to
sheltering an actor. In eternity, however, Shakespeare has been
morally useful: he has dramatized the earthly transgressions of sin-
ful ghosts with reluctant memories. He has also had time to read
some of the narrator's writing. The narrator and Shakespeare also
visit Hall's Croft, the house of Shakespeare's son-in-law; the graveyard of the church where Shakespeare is buried; and (both now
being invisible) the cottage where Shakespeare and Bacon are living. Bacon, dressed in Elizabethan clothes, argues vigorously and at
length against the modern theory that he wrote Shakespeare. Shakespeare privately tells the narrator that Bacon harps on this subject to
keep his mind off the dishonor of his own life, especially his be-
trayal of Aubrey and Essex. Suddenly Shakespeare disappears
again.

With his two unidentified companions the narrator eats regularly at a tearoom, and one day visits the home of Mary Arden, Shakespeare's mother, at Wilmecote. Alone, but missing Shakespeare, the narrator enjoys the atmosphere at the plays performed in the Memorial Theater. With the other two again, the narrator spends a day on the river. Later the narrator goes to the movies and sees a Western. When a little boy is frightened by the movie, Bacon materializes beside the narrator to comfort the child. Bacon expiates his lack of pity in life by practicing pity now. He finds the form of the cinema full of possibilities. He and the narrator discuss Macaulay's essay about Bacon's career. Bacon, too, has read some of the narrator's writing.

The next day Shakespeare and the narrator discuss the dramatist's method of composition, including his borrowing from other playwrights. They are interrupted by Bacon, who continues to feel guilty about his corruption, though he consoles himself with the fact that many people think of him only as the originator of the inductive method. He dismisses Shakespeare's literary glory as unreal because ordinary people don't care about him at all. To test this theory, the three of them go to a greengrocer, who says that the town couldn't live without Shakespeare.

The narrator visits Anne Hathaway's cottage, Shakespeare's school, and Holy Trinity Church, where Shakespeare tells him that Bacon has left and he is going soon, too. Shakespeare explains that whenever Bacon wants to return from eternity to time he comes with Shakespeare as his comforter, because in time Bacon can't forget his troubles as he can in eternity. The narrator says that now he really sounds like Shakespeare, but then the spirit disappears, this time for good.

> Sir Francis Bacon, boat boy, little boy, folk dancers, gardener, elderly gentleman, John Harvard, three young nuns, participants in Shakespeare Pageant, people at teahouses, young German priest, punters, William Shakespeare, tourists, verger, "we" (the narrator and his unspecified companions).

"The Selling and the Giving of Dinners," 1894 (1968).
Writing to his friend Cyril from New York City, Aristides Homos,

the Altrurian Emissary to the United States, describes the big department stores and deplores the ubiquity of advertising signs in the city and the country. There are also many different kinds of restaurants in New York. Cafeterias he approves of because the absence of waiters and cashiers' bills lowers the cost of the food and demonstrates the Altrurian trust in human nature. Homos describes lunch clubs, foreign restaurants, and kosher restaurants, defining the term "kosher." The big hotel dining rooms waste tons of food that hungry people could eat. Well-to-do housewives also let their cooks waste food and money. Inviting guests to share a meal is no longer considered enough; they must be offered some special entertainment, too.

Cyril, Aristides Homos.

The Shadow of a Dream, 1890.
Part First — Faulkner
In the small city of Muskingum, Ohio, in the 1850's, the then youthful narrator, Basil March, combines newspaper work with youthful dabblings in belles lettres. His best friend is a moody Virginian, Douglas Faulkner, a twenty-six-year-old lawyer and political editor, who lives with his widowed mother. At the Faulkner home March meets Faulkner's college friend, Rev. James Nevil, a handsome Episcopalian minister. During their rambling literary conversation, Faulkner confesses that sometimes he has terrible dreams which he cannot forget. Later Faulkner tells March what a good influence Nevil was on his life in his wild college days. Faulkner and March break apart after an exchange of angry notes about a political article March has written. Years later (probably the 1870's) March has married and settled in the insurance business in Boston when Faulkner, who has become very rich, sends him a newspaper describing his marriage to Hermia Winter, a New Englander. A friend also writes March that Faulkner intends to visit him in Boston, but he never does.

Seven or eight years later Dr. Wingate, the nerve specialist, tells March that Faulkner, one of his patients in Swampscott, is badly run down and has a bad heart. Because Faulkner has mentioned March, Dr. Wingate suggests that the Marches visit the Faulkners to cheer up Faulkner's lonely wife. The Marches go to lunch at the Faulkner

house on an isolated beach near Swampscott. Faulkner pretends to
be much healthier than he really is, but immediately after telling the
Marches that Nevil has been in Europe with him and his wife and
lives with them, Faulkner suffers a seizure. Recovering very
quickly, he introduces the Marches to his wife and Nevil. March
feels that Mrs. Faulkner is very beautiful and refined and that Nevil
is a sad and saintly man.

Everybody tries to pretend that nothing is really wrong with
Faulkner. As he talks to March about his friendship with Nevil and
his wife's tolerance of this friendship, March begins to feel that
there is something curious in the way Faulkner looks at and speaks
about them. Freshening up in their room for lunch, the Marches
agree that Faulkner's continued attachment to Nevil is a reflection
on his wife and must create conflicts among them. Mrs. March feels
that Mrs. Faulkner is a devoted wife, far superior to Faulkner. After
lunch Nevil tells March that Faulkner is in agony and may die at any
moment. Nevil insists, however, that all pain has meaning, has
some good for someone; but he admits that Faulkner rejects this
philosophy. Nevil then asks March if he has noticed anything peculiar in Faulkner's behavior. Because Nevil fears that Faulkner's
mind has been affected by his suffering, he is staying on to help
watch over him.

During a stroll in the old, untended garden of the Faulkner house,
March experiences a feeling of *déjà vu* but tells Faulkner that of
course it is as "unsubstantial . . . as the shadow of a dream." Faulkner wants to know why he calls the shadow of a dream unsubstantial and asks him whether he has ever had any recurrent dreams. He
insists that a dream which always recurs with exactly the same details is a warning of some impending calamity. March thinks that
Faulkner is illogical, but doesn't know how to refute his argument.
Dr. Wingate arrives shortly thereafter and tells March that such a
persistent dream is prophetic of insanity. As March walks away toward the beach he hears Dr. Wingate warn Faulkner that "it" will
not only drive him mad but kill him. A moment later, March appears alone on the cliff overlooking the beach. Mrs. Faulkner, Nevil,
and Mrs. March, who have walked down the beach, all misinterpret
Faulkner's absence; in spite of March's reassurance that nothing has
happened, they rush back toward the house. As Mrs. Faulkner out-
distances the rest of them, Nevil begins telling the Marches about

Faulkner's aversion to his wife. At first, he says, Faulkner loved his wife far more than she loved him; but her love grew, and they were very happy, even when Faulkner's heart condition began to develop. But then Faulkner's attitude changed mysteriously. Nevil hates watching Faulkner's antipathy and his wife's bewilderment. The three now enter the garden. They see that Faulkner, who seems to have had another seizure, is resting his head on his wife's shoulder. Suddenly he lifts his head, sees Nevil, glares at him, jumps to his feet, pushes his wife away, and collapses in a fatal attack.

Part Second — Hermia

All are stunned for a long moment. Finally Mrs. March bursts into tears and takes Mrs. Faulkner in her arms. When Dr. Wingate leaves and Nevil proves utterly helpless, the Marches stay and help Hermia through her trouble. That fall Dr. Wingate tells March that Hermia has gone to live with her mother-in-law in Muskingum, and Nevil is serving a mission church in Kansas. Wingate asks March whether Faulkner told him his dream, but refuses to reveal it. He does tell March, however, that Hermia came to ask him what he knew about her husband's mind. When he told her that Faulkner had had a recurring dream about her, she asked him whether it was something which, for Faulkner's sake, he wouldn't want her to know. Wingate agreed that it was, and Mrs. Faulkner accepted his decision to remain silent. Both men marvel at her goodness and heroic behavior. Later the Marches discuss the doctor's story and Nevil's behavior. When Mrs. March tells her husband that she has received a letter from Hermia announcing Nevil's engagement, March assumes that he is engaged to Hermia. Isabel, scandalized, tells him that Nevil is engaged to a young woman in his Kansas congregation. After discussing the letter, the Marches agree that now they can be sure that, whatever caused Faulkner's dream, Mrs. Faulkner and Nevil were completely innocent.

Later Mrs. Faulkner writes to Mrs. March again: a week before the wedding, Nevil's fiancée broke their engagement because she was sure she didn't love him. Newspaper stories about the affair left Nevil so shattered that he took refuge with the two Mrs. Faulkners in Muskingum. To the Marches it is incomprehensible but necessary that Mrs. Faulkner, who has already suffered so much, must now support her husband's friend in his suffering. Nevil recovers enough to sail for Europe with a wealthy parishoner for company. When March sees him off from East Boston, he is surprised to find him just as he was before, not broken at all. After Nevil's return from a year in Europe, Hermia announces her engagment to him. The Marches are uneasy: they can't help recalling the terrible scene of Faulkner's death. Mrs. Faulkner telegraphs them that she is coming to Boston to consult Dr. Wingate. As soon as Mrs. Faulkner arrives at the Marches', they see that she has changed: she seems younger and stronger, but seems to be holding her happiness in check. She begs them to be present at her consultation of Dr. Wingate, and the Marches, feeling apprehensive, ask him to come to their house.

When the doctor balks at telling Hermia what Faulkner's dream was, she says that she must know the dream in order to be sure that she is worthy to remarry; perhaps the dream was proof of evil in her. The doctor tries to refute her illogic, but she persists, showing him what she found among her husband's letters, a scrap of paper referring to a recurrent dream. Wingate tells her that Faulkner was insane when he wrote it, that the dream was the delusion of a maniac. She continues to insist. Finally the doctor agrees to tell her, but not in the Marches' presence. March is very much relieved to withdraw. Dr. Wingate leaves without telling March what he told Hermia, but she tells Mrs. March. Alone the Marches discuss the situation. Mrs. March feels that she ought not to tell her husband exactly what the dream was because he must accompany Hermia back to her mother-in-law's home; in her present state of mind she cannot travel alone. Mrs. March blames Faulkner for having Nevil live with them. She insists that his jealousy drove him insane and now his innocent widow is caught in a trap of fate. March agrees. He, too, is sure that Mrs. Faulkner never thought of Nevil while her husband was alive or long after, but he also understands that now she will feel guilty in spite of the facts. They agree that the whole situation might be different now if Mrs. Faulkner had insisted on knowing the dream the first time she consulted Dr. Wingate about it. Mrs. March blames the doctor for telling Mrs. Faulkner that the dream was about Nevil, but March says that he did not inform Dr. Wingate

of Mrs. Faulkner's engagement, and Mrs. March blames her husband. That night March is tormented by nightmares about Faulkner. The next day he and Mrs. Faulkner start west on the train.

Part Third — Nevil

During most of the journey Mrs. Faulkner sits passive and numb,
but when they near Muskingum, she revives and insists on inviting
March to the Faulkner home. March is impressed by the growth of
Muskingum and the sumptuous wealth of the Faulkners. Faulkner's
mother is a literary old lady who seems genuinely fond of her magnificent daughter-in-law. March is troubled by memories of Faulkner's death and feels that his widow's new love is monstrous. The
elder Mrs. Faulkner tells March that Hermia told her what she had
learned from Dr. Wingate, but that she still approves of Hermia's
engagement to Nevil, especially since she has always encouraged
Hermia not to be morbid about her dead husband. She admits that
her son was not in his right mind when he died. The scrap of Faulkner's notebook that Hermia showed Dr. Wingate accused his wife of
wishing his death. The dream, the doctor told Hermia, was one that
Faulkner had had for almost a year before he died. In it Nevil and
Hermia were in love and waiting for him to die so they could get
married. In the next scene of the dream Faulkner would see two ceremonies going on simultaneously in Nevil's own church: Nevil's
and Hermia's wedding and his own funeral. When Faulkner would
try to scream that he had not died, his wife would smile and tell the
people in church that she had known Nevil before she knew Faulkner; both ceremonies would continue. Faulkner's mother then asks
March if he told Dr. Wingate about the engagement. Feeling very
guilty once again, March thinks that the engagement must be broken off. But to his surprise the old lady says that Hermia has decided that Nevil must be told and the decision must be left to him.

Musing, March admits to himself that for their own sake the living must forget the dead, but he pities Faulkner and feels that there
is something weird in the affair. When Faulkner's mother asks him
to tell Nevil about the dream, March refuses in dismay, arguing that
he needn't be told because the dream wasn't real. If Dr. Wingate had
known of the engagement, he would have lied to Hermia about the
dream. But these arguments are wasted on the old lady. March visits

an old friend, a lady who was kind to him when he was a young man. March's friend doesn't know about Hermia's engagement, but she thinks that Nevil ought to marry Hermia, who married below herself before. She fears that Hermia is too loyal to her husband's memory to remarry. Without revealing his knowledge of the actual situation, March argues that if they were in love even Faulkner's ghost would not prevent their union. Back at the Faulkners' house, March decides to leave for Boston immediately: he can't describe the dream to Nevil. But, just as March comes down the staircase, he sees Nevil stagger out of Faulkner's den. Hermia follows him and kisses him passionately again and again. March realizes that Hermia has told Nevil about the dream and he has given her up. It is obvious that, though crushed, she admires Nevil for his decision.

When the two men meet in front of the house, Nevil drags March to his church study, where he insists on confiding in March. Nevil wonders whether he hasn't always been in love with Hermia. He introduced her and Faulkner, and before the marriage reassured Faulkner that he wasn't in love with her. He accuses himself of being a hypocrite, of living with the Faulkners because he loved Hermia. Perhaps his former fiancée recognized his duplicity. March protests against these self-accusations, but Nevil continues by saying that everything about Hermia's behavior can be explained by her secret love for him. March asks Nevil what harm there could have been in his unconscious, unconfessed love, but Nevil insists that Hermia agreed with him; if they couldn't convince themselves of their absolute innocence, then they were guilty of everything. *She* sent *him* away, and he went because he could not continue as a minister if he felt that he was a hypocrite. March argues that Nevil is only afraid that he is guilty, but this very fear proves that he could not be. He finally persuades Nevil to reconsider the situation and to see Hermia again. Nevil accompanies March to the railroad station and boards his train for a final word. Delayed by his rich parishioner friend, Nevil steps backwards from the car to the ground only as the train begins to move. As it enters a tunnel, he is crushed to death against the stone jamb of the archway.

Hermia accepts Nevil's death as a judgment and dies of a broken heart. The Marches feel that Faulkner's dream had power over his widow and his friend only because they were completely guiltless. March thinks that even if Nevil had lived he and Hermia would never have married. Isabel feels that if they had married, they couldn't have kept their self-respect or their respect for each other. March wonders whether their suffering had a purpose or was simply their fate; he clings to the former belief. Neither of the Marches is willing to admit the hypothesis that perhaps Faulkner's dream was based on fact, that perhaps Hermia and Nevil really were in love with each other while Faulkner was still alive.

Douglas Faulkner, Hermia Winter Faulkner, Mrs. Faulkner, Basil March, Isabel March, March's lady friend in Muskingum, Rev. James Nevil, Nevil's fiancée, a wealthy parishioner of Nevil's, Dr. Wingate.

"A Sleep and a Forgetting," 1906 (in *Between the Dark and the Daylight*, 1907).

Dr. Matthew Lanfear goes to San Remo to examine the place for a friend with a sick wife. At the station he assists an elderly American, who asks him to help his pretty daughter. She claims that she is alone, but the man returns and takes her off to the Hotel Sardegna, to Dr. Lanfear's amazement. Next morning he sees the two—Abner L. Gerald and Nannie Gerald—at their hotel. While Lanfear is talking to Nannie alone, a Mrs. Bell, whom Lanfear knows, arrives with her daughters. Nannie doesn't introduce them. The Bells talk to Lanfear and leave. When Mr. Gerald returns, Nannie says that no one has been there but Lanfear. Later Gerald says that Nannie had forgotten the Bells; he tells Lanfear that when Mrs. Gerald was killed before Nannie's eyes, Nannie fainted and woke up forgetful of her previous life and incapable of remembering anything for long.

Lanfear sends his friends elsewhere, and attends Nannie in the charming San Remo atmosphere. She says she has occasional glimpses of an earlier life. Lanfear wonders if Nannie's soul may not be eternal, since she is herself despite her loss of memory. Her memory begins to improve, but her health declines under the strain. Cool weather in January gives Nannie great vigor, which continues with the returning warmth. She upsets an English youth by forgetting him after several visits, and bows to an Italian lieutenant who then follows them around until Lanfear tells him the facts of the case.

In April they take a long expedition into the hills. Nannie says casually that her mother died long ago. They look at an old village abandoned after an earthquake; when Lanfear gets lost, she guides him out, seeming to use his memory of an earlier trip. They meet Gerald in the clutches of a madman, and Nannie collapses, saying her mother is killed. When she recovers, she has, gradually and painlessly, regained her full memory. Nannie and Lanfear marry. In the summer Gerald dies.

Mrs. Bell, Abner L. Gerald, Nannie Gerald, Dr. Matthew Lanfear, Italian lieutenant, madman, peasants.

"Somebody's Mother," 1915 (in *The Daughter of the Storage*, 1916).

On a December evening in New York, a man going out to dinner with his son and daughter sees an old woman half asleep on the steps of a brownstone. As they are trying to find out whether she is sick, a young black girl joins them and suggests that she must be somebody's mother. The black girl and the young man get the old woman to her feet and start to walk her along. When the old woman mutters that she lives in Harlem, they decide to put her on the Ninth Avenue streetcar and send her home, but suddenly she sits down on the steps of a black-people's boardinghouse. The young man goes off in search of a policeman, but it is his sister who finds one. When the policeman talks to the old woman, she announces that she lives only a block away and walks off unaided. Amused, the father wonders if the disreputable old woman really was somebody's mother.

The man's daughter, diners and dancers at a black board-inghouse, the father, young black girl, policeman, the man's son, old woman.

The Son of Royal Langbrith, 1904.

In Saxmills, a little New England factory town, Dr. Justin Anther, the leading local physician, has just proposed to Mrs. Amelia Langbrith, for nineteen years the widow of the local magnate, Royal Langbrith. She nervously puts him off, and Anther realizes with exasperation that her fear is that her son James, a Harvard senior, will

object to any remarriage. Anther blames her for allowing James to
walk over her. Mrs. Langbrith puzzles Anther: married at eighteen,
a wife for only three years, and now forty, does she still have any
feeling for Royal Langbrith? Anther and Amelia both agree that
James's reverence for his father's memory is sacrilege, because the
man was evil, but can't be destroyed while Langbrith's victims live.
She implores Anther not to tell James about Langbrith, because
James would hate Anther for that.

At Easter vacation, shortly thereafter, James brings home his Harvard friend Falk and acts very patronizing with the local girls and
his mother. Falk, a Midwesterner, finds James amusing and sometimes insufferable. Having overhauled the routine of the house to
suit his worldly tastes, James proposes a catered formal dinner, a
prospect beyond his mother's horizons. Looking at Royal Langbrith's grim puritan face in his picture, James praises him to Falk
and casually recalls that his mother has always evaded questions
about his father. James wonders aloud why he likes Falk, to which
Falk replies that only he has the courage to put James down when he
needs it. The young men speak admiringly of Hope Hawberk,
daughter of Langbrith's former partner, who, James says, took to
opium because of some unknown inner weakness. James likes Anther, but looks down disparagingly on his Uncle John, Royal's mis-
anthropic brother, who manages the family mills. James and Falk
call on Hope Hawberk, Susie Johns, and Jessamy Colebridge at the
latter's house. During the gay evening that follows, James finds
himself greatly attracted to Hope Hawberk.

James presides with dignity over the dinner party, at which
young and old unaccustomedly mix. At table James and Hope are
drawn to each other more and more. After dinner Falk tells Anther
of James's reputation at Harvard as a patronizing but friendly ass,
and analyzes the portrait of Royal Langbrith as tigerish. To the male
guests James recalls with satisfaction that his father squelched a
proposal to have Saxmills renamed Langbrith; however, James
wants a medallion of Langbrith put in front of the library that he
gave the town many years earlier. James is much put out by the lack
of interest taken in this proposal by the older men, especially Anther. During the dance that follows the dinner, James courts Hope,
who keeps him at arm's length. He walks her home and there encounters Hawberk, woozy and garrulous with opium.

Next morning, James, recalling Anther's coolness of the night before, asks his mother if Anther and Royal Langbrith were ever at odds; she puts him off and suggests he ask Anther. James still wants to put up the medallion. He wonders about Hawberk and the unknown reason for his addiction to opium. On the way back to Boston, James tells Falk of his love for Hope and his irritation with Anther. Falling into reverie, James wonders that his mother has never remarried, but assumes that she depends entirely on him.

Anther and Amelia feel guilty for not telling the world of Royal Langbrith's cruelty to Hawberk, whose addiction, they know, keeps him still in hopeless bondage to Langbrith. Amelia hopes that James and Hope can marry and break the chain of misery. She hasn't been able to speak to James about Anther's suit because of Anther's coolness to James at the dinner. She asks Anther to room at her house, but he says it's impossible. He urges her to let him tell James about his father, but she refuses, saying it's too late, and even asks Anther to be kind to James about the plan for the medallion. Grumbling that Royal Langbrith has the power to corrupt Amelia even now, Anther stalks out. Hawberk, tremulous with opium but still alert, comes to Anther's lodgings to ask him about Hope and James. Anther in turn presses Hawberk for the details of Royal Langbrith's swindle of and hold on Hawberk, but Hawberk can't remember.

Anther asks Judge Garley, an elderly local lawyer, his opinion of a man who would destroy another man's soul. Anther goes on to tell Garley, who moved to Saxmills after Royal Langbrith's death, the truth about Langbrith. Garley says he has had his suspicions ever since he ran across some curious details about Langbrith. Anther tells Garley that Hawberk was not, as the local legend has it, a mere opium-eating mechanic that Langbrith had to get rid of, but the inventor of the paper-making process on which the great prosperity of the mill and the town has been based; Hawberk was forced out by Langbrith's threat to expose a casual love affair of Hawberk's to his wife, and in his despair Hawberk then took to opium. Langbrith, says Anther, was living a double life complete with children in Boston by the woman Hawberk had merely flirted with; Langbrith would come back drunk from Boston, taunt Amelia with the woman, and beat her. Amelia, an ignorant country girl, had been a worker in Langbrith's mill, and was his slave. Anther says he has never felt able to tell the truth about Langbrith, and thus destroy the town's and James Langbrith's idol. No one would ever believe anything Hawberk might say. Garley advises Anther to keep quiet, even after Anther says that he hopes to get James's agreement to the marriage with Amelia by exposing Royal Langbrith. After leaving Garley, Anther stops at Amelia's house and apologizes to her for leaving so angrily the night before. Then he impulsively embraces her. Leaving, he feels more tolerant toward James. Meanwhile, Jessamy Colebridge and Hope tease Susie Johns about a letter from Falk, though Hope hasn't shown her letter from James.

On a warm spring day Hawberk has a horrible opium dream and is rescued by Hope. She arranges with Anther to control her father's addiction with laudanum. Hope tells Anther that Royal was Hawberk's best friend and willy-nilly Anther must agree. At Harvard, meanwhile, James broods over Hope's temporizing answers to his tender love letters, and tries out on her his ideas, which she generally ridicules, for the medallion of his father. Mrs. Enderby, the Episcopalian minister's wife, applauds to Hope the unknown person, actually Hope, who persuaded James not to have the medallion dedicated on Decoration Day. Rev. Enderby has suggested Royal Langbrith's birthday instead. Mrs. Enderby, a romantic soul, tries to help along the unacknowledged affair of James and Hope by advising Hope not to be so sharp with him.

Amelia thinks of her present genuine love for Anther and her past infatuation and misery with Royal Langbrith. She had been so ignorant and isolated that she thought her miserable state was the norm of marriage. She is still anxious at the thought of James's knowing about herself and Anther. Hope tells Amelia that James is so upset at her sarcasms about the medallion that he is planning to give it up. Hope asks Amelia if it is all right for her to ask Anther to write James and tell him to go on. Amelia agrees to speak to Anther. Mrs. Enderby asks Amelia if it is true that James will give up his plan, and is glad to hear the rumor is false, though Amelia seems oddly uninterested in the matter. Mrs. Enderby's interest is less a personal one than part of her duty toward her husband's parish, which drew him from a fashionable church in Boston. Mrs. Enderby passes on the good news of James's firm intentions to Anther, who is even less interested than Amelia. Mrs. Enderby concludes that Anther is jealous of Royal Langbrith's memory.

After pompously breaking with Hope, by letter, James examines the bas-relief of his father's head being done by a young sculptor he has discovered. The astute artist has made the face resemble James's; naturally the latter is enthusiastic, but Falk derisive. James tells Falk how Hope implored him to go on with the plan for the medallion, and he agreed; now he praises Hope extravagantly.

Hope's grandmother, Mrs. Southfield, grumbles to her about James; she has always vaguely suspected Royal Langbrith. To Anther, Hope gaily confesses her sin of gossiping about the medallion; Anther forgives and praises her. Before seeing Hawberk, Anther asks John Langbrith to make his nephew James drop his plan because only John can tell James the truth. John crossly says that he doesn't owe anybody anything and won't go outside his job. Garley advises Anther to drop the idea of telling James.

The date of the dedication being fixed for June 29, Royal Langbrith's birthday, the sculptor hastens to finish the bas-relief portrait, which turns out to be an idealization of the type of the post-Civil-War businessman. Still resenting Anther's indifference, James asks Garley instead of Anther to make the dedicatory address; however, everyone concerned comes to Anther for advice, forcing him to appear benevolent toward the affair. Mrs. Enderby presses Anther to come and help Rev. Enderby with some ideas about Royal Langbrith for Enderby's speech on Langbrith's altruism. Anther manages to stall until the night before the dedication. Talking to Anther, Enderby rejects the idea that truth should always out. Anther poses Royal Langbrith's case in a hypothetical way, and then names him openly. Anther says that he has been wrestling with himself about telling Enderby, and should have told him long before. Enderby is put on the spot. He decides to leave it to God to expose or not expose Langbrith. Anther has been planning to avoid the ceremony, but Amelia secretly leaves him a note begging him to attend.

The ceremony is simple and local, though James had yearned to have the governor there. To James's surprise and pleasure, both Anther and Hawberk appear and sit up front. Anther is impressed by Garley's agility in speaking at length of Royal Langbrith without giving him more than conventional praise. Enderby speaks mainly of the good Langbrith did the town. Good deeds, he says, take no color from their motive, good or bad. After a picnic for the whole

town at the Langbrith house, James tells his mother that it has been
a perfect day. He proposes again to Hope, who accepts him this
time, because he was kind to Hawberk at the ceremony. She says
she will wait for him while he studies playwriting in Paris. James
sympathizes with Hope's misery with her father, and she cries on
his shoulder. James then visits Anther, hoping to get him to help
Hope, and also planning to offer him the use of Royal Langbrith's
old office at the Langbrith house.

Anther is pleased by James's happiness during the day, and resigned to letting Royal Langbrith alone; but when he sees Amelia,
he says he must tell James the truth. When James comes in, Amelia
blurts out that she and Anther will be married. James is furious, and
accuses them of spoiling his day and of being afraid to tell him. He
accuses Anther of secretly hating Royal Langbrith and trying to sup-
plant him with Amelia. She manages to keep Anther from blurting
out the whole truth about Royal Langbrith. James accuses her of
being unfaithful to his father's memory. Amelia then tries to tell
James about his father, but he rushes out. Amelia is now in utter
revulsion from Royal Langbrith and his son, as she calls James; Anther must soothe her, and calm her anger toward James. In a nightmare of anger and frustration, James tells Hope about his mother
and Anther, and is horrified to find her applauding the idea and
deriding his belief that Anther and Amelia should unite only in
worship of Royal Langbrith's memory. Hope forces him to go back
to his mother and agree to tolerate her action, but when he speaks to
Amelia she says that she will not remarry.

Next day when Anther reads Amelia's note saying that she will
not marry him, he realizes that she has exhausted her little strength,
and he stays away until James has left for Paris. Anther tells Amelia
that he has decided that it's useless ever to expose Langbrith to
James, but that if Hawberk recovers, he might talk. For a moment
Amelia hints that Anther shouldn't cure Hawberk. Anther advises
John Langbrith to take a trip to cure his nervous dyspepsia, and rejoices with Hawberk on his greatly improved condition, but is torn
to see that Hawberk is beginning to recall Royal Langbrith's cruelty
to him. The author comments on the seeming absence or illogic of
moral law, in the vastness of its workings. Anther trembles to think
what Hawberk's remembering and telling the truth may do to
Hope. One day, upon Hawberk's direct question, Anther says that

Royal Langbrith was a scoundrel. Hawberk agrees, but decides to let the matter rest, or perhaps come out naturally some day, as Anther says.

At Anther's suggestion John Langbrith lets Hawberk run the manufacturing side of the mills. The town is skeptical about Hawberk. Eventually Amelia tells Anther bluntly that Hope should be told the truth because James might turn out to be like his father. When Anther says that she should first tell James, Amelia collapses again into weak passivity. Anther is puzzled at his calm acquiescence in the defeat of his hopes, which seem like something from the distant past; he is distressed, though, at the passing Darwinian thought that perhaps victims like Amelia are made for predators like Royal Langbrith. Anther realizes that James's bad behavior is his, Anther's, fault for not having the strength to tell him the truth about his father. Amelia says that she doesn't love James the way she did, and that she is willing to marry Anther; but he says that they should remain apart, because he thinks that her willingness doesn't go beyond the words. The winter passes. In April Hawberk suddenly catches pneumonia and dies.

A month earlier John Langbrith, unable to continue, wrote James to stop loafing and come back and look after the mills if he wanted them to go on. James replied that John Langbrith should leave the mills in Hawberk's care, and pompously regretted his uncle's inability to rise to the level of Royal Langbrith's character. Anther has typhoid fever; Amelia nurses him, and at John Langbrith's request she cables James to come home. John goes off for a few days; on his return, he meets James on the train from New York. They quarrel about each other's role in the mills. At last anger and indigestion drive John to tell James the truth about his father, especially the way he cowed and used people, and to relate the facts behind the celebration the previous summer. James is disgusted by his uncle, but knows that he is telling the truth. Reaching home, James at once tells his mother what has happened; in turn she tells him that Anther is dead. James realizes what a cruel fool he has been, and seizes on the idea of releasing Hope and telling the whole world about his father. Next day he tells Hope. She pities him for not knowing, says Hawberk had his reward in his inventions and work, and refuses to let him go. James agrees to take up with Rev. Enderby the question of publishing Royal Langbrith's guilt to the world. Enderby relieves

James of some of his misery by saying that Anther told him about Royal Langbrith, and says that he took part in the ceremony because he thought that no good would come of exposing Langbrith. Enderby says that James should remain silent until the will of God clearly requires him to speak.

The tone of Enderby's memorial speech for Anther is dampened by his memories of the doctor. Toward the end Anther had seen Royal Langbrith as merely a predatory beast. A few months later a last obstacle to the marriage of James and Hope perishes in Mrs. Southfield. The young couple are married soon thereafter, and live with Amelia, who gets along well with Hope. At present, Royal Langbrith's true nature is still concealed, but somehow the public has turned against his memory. James took over the mills while his uncle traveled abroad; in Paris he met Royal's former mistress. James reluctantly agrees to help his half sister study singing. Hope is curious about the girl until she sees her photograph and judges her character, negatively.

The young Langbriths have a child and may return to Paris. Mrs. Enderby continues to feel that Royal Langbrith's evil should be made public, but Enderby says that perhaps everything, given the mysterious complicity of human beings, has worked out for the best; certainly Hope's and James's teeth have not been set on edge by the sour grapes their fathers ate.

> Dr. Justin Anther, Mrs. Burwell, Jessamy Colebridge, daughter of Royal Langbrith, Rev. Enderby, Mrs. Enderby, Falk, Judge Garley, Mrs. Garley, Hope Hawberk, Lorenzo Hawberk, Susie Johns, Mrs. Amelia Langbrith, James Langbrith, John Langbrith, Royal Langbrith, Lilly, mistress of Royal Langbrith, Norah, Mrs. Southfield.

The Story of a Play, 1898.

Brice Maxwell, a young Boston newspaperman and playwright, explains his idea for a play to Launcelot Godolphin (pseud.), a handsome, self-centered young actor in town on tour. The play (title never given) is about the success, corruption, and fall of a businessman named Haxard, and has a good deal of spectacle, including a large public dinner at which Haxard dies, but no love element. Godolphin demands the latter, but is otherwise interested. During the winter Maxwell works on his play. In the summer Godolphin comes east, to Manchester-by-the-Sea, and its colony of actors, and works on the play with Maxwell, who is settled nearby in a modest cottage with his wife Louise, daughter of the wealthy Boston Hilarys. Godolphin wants many basic changes, making the play cheaply theatrical. Maxwell resists him, but not firmly enough to suit Louise, and they quarrel about it. Reconciled, they decry the state of the modern theater and praise the ideal of the drama. To herself Louise recalls her courtship and engagement, Maxwell's irreconcilable differences with her social world, and the well-contained disapproval of her parents. When Maxwell has trouble with the love element, he follows Louise's suggestion that they put themselves and their love into the characters Atland and Salome.

When Louise visits her father, Mr. Hilary, he conceals his great contempt for the theater and actors, though he is disturbed when she reveals her mixed feelings about Maxwell's total involvement in his work. Louise, somewhat confused, thinks that she loves Maxwell's talent, not his thin good looks. Meanwhile, Godolphin makes more trouble. First he writes saying that he relinquishes the play. Maxwell decides to increase the love interest and eliminate the businessman, and thus have a new play. Then Godolphin returns and negotiates with Maxwell again. Next Godolphin says he wants to play Atland. At the beach one day Maxwell and Louise notice a striking woman with smouldering eyes. They decide to keep the old play, with the love business subordinate in it. Returning to their cottage they find a telegram from Godolphin suggesting the same thing. With Louise's assistance, Maxwell reworks the love business to make it more realistic, but Godolphin finds it intrusive. Louise irritates Maxwell with her criticism of the love business, but they resolve the problem, and as is his habit Maxwell involuntarily keeps Louise's behavior in the back of his mind for future dramatic use. He finds Godolphin bafflingly and childishly capricious, but manages to get along with him. Though Louise fails to persuade Maxwell to go into society, she now is happy in his absorption in his work.

In the fall Godolphin takes the play and reports a success in the first tryout, in Midland, a Middlewestern town. The ecstatic Maxwells project huge profits, and impress Hilary with them. Mrs. Hilary, being a Boston Brahmin, is not impressed. Godolphin sends along some Midland papers with critical notices of the play and interviews in which he praises Maxwell highly. Louise puts them all in a scrapbook. The Midland critics have a low opinion of the actress who plays Salome, and are largely baffled by the play itself, missing its basis in nature and truth. The newspapers' play announcements reveal that Godolphin is not presenting the play anymore. He writes that he will present the play often, but not exclusively, and intends to shorten Salome's part. The Maxwells are horrified to think of Godolphin's revising the play. Maxwell concludes that Godolphin really lacks the ability to do that, and decides to wait and see what Godolphin does next. Maxwell is puzzled by Louise's demand that they tell everyone about the play not being so successful as they have been saying it is.

As fall comes, the life at the shore dwindles away, and the Maxwells move into a deserted hotel. Godolphin continues to present the play occasionally in the West. Maxwell exchanges a few letters with the most perceptive but anonymous critic of the play in Midland. Godolphin writes that he wants to give the play in Chicago and wants Maxwell to join him there for the rehearsals. Maxwell decides that he would do more harm than good by doing so; instead, he decides to go to New York with Louise and await Godolphin's eventual return. In a modest apartment in New York, Maxwell works very hard on a new play and worries about his dwindling savings. Godolphin occasionally performs the old play. The Boston *Abstract*, Maxwell's old paper, asks him to write a weekly New York letter. He and Louise quarrel over accepting the offer, but they are reconciled over a friendly letter from Godolphin with a check for $300 — Maxwell's first royalties. The quarrel gives Maxwell an idea for a play based on the idea of evil growing out of love.

Godolphin relinquishes the play, because of public and critical disfavor in Chicago. The Maxwells are stunned, but he courageously begins to take the script around to the theater managers. Louise is proud of Maxwell's industry, and nervous for his health and his future. At the local grocery she sees again the smouldering-eyed woman, whom the grocer calls Mrs. Harley; she lives in the Maxwells' building. The two women immediately detest each other. Maxwell leaves the play with Grayson, a manager whom he has met and liked before. Louise is sure that Grayson will take the play;

Maxwell, less optimistic, plans to write those New York letters. Louise now tells him that that woman lives in the building.

Maxwell familiarizes himself with the city in order to write his letter of comment for the *Abstract*. Grayson tells him that the play is really two incomplete and mixed plays, a comedy and a tragedy, and that he should make it into a vehicle for a star actress. Grayson says that he knows a good actress for the part, a Southern woman, but can't remember her name. Very disappointed at Grayson's remarks, Maxwell can't even take his usual step of turning the affair over with his wife. Grayson writes Maxwell that the actress is Mrs. Harley, who calls herself Yolande Havisham on the stage. This news greatly upsets Louise, and Maxwell accuses her of jealousy. She rushes out of the apartment, falls down on the stairs, and passes out. Mrs. Harley helps her. When Louise revives in her bed, she is first horrified that it was that woman who saved her, and then decides to be civil. Maxwell goes down to Mrs. Harley's flat and meets and thanks her. Later he studies the advertisements in a theatrical newspaper and feels alienated from the shabby and business sides of the theater; he considers himself a serious moralist. He broods meanwhile over his relations with Louise and her ambivalent feelings for his work, and wonders if he could turn his play into a novel, while continuing to visit the managers and write his letters.

Louise is eager to help Maxwell turn the play into a novel. While he is out, she finds an exciting want ad in the theatrical newspaper: Mr. L. Sterne, an agent, wants a play to suit an emotional actress. Certain that Maxwell's play will fill the bill and that time is of the essence, Louise answers the ad in Maxwell's name. When Maxwell returns after another unsuccessful round of the managers and Louise shows him the ad, his contempt for it is so great that Louise can't tell him about her letter and can't go on helping him with the novel. Maxwell continues working alone, on the novel version, and failing with the managers. No reply comes to Louise from the ad. She and Maxwell visit Mrs. Harley, who snubs Louise and devotes herself to Maxwell. When the Hilarys pay an unexpected visit, Hilary hints at Maxwell's going back to the *Abstract*, with Hilary's financial aid, but Maxwell misses the hint, and when told about it by Louise later, says that a newspaper could never be his real life.

Louise reluctantly declines several society invitations because of

Maxwell's unwillingness to go out. At a ladies' luncheon she meets a man who, missing her name, praises Maxwell's play; he is Mr. Ray of Midland, author and critic (see *The World of Chance*). Louise returns home to find a Mr. Laurence Sterne waiting, and she realizes that he must be the L. Sterne of the ad. He is the manager of a star who is interested in the play; he finally names her as Mrs. Harley, and leaves before Louise can say anything. When Maxwell returns she tells all, and is astounded when he replies that Godolphin is in town. Godolphin's company has gone bankrupt on the road, and he has returned to New York to rebuild his fortunes. Maxwell is happy to hear about Ray's praise of the play. At the Player's Club Maxwell finds Godolphin, who says a stronger actress is needed for the part of Salome to match the strong part of Haxard. Godolphin will take the play if Maxwell subdues the part of Salome while keeping it strong; they argue at length about this. Godolphin says that Grayson will help to back him. Grayson joins the group and says that Salome should be left alone and played strongly to reinforce Haxard; he and Godolphin say that Yolande Havisham should have the part, but that because she is engaged by Sterne, they should look for another actress, a Miss Petrell.

Grayson arranges with Sterne to have Miss Havisham consider the part. Louise is incensed, because Salome is based on her, and when Maxwell says he will agree to have Miss Havisham, Louise angrily decides to go home to Boston. Next day she decides to stay, even though Maxwell is fixed in his purpose. He arranges to have Miss Havisham hired. Rehearsals begin, with Louise still sulking and jealous. At last she relents, attends a rehearsal, and is impressed by Godolphin's skill as a director; she and Miss Havisham are cattily polite to each other, and later Louise says that Miss Havisham's version of her role is a deliberate parody of herself. She and Maxwell quarrel bitterly, and he stamps out of the apartment. Maxwell returns in the evening to find Louise friendly and Godolphin there singing the praises of Miss Havisham. After Godolphin leaves, the Maxwells are reconciled. A little later that evening, Grayson arrives with a note from Godolphin giving up his part, clearly out of jealousy of Miss Havisham's part. They decide to ask Godolphin to stay and Miss Havisham to go.

Miss Petrell is hired to play Salome. At the first night she is impressive in the part, partly because Godolphin has coached her in some of Miss Havisham's effective mannerisms. The play is a great popular and critical success. Godolphin soon marries Miss Petrell, and tours successfully in Maxwell's play.

Bellboy, Lancelot Godolphin, Grayson, Mrs. Harley, Eben Hilary, Mrs. Hilary, Brice Maxwell, Louise Hilary Maxwell, Miss Petrell, provision man, Ray.

"A Summer Sunday in a Country Village," 1859.
Unsigned. On a hot, slow, boring Sunday afternoon in a village (evidently based on Jefferson, Howells' Ohio home), the narrator analyzes the peculiar qualities of Sunday sunlight and sounds, waking up on Sunday, church, heat, and finally the cool twilight.

"I" (the narrator).

"Table Talk," in The Daughter of the Storage (1916). See "Editor's Easy Chair," June 1910.

"A Tale of Love and Politics. Adventures of a Printer Boy," 1853.
George Wentworth is a promising orphaned youth. He comes, seeking his fortune, to the upstate New York town of G—. While watching a political meeting he sees that the American flag has stuck halfway up its staff. He climbs up daringly and loosens the flag, thereby winning applause and the offer of a reward from the candidate, Judge S—. When George rejects the reward, the Judge, much impressed, takes him in and brings him up. Five years later, George, now twenty-one, and Ida, the Judge's daughter, are secretly in love. When George saves Ida from drowning, the Judge reads her face aright and is much distressed, because he considers George an inferior. The Judge makes George leave the house, but sets him up as a printer. Later George writes some brilliant unsigned editorials that help elect the Judge to Congress. Accidentally the Judge discovers George's authorship and George discloses his love for Ida and hers for him. The Judge now gives them his blessing and they are betrothed.

Ida S—, Judge S—, George Wentworth.

"A Tale Untold," 1917.

On a steamboat en route from St. Louis to Pittsburgh in 1857, a handsome elderly stranger leads the lady passengers in hymn singing. When he wanders past a group of gamblers on the hurricane deck, a losing gambler picks a fight with him by accusing him of helping someone to cheat. Looking on is Stephen West, a naïve young man whose sole experience of life has come from literature. He is troubled by his recent argument with the pilot, Captain Ryan, whom he admired until he argued that slavery was justified because blacks had no souls. Captain Ryan now invites Stephen into the pilothouse, where the stranger displays some jewelry he says he has just bought from a bankrupt's stock in Cincinnati. After asking Stephen's opinion about the value of a gold watch guard, the pilot buys it. The stranger warns Stephen against gambling and invites him to the hymn singing.

Convinced by the pilot's example and by the stranger's behavior, Stephen also buys a watch guard. Some of the ladies buy jewelry. When a planter boards the boat with his family and slaves, Stephen dreams about getting the planter to free his slaves. Just then he sees the second mate put the losing gambler off the boat. The elderly stranger runs to join him, and Stephen sees the two men laughing together and jeering at the passengers. In Pittsburgh a jeweler tells Stephen that his watch guard is worthless. He throws it away and a loafer picks it up in the street. Stephen muses about ways of putting his experience into a story, but because he never does, it remains a tale untold.

> Losing gambler, gamblers, jeweler, ladies, loafer, second mate, planter, Captain Ryan, slave women, elderly stranger, Stephen West, planter's wife and daughters.

Their Silver Wedding Journey, 1899.

In the New York office of *Every Other Week,* the literary magazine owned by Basil March and Fulkerson, the latter advises March to take off a sabbatical year, or at least a summer, in Europe. It is nine years since they took over the magazine from Dryfoos (see *A Hazard of New Fortunes*); although it has been quite successful, March has been tired and ill lately, and his doctor says he should go to Carlsbad for the cure. Mrs. March agrees, and wants to go herself. March's son Tom, an assistant editor of the magazine, can take over all the editing. March tells Isabel that they could call the trip their Silver Wedding Journey, a few years late (see *Their Wedding Journey*). She says that he could write an interesting and original book on it, mixing travel and fiction. They visit a ship, and keep changing their minds about going, but after studying Baedekers and phrase books and comparing ships, they finally reserve a stateroom on a German vessel, the *Norumbia*. About to leave New York, March finds that he suddenly likes the city and will miss it.

On the morning of sailing March can't believe that he is about to end his usual life. After the turmoil of departure the Marches go to breakfast and chat with the several Americans at their table; they include a humorous gentleman, R. M. Kenby; an aloof father and daughter, General E. B. Triscoe and Miss Triscoe; a young bridal pair, Mr. and Mrs. Leffers; a widowed mother and her young son, Mrs. Adding and Roswell Adding; and a handsome young man, L. J. Burnamy. March observes the crowd on board with the same gentle satire as in *Their Wedding Journey*. Burnamy turns out to be the author of a book of prose sketches and of a poem accepted recently by *Every Other Week*; he is bound for Carlsbad to be the secretary of an American businessman whose Chicago newspaper he has been working for. He is Triscoe's cabin mate. March studies the passengers in second class and steerage, and talks with Major Eltwin, an elderly invalid Ohioan. The ship sails on and the passengers live in an easy routine. Mrs. March introduces Miss Triscoe to Burnamy with no success; the Triscoes are society people and aloof. At dinner the group discusses a current best seller, and Mr. Triscoe unexpectedly joins in. Later Miss Triscoe unbends with Isabel and strolls with Burnamy, but the young people come no closer, as the ship continues, stopping in Plymouth. The group at table argue Triscoe's low opinion of America; he and Major Eltwin exchange sharp remarks, but make up. Triscoe, of an old but poor Rhode Island family, fought gallantly in the Civil War, married a rich girl, who died and left their daughter a fortune, and has since lived aimlessly, bringing his daughter up in New York and abroad, and holding aloof from American life. During the last days of the voyage, Burnamy and Miss Triscoe chat, but not enough to satisfy Isabel's matchmaking instinct.

As they disembark at Cuxhaven, the Marches notice that Burnamy is with the Eltwins, not with Miss Triscoe. On the train to
Hamburg they enjoy again the delightful strangeness of travel. In
Hamburg the Marches go to the circus, and enjoy the old city, and
look for evidence of Heine; then they take the train to Leipzig. On
the Leipzig battlefield the Marches meet the Triscoes, who think
they may go over to Carlsbad to cure the general's liver. Burnamy
has been in Leipzig, but Miss Triscoe says nothing about him. Later
the Marches observe the Leipzig students and the industrial fair.
On the train to Carlsbad they chat with Berliners with whom they
have mutual acquaintances, and enjoy the rustic countryside.

At Carlsbad the Marches are met by Burnamy, who says nothing
about Leipzig or Miss Triscoe. Carlsbad is a charming cosmopolitan
town in a wooded valley. At Pupp's Hotel, Burnamy introduces his
employer Stoller, a boorish *nouveau riche* originally from rural Indiana. He bullies Burnamy and makes him write letters to be
printed in Stoller's newspaper under Stoller's name. March, rising
at 5 A.M., begins his routine of waters and walks. Burnamy introduces the Marches to the Posthof, a café in the woods where everyone eats breakfast; there they meet Miss Triscoe, who later walks
in the woods and chats with Burnamy as March observes them. The
Marches help along the affair of the young people. Mrs. March chaperons them to the Kurhaus ball, and so astonishes them by waltzing
vigorously with an officer that they bump into another couple and
Burnamy hurts his leg. Mrs. Adding and her son Rose arrive; in Berlin, Kenby proposed to her, but she put him off.

As the pleasant days pass, the Marches linger over their midday
meal at Pupp's and watch the Carlsbad world, or stroll on the
wooded paths and through the streets. They observe visiting
"Highhotes," as they call *Hoheits* or dignitaries. One night Stoller
invites the Marches, the Triscoes, and Burnamy to share a box at the
opera. Afterwards the group stroll the deserted streets of Carlsbad,
have a late supper, and arrange an outing to a ruined castle, during
which Burnamy and Miss Triscoe drive and stroll together, irritating Stoller. He avenges himself by blaming Burnamy for not telling
him that the articles on European cities that Burnamy wrote under
Stoller's name implied that Stoller advocates municipal socialism,
which he abhors; American critics of Stoller's buccaneering business methods are jeering at him. Stoller fires Burnamy, who feels

guilty but won't help Stoller wiggle dishonestly out of his trouble, which may ruin his political prospects at home. The Triscoes, especially Miss Triscoe, are distressed by Burnamy's situation, but think he did right. He goes to Ansbach.

The Marches now see a great deal of Mrs. Adding and her son Rose. March meets Major Eltwin, who despondently tells him that the death of his last child made him finally willing to leave home. Miss Triscoe, who cherishes a handkerchief that Burnamy left behind, dazzles the audience when she sits in the Marches' box at the opera. Touring German theaters for an American paper, Burnamy appears at the box while March is out, and later rescues Miss Triscoe when she is lost in a crowd.

The Marches leave Carlsbad regretfully and go to Germany for the "after-cure." In Nürnberg they enjoy the old city, feel sorry for a German-American who has returned unhappily to Germany, visit Dürer's house, and run into the Lefferses, whose youthful style makes them want to be around people their own age. As the Marches wonder if Burnamy and Miss Triscoe are engaged, she tells her father that Burnamy has seen her, but that they are not engaged. Visiting Ansbach and Würzburg, the Marches note the way German women do physical work, and are amused by the arrogance of a Baroness they meet on the train. At Würzburg they run into Stoller and his equally vulgar daughters, and Kenby, with whom March visits the *Volksfest*. The Triscoes and the Addings also arrive. Stoller apologizes to the Marches for his behavior with Burnamy. The Marches, the Addings, Kenby, and Triscoe visit the Capuchin Church, where Rose Adding becomes ill and Triscoe can't summon the courage to propose to Mrs. Adding. Kenby decides it is decorous for him to help the Addings travel to Scheveningen.

The Marches watch the Kaiser's arrival for the military maneuvers, and then leave Würzburg for Weimar, where after visiting Goethe's house, they are upset to see Burnamy with Miss Etkins, a flirt who was on their ship. March is sure that Burnamy is merely passing the time with her. Burnamy feels ashamed of his flirtation, and is happy to see March, who gives him all the news. Mrs. March says that the Triscoes are coming, and as the Marches board the train for Berlin, they meet the Triscoes, who go off into the town with Burnamy.

The Marches find Berlin cold, uncomfortable, and pompous, and

Potsdam depressing in its display of relentless pride. In Weimar, meanwhile, Triscoe is ill, and Burnamy and Miss Triscoe are thrown together, which irritates the general. Burnamy finally proposes, disjointedly, to Agatha (Miss Triscoe), and is accepted. Greatly upset, Triscoe questions Burnamy unpleasantly about his expectations. Agatha, who is eavesdropping, interrupts, dresses down her father, and reduces him to silence. Triscoe consents to the engagement, but not to the marriage, until Burnamy earns more. Discovering flowers that Burnamy meant to give to Miss Etkins but didn't, and left in a closet in the hotel, Agatha breaks the engagement in a fit of jealousy.

The Marches travel from Berlin to Frankfurt, Mainz, and the Rhine. From Mainz the Marches retrace their travels of thirty years earlier, when they were first engaged. It is September, the weather is cold, and March is homesick for New York. They travel down the Rhine to Cologne and Düsseldorf, where they examine every place associated with Heine. At Düsseldorf the Marches receive letters announcing the engagements of Burnamy and Agatha, and Kenby and Mrs. Adding, and a letter from Fulkerson urging March to stay a year. But Mrs. March, weary and ailing, asks to go straight home, and they go to London to take the first ship. At Dover they meet and congratulate Kenby and his new wife. On the ship, March meets Major Eltwin, who is happy to be returning to his Ohio home, and the Triscoes. Agatha tells Mrs. March why she broke with Burnamy. Mrs. March encourages her to return to him, and finds that this interest revives her. Eltwin tells March that he has acquired a newspaper he doesn't want, needs an editor, and wonders if Burnamy could handle the job.

The arrival in New York involves the usual confusion. The day after, Burnamy arrives at the Marches' flat penniless; he has come over in steerage. March keeps him there while Mrs. March wills Agatha to appear. She does, and the lovers are reunited, to the great satisfaction of Mrs. March.

Roswell Adding, Mrs. Adding, August, L. J. Burnamy, Major Eltwin, Miss Etkins, Fulkerson, guides, R. M. Kenby, Leffers, Mrs. Leffers, Lili, Basil March, Isabel March, Tom March, Otterson, Mrs. Otterson, policemen, porters, Stoller, the Misses Stoller, Agatha Triscoe, General E. B. Triscoe.

Their Wedding Journey, 1872.

I. The Outset. The narrator ("I") modestly proposes not a sustained narrative but a succession of casual character sketches and descriptions; then he introduces Basil and Isabel March, thirty and twenty-seven, respectively. He is from the Midwest and works in a Boston insurance agency while he nurses his dream of becoming a literary man. She is a native Bostonian of highly respectable but not wealthy or Brahmin background. Eight years earlier, they met in Europe, traveled together, fell in love, became engaged, but were separated (for reasons unspecified); in America they met again, and in the spring of 1870 they were married. In June of that year they leave the Boston home of Isabel's aunt, where they have begun married life, to make their delayed wedding journey. In a cloudburst they reach the waiting room of the Worcester Depot (in Boston), where they assume the attitude of more or less critical observers, which they keep up througout the book. Isabel tries hard not to look like a newlywed, but of course fails, to Basil's amusement. After a nervous, wakeful trip by Pullman to New York, they observe the city and its people on a hot morning.

II. A Midsummer-Day's Dream. The Marches spend a few days with friends, the Leonards, in the New Jersey suburbs. Before taking the night boat to Albany, they spend a wretchedly hot day in New York paying visits and observing their fellow sufferers on the streets, in horsecars, and at a soda fountain.

III. The Night Boat. A storm relieves the heat as the gaudy side wheeler moves up the Hudson in the twilight. The Marches and the narrator enjoy the scenery and the widely varied American types on board, ranging from prostitutes to a group of ineffably conceited young people. Late at night the boat runs down a small craft, and while a dying man is brought aboard, the passengers run around in dishabille and make fatuous remarks.

IV. A Day's Railroading. After a wretched breakfast at the Albany depot, the Marches travel through the Mohawk Valley in a coach full of amusingly ordinary people, whom they and the narrator observe at length. The narrator finds the scenery so charming that he figuratively leaves the train and gambols through the countryside.

V. The Enchanted City, and Beyond. After a good lunch at Utica and a restful afternoon in a parlor car, the Marches survive the disdain of a Rochester hotel clerk, eat a hearty dinner, and roam the "enchanted" moonlit city. At the Genesee Falls they visit a noisy

German beer hall and Basil recites a poem about Sam Patch (who jumped to his death over the falls). Next day a tedious train ride brings the Marches to Buffalo and Niagara Falls.

VI. Niagara. The narrator finds the Falls bigger than any description but does not hesitate to describe them and their subsidiary features at length. Put off at first by the touristy atmosphere, the Marches find the Falls impressive, and visit all the usual sights, including the Three Sisters Islands and the Whirlpool. At the Three Sisters Isabel exasperates Basil by refusing to return to the mainland across a rickety bridge until she sees some tourists coming and her social shame conquers her fear.

VII. Down the St. Lawrence. On the boat across Lake Ontario the Marches meet formally the tourist group they saw at the Three Sisters: Colonel Richard Ellison and his wife Fanny, of Milwaukee, and their pretty young cousin Kitty Ellison, of western New York State. Mrs. March finds them charming, even if they don't come from Boston. The boat steams among the Thousand Islands, down the St. Lawrence, and through the rapids to Montreal.

VIII. The Sentiment of Montreal. The Marches are grateful for the foreign air of Montreal — markets, cathedrals, churches, a convent. Over a trifle they quarrel — their first quarrel! — but are quickly reconciled and afterwards find a tour of Mont Royal doubly enjoyable. Isabel shops passionately and plots to smuggle her purchases through the American customs. Basil meditates on the early history of Canada. Then the night boat takes them to Quebec.

IX. Quebec. The Marches and the narrator greatly admire Quebec — the old town, the citadel, the promenade on the terrace, the history, the falls of Montmorenci — and grow nervous at the sight of a troupe of British blondes staying at the hotel. When the Ellisons' room turns out to be next to that of the noisy blondes, Basil stays in it with Colonel Ellison (after a stray blonde has been cleared out) and the ladies take the Marches' room. March enjoys the adventure, which cements the intimacy of the two families.

X. Homeward and Home. Laden with Isabel's booty and accompanied by the gay troupe of blondes, the Marches take the train for Boston; the Ellison party continues by boat up the Saguenay (and into *A Chance Acquaintance*). A boring two-day ride brings the Marches back into the heat of Boston. The first friend March meets tells him he looks peaked and should take a vacation out of town.

(Twelve years later the Marches repeat part of the trip in "Niagara Revisited.")

Boatman, clerk, Private Drakes and family, Mrs. Fanny Ellison, Kitty Ellison, Colonel Richard Ellison, March's friend, Germans, girls and men, "I" (the commenting and acting narrator), Mr. and Mrs. Leonard, Basil March, Isabel March, Isabel March's aunt, New Yorkers, nun, passengers on steamboat who discuss accident, passengers on steamboat who flirt, passengers on trains, priests, tourists.

"Though One Rose from the Dead," 1903 (in *Questionable Shapes*, 1903).

In writing, Wanhope gives Acton, the narrator, the story of the Alderling affair. Alderling, a painter, and his wife Marion were a devoted couple living quietly on a cove on the New England coast. When Wanhope was down to see them, Marion said that she believed that she or Alderling could return from the dead if he or she willed it. They communicated frequently in thought; he had seen or felt her apparition when she was absent. Wanhope and the Alderlings discussed life after death and the relation of Christianity to it. Wanhope thinks now that the Alderlings' childlessness threw them too much together. Marion seemed to leave Alderling no mental privacy. Wanhope stayed with them for some time, and noted Marion's need for society. Each escaped somewhat from the mental pressure, Alderling by smoking, Marion by eating. Marion rowed and swam frequently in the cove; Alderling was never anxious about this, being telepathically in communication with her, but one foggy day he had to row out and fetch her back to shore.

From Minver at the club Wanhope later heard that Marion had died of typhoid in the Alderlings' house with only Alderling there. Then Alderling wrote Wanhope asking him to come down, and Rulledge insisted that he go. Wanhope found Alderling alone, shabby, and nervous. Next day Wanhope, in the presence of a roomful of paintings of Marion, was driven to ask about her, and Alderling leaped at the chance to talk about Marion's hope for a life after death for Alderling, not herself; he said that at the funeral he seemed to hear her saying, "I will come for you!" Alderling didn't think that he would ever be reunited with Marion, because he had killed the power of belief in himself.

Wanhope considers the subsequent events anticlimactic, but continues. A few days after the long talk, Wanhope was watching the fog when he heard Alderling shout, from his upstairs studio, "I am coming!", and there seemed to be an answering cry from the water. Then Alderling rushed out of the house and down to the shore, and rowed off into the fog. Later the boat was found, empty.

Acton, Marion Alderling, Alderling, minister, Minver, Dr. Norey, Rulledge, Wanhope.

Through the Eye of the Needle, 1907.

Introduction. The author begins by summarizing the American visit of Aristides Homos, an Emissary of the Altrurian Commonwealth, during 1893 and 1894, and his letters to his friend Cyril in Altruria. Because the Altrurians live for each other, Homos could not understand America, where people live upon each other. But since Homos wrote these letters, the author says that, as a result of the prosperity following the Spanish-American War, American society has improved. Homos would be pleased, the author ironically concludes, by the conditions of 1907: by the "affection" uniting capital and labor, by the philanthropy of millionaires, by the higher cultural level of businessmen, by improvements in tenements and transportation, and by the increased kindliness of employers to their servants. The first part of this book, the author says, is by Homos; the second part, by Mrs. Eveleth Strange, an American widow who married Homos and went back to Altruria with him. The importance of his story is sociological; of hers, psychological.

Part First. Homos tells Cyril that the Altrurians are the only people in the world who live logically. As a contrast, he cites the illogic of charity in America, where millionaires are applauded for giving away unearned money. He describes New York housing: the brownstones, the tenements, the elegant or shabby apartments. Mrs. Makely, a socialite, invites Homos to inspect her apartment. Like most apartment dwellers the Makelys are childless. Their apartment has eight rooms. She shows Homos the kitchen and introduces Lena, her cook, who has heard of Altruria and wants to go live there. Neither the kitchen nor the servants' bedroom has any natural light; the Makelys' rooms are of course large and sunlit. Mrs. Makely doesn't understand Homos' criticism of this arrangement and says that she will not employ American-born servants because they expect to be treated as members of the family. To show Homos how people live in separate houses, she promises to introduce him to Mrs. Strange, who is a kind of American Altrurian. Homos again condemns the illogicality of American life. Later Mrs. Makely describes a typical brownstone house for him. They are expensive to live in, but nice people must live expensively. Then Homos and Mrs. Makely renew their argument about servants.

After visiting some New York men's clubs, Homos discusses them with the Makelys. As Thanksgiving approaches, Homos wonders what the unemployed in the city have to be grateful for, and comments on American football. At Mrs. Makely's elaborate Thanksgiving dinner, Homos meets and at once likes Mrs. Eveleth Strange. When he says that in Altruria everybody works, she wishes that it were the same in America. Homos enjoys the men's after-dinner conversation because there are no coarse stories, but he doesn't like their smoking and drinking. After the men rejoin the ladies, Mrs. Strange quotes Longfellow's poem "The Challenge" to remind them of the people who have had no Thanksgiving dinner.

When Mrs. Strange invites Homos to dinner, Mrs. Makely tells him that Mrs. Strange married Bellington Strange, an elderly millionaire, because her father's business had failed and her family was dependent on her. A year after the marriage he died, and Mrs. Strange now lives with her mother, Mrs. Gray. At the dinner, Homos meets Mrs. Gray and Bullion and Twelvemough, the banker and the novelist he met before. The other guests include a painter and several ladies, who discuss poverty. The ladies don't want to read about poverty in novels. Homos tells them there is no poverty in Altruria. He feels guilty at eating another huge meal when so many people are hungry. Later, at Mrs. Strange's request, Homos stays and tells her and Mrs. Gray about Altruria. When Mrs. Strange says that charity is a failure and her money an incubus, Homos tries to explain how everybody has enough in Altruria. She says that her palatial house was an act of atonement to her by her husband for his wealth.

As time passes, Homos keeps meeting Mrs. Strange in society and calling on her. Finally he realizes that he has fallen in love with her.

When he calls again, Mrs. Gray confesses to Homos that she cannot believe Altruria exists, but Mrs. Strange assures him that she believes in him with all her soul. They become engaged, which makes them notorious, and they are attacked in some society papers. Homos wants Mrs. Gray to live with them when they are married, but she says that she does not want to move to Altruria permanently, and later he realizes that his fiancée does not expect to live there either. Since she does consider it her wifely duty to live in his country, they finally compromise on a year's visit to Altruria, followed by a return to New York. Then they will decide where to make their permanent home. In the meantime, Mrs. Strange wants to hang on to her money and property, but Homos, deeply upset, tells her that she must choose between her love and her money. After a sleepless night, Mrs. Strange sends him a note breaking their engagement, and Homos sails away without her.

Part Second. Mrs. Homos writes to Mrs. Makely from Altruria. She recalls that, after Homos had left New York, she visited the Makelys and implied that, although she had broken her engagement, she expected Homos to make her marry him anyway. Finally she decided to follow him to Liverpool, and disposed of her property. The lovers were reunited in Plymouth and married by a missionary. They took a trading ship to Altruria, and received a warm welcome. Mrs. Homos quickly adopted the classic Altrurian feminine costume; her American clothes were put in a museum as bad examples. After the sailors from their ship explored Altruria, they refused to return to America. During a hearing before the Altrurian Assembly the sailors' spokesman tells of his hard life, and then the crew do too. The captain says he had to mistreat the crew for the good of his family; only his children could draw him back to America. After the magistrates decide for the sailors and ask them to consider the captain's wishes, they all return to America to bring his children back. Mrs. Homos sends along an Altrurian costume for Mrs. Makely so that she can see what it means to be a free woman.

At first Mrs. Homos is indignant when the girls who serve her sit down with her at table, but her mother gets a nostalgic pleasure out of helping with the dishes. The Altrurians are vegetarians, and Mrs. Homos longs for meat until she and Homos have to kill a chicken themselves; then she is happy to go back to mushrooms, the Altrurians' meat substitute. The Altrurians use electric expresses for transportation, but travel little. Mr. and Mrs. Homos tour the country in an electric van to tell Altrurians about America. The people find American patriotism revolting because they do not understand how a poor man can be expected to die for his country if it will not provide for his family after his death. The Altrurians put on their idea of an American play. Mrs. Homos is amused by its misconceptions about money and poverty in America. She admires the national pastime of dancing and the artificially altered climate, which is like that of Italy.

One night while the Homoses are camping, Homos talks to a murderer. In Altruria murderers, if sane, are left free to expiate their crimes by doing good. Their only punishment is their own remorse. Later, at a conference in the Regionic capital, the Altrurians can hardly believe that American convicts' families are deprived of the convicts' wages and left to suffer. At another time Mrs. Homos observes an Altrurian wedding. Before young lovers are allowed to marry, they are instructed about marriage, and separated for a time to test their love. Divorce is possible, but is considered a social offense. After the wedding, the bride and groom join the others in the fields, although they may take a honeymoon later. At the end of each day's work, the Altrurians hold a service in their temples to consecrate their work. Mrs. Homos begins to learn and admire Altrurian, a simple language. The architecture in the Altrurian capitals is of classic beauty. Transportation is quiet and free. In the villages people do all their work cooperatively. Large kitchens are used in common. Every worker has a card recording work and entitling him or her to shop in the government stores. Fashions do not change, and Altrurians stay slim because they work and do not overeat, so shopping for clothes isn't a problem. Mrs. Homos also describes Altrurian art galleries, libraries, architecture, and highways, all built voluntarily by the people.

One day the Homoses meet an American couple whose yacht has been stranded on an Altrurian beach. Thrall, a New York millionaire, tells Mrs. Homos that he used to be a friend of Mr. Strange. Mrs. Thrall is very haughty. The Thralls' daughter, Lady Moors, and her husband, Lord Moors, are also with them. When Mrs. Thrall ignores Homos and calls the Altrurians "natives," Mrs. Homos is so put out that she makes her husband leave, and they return home to the Maritime Capital. Cyril Chrysostom, Homos's friend and a Regionic chief, summons the Homoses to help him decide what to do about the Thralls. Their yacht is useless. Its crew soon fit into Altruria, but the Thralls, the Moorses, and their servants insist on trying to buy provisions with money. The young Moors couple turn out to be on a honeymoon trip around the world. Chrysostom, when he was the Altrurian emissary to England, knew Lord Moors's father. So he explains to Mr. Thrall that the Altrurians are offended by his servants performing their work for money; in Altruria they must work for their living. Mrs. Thrall is furious at this. She cannot understand that the only currency in Altruria is work or love. If the American ship doesn't return from Boston, there may be no means of leaving Altruria for years. Thrall and his daughter are happy to help with the gardening, and Lord Moors, who did roadwork under Ruskin at Oxford, helps to build a culvert, but Mrs. Thrall is grumpy about having to cook. Anatole, the Thralls' French chef, is delighted to study mushrooms and finds new varieties for the Altrurians' use. Mrs. Homos feels increasingly Altrurian, although she still longs sometimes for meat and for sensational American news. Life in Altruria is eventless. There are no wars or crimes for the newspapers to report, but they do write about conditions in capitalistic countries. Altrurians cannot understand why American workers do not vote peaceful protection for themselves; unions, they feel, are too warlike.

The castaways, even Mrs. Thrall, are becoming Altrurianized. Anatole becomes engaged to Cecilia, an Altrurian widow. Thrall is so happy that he never wants to return to America, and Robert, Lord Moors's manservant, waits on the family just out of love. The American ship is sighted one day, and Mrs. Homos sends her last letter in great excitement.

Anatole, Bullion, Captain of the *Little Sally*, Captain's wife, Cecilia, Cyril Chrysostom, Mrs. Chrysostom, crew of the *Little Sally*, crew of the *Saraband*, gentleman, Mrs. Gray, Aristides Homos, Mrs. Eveleth Strange Homos, Lena, Dick Makely, Dorothea Makely, Lady Moors, Lord Moors, Robert, servants of the Thralls, spokesman for the crew of the *Little Sally*, Mrs. Eveleth Strange, Peter Bellington Strange, Mrs. Rebecca Thrall, Thrall, Twelvemough.

"Tonelli's Marriage," 1868 (in *A Fearful Responsibility,* 1881).

Tomasso Tonelli, a bachelor of forty-seven, works for an elderly Venetian notary, Cenarotti, and leads a regular and happy life, working, writing a little poetry, dining quietly, and lounging in a café. The notary has a pretty granddaughter whom Tonelli nicknames the Paronsina; she is kept in deep seclusion in an old palace. With her mother and Tonelli she sometimes visits the Molo and has an ice at Florian's. Tonelli arranges a correspondence between the Paronsina and a young doctor, and writes most of the letters leading up to the betrothal, but the doctor loses interest and the marriage is off.

Tonelli falls in love with a lady, Carlotta, whom he sees in the Piazza San Marco; he follows her around in the accepted fashion, and eventually they are betrothed, even though he regrets giving up his bachelor friends and pleasures. After a painful scene with the Cenarottis, when they learn of his betrothal, they all take a last walk together on the Molo, and the Paronsina gives Tonelli a Venetian chain, but the friendship is irrevocably broken, and when the Cenarottis hear that Tonelli's child is a girl, they are maliciously pleased.

Carlotta, Cenarotti, Signora Cenarotti, doctor, the Paronsina, Tomasso Tonelli.

A Traveller from Altruria, 1894.

At a New Hampshire resort hotel, Mr. Twelvemough, the narrator, interrupts his work on a novel to meet Aristides Homos, an Altrurian, at the depot. Homos, a vigorous, intelligent man with excellent English, rushes to help the porter with the heavy trunks, and Twelvemough is upset, and even more upset when Homos says he also helped the baggage man in Boston. He is delighted by the beautiful mountain scenery. At dinner in the hotel Twelvemough tells him that the headwaiter is a divinity student and the waitresses are country schoolteachers, and is therefore upset once again when Homos helps their young waitress with a heavy tray. Trying to explain his error to Homos, Twelvemough is forced to admit that, pace The Declaration of Independence (which Homos has read), America has evolved into a class society in which domestic service is considered degrading. The Altrurian replies that his countrymen have long outlived all that and is surprised to hear that successful

Americans feel no obligation to the weak. In Altruria, says Homos, all men are equal in duties and in rights. The American replies that all Americans are equal in opportunities. Then he tells him that he would like to introduce him to some of his friends, especially the ladies, the only leisure class in America.

During an after-dinner stroll, Homos is dismayed by the ugliness of a knoll stripped of trees. Twelvemough argues that since the woods were the man's property he could do what he wished with them. He sold them for building lots. Homos replies that in his country the community deprives a man of his property if he misuses it. When Twelvemough answers that Americans do not try to legislate personal virtue, Homos points out that there are many American laws, including the marriage laws, that do just that. Returning to the hotel, the Altrurian admires the well-dressed ladies and gentlemen. His host explains that summer resorts like this one are where such people relax. The Altrurian wonders what the ladies rest from, if they never work. Twelvemough admits that women have much more leisure than men. Novelists like him are read mostly by women; the men are too busy working. Homos is shocked that so many business and professional men are overworked in America, and puzzled that women have no influence on public affairs. Twelvemough insists that they don't want any. Asked where the manual laborers relax, Twelvemough wonders if his guest is a labor agitator in disguise, but replies that manual workers couldn't afford this resort. He knows very little about them but can introduce Homos to some people who can answer his question.

The novelist presents Homos to a group on the hotel piazza: Bullion, a banker; Professor Lumen, a teacher of political economy; and a minister, a lawyer, a doctor, and a retired manufacturer. Questioned about his country, Homos tells them that Altruria is an island with a Christian civilization introduced by a member of the first Christian commune after Christ. The banker, who says that he knows something about Altruria, describes it as preposterous, but adds that he respects the country. Then, offering to answer the visitor's questions, he tells him that workingmen have no leisure, except when striking or unemployed. All except the lawyer join in condemning strikes. The banker rates the social status of the American worker as nil. He criticizes the novelist for telling their visitor that Americans honor labor.

After summing up what he has learned so far, the Altrurian asks why workers are discontented. Twelvemough answers that the real cause is the "walking-delegate" (union representative) who blinds workers to their real interests and real friends. Disagreeing, the manufacturer tells them that the union leader in his own factory would not be satisfied until the manufacturer and the employees earned the same amount of money for the same amount of work. The manufacturer's answer was to smash the union. The lawyer feels that though the union has a certain justice on its side, it is directly opposed to the first principle of business. After the professor, the banker, and the manufacturer have defined this principle as various forms of selfishness, the Altrurian says that in his country trade unions were abolished after the nation had divided into a federation of labor unions and a federation of business syndicates; with everybody sharing in the manual labor, each person need work only a few hours every day and thus has time and energy for a cultivated leisure. The Altrurian can't imagine a country where making money is the most important goal. The group discusses whether an artist is concerned about money or about the quality of his work. The novelist argues that an artist who did not love his work couldn't do good work no matter how well he was paid. But the Altrurian feels that artists shouldn't have to work for their living. In Altruria everybody works for the living of others, and everybody's living is assured. No one has the power of economic life and death over another.

Mrs. Peggy Makely, a socialite friend of Twelvemough's, tries to ingratiate herself with Homos, who asks her why the young farmers and country girls sitting on the piazza aren't invited in to the hotel dance. Mrs. Makely explains that the young ladies inside would not dance with the farmers, even though they haven't enough dancing partners of their own social class. She discusses one of the country girls, Lizzie Camp, a dead soldier's daughter, who sews for her in the summer, and is very fond of books but still isn't a lady. When Homos asks her to define a "lady," Mrs. Makely says that a lady must have enough money for a well-staffed house and a fashionable wardrobe, must have cultivated artistic tastes, and must go in for something, such as charity or religion. When the Altrurian asks whether a lady isn't supposed to be completely idle, Mrs. Makely protests that ladies are endlessly busy. When the Altrurian protests that social activities are not useful work, Mrs. Makely argues that if ladies did their own housework, they would deprive their servants of their livelihood. Most ladies never take any exercise; as a result, Mrs. Makely boasts, most of them are never completely well. Makely now describes the almost empty dance floor inside. All the eligible young men are working in the cities or out West so they can afford to get married. But working-class people get married on nothing because they have no expectations. Mrs. Makely is surprised that toil-ridden working-class women keep healthy. The Altrurian answers that the solution to the problem is to do what they do in Altruria: everybody lives alike and shares everything equally, just like the members of a family. But Mrs. Makely holds that the members of a family always quarrel; it is human nature to do so.

Saying goodnight to Homos, Twelvemough feels bothered by his questions and nervous about the impression he must have made. Twelvemough tells himself that the American social system being divinely ordained, the Altrurian's questions are almost impious. The next morning the novelist is appalled to find that Homos has been helping the porter shine shoes, and lectures him on the meaning of being a gentleman. Homos is astonished to learn that although a gentleman is unwilling to shine his own shoes, his self-respect is not offended by letting somebody else do it for him.

Mrs. Makely takes Twelvemough and Homos to visit Lizzie Camp and her invalid mother. On their way they meet Reuben Camp, Lizzie's brother, at a farm deserted by its owners, who were defeated by depleted soil, high taxes, and competition with Western prices. The Altrurian hopes that they will be able to take up new land out of the public domain. The people have gone West, but their chances are poor because there isn't any good land left in the public domain, and mortgages on purchased farms are so high that farmers usually can't pay them off.

Driving on, the visitors nearly run over some ragged children, to whom Twelvemough condescendingly gives money for candy. Their mother says she is the English wife of a quarry worker too poor to finish their house. Mrs. Makely is indignant about the woman's supposed attempt to get a contribution for her cottage, and the novelist agrees that charity demoralizes the poor, but their visitor is sadly baffled by their attitude. There are no poor people in his country. Mrs. Makely triumphantly squelches him by citing scripture. She insists that Christ's statement "The poor ye have always with you" means that there ought to be poverty, for how else could the rich show any charity or love?

When the visitors praise the Camps' old-fashioned farmhouse, Reuben sarcastically offers to sell it to them. Mrs. Camp, an intelligent, bedridden woman, has read about Altruria and is deeply impressed by the Altrurian. The novelist remarks jokingly that he feels as if Homos were a bad conscience. Mrs. Makely repeats that Altrurianism is against human nature, but invites Homos to tell them about it. He answers that the first Christians practiced the same kind of altruism that the Altrurians have organized into a working economy, but Mrs. Makely insists it didn't work for the early Christians and wouldn't for individualistic Americans either. Reuben points out bitterly that only rich Americans can have individuality. But Mrs. Makely says fatuously that rich people can't have any individuality because it's considered vulgar and boring. The novelist tries to change the subject by praising Mrs. Camp's house and regretting that he hasn't been inside a farmhouse before. Homos is astonished by this lack of any real contact between the summer people and the natives. Reuben says that the summer visitors look down on the natives. Mrs. Makely protests that she doesn't look down on Lizzie, but the girl contradicts her. Mrs. Makely is hurt; but, although she apologizes for her children, Mrs. Camp insists that they cannot be untruthful in the Altrurian's presence. The novelist feels that Homos is a spiritual solvent precipitating sincerity out of people accustomed to polite hypocrisy. So when Mrs. Makely says that at least they all have the same country, Reuben disagrees: the rich have one country, the poor another. He cites a blacklisted man as an example, but Mrs. Makely doesn't even know the meaning of the term. When it is explained, the Altrurian is horrified. He feels that no crime is so terrible that the convicted criminal should lose his chance to earn a living. At this moment a tramp appears outside the farmhouse, and when Reuben goes out to give him some food, it is Mrs. Makely who is horrified. In her son's absence Mrs. Camp describes his experiences as a mill hand and her own hard work on the farm, which eventually paralyzed her. She had to put a mortgage on the farm, which will probably be foreclosed when she dies. She and her husband slaved to earn their farm, but now the bank owns it. Homos says that in Altruria everybody works hard for three hours a day and in this way they all keep well and strong. They help each other, because neighborliness is the essence of Altrurianism. Mrs. Makely interrupts to say that living in a big apartment building she doesn't know her neighbor. Homos tries to explain how it is in Altruria, but she interrupts again, this time to defend the practice of blacklisting, because the employers have their capital at stake. Reuben Camp argues that the men's work is just as important as capital and therefore employers and workers must be paid alike. Mrs. Makely pronounces this argument preposterous and gets up to go. On the way home she chatters patronizingly about the Camps' warped opinions, which she hopes the Altrurian won't misunderstand.

Homos spends that afternoon and all next day with Reuben Camp, comparing American and Altrurian farming methods. In the evening the minister, the lawyer, the manufacturer, Professor Lumen, Bullion, Twelvemough, and Homos get together for another discussion. Prof. Lumen asks Homos if he knows that some poor farmers sell their votes. Bullion, the banker, compares them to prostitutes, but in both cases, he says, the buyers are worse than the poverty-stricken sellers. Horrified, the Altrurian says that both things are unimaginable in his country. Next the professor asks him if he knows anything about rural paupers. The Altrurian replies that Reuben Camp feels the state should find them work. The minister feels that shutting paupers up with lunatics is humiliating, but the professor insists that any other treatment would be un-American. The lawyer asks whether a college education disables a man for business. The banker answers that a gentleman's education is incompatible with business principles because a businessman must seize his advantage without worrying about deceiving others. Reminded by this answer of a novel by another novelist, Twelvemough, without mentioning the title, summarizes the crisis in *The Rise of Silas Lapham*. Lapham could have saved himself from business failure if his conscience hadn't forced him to tell the truth to the other people involved. Real businessmen criticized this action because it wasn't business. The banker concludes that a university education equips a young man to use his own gifts, but if he goes into business he is forced to realize that to get rich he must exploit other men's gifts. He asks the Altrurian how rich his country is and how they define the ideal great man. Homos replies that everyone has enough and that the Altrurian great man is an artist, or poet, or inventor, or physician who has given the most happiness to the most people. The banker answers that the American ideal has changed several times. After the Revolution it was the great statesman, although writers like Longfellow were also honored later. During and after the Civil War the national hero was the great soldier, but in this era of prosperity, the American ideal is the millionaire.

When the group convenes again, its members return to the relationship between a college education and a business career. The banker, a Harvard man, jokingly implies that the reason he has only a million or two is that his education made him too moral. The banker also thinks that businessmen are asked to take part in public affairs because people feel that businessmen know how to make money and how to play it safe. Twelvemough feels that the banker's candor is produced by the Altrurian's mysterious control. The only people who have any real use for a gentleman's education, decides the banker, are women. Similarly, working-class children can't use their education to make a living. But the lawyer insists that in the long run it is education that will bridge the gap between the social classes, not religion, as people used to believe. The minister has to admit that there are no working-class people in his large congregation. If it ever came to an open conflict between the capitalists and the workers, the banker is sure that the capitalists would win. He cites the Haymarket riot as an example. The workers made their mistake by fighting instead of voting for what they want. Since they are in the majority, they could vote into law any change that they desired. The novelist blames the socialists for fomenting violence, but the banker disagrees because, he says, the socialist philosophy is not anarchy but the legislation of change. In the end, he feels, William Morris's prediction will come true: either the state or large corporations will own labor; but then he laughs, and Twelvemough decides that he has been joking. Homos says that in Altruria labor owns capital.

Mrs. Makely now plans to ask Homos to give a public lecture about Altruria, the proceeds to go toward redecorating the shabby village chapel. Mrs. Makely is sure that all the hotel servants and local farmers, who know and like Homos, will come to the lecture. At first he says that he thinks it is wrong to make money, but when the project is fully explained, he consents; however, he stipulates that nobody should be excluded from his lecture because of occupation or social status. Mrs. Makely agrees, secretly convinced that poor people won't be willing to pay a dollar to hear him. She has a hard time selling the tickets to the hotel guests, but the headwaiter and Reuben Camp sell many. The crowd is so great that on Homos's insistence the meeting is held out of doors.

Homos begins by outlining the conditions before the time of Altruria's Evolution. He describes how an apostle of Christ, cast away on the shore of Altruria, established a Christian commonwealth, which gave way to a long period of chaos and warfare. A kingdom arose and flourished until it was overthrown by a popular revolution which established a republic. An industrial revolution followed; enormous fortunes were made. Eventually the rich dominated; the Altrurians called their power "the Accumulation" because they were afraid to call it by its real name. The abuses of the Accumulation against labor became so great that the government legislated some improvements in working conditions, but the Accumulation became even stronger, forming huge monopolies. A series of financial panics ensued until it became necessary to legislate more controls. An old farmer interrupts to protest that he paid his dollar to hear about Altruria, not about America; after Reuben Camp quiets him, Homos says that he doesn't know enough about America to offer an allegory about American conditions.

Continuing, he says the unions in Altruria joined together in one large union only when the Accumulation had reduced all the monopolies to one enormous monopoly and political officials to mere figureheads. But finally the people rebelled, and the Accumulation's power was gradually voted out. Thus the Altrurian Evolution was achieved without any bloodshed, and a commonwealth was established. The manufacture of shoddy, obsolescent goods was stopped. Now only high-quality goods were made, and the amount of labor necessary was thus reduced, releasing people for farm work. With so many more farm laborers no one had to work himself to death on a farm. Honest and useful products became beautiful products as well because there was plenty of time to make them beautifully. At this point the professor whispers to the novelist that Homos is not an Altrurian at all, but simply a reader of William Morris.

Since there was no hurry anymore, Homos says, nine-tenths of the railroads fell into disuse, and many of the ugly railroad towns were burned down. The big cities were allowed to fall into ruin.

Only one part of one city is still preserved as a terrible example of how not to live. There are no Altrurian cities as such, but there are regional capitals and a capital of the commonwealth. These places, artistic centers with universities, theaters, museums, cathedrals, laboratories, and conservatories, are connected to the farming villages by electrical expresses operating at 150 mph. Nobody is classified by occupation; everybody does both obligatory work and voluntary work, and the same man may be both a shoemaker and a poet, but farming, which is shared by everybody, is honored above other occupations because tilling the soil strengthens a man's love of his home, which in Altruria is considered very important. There is no money; everybody works and everybody receives an equal share of food, clothing, and shelter. There is no international commerce either, because Altruria produces everything its people need. Fashions and domestic architecture are both of classic simplicity; anything else would be considered vulgar. The professor asks a question designed to trap Homos into admitting that Altruria exists only as a fraudulent rehash of Bacon's New Atlantis and More's Utopia. But Homos blandly agrees that these two writers anticipated certain aspects of Altrurian civilization. What is more, he continues, America could anticipate another Altruria. The Altrurians learned from their experience of competition and monopoly that labor-saving machines can be a good thing, but they have made their factories into beautiful places, and men who prefer to work with their hands instead of machines are freely permitted to do so. Both work and recreation are communal. Although family privacy is preserved, people eat together in large groups and meals become the occasion of long, pleasant discussions. Every man is a gentleman, and every woman a lady. There are no gentlemen in America, he implies, because under competitive conditions, a man is compelled to think of himself first, and a gentleman is by definition a person who thinks first of others. Women, however, can be ladies because their instincts are usually unselfish. Mrs. Makely shrieks her approval of this.

Homos continues his lecture by saying that in Altruria there are no wars and no religious denominations; everybody seeks to be a Christian, and everybody considers himself a member of one large family. There are sickness and death, of course, but Altrurians firmly believe in a reunion after death. Parents who have lost their children ask him sad and wondering questions about this belief. The Altrurian says that Altruria is the kingdom of heaven on earth mainly because it has no money. He insists that money truly is the root of all evil, and with no money in Altruria there is no crime or vice either. There is very little insanity. The professor interrupts again, but some railroad hands in the audience make him subside. The highest distinction in Altruria, Homos continues, belongs to the person who discovers a new way to serve the community, but such a benefactor shuns public recognition.

Finally Homos summarizes the achievements of Altruria and sits down. The working people in the audience clamor for him to continue. Reuben Camp says that Homos is too tired to go on, but he will be Mrs. Camp's guest for a week, and everybody is invited to visit. The working people line up to shake the speaker's hand, but the hotel guests go off to discuss him by themselves. The professor continues to criticize him, but Mrs. Makely insists on gushing to Homos that his speech was beautiful. The other guests make characteristic comments. The minister confesses dejectedly that he cannot believe that the kingdom of God will ever come on the earth. Twelvemough is polite, but secretly relieved that Reuben Camp has taken charge of his embarrassing guest. Eventually Homos is seen off for New York City by a host of lower-class admirers ardently convinced of the reality of Altruria, but the novelist and his friends are not so sure.

> Mrs. Bulkham, Bullion, Lizzie Camp, Mrs. Camp, Reuben Camp, children, doctor, a young Englishwoman, an old farmer, headwaiter, Aristides Homos, lawyer, Professor Lumen, Dorothea (Peggy) Makely, Richard Makely, retired manufacturer, minister, porter, Twelvemough, waitresses, railroad workers.

"Turkeys Turning the Tables," in *Christmas Every Day and Other Stories Told for Children*, 1893.

On Christmas Day a papa tells his small daughter about a family's Thanksgiving dinner. After helping to eat a huge turkey, one of the little girls of the family lies awake and sees hosts of angry turkeys badgering the family and blaming them for the fate of turkeys; then the turkeys seize her and plan to dine off her. Finally they let her go after she promises not to eat turkey anymore. Instead, she eats goose.

Little girl, little girl in the story, papa, turkeys.

The Undiscovered Country, 1880.

Indulging an interest in "spiritual manifestations," Ford and Phillips, two Bostonians, call on Dr. Boynton and his daughter Egeria, a nineteen-year-old medium, at the doctor's lodgings. Spirit raps are heard from "Giorgione" (the Venetian painter). In his habitual orotund manner Dr. Boynton discourses on the present stage of development of the phenomena. Ford is highly skeptical, Phillips less so. Guests and mediums arrive for a séance, along with Mrs. Le Roy, the doctor's landlady. In the darkness hands and flowers appear, and things float in the air. Finally the gas is lighted by a spirit hand, and something grabs at Egeria's ring and injures her finger so badly that she faints. The séance breaks up in confusion.

Phillips is a genial, wealthy man of leisure; Ford, a caustic man, is a poor journalist. Early one morning in the Public Garden, Ford is irritated first at a lecture by Eccles, a student of spiritualism, on the crudity of the previous séance, and then at the teasing of a fellow boarder, Mrs. Perham. Visiting the Boyntons to inquire about Egeria's condition, Ford is harangued by Dr. Boynton on the intermingling of genuineness and charlatanism in mediums and séances. Ford calls Dr. Boynton a quack; the doctor stands on his dignity. Ford claims that it was he who grabbed Egeria's ring. He vows to expose Dr. Boynton, who defies him theatrically.

Dr. Boynton angrily tells Egeria about Ford's attack. He thinks that through her efforts they could convert Ford, but she resists this idea, and wishes they could go away, back to their home in Maine. Egeria's passivity at the séance proves to the doctor that the phenomena were real. He rushes off to find Ford to arrange a proof of Egeria's psychic prowess. While the doctor is gone, Hatch, another medium, gets her views on the situation and goes to Ford to try to persuade him, for Egeria's sake, not to go along with Dr. Boynton's scheme. Hatch manages to reach Ford before Dr. Boynton does, and argues with him, in Phillips' presence. Ford won't give Hatch an an-

swer, because, as he tells Phillips, he thinks that Hatch was sent by
Dr. Boynton to get a refusal for the doctor's purposes. Before Phillips leaves for Mrs. Burton's salon, which Ford refuses to go to, Dr.
Boynton bursts in and harangues Ford, who refuses coldly to go to a
séance designed to test Egeria.

Returning home, Dr. Boynton announces Ford's refusal to a
much-relieved Egeria. Hatch derides the previous séance and advises Dr. Boynton to go home to Maine and stay there until he has
spiritualism really figured out. Hatch gets Mrs. Le Roy to admit that
she produced many of the phenomena of the séance. Dr. Boynton
realizes that he must approach spiritualism more impersonally. He
decides to leave with Egeria at once. He is so poor that Hatch must
help him pay his bill to Mrs. Le Roy and buy train tickets. As the
Boyntons leave, Egeria mails Ford a letter thanking him and admitting he was right to suspect the séance, though the Boyntons were
not responsible for what happened. Ford goes to Mrs. Le Roy but
finds the Boyntons gone; she doesn't have their address but offers
him a "see-aunts" anyway.

At the Fitchburg station in Boston, Dr. Boynton is fascinated by
two Shakers there. Hatch buys tickets for the Boyntons and travels
part way with them. Egeria is still wondering why Ford declined the
séance. At Ayer Junction Dr. Boynton talks so long to the Shakers
about their approach to psychic phenomena that he and Egeria miss
their train and get on the wrong one, which takes them back toward
Boston. Penniless, they are put off at the summer-resort village of
Egerton, cold and empty in April. People in Egerton are hostile, but
Dr. Boynton seems indifferent to their predicament. The forlorn pair
walk on in the night and gathering snowstorm into the country,
evade some tramps, and rest in a schoolhouse. In the morning
Egeria is awakened by the arrival of the teacher, who feeds them,
lends Egeria a coat, and sends them to Vardley Station. En route
they rest at Vardley Tavern, where the brutish landlord forces them
to stay because he is sure Egeria has escaped from a nearby reform
school. Even when enlightened by a police officer, the landlord is
surly and wants to keep them. Then, as Egeria sleeps fitfully, a ter-
rifying psychic visitation occurs—things fly around, and there is a
tremendous flash of lightning in the room. Egeria wakes and says
she has dreamt that the house was full of evil. This event reassures

the doctor of Egeria's psychic powers. Dr. Boynton and Egeria walk on in the rain, and are finally rescued by a Shaker who takes them to his village nearby.

The Shakers put the desperately ill Egeria to bed in a house for strangers called the office. Dr. Boynton at once tries to persuade a Shaker elder to allow Egeria and himself to enter the colony so that he can study spiritualism in a place based on it. When the elder refuses, the doctor, undaunted, gets a Shaker sister, Rebecca, to brief him on Shakerism. Next day, Egeria is put in the sick house. The doctor attentively watches the Shaker services and dances and then tells them about himself. He says that Egeria's character and certain vaguely specified events at the time of his wife's death, when Egeria was a baby, convinced him of the reality of spiritual phenomena, so that he dedicated Egeria and himself to the study of them. The hostility of the public and of his father-in-law destroyed the doctor's medical career and drove him and Egeria from Portland into a precarious wandering life. He asks to be taken in and allowed to continue his studies in the Shaker village.

As spring and summer pass, Egeria recovers amid the peace of the country. To the doctor's irritation, Egeria, once recovered, shows more interest in this world than in the spiritual one. She takes part in the Shaker activities, and from time to time thinks of Ford. Dr. Boynton is worried that the elders will turn against him, because he is planning to attack them, and he is upset to find that Egeria does not share his eagerness to do so. The doctor tells the Shakers that they should return to the world and provide the revelation beyond Christianity, but they see spiritualism as a means to the quiet end of Shakerism, and they and the doctor quarrel.

As the doctor and the Shakers prepare to put his psychic claims to the test (on Egeria), two strangers arrive for the night. At the evening meeting, the doctor tries and fails to make Egeria function as a medium. The Shakers say that the landlord at the tavern has spread the story that the doctor was drunk there and that the reported psychic occurrences never happened. Egeria can't prove they did, the Shakers are uncertain what to think, and the doctor, in a rage, storms off into the night. Egeria remains weeping in the office.

In Boston, earlier, Ford mopes through the summer until Phillips persuades him to join in a buggy trip to Brattleboro.

After a night of brooding and sleeping outdoors, Dr. Boynton is found in the morning by Ford and Phillips, the two recent arrivals. Convinced that it was Ford who made his mesmerism fail, the doctor attacks him, has an apoplectic fit, falls, and hits his head on a stone. Ford, feeling responsible, stays on; Phillips leaves. Word is received that Egeria's grandfather is dead, but the news is withheld from her. When the doctor sends for him, Ford broods about death; he fears the act of dying more than the state of death. Though weak, the doctor apologizes gracefully for attacking Ford and says he wants to be reconciled with his father-in-law. Ford tells Egeria and the doctor that her grandfather is dead. She apologizes to her father for not being able to help him, and involuntarily hints that Ford was the reason.

Ford patiently talks to the doctor, who thinks that they are alike under their opposing views. It is late August, and Ford goes with Egeria to gather the first autumn leaves. He apologizes for hurting her father, then cuts himself while cutting branches. This accident seems to make up for Ford's hurting Egeria earlier. She says that her powers and her father's obsession with them have isolated them from others and enslaved them. She and Ford agree that they wouldn't care to live the Shaker life. After a brief return to Boston, Ford brings grapes for the doctor and flowers for Egeria. He finds himself more and more drawn to her.

The doctor tells Ford that Egeria's power was real but that she lost it in her return to health. The doctor feels that he was a vampire in his relations with her. Ford clumsily tries to reassure him. Egeria and Ford wander about the woods and look down at the village from a hill. He teases her by saying he has her under a spell, and can't understand why the joke upsets her. Willy-nilly they are at cross-purposes. The Shakers conclude that Egeria and Ford love each other, and consider telling Ford the truth. Elihu, an elder, discusses the Shaker way with him, then tells him that Egeria loves him. Stricken and angry, Ford denies that he loves her. He explains that at the séance he had seized Egeria's hand thinking it was Mrs. Le Roy's. Finally Ford must admit his love. Elihu thinks that Ford should leave, and after hesitating, he decides to do so, and to return occasionally to check on the doctor.

But before Ford can speak, the doctor tells him that his faith in spiritualism has been destroyed by reading of a false case of possession strikingly parallel to Egeria's case. He now believes that she was merely overcharged with electricity and he has persecuted her for nothing. He is left with nothing but a precarious hope in Christianity. Ford agrees that there is no better hope. Boynton seems more cheerful now, though very weak. Phillips and Mrs. Perham drive by from a summer hotel to see what Ford is up to. She cattily tells Ford that Egeria never returned the coat lent her by the schoolteacher. At the hotel Miss Thorn, the teacher, tells Phillips and Mrs. Perham that it was her mother who spread around the coat story, which she herself regretted, because she regarded the coat as a gift and understood why the Boyntons forgot about it. Ford is angry at Mrs. Perham's malice and at Phillips' failure to check it. Egeria is away for the day; she expects Hatch the next day, Ford hears. Believing that she loves Hatch, Ford roams in misery through the woods. He decides to wait for her to choose between Hatch and himself. Next morning Ford learns that Dr. Boynton has died in his sleep. Hatch arrives and takes on the job of moving the doctor's body to Maine. Ford apologizes to Hatch for quarreling with him earlier.

Ford returns to Boston, takes new lodgings, and lives on in misery. Later he gets a note from Sister Frances: Egeria is back at the Shaker village. Going there at once, he gets Elihu's consent to speak to her. Next morning he learns that Hatch is engaged to a girl out West. Feeling free and confident now, he follows Egeria to the orchard. At first she wishes he hadn't come, and believes he has used some power against her. After they talk at cross-purposes, he bitterly says that he loves her, and begins to leave, but she tells him to stay, and they plight their troth. The Shakers don't know what to think of a betrothal taking place among them.

Soon Ford and Egeria marry. Eventually profits from one of his chemical discoveries allow them to live well. Egeria is now very stylish and in a literal way worldly, and Ford deliberately keeps her away from spiritualist affairs.

Egeria Boynton, Dr. Boynton, Mrs. Burton, Diantha, doctor, Eccles, Elihu, Elizabeth, Ford, Frances, Harris, Hatch, Brother Humphrey, Joseph, Brother Laban, Mrs. Le Roy, loafers, Mr. and Mrs. Merrifield, Mrs. Merrill, Mrs. Perham, Phillips, Rebecca, Shakers, Miss Thorn, townspeople, train conductor, tramps, Weatherby.

The Vacation of the Kelwyns: An Idyl of the Middle Eighteen-Seventies,
1920.

Elmer Kelwyn is a highly regarded lecturer in post-graduate
courses in Historical Sociology at a New England university. With
his wife Carry and his two sons, Francis and Carl, he lives modestly
but decently, thanks to his wife's private income. Both the Kelwyns
are genteel New Englanders, though Kelwyn is of farm stock. Although Kelwyn would be willing to spend the summer in town, the
family customarily board all summer at a farmhouse in the New
England hills. One spring day in 1876, before the Kelwyns have selected a summer place, Kelwyn is visited by a Shaker who knows
him by reputation and asks him to lecture on the Shakers. The man
says casually that his Shaker family, up in the Massachusetts hills
near the New Hampshire line, have farms for rent cheap. The Shakers agree to rent the Kelwyns a farm with a couple to do the
housework and cooking in return for housing and the use of the
farmland. Kelwyn finds the house, formerly a Shaker dormitory,
huge but clean and pleasant. The Kentons are glad to be able to help
some deserving farm couple. Kite, the farmer secured by the Shakers, visits the Kelwyns in the city. Kite is a raw-boned, surly man
whom Kelwyn dislikes and Mrs. Kelwyn nervously placates. Kite
takes Kelwyn's terms (which he can't read) home to his wife, whom
he vows to be an outstanding cook. The Kelwyns puzzle over the
fact that the Kites, like other working-class people, despise them.
They continue to worry about the scheme until Mrs. Kite writes politely accepting the terms.

In late spring the Kelwyns move into their farmhouse. Mrs. Kite,
who has one small son, Arthur, is agreeable, though countrified.
Supper, however, is a shattering experience. The food is skimpy
and unpleasant, and when the Kelwyns complain, Mrs. Kite oblig-
ingly makes them some awful eggs and biscuits. Rather than starve,
they desperately choke down this mess. Next day the Kelwyns eat a
poorly cooked breakfast. Mrs. Kelwyn refuses to do the work herself
or teach Mrs. Kite. For a few days the Kelwyns drift along, resigned
to the food and enjoying the comfort of the house. Eventually they
complain to the Shakers. While at the Shaker colony, they learn from
a letter that Mrs. Kelwyn's Cousin Thennie (Parthenope Brook) is
coming for a visit, and are confronted with a young man whom the
Shakers want them to take in as a roomer. Cousin Thennie suddenly

appears, and the Kelwyns rush off from the Shakers, forgetting the young man. Parthenope is the daughter of artists who died in Italy when she was a baby. She is pretty, energetic, and rather bossy, and has formed her romantic soul on the poetry and novels of the day.

The Kelwyns and Parthenope dine happily on storebought food until they realize that the boys are gone—riding on a stray horse, Mrs. Kite says. The horse and boys are brought back by Emerance, the young man from the Shakers. The Kelwyns have him in to dinner. To the Kelwyns' amazement, he says he has studied cooking and would like to start a cooking school. A bear and his French trainer come by the house and entertain the group. A storm comes up. Lightning stuns the bear and the trainer. The trainer revives, but not the bear, until Emerance and Parthenope give him coffee. As the rain continues, Emerance stays on, makes supper, and teaches Mrs. Kite some cooking in the process. Emerance chats with Kelwyn as if they were equals before returning to the Shakers for the night. The Kelwyns find Emerance puzzling; Parthenope finds him disturbing. Next day, on the road to the Shaker colony Emerance meets Kite, whose wagon has broken down, and stays to help him take the horses home. The bear is in the barn. The horses start to bolt and Emerance helps catch them, while Parthenope watches from her window. Emerance sleeps in the barn, to Parthenope's distress, and to the Kelwyns', when they hear about it next morning. A day later Emerance returns to Boston.

The days now pass calmly and identically for the Kelwyns and Parthenope. One day the Shaker sisters come to sample Parthenope's famous coffee and hear Mrs. Kelwyn lament about the Kites. The Shakers begin to arrange for another couple to take the Kites' place. Later the Shakers tell Kelwyn that Emerance has returned; meanwhile Parthenope and the Kelwyn boys watch an examination and program at the local school. Emerance is there, and criticizes the unnaturalness of sentimental literature by showing the schoolboy actors that they couldn't possibly say their lines naturally. Afterwards Emerance and Parthenope talk at length about education and themselves.

Next day the group from the farmhouse attend the Shaker meeting, where the speaker makes Parthenope feel self-conscious by attacking marriage. Back at the Kelwyns' place, the two young people are delighted when a gypsy van comes by. The gypsy woman tells Parthenope's future (marriage to a man who resembles Emerance). Parthenope has no money, and Emerance pays. They talk more about life and themselves. Later Mrs. Kelwyn asks Emerance to stay on until the Shakers can put him up.

As the idyllic summer days pass, the group is visited by an Italian organ-grinder, an Irish linen peddler, and numerous tramps. One of these is a huge, sullen black man who puts them all in a tizzy; but then Kelwyn waves his pistol around until Emerance persuades him to throw it away. Meanwhile Emerance takes over the kitchen. He and Parthenope are much together, in the simple, innocent manner of the period. They wander widely through the sleepy countryside. Mrs. Allson, the local drunkard's wife, tells Parthenope that her marriage is worthwhile, despite its miseries, because of the children. Emerance tells Parthenope that he should go to the Centennial celebration and try to be of use to the world; he thinks he might act, or write a play based on the Shakers. Mrs. Kelwyn and Parthenope reluctantly give up a discussion of Emerance to deal with the Kites, who don't want to be put out. Elder Nathaniel of the Shakers tells Parthenope that people should wait before marrying, though he doesn't disapprove of successful marriages.

Though everyone in the area seems to be sure that the Kites are about to be forced out, the couple puzzle the Kelwyns by acting very friendly. As time passes, Kelwyn realizes that the Shakers are leaving to him the responsibility of dealing with the Kites. Finally Kelwyn forces Elder Jasper to go with him to speak to Kite. Saying that the Kelwyns are impossible to please, Kite responds bitterly to Kelwyn's accusations. Kite says that he will go to law, but later in the day Elder Nathaniel assures Kelwyn that the Kites will leave peaceably. Now the Kelwyns begin to feel sorry for the Kites. Kelwyn discusses the affair with Emerance, as Parthenope eavesdrops. That night Emerance and Parthenope talk alone in the moonlight. She thinks that he is going to propose, but he doesn't, and she is left with a mixture of relief and disappointment. Next day the Kelwyns, after a sleepless night, decide to move themselves and let the Kites stay. Kelwyn takes a cottage that Parthenope and Emerance saw during a drive. After he tells the Shakers what he is going to do, they casually say that Emerance has gone with the local schoolteacher, a girl, to the Centennial celebration in Boston. Parthenope is upset to find herself upset at this news. Parthenope tells Mrs. Kelwyn that she is not seriously interested in Emerance. Mrs. Kelwyn says she's glad, because Emerance isn't of Parthenope's social class; Parthenope is miffed under her carefully studied coolness. The next moment, Emerance suddenly reappears; he has not gone to Boston, because of a letter he found at the post office. He and Parthenope go to the other cottage to clinch the deal for Kelwyn. On the way Emerance tells Parthenope that his letter is from a man who likes his idea for a play and will come up to talk about it. Emerance arranges with the cottager for the Kelwyns to move in next day. When Parthenope voices a dislike of the local people, Emerance rebukes her. Parthenope finds she rather likes that.

In the evening Emerance seizes on the pretext of running errands to take Parthenope for a drive. He proposes; Parthenope is thrilled but puts him off. Then she feels ashamed. They talk more; he presses his suit, and she yields. Mrs. Kelwyn is amazed at the news. Next morning several neighbors and the bear trainer see the Kelwyns off. Mrs. Kite seems friendly; even Kite is fairly courteous. Driving off, Parthenope and Emerance feel that they are starting life together, and the Kelwyns feel that they are doing the right thing in leaving.

> Mrs. Ager, Tad Allson, Mrs. Allson, bear trainer, Parthenope (Thennie) Brook, cottager, Elihu Emerance, Jasper, Carl Kelwyn, Carry Kelwyn, Elmer Kelwyn, Francis Kelwyn, Alvin Kite, Arthur Kite, Mrs. Kite, linen peddler, Nathaniel, Miss Nichols, organ-grinder, René, Saranna, black tramp, French-Canadian tramp, gypsy woman.

A Woman's Reason, 1883.

Joshua Harkness is an elderly, ailing widower in the India trade; he shields Helen, his pretty young daughter, from his tangled business affairs. Unsure that she loves Robert Fenton, a naval lieutenant deeply in love with her, she writes him to forget her, and receives a disappointingly short reply. Furiously hurt, Robert exchanges assignments with a newly married fellow officer ordered to China, and goes to China for three years. Since Robert's father, a captain of one of Harkness's ships, drowned at sea, Harkness has been Robert's guardian. Paying little attention to Helen's affairs, and worried about business, Harkness dreams of moving to the country, and talks with an old friend, Captain Jack Butler, about the old days of the India trade.

While yachting with her friend Marian Butler and Marian's wealthy fiancé, Edward Ray, Helen meets Lord Rainford, a young Englishman, but the same day learns that Joshua Harkness died that afternoon. Helen broods about her self-centered ignorance of her father's illness, and learns from Captain Butler that her father died intestate, leaving his business in confusion; he does not tell her and she does not realize that Harkness died insolvent and probably left Helen a beggar. Captain Butler asks Helen to come live with them and also offers Margaret, the elderly Harkness cook, a position in his household, but Margaret refuses. After a tearful farewell scene with Margaret, Helen learns that Margaret has paid all the household bills out of her own pocket.

Mortimer, a vulgar young auctioneer, sells the Harkness possessions and auctions off the house to an old man named Everton. Captain Butler thinks Mortimer may not have been honest, but he is pleased that Helen will net $5,000. Helen thinks she will get $5,000 annually, and the Butlers can't bring themselves to explain. Now Helen writes Robert that she has loved him all the time.

Finally realizing her financial position, Helen tells Mrs. Butler she wants to leave, and earn her living, though her training in languages, music, and painting is that of an amateur, a lady, and the Butlers are dubious about her prospects. She meets Lord Rainford briefly before he sails for England.

Leaving her own Boston world, Helen tries to get a room with the Misses Amy, decayed Boston gentlewomen who take boarders, but is sent to see Mrs. Hewitt, who rents her an attic room. There she meets Miss Cornelia Root, an art student, and Mr. and Mrs. Evans and their little boy. Helen finds out that Mrs. Hewitt is a deserted wife and a delinquent debtor. The Butler girls suggest that Helen decorate pottery for a living. She decorates some jars with designs copied from an illustrated Homer, but has great trouble getting storekeepers to display her wares. Then Helen receives two letters from Robert. Robert did not understand Helen's first letter because, being a man, he naturally took her refusal at face value. Committed to his three-year assignment, he is utterly wretched but sends two letters from Rio, the second after learning of Harkness's death. The first letter is a love letter that fills Helen with passionate joy, but the second letter, asking to share her mourning as her brother, strikes Helen as a rebuff. Asked for advice, Mrs. Butler says that Helen should answer only the first letter and consider herself engaged. Marian and Mrs. Butler urge Helen to go abroad with them, but Helen feels that she must wait in Boston for Robert's return.

In Hong Kong Robert receives Helen's avowal of love. The frustration of being unable to return to her makes him ill. When he sees Helen's ghost in the presence of Simmons, the navy doctor, the doctor intercedes with the Admiral, who sends Robert to Washington with naval dispatches. On his way to San Francisco, Robert confides his love story to another passenger, Mrs. Bowers. When the ship breaks a shaft and returns to Yokohama, Robert is transferred to the *Meteor*, a clipper ship, Captain Rollins commanding.

In a terrible storm the clipper is driven far off course, and is shipwrecked on a coral reef. Robert helps in the rescue of the passengers before the ship breaks in half and some Chinese drown. During the night Robert and the other men fight off sharks. When their only lifeboat is found to be too small for all the passengers, Robert offers to stay behind on the atoll. He gives Captain Rollins a note to mail to Helen. Three other men stay behind with him: Giffen, an American; a Portuguese sailor who calls himself John Jones; and an Icelander. The four men find another lifeboat and the captain's bag of gold. They repair the lifeboat, and after many miseries, reach an inhabitable island, but while Robert and Giffen are asleep, the two sailors desert with the boat and the gold.

Meanwhile Helen meets an old friend, Miss Clara Kingsbury, but otherwise her old life has dropped away. She writes often to Robert. Lumley, a jeweler, sells her vases to Trufitt, a former suitor whom she disliked so much that she determines to get the vases back. Lord Rainford brings her gold jewelry from Marian Ray in Egypt, but he hasn't paid duty on it, and to do so Helen spends the money earned from selling vases. Lord Rainford calls more than once, and Clara Kingsbury invites him and Helen to lunch. Eventually he confesses that he returned to America to see her; he loves her and doesn't mind her loss of position. But he leaves when Helen tells him that she is engaged.

Everton, the purchaser of the Harkness house, complains to Helen

that he was tricked by the auctioneer into overbidding. Everton
shows a written confession from the auctioneer to Helen's lawyer,
Hibbard. But he says that Mortimer, needing money, sold the confession to Everton. Everton tells Helen that his loans helped save her
father from bankruptcy, but Hibbard denounces him as a usurer
and tells Helen to ignore him. However, when she finds out that
Captain Butler was also concerned about Mortimer's honesty, she
refuses to touch her inheritance because she feels that Everton may
have a prior claim to it. Cornelia Root advises Helen to color photographs for a friend of hers, Zenas Pearson. Helen does some, but
Pearson is dissatisfied. Then, with Cornelia's help, Helen gets three
novels to review for Evans, the book-review editor of *Saturday Afternoon*. Hibbard receives a telegram from Captain Butler instruct-
ing him to pay Everton's claim according to Helen's wishes, and she
says he must be paid. Everton thanks Helen for the money and then
asks her to marry him; Helen thinks he is insane and flees. Evans
sends Helen a check for the reviews, but rewrites them. In *Saturday
Afternoon* Helen reads a story of the wreck of the *Meteor* in which
the two deserting sailors said that both Fenton and Giffen had died
while trying to free the second lifeboat from the wreck. Convinced
that Robert has been murdered, Helen becomes delirious. Clara
Kingsbury nurses her and when Helen is better takes her home.
Helen has received the note Robert sent her through Captain Rollins. Still trying to support herself, Helen makes bonnets; but the
Beacon Street ladies find her work amateurish, and the scheme fails.
Moving in with the recently married Margaret and her Irish husband in East Cambridge, Helen begins successfully to make bonnets for servant girls.

A year passes. The Rays return from Europe with their little boy
and make Helen, who is in bad health, come to them in Beverly.
Marian urges Helen to marry Lord Rainford now that Robert is
dead. Though Helen dislikes and evades Marian's plan to bring
Lord Rainford to the house, the two meet and Helen refuses him
again but leaves him with some hope.

Meanwhile, on the atoll, Robert and Giffen live like Robinson
Crusoe. Three months later, Robert finds the lifeboat the two sailors
left in. He and Griffen repair it and sail to what they think is another
atoll, only to discover that they are back on their own island. Eighteen months later, a hurricane wrecks the island but does not destroy

their boat. They repair it and preparing to leave stock it again, but Giffen falls ill and dies. The same day Robert is rescued by a New Bedford whaler.

Helen decides to refuse Rainford because she doesn't love him; her friends agree. Her millinery customers decrease. Margaret's husband threatens to evict Helen, but is killed in an explosion, and Margaret becomes a servant again. In a restaurant Helen overhears Mrs. Bowers talking, and gets the impression that Robert flirted with her because it was his last chance before marriage. Heartbroken, Helen goes to the Butlers', and Robert is waiting for her there.

Helen and Robert are married, and Helen rehires Margaret. Everton turns the old Harkness home into the Everton Institute of Industrial Arts for Young Ladies. Helen tells her own story to one of the students. She says that women must learn to do something well, just like men. But she tells her husband that love and marriage are more important for her. Robert is appointed commandant of the Narragansett Navy Yard. Helen is glad to have solved her problems through marriage.

> Admiral, the Misses Amy, Mrs. Bowers, Bridget, Mrs. Catherine Butler, Captain Jack Butler, Jessie Butler, Marian Butler, the Misses Butler, Chinese, Tom Evans, Evans, Mrs. Evans, Everton, Lieutenant Robert Fenton, Professor Fraser, Mrs. Fraser, Giffen, Helen Harkness, Joshua Harkness, Mrs. Hewitt, Hibbard, Icelander, Irishman, John Jones, Kimball, Miss Clara Kingsbury, leader of the rescue party, Lumley, Margaret, Mortimer, Newell, Zenas Pearson, Lord Rainford, Edward Ray, Rogers, Captain Rollins, Miss Cornelia Root, Dr. Simmons, student at the Everton Institute, Mrs. Sullivan, Trufitt, Wetherall, Wheeler, White, Wilson, Mrs. Wilson.

The World of Chance, 1893.

The Midland *Echo,* a Midwestern paper, cuts its staff, and (Percy Bysshe) Shelley Ray, a young reporter, loses his job. He takes the sleeper for New York, where he hopes to find a publisher for his novel, and to write letters for the *Echo.* On the train the next morning he watches two young women, each with a baby. One baby throws his mother's purse out the window. Although the mother wails that all her money was in her purse, the conductor refuses to stop the train. Learning from the conductor that the women are going to New York, Ray secretly gives him a dollar for their carfare from the ferry station. On the ferry boat from Jersey City to New York, Ray watches the two young women. Then he goes to a hotel recommended by his friend Sanderson of the *Echo* and at once begins to revise his manuscript, which has been rejected by many magazines. Homesick, Ray doubts that he will get it published. When he overhears a worried country storekeeper, talking in the hall, tell his friend that he is overstocked and going bankrupt, Ray incorporates the incident into his first letter to the *Echo*; but he doesn't consider it as important as his own disappointment in love, the basis of his novel.

Walking up Broadway the next morning on his way to a publisher, Ray begins to plot a novel about one of the young mothers. He sees a policeman arrest a man accused by a shopkeeper of trying to steal a traveling bag. He decides to include the incident in his letter to the *Echo*. The shopkeeper is questioned by an elderly gentleman, who falls into step with Ray and says that if the thief had stolen a street instead of a bag, he might have been regarded as a public benefactor instead of a thief. It turns out that the old gentleman is also calling on the publishers Ray wants to see.

Although Ray has a letter of introduction to the firm's Mr. Brandreth, he first meets the owner of the publishing company, Henry C. Chapley, a gloomy old gentleman who tells him that they wouldn't think of considering the manuscript of an unknown author. Then Brandreth, Chapley's son-in-law, arrives. Full of excitement about the birth of his son, he talks to Ray in such a friendly way that Ray finally feels emboldened to announce that he has a novel he would like to submit. Brandreth's attitude changes immediately, but he politely asks Ray what his novel is about. When Ray tells him that its story parallels the plot of *Romeo and Juliet*, Brandreth says that he and his wife once played the leading roles in an amateur production of the play (see *Annie Kilburn*). Ray's attempts to summarize his novel are repeatedly interrupted by Brandreth's reminiscences. Finally he agrees to have Ray's manuscript read. He also introduces Ray to Kane, the elderly gentleman he has already met. One of the company's authors, Kane indulges in elaborate pleasantries about Ray's literary ambitions. When Kane has left,

Brandreth tells Ray that Kane is a queer genius who has written an unpopular book of aphorisms.

While waiting to hear from Chapley or Brandreth, Ray visits other publishers, one of whom tells him that no one can predict whether a book will be a popular success. Letters from home increase Ray's loneliness. One evening he sees Kane dining with some young authors in a restaurant. When Kane invites him to join them, Ray declines; he is ashamed to let them see how terribly lonely he is. When Kane visits him and asks him why he refused the invitation, Ray confesses the truth. Kane then asks Ray to visit an old friend with him. On the uptown elevated train Kane tells Ray about David Hughes, an altruist who began his career at Brook Farm and has lived in many similar communities since. Now old and sick and poor, but still full of hope, he is writing a book about his utopian beliefs.

At Hughes's tenement apartment Ray meets Ansel Denton, a gloomy young man and father of twin babies. Hughes is arguing about Tolstoy with Chapley, who does not recognize Ray, but in spite of this, Ray is relieved that Chapley knows Hughes because he himself finds Hughes and his tenement apartment rather queer. When Hughes finds out that Ray has written an unpublished novel, he is impatient. He has no time for novels or for his friend Kane's essays either. Arguing with Hughes about the possibility of "the Altruistic Man," Kane says that he cannot exist as long as people have to eat three times a day. Ray doesn't pay attention to them because he overhears two women talking who turn out to be the two young women on the train. Mrs. Jenny Denton, David Hughes's older daughter, tells Ray that until recently she and her husband lived in a community. She explains to him her father's belief that everybody should be part of a family and sure of a living as long as he is willing to work. Peace Hughes, her sister, who is employed by Chapley, has already recognized Ray as the passenger whom she suspected of giving them their carfare. She tries to repay Ray, but he asks her to give the dollar to somebody who really needs it. Ray finds Peace beautiful and innocent, and their conversation soon becomes personal.

In the front room Hughes argues with his motley crowd of visitors. He has rejected the idea of communities, and believes that all men willing to work must gradually be organized into one great human family. Though rather put out to find Ray indifferent to social questions, he invites Ray to come again. Resenting Hughes's attempt to involve him in the discussion, Ray tells Kane that Hughes and his friends are cranks. Kane tells him that Jenny Hughes nursed Denton when he fell sick while visiting their community, and Denton later married her. Denton believes that cities must be eliminated; Kane disagrees with him.

When Ray calls at the publishers, Brandreth casually informs him that the readers' reports are in and will be put in shape over the weekend by Peace Hughes, whose literary acumen he praises. Brandreth explains that Hughes and Chapley have been friends since their Brook Farm days together and meet every Sunday to discuss political economy. The firm hasn't decided yet whether to publish Ray's novel, but Brandreth invites Ray to go home with him for dinner. Although anxious to rush off to see Peace and the readers' reports, Ray feels that he can't refuse the invitation. At home, Brandreth proudly displays his baby son, and introduces Ray to his wife and mother-in-law, Mrs. Chapley, who questions Ray about her husband's friend Hughes. When Mrs. Brandreth invites Ray to stay for dinner, he sees that her husband hasn't told her of *his* invitation; so he seizes his opportunity to decline.

Ray rushes to the Hughes's apartment, but Peace is out. Waiting for her, he is forced to listen to David Hughes talk about *his* book, a criticism of modern life, which he hopes Chapley will publish. When Peace returns, Ray begs her for her opinion of his novel, but she declines to interfere with the official readers' opinions. On the elevated train, Ray reads their six reports and is humiliated by their combined effect: each condemns his novel for a different reason. During the sleepless night that follows, he decides that his career as a novelist is over. The next morning Kane tells Ray that he has had many of his novels rejected. After reading the reports, he asks Ray encouraging questions and suggests other publishers.

Brandreth formally rejects Ray's manuscript in its present form. When Ray offers it to other publishers, they reject it for a bewildering variety of general economic reasons. Kane reads it and has a mixed reaction: he can't quite bring himself to offer it to a publisher friend. Brandreth asks for the return of the manuscript, then tells Ray that he was going to ask a friend of Ray's to read it, but the friend has already read it and doesn't exactly like it.

Disappointed, Ray writes a poem about his experiences, takes it to show Peace, and is invited to share a frugal meal with the family. Ansel Denton is upset because engraving processes are putting many engravers like himself out of work. Uninterested in this topic, Ray reads his poem to Peace. Mrs. Denton privately tells Ray that her husband hears a voice giving him commands, and in Denton's presence she tells Ray that *he* has invented an engraving process that will throw engravers out of work. When Denton says that he is unsure about the morality of trying to get his invention accepted, his wife jokingly urges him to consult his voice. Peace tries to comfort Denton; Ray would prefer her to comfort him.

Kane feels Ray's coldness, but Ray refuses to reveal his suspicion that it was Kane who advised Brandreth against accepting his novel. When the owners of the *Echo* ask for more social gossip in Ray's letters, he replies sarcastically and loses his assignment. He asks Brandreth for a job, and the publisher says that he has already suggested him to the editor of *Every Evening*, who needs a synopsis of a French book. Overjoyed, Ray gets the book, works all night, and delivers the review the next morning as ordered, but is infuriated by the editor's critical comments and the small pay. Concealing his rage from Brandreth, Ray tells the story to Kane, who defends the editor's behavior as an inevitable product of his circumstances. Ray begins to like Kane again.

Ray becomes a reader for Chapley's, and also begins writing short pieces, most of which are rejected, but he sells some jokes and humorous verse. When he begins to neet other aspiring young writers who give him practical advice, he loses his homesickness. He also begins to have a social life. Through Mrs. Chapley he meets Mrs. Mayquait, who likes him and gets him invited to dinners and balls. He has a brief interlude with a rich girl who seems interested in him until he tells her about the Hughes family.

Hughes reads him his book and, after some argument, adopts some of the changes Ray suggests. Denton is increasingly gloomy and irritated by his wife's frivolity, and Ray overhears him talking to himself. Denton plays the violin and dances for his twins, but when Ray asks him whether it is a Shaker dance, Denton is insulted by his ignorance of the fact that the Shaker dance is a rite. Mrs. Denton explains that her husband had to leave the Shakers after painting a bull on a shingle (thus violating the Shaker rule against graven images), but she believes that he would return to them if he could be relieved of his family. Later, Mrs. Denton tells Ray that Kane is sick, and Ray recounts Brandreth's consulting a friend about Ray's novel. He still believes the friend was Kane. Denton is strangely excited by the progress of his invention, but when his wife urges him to finish it so he can make enough money for them to go into society, he suddenly seems to hear his voice again. Discussing the Dentons with the convalescing Kane, Ray tells him of Denton's voice, and then impulsively mentions Kane's refusal to reread his novel at Brandreth's request. Kane is astonished: Brandreth never asked him to do that, but if he had, Kane would have urged Brandreth to accept the novel. They wonder whom Brandreth did ask.

Suspecting that it was Peace whom Brandreth asked, Ray is upset by her double role. Brandreth comes to tell him that it wasn't Kane and that he is now authorized to reveal the person's identity, but Ray says that he doesn't want to know. Peace tells him that Brandreth asked her but she felt it was too much for her to decide his fate. Angry and sarcastic, Ray reduces her to tears and leaves, but then he is ashamed and returns to apologize. At the apartment he finds only Hughes, who tells him that Denton, at the command of his voice, has destroyed his invention. Denton feels that he must atone for the sin of his invention by making some kind of expiation. Peace tries to calm him by telling him the voice is wicked and he must remember his family. She finally succeeds in soothing him. She is weeping from the strain, and Ray wants to do something, but Hughes sends him away without letting him see Peace.

Ray tells Kane what he has overheard, and Kane promises to inform Chapley. Later Ray also confesses to Kane how he treated Peace because of her behavior in the manuscript affair. Kane tells Ray that if he doesn't understand why Peace wouldn't reread his novel he should not see her again.

Denton exposes his twins to scarlet fever. The twins die, and Denton, who has diphtheria, is too sick to attend their funeral. He recovers, but the children's deaths embitter his wife. Denton gives up his job to another man. When Ray meets Denton in Central Park, Denton blames himself for the twins' deaths and says he hears them talking to him; then he runs away, babbling wildly to his voice about atonement. While Ray is at the Hugheses' later, Denton hears his voice order him to smash his violin. His wife and his father-in-law are very unsympathetic; only Peace defends him. But suddenly

Denton flings himself upon Peace and tries to force something into her mouth. When Ray and Hughes fight him off, Peace faints and Denton rushes into the next room, where he swallows some prussic acid and dies instantly. Later, Hughes has a hemorrhage.

The next morning Brandreth tells Ray that the editor of *Every Evening* wants to offer him a job, which might even mean a serialization of his novel. Brandreth thinks he might even accept it for Chapley's. Ray tells him about Denton's suicide. Brandreth asks Ray to help him break the news to his wife and the Chapleys. He is afraid that there will be a scandal involving all of them, and changes his mind about considering Ray's novel for publication. Chapley and Mrs. Brandreth, on the other hand, are unselfishly sympathetic. As a result, Brandreth's attitude is somewhat changed. There is no publicity or scandal, and Ray gets the job with *Every Evening*.

Ray spends a lot of time visiting Hughes, who is dying. For a while Ray toys with two fantasies, that Peace was in love with Denton and that he himself is in love with Mrs. Denton. Tortured by the heat and noise of the city, Hughes continues to try to write about his dream of an urban utopia. Full of pity for Hughes and Peace, Ray kisses her hand.

When Ray is asked by his chief to decide whether *Every Evening* should serialize his novel, Ray is forced to conclude that it should not. Then Brandreth wants to reconsider the novel for Chapley's, and Kane tells Ray that Brandreth's change of heart has probably been caused by Chapley's declining interest in business. Ray wonders if under these circumstances he ought to let Brandreth take a chance on his book, but Kane says that chance may be a larger law of life. Now Brandreth tells Ray that he could not put his novel down. And if his wife likes it, too, then he will accept it. By that evening Mrs. Brandreth has decided in his favor, but Ray has been waiting so long that he finds himself strangely unexcited. He goes to tell Kane, then Peace. Her father has had another hemorrhage and cannot speak, and Ray is ashamed of himself for discussing his book. Peace tells Hughes Ray's news, and the old man scribbles Ray a note asking him to try to get *his* manuscript published. Ray promises, and later asks Brandreth to publish Hughes's book instead of his own, but Brandreth says it is too late for that now, though he promises to consider Hughes's manuscript. Ray tells Peace and Mrs. Denton about Brandreth's refusal. But at her father's bedside, with the end near, Mrs. Denton tells Hughes that Brandreth has agreed to publish his book right away, and the old man is overjoyed. Hughes dies and Kane pays for his funeral.

When Ray's novel is published, the influential journals do not review it, though his friend Sanderson praises it in the Midland *Echo*. Ray, Kane, and Brandreth discuss the novel's failure to sell; Brandreth is still hopeful it will succeed. In the new apartment of Peace and Mrs. Denton in Greenwich Village, Ray tries to learn Peace's opinion of his novel, but once again she evades his questions, and he must be content with asking her to let him be her best friend.

Then a laudatory review appears in the *Metropolis*, comparing Ray to both Thackeray and Hawthorne. Brandreth has excerpts printed as ads in the leading morning papers. He tells Ray that the review was written by a young man named Worrell, substituting for the regular reviewer on sick leave. Now other friendly reviews appear in influential papers throughout the country. When Ray is interviewed by a girl reporter for a Southern paper, her story starts a wave of interviews, photographs, and romantically inaccurate biographies. *Every Evening* raises his salary. But after 43,000 copies the book stops selling. Brandreth wants to publish Ray's next novel, and praises Peace very highly.

Ray proposes to Peace, who says that she doesn't love him, although she did when Brandreth asked her to read the manuscript. She says that she will never marry and never love anyone again. Though Ray says the same thing, he feels relieved by her rejection. On his way home to Midland for his vacation, Ray muses about his changing relationship with Peace. He decides that the change was caused only by chance and that he will write a story about it. The success of his book has also been the result of chance, but chance, he feels, is really the operation of Providence. As he falls asleep on the train, he realizes that his last idea is Kane's.

> Bella Chapley Brandreth, Percy Brandreth, Sr., Percy Brandreth, Jr., Henry C. Chapley, Mrs. Henry C. Chapley, train conductor, Ansel Denton, Jenny Hughes Denton, Denton twins, editor of *Every Evening*, Hanks brothers, David Hughes, Peace Hughes, Kane, rich young lady, old black man, young man, Mrs. Mayquait, policeman, Percy Bysshe Shelley Ray, S. Ray, girl reporter, Sanderson, shopkeeper, Mr. and Mrs. Simpson, country storekeeper, storekeeper's friend, visitors, waiter, Worrell.

CHARACTERS

Acton. Author, novelist, writer. "The Angel of the Lord," "A Case of Metaphantasmia," "Braybridge's Offer," "The Chick of the Easter Egg," "A Memory that Worked Overtime," "A Presentiment": the narrator. "Though One Rose from the Dead": the narrator, to whom the story was told earlier by Wanhope.

Adding, Roswell. *Their Silver Wedding Journey*. Called Rose, son of Mrs. Adding.

Adding, Mrs. *Their Silver Wedding Journey*. Widowed mother of Roswell Adding.

Admiral. *A Woman's Reason*. Commander in the western Pacific who sends Lt. Fenton to Washington with dispatches.

Agent, Freight. "The Pursuit of the Piano." Small-town New Englander who is sarcastic to Hamilton Gaites.

Agent, Insurance. "An Experience." The man who dies in the narrator's office.

Ager, Mrs. *The Vacation of the Kelwyns*. A farmer's wife.

Agnew. *The Coast of Bohemia*. A guest of Wetmore the painter.

Aide to the Governor of New York. *A Foregone Conclusion*. Ferris's friend who helps him exhibit his paintings.

Al. "The Father." The Talberts' gardener.

Albers, Jane. "The Pursuit of the Piano." A girl whom Hamilton
Gaites dallies with at Kent Harbor, Maine.

Aldeano, Perez Armando. "The Amigo." A mischievous small Ecuadorian boy nicknamed the "amigo."

Alden, Mrs. *Mrs. Farrell.* A boarder at the Woodward farm.

Alderling, Marion. "Though One Rose from the Dead." Alderling's
wife, a believer in life after death.

Alderling. "Though One Rose from the Dead." A painter, who,
summoned by his dead wife, joins her.

Aldgate, Rhoda. *An Imperative Duty.* A beautiful young orphan,
one-sixteenth black, who eventually marries Dr. Olney after
agonies over her ancestry.

Alford, Brooks. "The Eidolons of Brooks Alford." A nervous Bostonian who has disconcerting visions.

Alfred, Elder. *A Parting and a Meeting.* A Shaker elder.

Alger, Mrs. *Dr. Breen's Practice.* A boarder at Jocelyn's resort hotel.

Allson, Tad. *The Vacation of the Kelwyns.* A slovenly New England
back-country farmer.

Allson, Mrs. *The Vacation of the Kelwyns.* Patient wife of Tad Allson.

Alverly. "EEC," O 12. Anguished man who once killed a child with
his car.

Amsden, Mrs. *Indian Summer.* American living in Florence.

Americans. See especially the March narratives. Citizens — at home
or traveling, male and female, young and old, working or
loafing or talking or courting — observed by the Marches
and/or Howells' narrators.

Amy, Misses. *A Woman's Reason.* Decayed Boston gentlewomen
who take boarders.

Anatole, Monsieur. *Through the Eye of the Needle.* Mr. Thrall's
French chef, quickly at home in Altruria.

Andersen, Herbert. *A Fearful Responsibility.* A shy Dane whom Lily
Mayhew refuses.

Anderson, Julia. *April Hopes.* A lively New York girl, friend of Dan
Mavering and sometime rival of Alice Pasmer.

Andrew. *The Landlord at Lion's Head.* The Lyndes' butler.

Andrews, Miss. *Fennel and Rue.* An earnest young woman whom
Verrian meets at a house party and whom Verrian's mother
wants him to marry.

Angelina. "Romance of the Crossing." Girl who is reconciled to Edwin by his gallantry.

Angels. "The Archangelic Censorship." Observers of the world who discuss the beginning of World War I.

Annie. *No Love Lost.* Sister (or friend) of Fanny.

Anther, Dr. Justin. *The Son of Royal Langbrith.* Intelligent, middle-aged physician who for many years hopelessly loves Mrs. Amelia Langbrith, a widow, and who dies suddenly of typhoid fever.

Arabella. "A Perfect Goose." Girl who angrily calls Charles a perfect goose.

Arbuton, Miles. *A Chance Acquaintance.* A priggish Bostonian whose snobbery loses him Kitty Ellison.

Ardith, Wallace. *Letters Home.* Young writer from Iowa who goes to New York to make his fortune.

Arkwright, Millicent. "The Pursuit of the Piano." Girl from Merritt, N.H., whom Hamilton Gaites confuses with Phyllis Desmond but later courts.

Armiger. *Fennel and Rue.* Verrian's editor.

Arthur. "Not a Love Story." Small-town youth who too casually courts Fanny.

Artist, young. "EEC," Ag 12. Participant in discussion of the American *mañana* habit.

Atherton, Clara (Kingsbury). (See also Kingsbury.) A wealthy, fluttery Bostonian socialite. *An Imperative Duty:* friend and confidante of Dr. Edward Olney, she takes Rhoda Aldgate into her Beverly home after the death of Rhoda's aunt, Mrs. Meredith. *A Modern Instance:* the whimsical, exasperating client of Eustace Atherton, whom she later marries. She gives a party for the Hubbards and helps Marcia Hubbard after Bartley's desertion. *The Rise of Silas Lapham:* a guest at the Coreys' dinner party for the Laphams. *A Woman's Reason:* friend of Helen Harkness whom she nurses when Helen is ill.

Atherton, Eustace. A dignified, thoughtful Boston lawyer. *An Imperative Duty:* helps Rhoda Aldgate after the death of her aunt, Mrs. Meredith. *A Modern Instance:* friend and confidant of Ben Halleck, and attorney and eventually husband of Clara Kingsbury, with whom he discusses the Hubbards; helps Marcia Hubbard after Bartley's desertion.

Atwell. *Ragged Lady.* Owner of summer hotel where Clementina Claxon works.

Atwell, Mrs. *Ragged Lady*. Atwell's wife; hotel manager.

Audience. "EEC," Ap 20. Listeners who start a riot at the Martians' lecture.

August. *Their Silver Wedding Journey*. A helpful porter at Weimar.

Andersen's aunt. *A Fearful Responsibility*. An elderly woman who visits the Elmores with her nephew.

Aunt of Isabel March. *Their Wedding Journey*. Boston woman with whom the Marches stay when first married.

Aunt, Minver's. "A Presentiment." Beautiful young wife of Minver's Uncle Felix who dies while he is away on a trip.

Author. "The Critical Bookstore." Visitor to the store to protest against Erlcort's failure to stock his books.

Author, aged. "EEC," N 19. An experienced writer, he is startled at an invitation to join a correspondence-school writing course.

Author, famous. "EEC," My 07. A friend of the Easy Chair; he discusses breaking into print.

Author, very old. "EEC," Mr 12. A writer who is upset by criticism.

Authors. "The Critical Bookstore." Writers who want Erlcort to stock their books.

Authors, creative and visiting. "ES," D 90. Members of an imaginary parade to celebrate the copyright law.

Bachelor, American. "EEC," Ag 12. Participant in the discussion of the American *mañana* habit.

Bachelor, elderly. "EEC," Je 10. A guest at a dinner where divorce is discussed.

Bacon, Sir Francis. *The Seen and the Unseen at Stratford-on-Avon*. Spirit who talks and tours with Shakespeare and the narrator.

Baker, Frank. *The Flight of Pony Baker*. Responsible older cousin of Pony Baker.

Baker, Frank ("Pony"). *The Flight of Pony Baker*. Small boy who lives a difficult life in Boy's Town.

Baker, Henry. *The Flight of Pony Baker*. Father of Pony Baker.

Baker, Lucy. *The Flight of Pony Baker*. Mother of Pony Baker.

Baker. *The Flight of Pony Baker*. Father of Frank Baker.

Baker, Mrs. *The Flight of Pony Baker*. Mother of Frank Baker.

Baptiste. *The Quality of Mercy*. Northwick's sleigh driver.

Barker, Lemuel. *The Minister's Charge*. Naïve farm youth who is drawn by his fatuity and Rev. Sewell's careless praise into an adventurous life in Boston.

Barker, Mrs. *The Minister's Charge*. Lemuel's grim mother.

Barlow. *Dr. Breen's Practice*. Rustic hotel handyman.

Bascom, Editha. "Editha." Selfishly idealistic fiancée of George Gearson.

Bascom. "Editha." Editha's prosaic father.

Bascom, Mrs. "Editha." Editha's mother.

Baysley, Abner J. *Letters Home*. Iowa businessman moved to New York by his employer Ralson.

Baysley, Mrs. Abner J. *Letters Home*. Wife of Abner J. Baysley.

Baysley, Essie. *Letters Home*. Naïve daughter, aged sixteen, of Abner J. Baysley.

Baysley, Jenny. *Letters Home*. Young daughter of Abner J. Baysley.

Baysley, Rev. William. *Letters Home*. Brother of Abner J. Baysley.

Baysley, Mrs. William. *Letters Home*. Wife of Rev. William Baysley.

Bear trainer. *The Vacation of the Kelwyns*. An itinerant who entertains the Kelwyns with his bear.

Beaton, Angus. *A Hazard of New Fortunes*. A handsome, peevish, selfish artist romantically involved with Alma Leighton, Christine Dryfoos, and Margaret Vance.

"Beats" (confidence-men). *The Minister's Charge*. Plausible rascals who swindle Lemuel Barker of his last $10.

Bell, Mrs. "A Sleep and a Forgetting." Voluble American socialite with numerous daughters.

Bellam, Jimmy. *New Leaf Mills*. The only Bellam child to survive an epidemic.

Bellam. *New Leaf Mills*. A sawmiller who dies in an epidemic.

Bellam, Mrs. *New Leaf Mills*. Bellam's wife.

Bellard, Lillian. *Miss Bellard's Inspiration*. Lovely and independent niece of Mrs. Crombie.

Bellingham, Charles. Intelligent Boston businessman and Brahmin. *The Rise of Silas Lapham:* Mrs. Corey's cousin and a guest at her dinner for the Laphams; helps Lapham in business. *The Minister's Charge:* helps Bromfield Corey test Lemuel Barker's reading ability. *April Hopes:* a friend of Bromfield Corey; attends a reception. *The Quality of Mercy:* attends a dinner given by Eben Hilary.

Bellingham, Mrs. Charles. *The Rise of Silas Lapham*. Wife of Charles; attends the Coreys' dinner.

Bellingham, James. *The Rise of Silas Lapham*. Mrs. Corey's brother; attends her dinner for the Laphams.

Bellingham, Jane (Mrs. James). *April Hopes.* Boston lady who gives a party at which Dan Mavering gets into trouble with Alice Pasmer.

Belsky, Baron. *Ragged Lady.* Emotional Russian who admires Clementina Claxon in Florence.

Bennam. *Ragged Lady.* Elderly, helpful American vice-consul in Venice.

Bentley, Mrs. "A Pair of Patient Lovers." Domineering mother of Miss Bentley.

Bentley, Miss. "A Pair of Patient Lovers." Fiancée and finally wife of Rev. Glendenning.

Berry, Alonzo W. *The Minister's Charge.* Law student who introduces Lemuel Barker to Miss Carver.

Berson, Annie. "The Independent Candidate." George Berson's old-maid sister and housekeeper.

Berson, George. "The Independent Candidate." Independent candidate for Congress against Cuffins; has a breakdown on his night of triumph.

Bertha. *No Love Lost.* American girl traveling in Italy.

Betterson, Jenny. "The Boarders." Mrs. Betterson's sickly daughter.

Betterson, Minervy. "The Boarders." Mrs. Betterson's pretty daughter.

Betterson, Mrs. "The Boarders." An elderly widow who runs a boardinghouse.

Bevidge, Mrs. *The Landlord at Lion's Head.* Boston hostess at whose house Jeff Durgin meets Bessie Lynde again.

Bickler, Captain Harrison. *New Leaf Mills.* Young lawyer and politician who tries to seduce Rosy Hefmyer.

Billard, Hen. *The Flight of Pony Baker.* Friend of Pony.

Billings, Baby Girl. *The Leatherwood God.* Daughter of Laban and Nancy Billings.

Billings, Joey. *The Leatherwood God.* Bright son of Dylks and Nancy Gillespie (Dylks) Billings.

Billings, Laban. *The Leatherwood God.* Nancy Gillespie's decent second husband.

Billings, Nancy Gillespie Dylks. *The Leatherwood God.* Sister of David Gillespie, married first to Joseph Dylks and then (after he runs off and is presumed dead) to Laban Billings.

Billy. "Buying a Horse." A horse that satisfies the friend of the narrator until it runs away and smashes the friend's phaeton.

Bingham, Juliet. "The Magic of a Voice." A bossy girl whose appearance Langbourne wrongly links with the voice of Barbara Simpson.

Binning, Otis. *Letters Home*. A prissy, middle-aged Boston bachelor.

Binning, Mrs. Walter. *Letters Home*. Otis Binning's sister-in-law, a Bostonian.

Bird (Oiseau). *The Quality of Mercy*. A tavern keeper of Haha Bay, P.Q., with whom Northwick stays the winter. (Also appears, unnamed, in *A Chance Acquaintance;* see Guide, French-Canadian.)

Bird, Henry. *A Modern Instance*. A young printer, in love with Hannah Morrison; knocked down by Bartley Hubbard.

Bird, Mrs. *A Modern Instance*. The mother of Henry Bird.

"Birds of Prey." "The Mother-Bird." Two loud male passengers on a ship who make fun of a woman called "the Mother-Bird."

Birkwall. "The Pursuit of the Piano." The Harvard classmate of Hamilton Gaites, now living in Burymouth, N.H.

Birkwall, Mrs. "The Pursuit of the Piano." The helpful, charming wife of Gaites's friend.

Bittridge, Clarence. *The Kentons*. Pushy, malicious reporter who insults Ellen Kenton and Judge Kenton.

Bittridge, Mrs. *The Kentons*. Bittridge's fatuous mother.

Black, Dave. *The Flight of Pony Baker*. A boy, friend of Pony.

Black. *The Flight of Pony Baker*. The father of Dave Black.

Bladen, Lizzie. *New Leaf Mills*. The daughter of a retired merchant.

Bladen. *New Leaf Mills*. A retired merchant.

Blake, Hughey. *The Leatherwood God*. A clumsy youth who courts and loses Jane Gillespie.

Blakely. "The Boarders." A law student and boarder.

Blakely. *New Leaf Mills*. A guest at the Powells' house-raising.

Blakey. "A Memory that Worked Overtime." A painter.

Blood, Lydia. *The Lady of the* Aroostook. A charming, independent New England girl who meets her future husband on a small sailing ship, the *Aroostook.*

Bloomingdale, Josie. *An Imperative Duty*. A sister of Rev. Bloomingdale.

Bloomingdale, Roberta. *An Imperative Duty*. A sister of Rev. Bloomingdale.

Bloomingdale, Rev. *An Imperative Duty*. A stuffy young clergyman refused by Rhoda Aldgate.

Bloomingdale, Mrs. *An Imperative Duty.* The widowed mother of Rev. Bloomingdale.

Bloomingdale, Miss. *An Imperative Duty.* The oldest sister of Rev. Bloomingdale.

Boardman. *April Hopes.* A reporter; a classmate and confidant of Dan Mavering.

Boat boy. *The Seen and the Unseen at Stratford-on-Avon.* A boy hired by the narrator and his companions to take them up the Avon to a teahouse.

Boatman. *Their Wedding Journey.* A man who is injured in a collision with the Marches' steamboat.

Bob, Blue. *The Flight of Pony Baker.* A man who once saved a boy in a flood.

Bobby. "Bobby. Study of a Boy." An energetic scamp of twelve.

Bolton, Oliver. *Annie Kilburn.* A rustic farmer who takes care of the Kilburn place.

Bolton, Pauline. *Annie Kilburn.* Bolton's drily opinionated wife, cook for Annie Kilburn.

Bostonian, Young. "EEC," O 10. A man who appears in the Easy Chair's dream.

Bostonian, Young. "EEC," N 10. A man who discusses a book about hunting with the Easy Chair.

Bowen, Effie. *Indian Summer.* The ladylike small daughter of Mrs. Bowen.

Bowen, Mrs. Evalina (Ridgely). *Indian Summer.* Once a companion of the girl Colville courted; now a charming widow in her mid-thirties whom Colville finally loves.

Bowers, Mrs. *A Woman's Reason.* A passenger in whom Lt. Fenton confides.

Boy, Christmas. "ES." D 91: an Altrurian in an allegory of Christmas. Mr 92: the paulo-post-future's helper in cleaning out the Study's office.

Boy, German-American. "The Amigo." A playmate of the "amigo."

Boy, Little. "The Pony Engine and the Pacific Express." The boy to whom the story is told.

Boy, Little. "The Pumpkin-Glory." The boy to whom the story is told.

Boy, Little. *The Seen and the Unseen at Stratford-on-Avon.* The boy to whom Bacon talks kindly at the movies.

Boy, Scrooge's. "ES," D 90. The bright lad from *A Christmas Carol*, he briefs the Study, in a dream, about conditions in Altrurian America.

Boynton, Egeria. *The Undiscovered Country*. Dr. Boynton's pretty daughter, a medium and the subject of his experiments; she loves Ford after eventful months in Boston and a Shaker village.

Boynton, Dr. *The Undiscovered Country*. Formerly a medical doctor of Portland, Maine; later a determined but scatterbrained mesmerist and student of spiritualism who eventually dies a Christian in a Shaker village.

Bragg. "The Emigrant of 1802." Farmer who helps the M. family in "New Connecticut."

Braile, Matthew. *The Leatherwood God*. Local "Squire" and Justice of the Peace; sarcastic spokesman for rationalism.

Braile, Mrs. *The Leatherwood God*. Wife of the Squire.

Brandreth, Bella Chapley. *The World of Chance*. Daughter of New York publisher, and wife of Percy Brandreth; she reads Shelley Ray's novel and persuades her husband to publish it.

Brandreth, Percy, Sr. *Annie Kilburn:* social butterfly in South Hatboro'. *The World of Chance:* junior member of father-in-law's New York publishing firm; he takes Shelley Ray's book.

Brandreth, Percy, Jr. *The World of Chance*. Brandreth's newborn son, who takes his mind off publishing.

Brandreth, Mrs. *Annie Kilburn*. Socialite mother of Percy Brandreth, Sr., in South Hatboro'.

Braybridge. "Braybridge's Offer." Misogynistic lover of Miss Hazelwood.

Brayton, Dr. *The Coast of Bohemia*. One of General Westley's dinner guests.

Bream, Peter. "The Daughter of the Storage." Mrs. Bream's son, who falls in love with Charlotte Forsyth.

Bream, Mrs. "The Daughter of the Storage." A wealthy Middle Westerner, wife of an international insurance inspector.

Breckon, Rev. Hugh. *The Kentons*. A droll young minister from New York who slowly comes to love Ellen Kenton.

Breen, Dr. Grace. *Dr. Breen's Practice*. A young, pretty homeopathic physician who gives up an unsatisfactory practice to marry.

Breen, Mrs. *Dr. Breen's Practice*. Dr. Breen's mother.

Brews, Margery. "An Old-Time Love Affair." A fifteenth-century English girl who loves John Paston.

Brews. "An Old-Time Love Affair." A fifteenth-century Englishman who gives his daughter in marriage to John Paston.

Bridget. *A Woman's Reason*. Mrs. Hewitt's servant.

Briggs. "The Boarders." A young newspaperman, boarder, and friend of Phillips.

Briggs. *The Leatherwood God*. The regular local minister whose flock is stolen away by Dylks.

Brinkley. *April Hopes*. The genial but tactless husband of Mrs. Brinkley.

Brinkley, Mrs. *April Hopes*. Worldly, cynical Boston woman; major catalyst in the action of the novel.

"British blondes." *Their Wedding Journey*. Showgirls whose presence in the hotel distresses the Marches in Quebec.

Broker, Real-estate. *The Rise of Silas Lapham*. A Bostonian who fails to sell Lapham's unfinished new house.

Brook, Parthenope ("Thennie"). *The Vacation of the Kelwyns*. Mrs. Kelwyn's pretty young cousin who pays a visit to their summer place and catches a husband.

Brother of a young woman. "EEC," S 10. Her chaperon.

Brother and sister, Elderly. "EEC," Jl 09. Observers of the other passengers on a steamboat.

Brown, Sister Althea. *The Day of Their Wedding*. A Shaker who runs off to marry Lorenzo Weaver but returns after adventures in Saratoga Springs.

Brown, Jerusha Peregrine. *Fennel and Rue*. A village girl who writes to the novelist Verrian with the help of Miss Shirley.

Bulkham, Mrs. *A Traveller from Altruria*. A guest in the summer hotel.

Bullion. *A Traveller from Altruria*, "Letters of an Altrurian Traveller," *Through the Eye of the Needle*. An intelligent Boston banker.

Burnamy, L. J. *Their Silver Wedding Journey*. A handsome young newspaper man and author who courts Miss Triscoe.

Burton, James. *The Coast of Bohemia*. A friend of the visiting artist Walter Ludlow in Pymantoning, Ohio.

Burton, Mrs. Polly. *The Coast of Bohemia*. The spirited wife of James Burton; a friend of Cornelia Saunders and a confidante of Mrs. Saunders.

Burton, Roger. *A Parting and a Meeting.* A teacher at an academy who gives up his beloved to become a Shaker.

Burton, Mrs. *The Undiscovered Country.* A Boston society lady.

Burwell, Mrs. *The Son of Royal Langbrith.* Dr. Anther's obliging landlady.

Bushell. *The Flight of Pony Baker.* A merchant who successfully entrusts money to Frank Baker.

Bushwick. *Fennel and Rue.* A vigorous young man who is more successful with Miss Shirley than Verrian is.

Businessmen, English. *The Rise of Silas Lapham.* Mysterious parties, introduced to Lapham by Rogers, who unsuccessfully tempt Lapham to perform an easy swindle and recoup his fortunes.

Butcher. "The Independent Candidate." A tough Whig, who is angered by Wat Larrie's campaign oratory and beats him up.

Butler, Mrs. Catharine. *A Woman's Reason.* Captain Butler's wife, Helen Harkness's confidante.

Butler, Captain Jack. *A Woman's Reason.* Joshua Harkness's old friend who tries to help his daughter Helen after Harkness dies.

Butler, Jessie. *A Woman's Reason.* The youngest Butler daughter.

Butler, Marian. *A Woman's Reason.* Capt. Butler's daughter who marries Edward Ray.

Butler, Misses. *A Woman's Reason.* Other Butler daughters, intrigued by their sister's and Helen Harkness's love affairs.

Butterflyflutterby. "Butterflyflutterby and Flutterbybutterfly." Prince of an imaginary kingdom.

Cabdrivers. "At the Sign of the Savage." Austrians who carry the characters all over Vienna.

Camp, Lizzie. *A Traveller from Altruria.* A young seamstress, daughter of Mrs. Camp.

Camp, Reuben. *A Traveller from Altruria.* A poor but intelligent young farmer.

Camp, Mrs. *A Traveller from Altruria.* A poor, widowed invalid; mother of Lizzie and Reuben.

Candace. *A Parting and a Meeting.* A Shaker sister.

Captain of the *Little Sally. Through the Eye of the Needle.* Captain of the ship that takes Mr. and Mrs. Homos to Altruria.

Captain, Off-duty ship. "The Amigo." An elderly man who spanks the "amigo."

Cargate, Mrs. George. *The Day of Their Wedding*. A vivacious young newlywed at a Saratoga Springs hotel.

Carlotta. "Tonelli's Marriage." A Venetian lady who marries Tonelli.

Carpenter. "Buying a Horse." A neighbor who helps the friend of the narrator buy Billy, a horse.

Carver, Miss Jessie. *The Minister's Charge*. A beautiful art student, boarder at Lemuel Barker's hotel, who eventually falls in love with him.

Casman. *Letters Home*. Editor of the New York *Signal*, at whose home the other characters meet and talk.

Cazzi. *A Fearful Responsibility*. A *valet de place*.

Cecilia. *Through the Eye of the Needle*. An Altrurian widow, M. Anatole's fianceé.

Cenarotti. "Tonelli's Marriage." An aged Venetian notary.

Cenarotti, Signora. "Tonelli's Marriage." Wife of the notary.

Chapley, Miss Bella. *Annie Kilburn*. A young South Hatboro' socialite who falls in love with Percy Brandreth.

Chapley, Henry C. *The World of Chance*. An elderly New York publisher whose company accepts Shelley Ray's first novel.

Chapley, Mrs. Henry C. *The World of Chance*. The wife of the publisher.

Characters in modern Christmas fiction. "EEC," Ja 18. Visitors who discuss frankness in literature with the Easy Chair.

Charles. "A Perfect Goose." The man whom Arabella angrily calls a perfect goose.

Charley. "How I Lost a Wife." A friend of "I" and of Mary, the girl that "I" loves but loses, thanks to a dog.

Charley. "Not a Love Story." Fanny's brother, who impedes her courtship when she strolls in the garden with Arthur.

Chef. *Ragged Lady*. An employee at the summer hotel who teases Clementina Claxon.

Child. "Life and Letters," Ja 23, 1897. A person to whom "he" shows a breadline in New York.

Child, Frank's small. "A Day's Pleasure." One of the excursionists.

Child, German immigrant. "The Lost Child." A small boy lost in an American town, who is helped by a friendly German.

Child, Lost. "A Day's Pleasure." A boy who is at Frank's house when the characters get home in the evening, and who is later restored to his father.

Children. *A Traveller from Altruria.* Poor farm children whom Twelvemough gives money for candy.

Children, Slum. "A Day's Pleasure." Loafers on the pier; they irritate the characters with their loud coughing.

Chinese. *A Woman's Reason.* Passengers who drown when the *Meteor* is shipwrecked.

Chispa. "A Perfect Goose," "Romance of the Crossing." The narrator.

Chrysostom, Cyril. "Letters of an Altrurian Traveller," "The Selling and the Giving of Dinners," *Through the Eye of the Needle.* Homos' Altrurian correspondent; a Regionic Chief there.

Chrysostom, Mrs. Cyril. *Through the Eye of the Needle.* The wife of Homos' friend.

Circus-man. *The Flight of Pony Baker.* A malicious man who teases and scares Pony Baker.

Citizen, First. "EEC," Ap 13. An American who discusses travel books with the Easy Chair.

Citizen, the Good. "EEC," D 11. A concerned man who discusses with the Easy Chair the easy availability of firearms in America.

Citizen, Second. "EEC," Ap 13. An American who discusses travel books with the Easy Chair.

Citizens. "EEC," My 10. Americans who discuss cleanliness in public places with the Easy Chair.

Clara. *No Love Lost.* A friend of Fanny, in America.

Clara. "A Perfect Goose." A young lady who fondly calls her beloved Frederick a perfect goose.

Claxon, Clementina. *Ragged Lady.* A beautiful country girl who is taken out into the world but retains her simplicity.

Claxon, Jim. *Ragged Lady.* Clementina's little brother.

Claxon. *Ragged Lady.* Clementina's philosophical father.

Claxon, Mrs. *Ragged Lady.* Clementina's mother.

Clayton. *A Modern Instance.* The managing editor of the Boston *Events;* replaced by Bartley Hubbard.

Clementine. "A Perfect Goose." A young lady who contemptuously calls Clumsie a perfect goose when he steps on her dress.

Clerk, Hotel. *The Day of Their Wedding.* A Saratoga man who has trouble getting Lorenzo Weaver to register correctly.

Clerk, Hotel. "The Magic of a Voice." A New Englander who tells Stephen Langbourne about Barbara Simpson.

Clerk, Hotel. *The Minister's Charge.* A Bostonian who tells Lemuel Barker his last bill is counterfeit.

Clerk, Hotel. *Their Wedding Journey.* One of the "Rochesterese"; he treats Basil March with great disdain when he registers.

Clumsie. "A Perfect Goose." A youth who annoys Clementine when he steps on her skirt.

"The old codger." "The Critical Bookstore." The bookstore owner who sells out to Erlcort.

Colebridge, Jessamy. *The Son of Royal Langbrith.* Vivacious Saxmills friend of Hope Hawberk.

Colville, Theodore. *Indian Summer.* A former Indiana newspaper editor who at forty-one returns to Florence to renew his youth, becomes infatuated with Imogene Graham, and then really falls in love, with Mrs. Bowen.

Concierges. "At the Sign of the Savage." Viennese involved in Kenton's search for his hotel.

Conductor, Horsecar. *The Minister's Charge.* A Bostonian who tells Lemuel Barker all about his job.

Conductor, Train. "A Case of Metaphantasmia." A late arrival to the mass hysteria in the Pullman car; he calms the passengers.

Conductor, Train. "Incident." An official whose distaste for the smell of paint leads indirectly to a house painter's death.

Conductor, Train. "The Pursuit of the Piano." A New Englander who lets Gaites ride in his caboose.

Conductor, Train. *The Undiscovered Country.* The man who tells the Boyntons they are on the wrong train.

Conductor, Train. *The World of Chance.* An official who refuses to stop the train when Mrs. Denton's baby throws her purse out the window.

Conductors, Train. *The Quality of Mercy.* The railroaders of whom Northwick asks many questions during his flight to Canada.

"A contributor to the magazines." "A Romance of Real Life," "Scene." A rather romantic writer who finds real life stranger than books.

Contributor, Rejected. "EEC," Ap 03. The writer of an unwanted essay about vaudeville.

Cooper. *A Chance Acquaintance*. A shopkeeper in Quebec at whose door Arbuton saves Kitty from a savage dog.

Corey, Anna Bellingham. *The Rise of Silas Lapham*. Bromfield's wife, who finds everything about the Laphams distressing.

Corey, Bromfield. A charming Boston Brahmin and man of leisure. *The Rise of Silas Lapham:* no longer wealthy, he watches his family's involvement with the Laphams with amused irony. *The Minister's Charge:* again rich, thanks to his stock in his son's paint company; he employs Lemuel Barker as a reader. *April Hopes:* now garrulous and slightly senile. *The Quality of Mercy:* attends dinner given by Eben Hilary.

Corey, Lily. *The Rise of Silas Lapham, The Minister's Charge*. The older daughter of the Coreys.

Corey, Nanny. *The Rise of Silas Lapham, The Minister's Charge*. The younger daughter of the Coreys.

Corey, Tom. *The Rise of Silas Lapham*. The able, agreeable son of Bromfield Corey. Works for Silas Lapham, marries Penelope Lapham (after everyone thinks he loves Irene Lapham), makes a success of new job and investment with the West Virginians who drive Lapham out of business.

Cottager. *The Vacation of the Kelwyns*. The summer visitor who rents his house to the Kelwyns when they part from the Kites.

Cotton, Miss. *April Hopes*. A severe old maid, advisor of Alice Pasmer.

Couple, English. *A Chance Acquaintance*. Passengers, with their daughter, on the ship that takes Arbuton and the Ellisons up the Saguenay.

Cousin, Minver's. "A Presentiment." Daughter of Minver's Uncle Felix.

Craybourne, Edmund. *Miss Bellard's Inspiration*. An agreeable young English aristocrat who wins Miss Bellard despite her reluctance.

Crew, The Motley. "EEC," D 15. Stereotyped characters in old-fashioned Christmas stories who appear to the Easy Chair.

Crew of the *Little Sally*. *Through the Eye of the Needle*. Men who want to stay in Altruria once they get there.

Crew of the *Saraband. Through the Eye of the Needle.* The crew of
    Thrall's yacht; they are very happy to be shipwrecked in Al-
    truria.

Critic. *Mrs. Farrell.* A Boston amateur who judges Mrs. Farrell's act-
    ing very severely.

Critic, Anonymous. "ES," D 90. An argumentative reviewer who
    fires blank cartridges at authors.

Critics, Dramatic and Literary. "ES," D 90. A varied group who pass
    in review before the Study.

Crombie, Archibald. *Miss Bellard's Inspiration.* An elderly Boston
    gentleman whose summer peace is broken by the appearance
    and courtship of his niece Miss Bellard.

Crombie, Mrs. Hester. *Miss Bellard's Inspiration.* Crombie's wife,
    blood aunt of Miss Bellard.

Cuffins. "The Independent Candidate." Whig candidate for Con-
    gress.

"Customer, The favorite." "The Return to Favor." A man, the narra-
    tor.

Customers. "The Return to Favor." Ladies who complain about
    their unfinished clothes.

Customers. "The Critical Bookstore." Ladies who don't like the
    choice of books; elderly men, who use the store as a club.

"Cynic, The." "EEC," N 11, F 12, J1 12. An imagined figure with
    whom the Easy Chair discusses American justice, women's
    suffrage, and the differences between poetry and prose.

Cyril. See Chrysostom.

Dale, Miss. *An Open-Eyed Conspiracy.* A cottager in Saratoga
    Springs whom the characters visit.

Dan. "The Pearl." Stephen West's cousin, a young man who loses
    his scarf pin.

Daughter of Basil and Isabel March. "A Circle in the Water." A little
    girl, unnamed here (see March, Bella).

Daughter of old gentleman. "EEC," D 16, Ja 17. A young lady who
    talks to Florindo and Lindora during their automobile trip
    through Maine.

Daughter of Royal Langbrith. *The Son of Royal Langbrith.* Daughter
by his mistress; now a young woman studying singing in
Europe.

Daughter of Tedham. "A Circle in the Water." A girl, later a young
woman, who keeps faith in her father while he is in jail for
ten years.

Davis. "At the Sign of the Savage." The American consul in Vienna
who helps Kenton look for his hotel.

Dealer. "Buying a Horse." A horse dealer who has just sold the perfect horse for the narrator's friend.

Deering, Rufus. *An Open-Eyed Conspiracy.* Well-to-do lumber dealer
who helps chaperon Julia Gage.

Deering, Mrs. *An Open-Eyed Conspiracy.* The second wife of Deering, who helps chaperon Julia Gage.

Denbigh, Dr. "The Father." The village doctor.

Dennam, Mrs. Ansel G. *Letters Home.* The mother of Frances Dennam, from upstate New York.

Dennam, Frances. *Letters Home.* An energetic young lady who seeks
her and her family's fortune in New York.

Dennis. *The Rise of Silas Lapham.* Lapham's office porter.

Denton, Ansel. *The World of Chance.* An ex-Shaker, a young wood
engraver and inventor who goes insane and kills himself.

Denton, Jenny Hughes. *The World of Chance.* The devoted older
daughter of David Hughes; unsympathetic wife of Ansel
Denton and mother of his twin children.

Deschenes, Caroline. *Letters Home.* An Iowa girl whose jilting of
Wallace Ardith drives him to New York and begins the action
of the book.

Desmond, Phyllis. "The Pursuit of the Piano." A New Hampshire
girl, once rich and now poor, to whom a piano is sent from
Boston.

Detectives, Dutch. *The Kentons.* Authorities who arrest Boyne
Kenton after he runs toward the Queens of Holland.

Dewey, Hen. *The Rise of Silas Lapham.* A drunken sailor, husband of
Zerrilla Millon.

Dewey, Zerrilla Millon. *The Rise of Silas Lapham.* Silas Lapham's typist, the daughter of the man who saved Lapham's life in the
Civil War.

Diantha. *The Undiscovered Country.* A Shaker sister.

Dickerman, Chloe Mason. *A Parting and a Meeting.* The betrothed of Roger Burton, later the wife of Ira Dickerman after Burton becomes a Shaker.

Dickerman, Ira. *A Parting and a Meeting.* The man who marries Chloe Mason after her parting from Roger Burton.

Dickerson, J. B. *The Coast of Bohemia.* An art-goods salesman who courts Cornelia Saunders, marries and divorces someone else, and returns to plague Cornelia with his attentions.

Dickery, John. "The Magic of a Voice." A New England lumber-mill owner who courts Juliet Bingham.

Dixmore, Laura. *A Modern Instance.* A friend of Ben Halleck.

Doan. "The Independent Candidate." Printer and editor who bolts the Cuffins party to support Berson.

Doctor at a resort hotel. "EEC," O 12. Alverly's physician, who discusses the social and psychological effects of the automobile.

Doctor at a New Hampshire resort hotel. *A Traveller from Altruria.* A vacationer who joins in the discussions with Homos and other guests.

Doctor. "A Difficult Case." A New England physician who tries and fails to get the dying Hilbrook to eat.

Doctor. "An Experience." A physician called to aid a man who dies on the floor of a publisher's office.

Doctor. "A Pair of Patient Lovers." A small-town physician who treats the neurotic Bentley ladies.

Doctor. "Tonelli's Marriage." A Venetian, once betrothed to the Paronsina.

Doctor. *The Undiscovered Country.* A country doctor who treats Dr. Boynton after he falls and hurts his head.

Drakes, Private, and family. *Their Wedding Journey.* An English soldier, his wife, and his children, who talk to and are observed by the Marches at the fort in Quebec.

"Dreamer, The." *New Leaf Mills.* Owen Powells' quiet, observant second son (based on Howells as a boy).

Driver, Carriage. *The Day of Their Wedding.* A shrewd hustler who takes Lorenzo Weaver and his beloved for a ride around Saratoga Springs and later takes them to a minister and a hotel.

Dryfoos, Christine. *A Hazard of New Fortunes.* The selfish, fiery older daughter of Jacob Dryfoos; her quarrel with him over Beaton leads to tragedy.

Dryfoos, Conrad. *A Hazard of New Fortunes.* The only surviving son of Jacob Dryfoos; an idealistic, unworldly young man, nominal publisher of *Every Other Week*; he is bullied by his father and killed by a stray bullet during a strike.

Dryfoos, Mrs. Elizabeth. *A Hazard of New Fortunes.* The quiet, countrified wife of Jacob Dryfoos; she mourns her lost life in Ohio.

Dryfoos, Jacob. *A Hazard of New Fortunes.* A crude, irascible, elderly capitalist, former Ohio farmer, backer of *Every Other Week*; quarrels with and loses his only son, Conrad.

Dryfoos, Mela. *A Hazard of New Fortunes.* The genial, silly younger daughter of Jacob Dryfoos.

Dudley, Statira. *The Minister's Charge.* A pretty, clinging girl, nineteen, who first accuses Lemuel Barker of stealing her satchel, then becomes his friend and fiancée, but loses him to Miss Carver.

Dunham, Charles. *The Lady of the* Aroostook. A kindly young Bostonian and Harvard graduate, friend and confidant of James Staniford and of Lydia Blood; his injury keeps the lovers apart for a time in Italy.

Dunham, Mrs. (*née* Hibbard). *The Lady of the* Aroostook. The fiancée and later the bride of Dunham.

Durgin, Andrew Jackson. *The Landlord at Lion's Head.* Called Jackson. The tubercular older Durgin son who lingers for some years and builds the first Lion's Head House.

Durgin, James Monroe. *The Landlord at Lion's Head.* Mrs. Durgin's tubercular husband, who dies early in the novel.

Durgin, Mrs. *The Landlord at Lion's Head.* A determined middle-aged woman who preserves the family's hill farm by taking summer boarders and then building a hotel.

Durgin, Thomas Jefferson. *The Landlord at Lion's Head.* Called Jeff. The sturdy, coolly impudent youngest son of Mrs. Durgin; he spends some years at Harvard, flirts with Cynthia Whitwell and Bessie Lynde (to Jere Westover's distress), marries Genevieve Vostrand, and eventually becomes the landlord at the swank new Lion's Head Hotel.

Durgin daughters. *The Landlord at Lion's Head.* Girls who die of tuberculosis.

Durgin sons. *The Landlord at Lion's Head.* Three older sons who go West.

Dylks, Joseph. *The Leatherwood God.* A native of Leatherwood who deserts his wife Nancy, returns years later claiming godhead, and causes much havoc before his death.

Easton, Wayne. *Mrs. Farrell.* A shy New York man of leisure who becomes involved with the *femme fatale* Mrs. Farrell.

Easy Chair, The Editor's. "EEC." A persona of Howells in dialogue and symposia in *Harper's Monthly*, 1900–1920. D 00: chats with Howells in the first of these monthly pieces. Jl 05: discusses writing with Eugenio. D 06: takes a trip in New England. My 07: talks with a famous author. Jl 07: discusses spring with a poet. S 07: discusses conscience with a friend. O 07: pretends to be a reporter. J 08: discusses the opinions of critics. Jl 09: describes steamboat passengers. Mr 10: listens to a friend's story about an ex-convict. My 10: discusses books about smart society. Jl 10: speculates about a couple described to him by a friend. O 10: dreams that he is in London. N 10: discusses a hunting book with a young Bostonian. D 10: discusses his consulship in Torcello with a successor. Ja 11: discusses ship and air travel with the Torcello consul. F 11: talks about E. C. Stedman. Ap 11: discusses autobiography. S 11: discusses Havelock Ellis with an editor. O 11: talks with a friend about the easy availability of firearms in America. N 11: discusses American justice as reflected in a novel by Valdés. F 12: discusses women's suffrage with the Cynic. Mr 12: describes a very old author upset by criticism. My 12: discusses capitalism with the Reviewer. Je 12: discusses publishing with the Reviewer. Jl 12: chats with a friend about the differences between poetry and prose. N 12: discusses spiritualistic phenomena. D 12: discusses the recent election with an eighteenth-century Chinese philosopher. Ap 13: discusses travel books with the First and Second Citizens. N 13: discusses newspaper crime stories with a favorite author. Ap 14: on his way to London, observes and identifies with two men, aged fifty-eight and eighty-five. Jl 14: discusses romance and realism in American literature. S 14: listens to the Idealist's description of the good treatment of a wrongly convicted person in Barataria. Jl 15: discusses books with an elderly sage. N

15: discusses recent American fiction with the sage. D 15: discusses stereotyped Christmas stories with the characters from them. N 16: discusses ideas about republics with a nondescript presence. S 17: discusses ways of talking about the war. Ja 18: visited by characters in modern Christmas fiction. My 18: discusses cleanliness in public places. Jl 19: discusses the American and European plans in hotels with a traveler. S 19: discusses the idea that people always get what they want when they want it. (D 08; Ja, F, Mr, Ap, Je 09; F, Ap, Jl, S 10; Ap 20: see "We. 'EEC.' ")

Eccles. *The Undiscovered Country*. A student of spiritual phenomena at the séance in Boston.

Ecuadorian. "The Amigo." Tutor or uncle of the "amigo."

Editor. "EEC." A Howells persona. My 04: goes to the opera with a reader. Ja 08: discusses servants with "the satirical reader." S 11: discusses Havelock Ellis with the Easy Chair.

Editor. "Hot." A newspaperman who interrupts the meditations of the narrator and calls for copy.

Editor. *The World of Chance*. A New Yorker who hires Ray to work for *Every Evening*.

Editor, Magazine. "EEC," N 19. An experienced man who discusses, with an aged author, ways of learning to write.

Editor, The Unreal. "ES," Ja 86: the inhabitant of a fabulous room, the Editor's Study. "EEC," Ap 03: a spokesman for editors in general, who talks to a rejected contributor.

Editor's Easy Chair. See Easy Chair, The Editor's.

Editor's Study. See Study, The Editor's.

Edwin. "Romance of the Crossing." A village swain who wins back his beloved Angelina by stepping into the mud to let her by.

Ehrhardt, Captain Ernst von. *A Fearful Responsibility*. A dashing Austrian who courts Lily Mayhew to the distress of Professor Elmore. He may be the unknown Austrian officer who dances with Lily at a ball.

Elihu. *The Undiscovered Country*. A Shaker elder with whom Dr. Boynton often talks.

Elizabeth. *The Undiscovered Country*. A Shaker sister.

Ellett, Charles. "The Pursuit of the Piano." A New Hampshire youth who courts Phyllis Desmond.

Ellida. *Ragged Lady*. The maid in Italy of Mrs. Lander and Clementina Claxon.

Ellison, Mrs. Fanny. *Their Wedding Journey, A Chance Acquaintance.* Vivacious wife of Col. Richard Ellison; she lends Kitty Ellison her clothes and her sympathetic ear.

Ellison, Kitty. *Their Wedding Journey, A Chance Acquaintance.* A charming, unworldly, perceptive girl from upstate New York; in her impromptu trip from Niagara to Quebec and the Saguenay with her cousins Richard and Fanny Ellison, she meets, is courted by, and finally rejects the aloof Bostonian Miles Arbuton.

Ellison, Colonel Richard. *Their Wedding Journey, A Chance Acquaintance.* A Milwaukee businessman escorting his wife and cousin Kitty on a trip; he meets the Marches in Niagara Falls, travels to Quebec with them, and later watches uncomprehendingly the affair of Kitty and Miles Arbuton.

Elmore, Mrs. Celia. *A Fearful Responsibility.* Elmore's wife, who looks out for Lily Mayhew better than Elmore does.

Elmore, Owen. *A Fearful Responsibility.* A history professor from (and later president of) a college in upstate New York; he goes to do research in Venice and finds himself responsible for his much-courted charge Lily Mayhew.

Elroy. *The Kentons.* A young Tuskingum lawyer who marries Lottie Kenton.

Eltwin, Major. *Their Silver Wedding Journey.* An elderly, ailing businessman traveling unwillingly in Europe after having to leave his Ohio home.

Eltwin, Mrs. *Their Silver Wedding Journey.* The shy wife of Major Eltwin.

Emerance, Elihu. *The Vacation of the Kelwyns.* A firm-minded young man who courts and wins Parthenope Brook.

Enderby, Mary (Molly). *The Landlord at Lion's Head.* Bessie Lynde's friend who warns her about Jeff Durgin.

Enderby, Dr. "The Eidolons of Brooks Alford." Alford's doctor, who advises him to marry Mrs. Yarrow, thus banishing his apparitions.

Enderby, Rev. *The Son of Royal Langbrith.* An earnest minister who advises against exposing the sins of Royal Langbrith.

Enderby, Mrs. *The Son of Royal Langbrith.* The meddlesome, uncomprehending wife of Rev. Enderby.

Engine, Papa and Mother. "The Pony Engine and the Pacific Express." Anxious parents who try in vain to make their son behave.

Engine, Pony. "The Pony Engine and the Pacific Express." An ignorant little engine who leaves the home roundhouse against his parents' advice and races the Pacific Express all the way to the West Coast.

Englishman, Young. *Indian Summer.* An energetic youth who dances expertly with Imogene Graham and is contemptuous of Colville's dancing.

Englishwoman. *A Traveller from Altruria.* The young wife of a quarry worker.

Enraghty, Richard. *The Leatherwood God.* A respected citizen who joins Dylks's flock and is renamed St. Peter.

Erlcort, Fred. "The Rotational Tenants." A summer resident who stays on at his seaside cottage until Hallowe'en and is visited by spirits.

Erlcort, Frederick. "The Critical Bookstore." The idealistic, problem-ridden owner of the bookstore.

Erlcort, Margaret. "The Rotational Tenants." Fred Erlcort's wife, who shares his strange experience.

Erwin, Henshaw. *The Lady of the* Aroostook. Lydia Blood's English uncle, fascinated by American slang.

Erwin, Mrs. Josephine. *The Lady of the* Aroostook. Lydia Blood's paternal aunt, who introduces her to Venice and is disturbed at her dislike of it.

Essayist, Elderly. "EEC," Mr 17. A writer who discusses solecisms with a lady and his niece.

Étienne, Père. *The Quality of Mercy.* A parish priest in a French-Canadian village who can't understand Northwick's character or actions.

Etkins, Miss. *Their Silver Wedding Journey.* A shipboard flirt whom the Marches call the pivotal girl.

Eugenio. "EEC." An author and critic, a Howells persona. N 04: advises young writers. My 05: comments on the critics of Howells' fiction. Jl 05: discusses writing with the Easy Chair. Ag 05: eavesdrops on the conversations of unemployed fictional characters. Ja 06: studies the guests at a famous seaside resort. Ap 08: voyages on the Great Lakes.

Europeans. *A Foregone Conclusion,* "At the Sign of the Savage," *A*

Fearful Responsibility, The Lady of the Aroostook, *Indian Summer, Ragged Lady, Their Silver Wedding Journey, The Kentons, The Seen and the Unseen at Stratford-on-Avon,* "A Sleep and a Forgetting." Officers, soldiers, gondoliers, carriage drivers, couriers, porters, railway guards, hotel keepers, peasants, holiday makers, audiences, priests, churchgoers, diners, cure takers, in the background, or observed by the Marches (and others) or by the narrator.

Evans, Tom. *A Woman's Reason.* The Evanses' little boy.

Evans. *A Woman's Reason, The Minister's Charge.* Theater and book-review editor of *Saturday Afternoon;* later its editor, and friend of Lemuel Barker.

Evans, Mrs. *A Woman's Reason:* the editor's wife. *The Minister's Charge:* the editor's invalid wife.

Evarts, Mrs. "The Father." Mrs. Talbert's mother.

Everton. *A Woman's Reason.* A greedy old man who buys the Harkness house at auction and later complains that the auction was rigged; he proposes to Helen Harkness and is refused.

Ewbert, Rev. Clarence. "A Difficult Case." A minister who wears himself out on the atheist Ransom Hilbrook.

Ewbert, Emily. "A Difficult Case." Ewbert's wife, who fails to get him to drop Ransom Hilbrook.

Ewins. *Ragged Lady.* A young man who is attentive to Clementina Claxon on the ship and in Florence.

Ex-consul for Torcello. "EEC," D 10, Ja 11. One of the Easy Chair's separable selves, who discusses ship and future air travel with him.

Fairy, Christmas. "Christmas Every Day." An apparition who grants a little girl's wish for an eternal Christmas.

Falk. *The Son of Royal Langbrith.* James Langbrith's Harvard friend and conscience.

Fane. *Ragged Lady.* An insinuating hotel clerk, who courts Clementina Claxon, to her irritation.

Fanny. *No Love Lost.* A young American girl traveling in Italy.

Fanny. "Not a Love Story." A high-spirited girl who favors Arthur but marries the dull Job Green after Arthur fails to propose to her.

Farmer. "Buying a Horse." A wealthy fruit grower who sells Frank, a horse, to the narrator's friend.

Farmer. "The Pumpkin-Glory." The head of a large family who grows the two pumpkins that are the center of interest at Thanksgiving dinner.

Farmer. *Ragged Lady.* A back-country man who tells the Landers all about Clementina Claxon.

Farmer. *A Traveller from Altruria.* A poor New Englander who asks Homos questions.

Farrell, Mrs. Rosabel. *Mrs. Farrell.* A beautiful, willful, selfish widow, aged twenty-four, who boards at the Woodward farm, makes trouble among the men there, and later acts Juliet badly in Boston.

Father. "A Day's Pleasure." A man who claims the lost child at Frank's house.

Father. *No Love Lost.* The father of Fanny, with her in Italy.

Father. "Somebody's Mother." A passerby, who with his son and daughter tries to help a disreputable-looking old woman.

Faulkner, Douglas. *The Shadow of a Dream.* A wealthy, moody lawyer of Virginia background; friend of Basil March in their Midwestern young manhood; later married to Hermia Winter; dies of heart failure after long miseries over the recurring dream of her love for his best friend, Nevil.

Faulkner, Hermia Winter. *The Shadow of a Dream.* A Midwestern girl, extremely beautiful; wife and later widow of Douglas Faulkner, loves and loses Rev. James Nevil.

Faulkner, Mrs. *The Shadow of a Dream.* Douglas Faulkner's dignified widowed mother, who tells March about Faulkner's dream.

Felix, Uncle. "A Presentiment." Minver's uncle, a merchant, who during a trip has a presentiment that his wife will die.

Fenleigh, Lady. *The Lady of the* Aroostook. An English social leader in Venice; her style disgusts Lydia Blood.

Fenton, Lt. Robert, U. S. N. *A Woman's Reason.* Joshua Harkness's ward, in love with Helen Harkness; wins her after endless complications.

Ferris, Henry. *A Foregone Conclusion:* a painter, the American consul in Venice, who loves, loses, and finally wins Florida Vervain. *A Fearful Responsibility:* the former American consul in Venice.

Fiancée of Rev. James Nevil. *The Shadow of a Dream.* A Kansas girl
who breaks her engagement.

Filbert, General. "A Memory that Worked Overtime." A friend
whom Joe Minver meets on a Boston horsecar.

Fishermen, Italian. *A Foregone Conclusion.* Men that Ferris and his
party talk to during the disastrous excursion on the lagoon.

Fish man. "A Difficult Case." A man making deliveries who sends
neighbors to help Ransom Hilbrook.

Florindo. "EEC." A prosperous New Yorker, husband of Lindora. S
03: has many unsatisfactory summer vacations with Lindora.
O 14: tries to save money during their summer in a cottage. O
15: discusses society dinners with Lindora, who then gives a
foodless party. D 16: during an automobile trip he talks to
guests at a roadside hotel. Ja 17: he proposes state-run motor
hotels.

Flutterbybutterfly. "Butterflyflutterby and Flutterbybutterfly."
Princess of an imaginary kingdom, won by the Khan of Tartary.

Fogle, Mrs. *The Flight of Pony Baker.* The mother of a dead boy
whose ghost some other boys see.

Ford. *The Undiscovered Country.* A stern, awkward man of country
origin, living in Boston and doing literary hack work and
chemical experiments when he becomes involved with
Egeria Boynton; he eventually narries her and becomes rich
through chemical discoveries.

Foreman. "The Journeyman's Secret." The man who runs the print
shop.

Forsyth, Ambrose. "The Daughter of the Storage." A painter, father
of Charlotte Forsyth.

Forsyth, Charlotte. "The Daughter of the Storage." Called Tata as a
child. A child and later a young woman who during her
courtship has trouble making up her mind, but eventually
gets married in a storage warehouse.

Forsyth, Mrs. "The Daughter of the Storage." The mother of Charlotte.

Frances. *The Undiscovered Country.* A Shaker sister.

Frank. "Buying a Horse." A docile horse that finally satisfies the
friend of the narrator.

Frank. "A Day's Pleasure." The harassed young father of a family that tries to take an outing at the seashore.

Fred. *No Love Lost*. Brother of Fanny, with her in Italy.

Frederick. "A Perfect Goose." A young man whose beloved Clara fondly calls him a perfect goose.

Friend, A. "Life and Letters." A figure who appears to discuss topics with "I," the narrator. Jl 6, 13, 1895: discusses the influence of housekeeping and household effects on women. Ap 25, 1896: discusses the popular theater. My 9, 1896: discusses advertising.

Friend of Basil March. *Their Wedding Journey*. A Bostonian who, just after March's return, suggests that March looks run-down and should take a trip.

Friend of country storekeeper. *The World of Chance*. A visitor to New York whom Shelley Ray overhears commiserating with the storekeeper's financial problems.

Friend of the Easy Chair. "EEC." A convenient conversationalist and surrogate. S 07: discusses conscience with the Easy Chair. D 08: talks with him after return from Europe. Ja 09: talks with him after return from Boston. F 09: discusses New York's sublimity with him. F 10: eavesdrops on an elderly couple. Mr 10: tells the Easy Chair a story about an ex-convict. Ap 10: has overheard two girls discussing a gentleman caller. Jl 10: tells the Easy Chair about a couple he has seen in the park. S 10: discusses with him the idea that people always get what they want when they want it.

Friend of Eugenio. "EEC," Jl 06: a fellow vacationer at a summer resort.

Friend of the higher journalist. "Entertaining on Thirty-Five Hundred a Year." A New Yorker who discusses entertaining with that journalist.

Friend of the narrator. "Buying a Horse." A suburbanite who has endless trouble buying a suitable horse.

Friends, Two. "EEC," Ja 10. Men who discuss ideals of duty.

Frobisher, Mrs. *April Hopes*. A Portland lady, a friend of Daniel Mavering, whose friendliness with her and her friend Miss Wrayne gets him into trouble with his jealous fiancée, Alice Pasmer.

Frost, Mrs. *Dr. Breen's Practice.* Boarder at the seaside hotel who en-
    courages Dr. Breen.

Fulkerson. *A Hazard of New Fortunes:* a Western man, a dynamic
    journalist and syndicator, business manager of *Every Other
    Week,* who encourages March to leave Boston to work for the
    magazine; an easygoing man who dislikes controversy. *Their
    Silver Wedding Journey:* still business manager, and now part-
    owner of *Every Other Week,* he encourages March to take a
    vacation.

Future, The paulo-post. "ES," Mr 1892. An imaginary figure who,
    helped by the Christmas Boy, strips the vacated Editor's
    Study of all traces of literary realism.

Gage, Julia. *An Open-Eyed Conspiracy.* A beautiful, willful girl,
    helped socially at Saratoga Springs by the Marches, and
    courted by Kendricks.

Gage. *An Open-Eyed Conspiracy.* Rich, miserly, disagreeable father
    of Julia Gage.

Gaites, Hamilton. "The Pursuit of the Piano." A young lawyer who
    pursues a crated piano to its distant New England destina-
    tion and winds up with a wife.

Gambler, the losing. "A Tale Untold." A steamboat hustler in league
    with the confidence man who fleeces Stephen West.

Gardener. "His Apparition." A country-house servant who is
    amazed to see Hewson jump out a window at dawn.

Garley, Judge. *The Son of Royal Langbrith.* An elderly Saxmills law-
    yer, much perplexed by the problem of dealing with Lang-
    brith's legacy of evil.

Garley, Mrs. *The Son of Royal Langbrith.* Wife of the Judge.

Garofalo, Prof. *An Imperative Duty.* Dr. Olney's Florentine friend, at
    whose home Olney first meets Rhoda Aldgate.

Gates. *Annie Kilburn, The Quality of Mercy.* A prosperous grocer in
    Hatboro', who defends the Rev. Peck.

Gaylord, Squire Flavius Josephus. *A Modern Instance.* A sardonic
    Maine lawyer, father of Marcia Gaylord Hubbard; opposes
    her marriage to Bartley Hubbard and drives himself into a
    stroke getting his revenge on Bartley.

Gaylord, Miranda. *A Modern Instance.* The meek, retiring wife of Squire Gaylord.

Gearson, George. "Editha." A realistic but weak young man who allows his love for Editha Bascom to sweep him into the war hysteria that she shares; he enlists and is killed.

Gearson, Mrs. "Editha." George Gearson's widowed mother, who hates war and attacks Editha for getting George killed.

Gentleman, elderly. *The Seen and the Unseen at Stratford-on-Avon.* An Englishman who puzzles the narrator by waiting on a lady and a young man rather than being waited on.

Gentleman, Martian. "EEC," Ap 20. A visitor to Earth.

Gentleman, Old. A traveling motorist. "EEC," D 16: chats with Florindo and Lindora about roads. Ja 17: chats with them about state-run hotels for motorists.

Gentleman, Young. "Incident." A train traveler who observes a fellow passenger, a house painter, and his accidental death.

Gentlemen, Italian. *Indian Summer.* Guests of Mrs. Bowen who admire Imogene Graham.

Gerald, Abner L. "A Sleep and a Forgetting." An American in Italy who consults Dr. Lanfear about his amnesiac daughter Nannie.

Gerald, Nannie. "A Sleep and a Forgetting." A lovely girl whose memory was destroyed when she saw her mother killed; she is cured and married by Dr. Lanfear.

Germans. *Their Wedding Journey.* Habitués of a Rochester café whose good-natured table-pounding the Marches enjoy.

Gerrish, Emmeline. *Annie Kilburn, The Quality of Mercy.* A childhood friend of Annie Kilburn in Hatboro', Mass.; later the smug wife of a rich merchant there.

Gerrish, William. *Annie Kilburn, The Quality of Mercy.* A narrow, self-made, rich drygoods merchant in Hatboro', Mass.; in *Annie Kilburn* he tries to remove Rev. Peck from his church because of his radical social views.

Giffen. *A Woman's Reason.* A passenger who is shipwrecked with Lt. Fenton on a Pacific atoll and dies just before rescue arrives.

Gilbert, Mrs. Susan. *Mrs. Farrell.* A middle-aged, semi-invalid boarder at the Woodward farm; sister-in-law of William Gilbert and pained observer of his affair with Mrs. Farrell.

Gilbert, William. *Mrs. Farrell.* A self-possessed New York lawyer

who falls uncomfortably in love with Mrs. Farrell and quarrels over her with his friend Easton.

Gilbert. *Mrs. Farrell.* A Bostonian, husband of Susan Gilbert, who
agrees with her that Mrs. Farrell can't act.

Gilky, Angelica. "The Independent Candidate." The wife of Moro
Gilky.

Gilky, Moro. "The Independent Candidate." A weak, incompetent
man whom George Berson persuades to stump for him.

Gillespie, David. *The Leatherwood God.* A dour, elderly widower,
brother of Nancy Dylks and enemy of Dylks.

Gillespie, Jane. *The Leatherwood God.* David Gillespie's beautiful,
headstrong daughter who is infatuated with Dylks but later
marries Jim Redfield.

Gillespie, Nancy. *The Leatherwood God.* See Nancy Billings.

Girl. "A Case of Metaphantasmia." A young lady who resembles a
girl Newton had once known.

Girl. "EEC," Je 10. A dinner guest who argues with the stopgap
guest about marriage and divorce.

Girl, Fifteen-year-old. *The Landlord at Lion's Head.* A country girl
with whom the adult Jeff Durgin flirts at Lion's Head.

Girl, Irish. "Scene." A suicide whose drowned corpse the contributor sees brought up from the (Charles) river in a
wagon.

Girl, Little. "Christmas Every Day." A child who wants eternal
Christmas but regrets it when she has it.

Girl, Little. "Christmas Every Day." The child to whom the story is
told.

Girl, Little. "The Critical Bookstore." A child who wants to buy an
egg beater at a bookstore that was a hardware store.

Girl, Little. "The Pony Engine and the Pacific Express." The child to
whom the story is told, with her brother.

Girl, Little. "The Pumpkin-Glory." The child to whom the story is
told, with her brother.

Girl, Little. "Turkeys Turning the Tables." The child whose father
tells her the story.

Girl, Little. "Turkeys Turning the Tables." A child who in the story
is seized by angry turkeys.

Girl, Young. "Reading for a Grandfather." An opinionated girl who
quizzes her grandfather about his literary tastes so that she
can pick out a Christmas book for him.

Girl, Young black. "Somebody's Mother." A passerby who thinks that the unknown old woman may be somebody's mother.

Girls. "How I Lost a Wife." Guests at the house of Mary and Charley; they think "I" is dead, but are horrified to have him fall at their feet half-naked.

Girls, Two, in Central Park. "EEC," Ap 10. Young women whom the Easy Chair's friend overhears discussing a man.

Gleason, Miss. *Dr. Breen's Practice*. A feminist boarder at the resort hotel.

Glendenning, Rev. "A Pair of Patient Lovers." An Episcopalian minister who marries Miss Bentley after a long and tortuous engagement.

Godolphin, Lancelot. *The Story of a Play*. The handsome, talented, and conceited actor-manager who puts on Maxwell's play.

Graham, Imogene. *Indian Summer*. A beautiful, energetic girl of twenty whose streak of self-sacrificing idealism leads her to believe that she loves Colville.

Graham, Mrs. *Indian Summer*. The brisk, sensible nother of Imogene Graham.

Granddaughter. "EEC," F 16. A young lady who scolds her grandfather for not being on the bench where he was supposed to wait for her.

Granddaughter. *A Parting and a Meeting*. A little girl who accompanies her grandmother, Chloe Mason Dickerman, to the latter's poignant meeting with her old lover Roger Burton at a Shaker village.

Grandfather. "EEC," F 16. The elder sage who chats in Central Park with a friend.

Grandfather. "Reading for a Grandfather." An elderly man whose literary tastes are much too old-fashioned for his granddaughter.

Grandmother. "The Pumpkin-Glory." A farm woman who makes delicious pies out of the good little pumpkin.

Grassi, Captain Count. *The Landlord at Lion's Head*. Called Gigi. A penniless, charming Italian aristocrat who marries the wealthy Genevieve Vostrand, is later separated from her, and then dies.

Gray, Mrs. *Through the Eye of the Needle*. Mrs. Strange's mother, who accompanies her and Homos to Altruria and becomes completely at home there.

Grayson. *The Story of a Play.* A New York theater manager who puts on Maxwell's play.

Great-niece, The novelist's. "EEC," Ag 06. A young lady who discusses his fiction with him.

Green, Mrs. Grosvenor. *A Hazard of New Fortunes.* A rich New Yorker from whom the Marches rent a flat stuffed with "Jamescracks."

Green, Margaret. "The Critical Bookstore." A painter, Erlcort's friend and later his fiancée.

Greengrocer. *The Seen and the Unseen at Stratford-on-Avon.* A woman who says that Shakespeare helps support Stratford.

Gregory, Frank. *Ragged Lady.* A severe man who as a college student works in a country hotel and falls in love with Clementina Claxon; later he becomes a minister and wins her love after she becomes a widow.

Grier, Amanda. *The Minister's Charge.* Statira Dudley's vulgar, possessive friend, and Lemuel Barker's enemy.

Griswell, Elder. *New Leaf Mills.* A farmer for whom Bellam works.

Grove, Elder. *The Leatherwood God.* A Leatherwood preacher pushed into the shadow by Dylks.

Guard, Subway. "The Critical Bookstore." The recipient of a book that Erlcort finds unbearably boring.

Guest, A stopgap. "EEC," Je 10. A dinner guest who believes that marriage, not divorce, should be made more difficult.

Guests at Lindora's party. "EEC," O 15. Summer people who are mystified by her failure to provide refreshments.

Guests at a resort hotel. "EEC," O 12. Motorists, largely, who discuss the social effects of the automobile.

Guests at Thanksgiving Dinner at the Makelys. *Through the Eye of the Needle.* Wealthy New Yorkers who discuss America and its mores with Homos.

Guide, French-Canadian. *A Chance Acquaintance.* A *habitant* who takes the American tourists around Tadoussac (See Bird).

Gypsy woman. *The Vacation of the Kelwyns.* An itinerant who tells Parthenope Brook's fortune.

Habitants and their wives. *The Quality of Mercy.* French-Canadian settlers along the Saguenay with whom Northwick stays during his flight.

Halleck, Anna. *A Modern Instance.* The middle Halleck daughter.

Halleck, Ben. *A Modern Instance.* Crippled son of Ezra B. Halleck; acquaintance of Bartley Hubbard at college; hopelessly and neurotically in love with Marcia Hubbard; becomes a backwoods minister at the end.

Halleck, Ezra B. *A Modern Instance.* A rich, old-fashioned, kindly leather merchant.

Halleck, Mrs. *A Modern Instance.* The simple, retiring wife of Ezra B. Halleck.

Halleck, Louisa. *A Modern Instance.* The oldest Halleck daughter.

Halleck, Olive. *A Modern Instance.* The youngest Halleck daughter; a vivacious, perceptive girl; confidante of Ben Halleck.

Halson. A New York clubman. "Braybridge's Offer": tells part of the story. "A Case of Metaphantasmia": brings Newson to the club to tell his story.

Hanks brothers. *The World of Chance.* Joe, Martin, and a third unnamed. The purchasers of the Midland *Echo.* Their reduction of the editorial staff results in the firing of Shelley Ray and his going to New York.

Hapford, Mrs. "A Romance of Real Life." The keeper of the lodging house where Julia Tinker lives.

Harkness, Helen. *A Woman's Reason.* Joshua Harkness's pretty young daughter, who has to make her way alone after her father's death and after many vicissitudes winds up marrying Lt. Fenton.

Harkness, Joshua. *A Woman's Reason.* A once well-to-do Bostonian in the India trade, father of Helen Harkness and guardian of Lt. Robert Fenton; his sudden death precipitates the action of the novel.

Harley, Mrs. *The Story of a Play.* A smouldering-eyed actress who plays under the name of Yolande Havisham and for a time has the feminine lead in Maxwell's play.

Harmon, Mrs. *The Minister's Charge.* The landlady of a Boston hotel who gives Lemuel Barker a job.

Harris. *The Undiscovered Country.* The brutish landlord of the Elm Tavern, Vardley, Mass., who tries to keep the Boyntons prisoner and is punished by a supernatural visitation.

Harry. "The Independent Candidate." A girl, a friend of Merla Cuffins.

Harvard, John. *The Seen and the Unseen at Stratford-on-Avon.* A spirit which, the spirit of Shakespeare says, appeared at Harvard's house and talked to Shakespeare and Bacon.

Hasker. "The Independent Candidate." A Beauville storekeeper, who chats with Wat Larrie.

Hatch. *The Undiscovered Country*. A Boston medium, friend of Dr. Boynton.

Hathaway. *A Modern Instance*. A lawyer in Tecumseh, Indiana, who helps Squire Gaylord in court.

Havisham, Yolande. *The Story of a Play*. The stage name of Mrs. Harley, which see.

Hawberk, Hope. *The Son of Royal Langbrith*. The beautiful, noble daughter of Lorenzo Hawberk; she cares for him until his death, and later marries James Langbrith.

Hawberk, Lorenzo. *The Son of Royal Langbrith*. A brilliant inventor tricked out of his rights and profits by Royal Langbrith; he turns to opium and degenerates into a pathetic wreck.

Hawkins, Archy (Old). *The Flight of Pony Baker*. A friend of Pony in the Boy's Town.

Hazelwood, Miss. "Braybridge's Offer." A young lady who may or may not have subtly attracted Braybridge to herself.

"He." "EEC," Je 08. A man who discusses organized charity with "She."

"He." "Life and Letters," Ja 23, 1897. The narrator's friend, who observes a bread line with a child.

Headwaiter. "The Pursuit of the Piano." A college student at a summer hotel who gives Gaites information.

Headwaiter. *A Traveller from Altruria*. A resort-hotel employee to whom Homos is friendly, thus scandalizing everyone.

Hefmyer, Rosy. *New Leaf Mills*. The Powells' hired girl, young, pretty, and naïve; she almost lets herself be seduced by Captain Bickler.

Hefmyer, Mrs. *New Leaf Mills*. Rosy's drunken old mother, who takes her away from the Powells.

Hernshaw, Rosalie. "His Apparition." A beautiful, rich, painfully frank girl who causes trouble for and then marries Arthur Hewson.

Hernshaw. "His Apparition." The very rich and affable father of Rosalie Hernshaw.

Hero and heroine, unemployed fictional. "EEC," Ag 05. Characters whom Eugenio overhears complaining about their lot.

Hesketh. "A Circle in the Water." The elderly, well-meaning, weak husband of Mrs. Hesketh.

Hesketh, Mrs. "A Circle in the Water." The now elderly sister of Tedham's long-dead wife, and the anxious protector of Tedham's daughter while he is in jail.

Hewitt, Mrs. *A Woman's Reason.* A landlady who rents Helen Harkness an attic room.

Hewson, Arthur. "His Apparition." A man who sees a ghost which, in a roundabout way, gains him a wife.

Hibbard. *A Woman's Reason.* The lawyer in charge of the Harkness estate.

Hibbard, Miss. *The Lady of the* Aroostook. See Mrs. Dunham.

Hicks. *The Lady of the* Aroostook. A young alcoholic who is sent to sea on the *Aroostook* for his health; he gets drunk, falls in, and is rescued by Staniford, who finds the whole episode disgusting; later he laments his doom and leaves the ship.

Hilary, Eben. *The Quality of Mercy:* the choleric but good-hearted president of the Ponkwasset Mills. *The Story of a Play:* Louise Maxwell's father.

Hilary, Mrs. *The Quality of Mercy* and *The Story of a Play.* The socialite mother of Louise Hilary, whose affair with Brice Maxwell she deeply disapproves of although she resigns herself to accepting him as Louise's husband.

Hilary, Louise. *The Quality of Mercy.* Eben Hilary's beautiful daughter, who later marries Brice Maxwell.

Hilary, Matt. *The Quality of Mercy.* Eben Hilary's son, aged twenty-eight; an earnest radical who helps the Northwick girls and falls in love with Sue.

Hilbrook, Ransom. "A Difficult Case." An elderly man in the town of Hilbrook who wears out Rev. Ewbert arguing over the question of immortality, relapses into apathy, and dies.

Hingston, Benny. *The Leatherwood God.* The small son of Peter Hingston.

Hingston, Peter. *The Leatherwood God.* A rich, respected miller who becomes St. Paul in Dylks's flock.

Hinkle, George W. *Ragged Lady.* An Ohio inventor whom Clementina Claxon meets in Florence, eventually marries, and is widowed by.

Hinkle. *Ragged Lady.* George Hinkle's father.

Holly, Miss Custis. *Letters Home.* An energetic Southern journalist,

working for the New York *Signal,* who rooms with and helps
Frances Dennam.

Homos, Aristides. *A Traveller from Altruria,* "Letters of an Altrurian
Traveller," "The Selling and the Giving of Dinners," *Through
the Eye of the Needle.* An emissary from the Altrurian Commonwealth who visits the United States twice (staying in a
resort hotel in New England, and in New York) to explain Altruria to Americans; eventually he marries Mrs. Strange and
takes her back to Altruria.

Homos, Mrs. Eveleth Strange. *Through the Eye of the Needle.* An attractive, young, wealthy New York widow who meets and is
fascinated by Homos, falls in love, reluctantly gives up her
riches, marries him, goes with him to Altruria, and to her
surprise enjoys it greatly.

Horn, Mrs. *A Hazard of New Fortunes.* A New York socialite and
hostess, friend of the Marches, reluctant and distressed hostess to the Dryfoos girls.

Hoskins. *A Fearful Responsibility.* A sculptor, American consul in
Venice after Ferris, friend of the Elmores.

Host and hostess. "EEC," Je 10. New Yorkers at whose table many
people discuss marriage and divorce.

Housekeeper, American. "EEC," Ag 12. One of the group discussing the American *mañana* spirit.

"Howadji, The." "EEC," Mr 09: the traveling friend of "we," the
Easy Chair. Ap 09: discusses New York rents with "we," the
Easy Chair.

Hubbard, Bartley. *A Modern Instance:* a talented, coolly arrogant,
self-seeking, self-indulgent young man; an orphan who is
sent to a freshwater college (where he meets Ben Halleck), becomes editor of the Equity *Free Press,* meets and indolently
courts Marcia Gaylord, loses his job when he gets into a fight
with the weakling Bird, marries Marcia when she follows
him, works on Boston newspapers, leaves Marcia after the
last of many spats, tries and (thanks to Squire Gaylord's intervention) fails to divorce Marcia in Indiana, flees to Ari-
zona, and is shot there by a man irritated by his newspaper
squibs; Howells' greatest negative lesson in the importance
of character training. *The Rise of Silas Lapham:* he interviews
Silas Lapham for his Boston paper.

Hubbard, Flavia. *A Modern Instance.* The child of Bartley and Marcia Hubbard.

Hubbard, Marcia Gaylord. *A Modern Instance:* a beautiful, passionate, hot-tempered, possessive girl and woman; insists on having Bartley Hubbard against her father's advice, and after several years finds herself a deserted wife and mother, later a widow. *The Rise of Silas Lapham:* is just married and happy at the success of Bartley's interview of Lapham.

Hughes, David. *The World of Chance.* An elderly altruist who began his career at Brook Farm; the author of a utopian manuscript; friend of Shelley Ray.

Hughes, Peace. *The World of Chance.* David Hughes' beautiful younger daughter, who rejects Shelley Ray's proposal.

Humphrey, Brother. *The Undiscovered Country.* A Shaker involved with the Boyntons.

Hubbell. *A Hazard of New Fortunes.* The representative of March's insurance company who comes to tell him that he has been kicked upstairs.

Husbands, Two. "EEC," Je 10. They join in the discussion of marriage and divorce.

"I." "The Amigo." The narrator, who observes the "amigo."

"I." "Bobby. Study of a Boy." The narrator, who discusses Bobby.

"I." "By Horse-Car to Boston," "Doorstep Acquaintance," "Flitting," "Mrs. Johnson," "A Pedestrian Tour." For some time an observant resident of "Charlesbridge" (Cambridge, Mass.); narrator and central character of these sketches.

"I." "A Day's Pleasure," "A Romance of Real Life." The narrator and commentator.

"I." "EEC," F 20. The narrator, a friend of the editor, who recalls a servant in San Remo.

"I." "An Experience." The narrator, a publisher's editor who sees a man die in his office.

"I." "The Fulfilment of the Pact." The narrator and a listener; a clubman.

"I." "How I Lost a Wife." A bachelor who explains how he lost his beloved when a dog tore up his clothes.

"I." "The Independent Candidate." The narrator, who interrupts the story to argue about it with Old Smith and to tell an anecdote about Stub.

"I." "The Journeyman's Secret." A journeyman printer who tells about a mysterious colleague in his shop.

"I." "Life and Letters." The narrator, and usually the protagonist. Jl 6 & 13, 1895: with a friend, discusses the influence of household effects on women. D 14, 1895: is visited by the Christmas Muse. Ap 25, 1896: discusses popular theatre with a friend. My 9, 1896: discusses advertising with a friend. D 19, 1896: must write a Christmas essay. Ja 23, 1897: is visited by a friend who observed a bread line. D 25, 1897: with the Christmas Muse and Santa Claus, argues that Santa is a superstition.

"I." "The Lost Child." The observer of the street scene involving a lost German child.

"I." "An Old-Time Love Affair." A modern reader who speculates about the fifteenth-century love affair of John Paston and Margery Brews.

"I." *The Seen and the Unseen at Stratford-on-Avon.* A seventy-six-year-old author visiting Stratford who becomes involved with the spirits of Shakespeare and Bacon.

"I." "A Summer Sunday in a Country Village." The narrator, who experiences and analyzes a sleepy summer day.

"I." *Their Wedding Journey.* The commenting and acting narrator.

Icelander. *A Woman's Reason.* A member of the *Meteor* crew who deserts Lt. Fenton and Giffen.

Idealist, The. "EEC," S 14. A man who describes to the Easy Chair the good treatment of a wrongly convicted man.

Immigrant, German. "The Lost Child." A passer-by who helps the lost German child.

Irishman. *A Woman's Reason.* The husband of Margaret; killed in an explosion.

Jailers. *The Minister's Charge.* Boston men who look after Lemuel Barker after he is arrested.

James. *The Quality of Mercy.* Northwick's servant.

Jane. *Dr. Breen's Practice.* Bella Maynard's nurse.

Jane. *The Minister's Charge*. Miss Vane's cook during Lemuel Barker's employment there.

Janitor. *A Hazard of New Fortunes*. A pleasant man who charms the Marches during their house hunting in New York.

Janitor. *A Hazard of New Fortunes*. An irritating man encountered by the Marches during their house hunting in New York.

Janitress. *The Coast of Bohemia*. A worker in the ladies' parlor in a New York railroad station.

Jasper. *The Vacation of the Kelwyns*. A Shaker elder whom the Kelwyns meet.

Jeffers. "The Critical Bookstore." A department-store floorwalker who tells Erlcort the store gives no refunds on books.

Jenner, Dr. *New Leaf Mills*. A doctor who treats Overdale and others.

Jenness, Captain. *The Lady of the* Aroostook. The crusty, kindly captain of the *Aroostook*.

Jenny. "Mrs. Johnson." An Irish cook who leaves the narrator's employ.

Jerry. *The Minister's Charge*. The surly porter at Lemuel Barker's hotel, who enjoys getting Lemuel in trouble.

Jerry. *The Rise of Silas Lapham*. Lapham's carriage driver.

Jessup, Rev. *A Modern Instance*. An elderly small-town minister who marries Bartley and Marcia Hubbard.

Jeweler. "A Tale Untold." A Pittsburgh man who tells Stephen West that his watch guard is worthless.

Jewett, Miss. *Mrs. Farrell*. A boarder at the Woodward farm.

Jim. "The Pearl." A black cabin boy who is accused of stealing a scarf pin.

Joe. *April Hopes*. The Maverings' Portuguese cook.

John and his wife. "EEC," F 10. Elderly villagers who yearn to ride in a parlor car.

Johns, Susie. *The Son of Royal Langbrith*. A vivacious Saxmills girl who has a brief affair with Falk.

Johnson, Hippolyto Thucydides. "Mrs. Johnson." Mrs. Johnson's irritating son.

Johnson, Naomi. "Mrs. Johnson." The saucy small daughter of Mrs. Johnson.

Johnson, Mrs. "Mrs. Johnson." The narrator's excellent cook.

Jombateeste. *The Landlord at Lion's Head*. The wiry French-Canadian handyman at Lion's Head.

Jones, John. *A Woman's Reason.* The assumed name of a Portuguese sailor who deserts Lt. Fenton in a crisis.

Joseph. *The Undiscovered Country.* A Shaker elder with whom Dr. Boynton confers.

Journalist, Girl. "The Critical Bookstore." An interviewer of Erlcort, for the Sunday supplement.

Journalist, The higher. "Entertaining on Thirty-Five Hundred a Year." A writer who discusses entertaining with his friend.

Journeyman, Tailor's. "The Return to Favor." The buyer of Mr. Morrison's tailoring business.

Judge. *The Minister's Charge.* A Bostonian who tries Lemuel Barker's case and frees him.

Kane. *The World of Chance.* A philosophical writer, Shelley Ray's elderly friend and mentor.

Katy. *The Coast of Bohemia.* The Burtons' servant.

Kelwyn, Carl. *The Vacation of the Kelwyns.* The Kelwyns' small younger son.

Kelwyn, Carry. *The Vacation of the Kelwyns.* Kelwyn's wife, an earnest New Englander.

Kelwyn, Elmer. *The Vacation of the Kelwyns.* A professor who rents a summer house and has an eventful vacation.

Kelwyn, Francis. *The Vacation of the Kelwyns.* The Kelwyns' small older son.

Kenby, R. M. *Their Silver Wedding Journey.* An American tourist in Europe, an acquaintance of the Marches, who later marries his fellow tourist Mrs. Adding.

Kendricks. *A Hazard of New Fortunes:* a young contributor to *Every Other Week. An Open-Eyed Conspiracy:* now twenty-seven, a writer and New York socialite whom the Marches introduce to his future bride in Saratoga.

Kenton, Mrs. Bessie. "At the Sign of the Savage." Col. Edward Kenton's wife, who waits for him at their Viennese hotel.

Kenton, Boyne. *The Kentons.* The adolescent son of Rufus Kenton who imagines that he is in love with the young Queen of Holland.

Kenton, Colonel Edward. "At the Sign of the Savage." (No relation to Judge Rufus Kenton.) An American tourist who gets lost in Vienna.

Kenton, Ellen. *The Kentons.* Rufus Kenton's intense, oversensitive older daughter, who marries Rev. Hugh Breckon.

Kenton, Lottie. *The Kentons.* Pert, pretty, and popular sixteen-year-old daughter of Rufus Kenton.

Kenton, Mary. *The Kentons.* The wife of Richard Kenton.

Kenton, Richard. *The Kentons.* Rufus Kenton's oldest son, a lawyer who cowhides Bittridge.

Kenton, Judge (or Colonel) Rufus. *The Kentons.* A retired lawyer, judge, and Civil-War officer, driven from his Ohio home to New York and to Europe by the bounder Bittridge.

Kenton, Sarah. *The Kentons.* The long-suffering wife of Rufus Kenton.

Khan, Prince of Tartary. "Butterflyflutterby and Flutterbybutterfly." A handsome prince who marries Flutterbybutterfly; brother of Khant.

Khant, Princess of Tartary. "Butterflyflutterby and Flutterbybutterfly." A beautiful princess who marries Butterflyflutterby; sister of Khan.

Kilburn, Annie. *Annie Kilburn.* An earnest, well-to-do, thirty-one-year-old woman who comes back to Hatboro', Mass., to serve mankind, and who after many troubles marries Dr. Morrell.

Kilburn, Rufus. *Annie Kilburn.* A wealthy retired American, living in Rome, who dies when his daughter Annie is thirty-one.

Kimball. *A Woman's Reason.* A policeman and later a Custom-House officer.

Kingsbury, Clara. *A Woman's Reason.* A wealthy Boston socialite, a friend of Helen Harkness who helps Helen when the latter thinks Lt. Fenton is dead. (See Clara Kingsbury Atherton.)

Kinney. *A Modern Instance.* The garrulous logging-camp cook whose ideas Bartley Hubbard steals for an article.

Kite, Alvin. *The Vacation of the Kelwyns.* An oafish New England hill farmer who works for the Kelwyns.

Kite, Arthur. *The Vacation of the Kelwyns.* The Kites' small son.

Kite, Mrs. *The Vacation of the Kelwyns.* Kite's wife, whose wretched cooking drives the Kelwyns to distraction.

Kitty. *A Modern Instance.* A girl who works at the Equity *Free Press.*

Laban, Brother. *The Undiscovered Country.* A young Shaker.

Lacy, Dr. *The Landlord at Lion's Head.* The Lyndes' doctor, who sends Alan Lynde off for a cure near Lion's Head.

Ladies, American. "EEC," Ag 12. People who join in the discussion of the American *mañana* habit.

Ladies, Hymn-singing. "A Tale Untold." Steamboat passengers who are duped by the confidence man.

Ladies, Old. "The Pursuit of the Piano." Small-town gossips on whom Gaites eavesdrops for information about Miss Desmond.

Ladies, Two. "EEC," Je 10. Dinner guests who discuss marriage and divorce.

Ladies, Two Boston. *A Chance Acquaintance.* Friends, one mature and one young, of Miles Arbuton, who loses Kitty Ellison because he talks to them and ignores her.

Landini, Miss. *The Lady of the* Aroostook. A young Venetian woman whose behavior upsets Lydia Blood.

Lady. *Annie Kilburn.* An elderly American in Rome who tells Annie that she should stay there.

Lady. "EEC," N 12. A woman who discusses spiritualistic phenomena.

Lady. "EEC," Mr 17. A woman who discusses solecisms.

Lady. *The Shadow of a Dream.* An old friend of Basil March in Ohio with whom he discusses the Faulkners.

Lady, Lively. "EEC," Ja 18. A character in modern Christmas fiction.

Lady, Martian. "EEC," Ap 20. The wife of a Martian visitor.

Lady, Old Genoese. "Doorstep Acquaintance." One of the narrator's congenial visitors.

Lady, A rich young. *The World of Chance.* A New Yorker temporarily interested in Shelley Ray during his social phase.

Lady, Young. "Incident." The companion of the young gentleman.

Lancaster, Freddy. *The Landlord at Lion's Head.* A Harvard student who gets Jeff Durgin invited to a fashionable tea.

Lander, Albert Gallatin. *Ragged Lady.* A retired and retiring self-made rich man.

Lander, Mrs. *Ragged Lady.* Lander's wife and later his widow, a selfish, rich old woman who makes Clementina Claxon her protegée.

Lanfear, Dr. Matthew. "A Sleep and a Forgetting." A young doctor from New York interested in psychopathology, who treats and marries Nannie Gerald in Italy.

Langbourne, Stephen M. "The Magic of a Voice." A New York businessman who carries on with Barbara Simpson a love affair based on miscomprehension.

Langbrith, Amelia. *The Son of Royal Langbrith*. The weak widow of Royal Langbrith, doting mother of James Langbrith, reluctant beloved of Dr. Anther.

Langbrith, James. *The Son of Royal Langbrith*. The conceited but essentially decent son of Royal Langbrith.

Langbrith, John. *The Son of Royal Langbrith*. The grumpy, dyspeptic brother of Royal Langbrith who runs the family's mill and tells James Langbrith the truth about his father Royal.

Langbrith, Royal. *The Son of Royal Langbrith*. An evil New England mill owner who controls the action of the novel, although he dies many years before it begins.

Langham, Lily. *April Hopes*. A friend of Alice Pasmer who dances with Dan Mavering and thus almost causes a quarrel.

Lapham, Irene. *The Rise of Silas Lapham*. The Laphams' beautiful younger daughter who everyone, including herself, mistakenly believes is loved by Tom Corey.

Lapham, Penelope. *The Rise of Silas Lapham*. The Laphams' older daughter, who charms and marries Tom Corey.

Lapham, Persis. *The Rise of Silas Lapham*. Lapham's schoolteacher, who marries him and reluctantly participates in his success in Boston.

Lapham, Silas. *The Rise of Silas Lapham*. A self-made paint millionaire whose pride leads him into catastrophe but whose decency proves greater than his greed.

Larker, Elfred. "The Independent Candidate." A young printer in Doan's shop and a friend of Wat Larrie.

Larrabee brothers. *New Leaf Mills*. Country millers who sell out to Owen Powell.

Larrie, Walter (Wat). "The Independent Candidate." A young lawyer who stumps for George Berson.

Last of the Romanticists, The. "ES," D 90. A picturesque writer who defends his type of fiction to the Study.

Latham, Miss Maria. *The Lady of the* Aroostook. Lydia Blood's maternal aunt.

Latham, Deacon. *The Lady of the* Aroostook. Lydia Blood's rustic grandfather, who accompanies her to Boston.

Lawyer. *A Traveller from Altruria.* A guest at a summer hotel who discusses America with Homos and others.

Leader of the rescue party. *A Woman's Reason.* The rescuer of Lt. Fenton from an atoll.

Leffers, Mr. and Mrs. *Their Silver Wedding Journey.* Newlywed shipmates of the Marches.

Leighton, Alma. *A Hazard of New Fortunes.* A pretty, independent art student who is involved with Angus Beaton but finally drops him.

Leighton, Mrs. *A Hazard of New Fortunes.* A widow who comes to New York to support herself and her daughter Alma by taking boarders.

Lena. *Through the Eye of the Needle.* The Makelys' New York cook who would like to live in Altruria.

Leonard, Jim. *The Flight of Pony Baker.* A sly boy in the Boy's Town who eggs Pony on into trouble.

Leonard, Mr. and Mrs. *Their Wedding Journey.* Friends of the Marches with whom the latter stay near New York.

Leonard, Mrs. *The Flight of Pony Baker.* Jim Leonard's widowed mother.

Lereo. "The Emigrant of 1802." The narrator.

Le Roy, Mrs. *The Undiscovered Country.* The Boyntons' landlady, also a medium and an organizer of "see-aunts."

"Letters." "Life and Letters." Ag 10, 1895: a man who discusses women cyclists at a Long Island summer resort. Ag 24, 1895: a man who discusses with "Life" summer hotels and separation in marriage.

Libby. *Dr. Breen's Practice.* A handsome, wealthy young man who courts and marries Dr. Grace Breen.

Lida. *The Coast of Bohemia.* A New York art student and friend of the heroine.

Lieutenant, Italian. "A Sleep and a Forgetting." A dashing youth who follows Nannie Gerald after she absentmindedly bows to him, until Dr. Lanfear tells him of Nannie's amnesia.

"Life." "Life and Letters." Ag 10, 1895: a man who discusses women cyclists with "Letters" at a Long Island summer resort. Ag 24, 1895: a man who discusses with "Letters" summer hotels and separation in marriage.

Lili. *Their Silver Wedding Journey.* The charming waitress at the Posthof Café near Carlsbad.

Lilly. *The Son of Royal Langbrith.* A sculptor who does a bas-relief of Royal Langbrith.

Lindau, Berthold. *A Hazard of New Fortunes.* An elderly German refugee (of 1848), an old friend of Basil March in the West, who lost a hand in the Civil War; the cause of friction between March and Dryfoos; dies after a beating by the police.

Lindora. A middle-aged society woman, wife of Florindo. "EEC," S 03, O 14, O 15, D 16, Ja 17: see Florindo.

Lindsley, Elder. *A Parting and a Meeting.* A Shaker elder who influences Roger Burton's decision to be a Shaker.

Linen peddler. *The Vacation of the Kelwyns.* An itinerant who sells wares to the Kelwyns at their summer house.

Lioncourt, Lord. *Ragged Lady.* An Englishman who is attentive to Clementina Claxon on the ship and in Florence.

Listeners. "EEC," N 12. People who discuss spiritualistic phenomena.

Lizzy. "The Independent Candidate." Wat Larrie's cousin, who introduces him to Merla Cuffins.

Loafer. "A Tale Untold." A Pittsburgh man who picks up the worthless watch guard discarded by Stephen West.

Loafers. *The Undiscovered Country.* Yokels who jeer at the Boyntons in the Vardley Tavern.

Lohndiener, A. "At The Sign of the Savage." A Viennese servant who assists Edward Kenton.

Lorry. "The Pearl." Stephen West's cousin; a young man who sketches.

Lovers, A pair of thirtyish. "EEC," Jl and S 10. New Yorkers observed in the park by the Easy Chair's friend.

Lucrexia, Gianetta. "The Bag of Gold." The daughter of Madonna Lucrexia.

Lucrexia, Madonna. "The Bag of Gold." An Italian innkeeper involved with three ruffians and their stolen gold.

Lucy, Cousin. "A Day's Pleasure." A young lady who accompanies the family on their excursion.

Ludlow, Walter. *The Coast of Bohemia.* A young impressionist painter trained in France and working in New York; he sees Cornelia Saunders in Pymantoning, Ohio, attracts her to his class in New York, and eventually marries her.

Lumen, Prof. *A Traveller from Altruria.* A conceited professor of political economy who lectures Homos.

Lumley. *A Woman's Reason*. The proprietor of a jeweler's shop who sells Helen Harkness's vases to Trufitt.

Lynde, Alan. *The Landlord at Lion's Head*. Bessie's handsome, alcoholic brother, who tangles with Jeff Durgin and is lucky to escape alive.

Lynde, Bessie. *The Landlord at Lion's Head*. A bored Boston society girl of twenty-five who flirts with Jeff Durgin, to her sorrow.

Lynde, Louisa. *The Landlord at Lion's Head*. Bessie's and Alan's doddering aunt and guardian.

M., Mr. and Mrs. "The Emigrant of 1802." A New England farm couple who make a new home in "New Connecticut" near a lake (Erie).

McAllister, Mrs. *A Modern Instance*. The wife of a Montreal friend of Willett; she flirts twice with Bartley Hubbard, the second time enraging Marcia.

McAllister, Miss. *A Modern Instance*. The daughter of Mrs. McAllister.

Macroyd, Julia. *Fennel and Rue*. A self-centered society girl.

Maddalena. *Ragged Lady*. A Florentine maid, friendly to Clementina Claxon.

Madman. "A Sleep and a Forgetting." An unattended lunatic who attacks Mr. Gerald in an Italian village.

Magistrate, Dutch. *The Kentons*. An official at the Hague who lets Boyne Kenton go after Breckon explains why Boyne ran out to speak to the Dutch queens.

Makely, Dorothea. *A Traveller from Altruria, Through the Eye of the Needle*. Called Dolly or Peggy. A superficial society woman, wife of Richard Makely; she explains social life and its demands to Homos.

Makely, Richard. *A Traveller from Altruria, Through the Eye of the Needle*. A wealthy businessman, Homos' friend and host; more worldly and tolerant than his wife.

Man, aged eighty-five. "EEC," Ap 14. A traveler with whom the Easy Chair identifies.

Man, aged fifty-eight. "EEC," Ap 14. A traveler with whom the Easy Chair identifies.

Man, Circus. *The Flight of Pony Baker*. A worker in a circus that visits the Boy's Town; he teases Pony Baker cruelly.

Man, Old. "The Day of Their Wedding." A passenger on the train to Saratoga who talks to Althea Brown.

Man, Old Black. *The World of Chance*. A begging performer on the ferry which Shelley Ray takes from New Jersey to Manhattan.

Man, Provision. *The Story of a Play*. A New York grocer who supplies information to Mrs. Maxwell and Mrs. Hilary.

Man, Young. "EEC," F 16. The escort of the granddaughter.

Man, Young. "EEC," Ja 18. A character in modern Christmas fiction who visits the Easy Chair.

Man, Young. *No Love Lost*. Bertha's suitor in Europe.

Man, Young. *The Seen and the Unseen at Stratford-on-Avon*. The companion of an older woman; observed by the narrator and his friends.

Man, Young. *The World of Chance*. A thief whom Ray and Kane see trying to steal a suitcase, thus causing Ray and Kane to meet.

Manager, Warehouse. "The Daughter of the Storage." The manager of the warehouse patronized by the main characters.

Mandel, Mrs. *A Hazard of New Fortunes*. A genteel widow hired by Fulkerson to civilize the Dryfooses.

Mandeville, T. J. *The Leatherwood God*. An Eastern scholar who comes to Leatherwood to ask about the Dylks cult years after Dylks's death.

Manton. *The Quality of Mercy*. A detective hired by the Ponkwasset Mills to track down Northwick.

Manufacturer, Retired. *A Traveller from Altruria*. A perceptive man who joins in the discussions with Homos and others at the resort hotel.

Manufacturers, Paint. *The Rise of Silas Lapham*. Young West Virginians whose cheap paint ruins Lapham.

March, Basil. Howells' major embodiment of the decent, hardworking, socially concerned, sometimes baffled or faulty middle-class American. *Their Wedding Journey*: a former Westerner, now working in Boston; on his honeymoon to Niagara and Quebec with his bride, Isabel, to whom he was briefly engaged in Europe. "Niagara Revisited": a Boston businessman retracing, with his wife and two children, parts of his wedding journey, twelve years later. "A Circle in the Water": the narrator, for some years a Boston insurance agent, who becomes entangled again with Tedham, his criminal former business associate. "A Pair of Patient Lovers": the narrator, who repeats with his wife Isabel their honeymoon trip down the St. Lawrence, and becomes involved in the interminable courtship of two young people. *The Shadow of a Dream:* the narrator, still in Boston, who becomes involved, to his great distress, in the obsessions of his old friend Faulkner and their repercussions on Faulkner's wife and best friend. *A Hazard of New Fortunes:* a reflective middle-aged man, demoted by his insurance company, who moves to New York, becomes editor of *Every Other Week,* and sees firsthand, on many levels, the qualities of modern life and employment in a metropolis. *An Open-Eyed Conspiracy:* the narrator, now fifty-two and part owner of *Every Other Week,* who vacations with his wife in Saratoga Springs and helps along Kendricks' courtship of Julia Gage. *Their Silver Wedding Journey:* a tired editor of fifty-eight, who takes Isabel on a sabbatical from *Every Other Week,* crosses the Atlantic on an elegant ship, takes the cure at Carlsbad, tours Germany, and helps along Burnamy's courtship.

March, Bella. "Niagara Revisited": March's small daughter. *A Hazard of New Fortunes:* a fourteen-year-old, reluctant to leave Boston for New York. (See also Daughter of Basil and Isabel March.)

March, Isabel. Howells' major embodiment of the good breeding, moral earnestness, and occasional stuffiness of Boston upper-middle-class womanhood. *Their Wedding Journey:* Basil March's twenty-seven-year-old bride. "Niagara Revisited": now the mother of two young children. "A Circle in the Water": a matron who reluctantly helps Tedham recover his daughter. "A Pair of Patient Lovers": the tireless pusher of the courtship. *The Shadow of a Dream:* a concerned observer of the distressing affair of Faulkner, Hermia, and Nevil. *A Hazard of New Fortunes:* a middle-aged woman, now less resilient, who moves reluctantly to New York and has trouble backing Basil in his quarrel with Dryfoos over Lindau. *An Open-Eyed Conspiracy:* an energetic matchmaker again. *Their*

Silver Wedding Journey: a woman approaching old age, she finds travel tiring but matchmaking still enjoyable.

March, Tom. The Marches' son. "Niagara Revisited": a small boy who enjoys train travel. *A Hazard of New Fortunes:* a sixteen-year-old who leaves Boston reluctantly but soon finds New York absorbing. *Their Silver Wedding Journey:* the capable assistant editor, now in his mid-twenties, of *Every Other Week,* who runs it while his parents are in Europe.

Margaret. *A Woman's Reason.* The Harknesses' loyal cook.

Maria. "EEC," F 20. An elderly widow, a servant in Italy, discussed by the Easy Chair's friend.

Marilla. *A Modern Instance.* One of the girls working at the Equity *Free Press.*

Markham. *The Quality of Mercy.* A Canadian businessman who gives Northwick the idea of investing his stolen money up the Saguenay.

Martelli, Lorenzo. "The Bag of Gold." A young Italian lawyer who cleverly gets Madonna Lucrexia off in court.

Marven, Mrs. *The Landlord at Lion's Head.* A woman boarder at Lion's Head whose patronizing manner so infuriates Jeff Durgin and his mother that Mrs. Durgin throws her out.

Marvin, Colonel. *Annie Kilburn.* A Hatboro' businessman.

Mary. "How I Lost a Wife." The narrator's beloved, lost along with his clothes.

Mason, Chloe. *A Parting and a Meeting.* See Dickerman, Chloe Mason.

Mason, David. *The Leatherwood God.* A sick child healed by Dylks.

Mason. *The Lady of the Aroostook.* The second mate on the ship; an admirer of Lydia Blood.

Mate, second. "A Tale Untold." A riverboat man who throws the confidence men off.

Mavering, Daniel. *April Hopes.* An agreeable, easygoing young Harvard graduate, suitor of the umbrageous Alice Pasmer.

Mavering, Elbridge G. *April Hopes* The father of Dan Mavering; a wealthy New England manufacturer and Harvard graduate.

Mavering, Eunice. *April Hopes.* The older sister of Daniel Mavering.

Mavering, Minnie. *April Hopes.* The younger sister of Daniel Mavering.

Mavering, Mrs. *April Hopes.* The invalid wife of Elbridge Mavering; possessive mother of Daniel Mavering.

Maxwell, Brice. *The Quality of Mercy:* a shabby-genteel reporter and would-be dramatist who courts Louise Hilary. *The Story of a Play:* a young dramatist, married to Louise Hilary; his play finally is a success.

Maxwell, Louise Hilary. *The Story of a Play.* The pretty wife of Brice Maxwell, jealous, and often confused by the theater world. (See also Hilary, Louise.)

Maxwell, Mrs. *The Quality of Mercy.* A genteel Boston boarding-house keeper, the mother of Brice Maxwell.

May, Aunt. *No Love Lost.* Fanny's aunt, with her in Italy.

Maybough, Charmian. *The Coast of Bohemia.* A very wealthy young art student, a New Yorker, much more interested in casual Bohemianism than serious art; Cornelia Saunders' confidante.

Maybough, Mrs. *The Coast of Bohemia.* Charmian's widowed stepmother who commissions Walter Ludlow's portrait of Charmian.

Mayhew, Lily. *A Fearful Responsibility.* A beautiful American girl, daughter of friends of the Elmores; she visits the latter in Italy and causes them many worries.

Maynard, Bella. *Dr. Breen's Practice.* Mrs. Maynard's small daughter.

Maynard, Louise. *Dr. Breen's Practice.* A peevish invalid, friend and patient of Dr. Breen.

Maynard. *Dr. Breen's Practice.* A Wyoming cattleman, the long-suffering husband of Louise Maynard.

Mayquait, Mrs. *The World of Chance.* Mrs. Chapley's old friend, who befriends Ray in New York.

Maze, Elaine W. "The Pursuit of the Piano." A Kent Harbor summer resident who helps Gaites pursue the errant piano.

Melford. "A Case of Metaphantasmia." Newton's former Harvard roommate who has a recurrent nightmare.

Melissa, Aunt. "A Day's Pleasure." A helpful member of the family's bungled outing.

Meredith, Mrs. Caroline. *An Imperative Duty.* The silly, nervous, widowed aunt of Rhoda Aldgate; she tells Rhoda that the girl is part black and then dies of an overdose of a sleeping draught.

Meredith. *An Imperative Duty*. Mrs. Caroline Meredith's deceased
husband; he adopted her orphaned niece, Rhoda Aldgate,
and took the girl to live in Italy.

Meredith. *The Minister's Charge*. Charles Bellingham's friend, who
helps test Barker's reading skill.

Merrifield, Mr. and Mrs. *The Undiscovered Country*. Members of Dr.
Boynton's séance in Boston.

Merritt, Mrs. *Dr. Breen's Practice*. A guest at the summer hotel.

Mevison, Arthur. *Miss Bellard's Inspiration*. A painter, an old friend
of Archibald Crombie's bachelor days; the sight of Mevison's
unhappy marriage nearly destroys Miss Bellard's desire for
marriage.

Mevison, Clarice. *Miss Bellard's Inspiration*. The passionately jealous
wife of Arthur Mevison.

Miller. *New Leaf Mills*. A Pennsylvania German who takes over from
Overdale after the latter's accident.

Miller, Mrs. Secretary. *April Hopes*. A Washington hostess of Dan
Mavering and Julia Anderson.

Millon, Corporal Jim. *The Rise of Silas Lapham*. A friend of Lapham's
old Vermont days who is killed during a Civil War battle
while warning Lapham about a rebel sharpshooter.

Millon, Molly. *The Rise of Silas Lapham*. Jim Millon's disreputable
widow, whom Lapham feels obliged to help.

Milrace, Jake. *The Flight of Pony Baker*. A boy and a friend of Pony in
the Boy's Town.

Milray. *Ragged Lady*. A shrewd ex-politician, nearly blind, who employs and befriends Clementina Claxon.

Milray, Mrs. *Ragged Lady*. Milray's gay, scheming wife, who alter-
nately helps and bothers Clementina.

Milray, Miss. *Ragged Lady*. The brilliant, worldly maiden sister of
Milray, a socialite in Florence, and an adviser of Clementina
Claxon.

Minister. *The Day of Their Wedding*. A Saratoga Springs man who
marries Lorenzo Weaver and Althea Brown.

Minister. "Though One Rose from the Dead." The preacher of Marion Alderling's funeral sermon.

Minister. *A Traveller from Altruria*. A thoughtful man who discusses
America with Homos and others at the summer hotel, and
can't believe that Altruria is here on earth.

Minver, Joe. "A Memory that Worked Overtime." Minver's brother, a painter who loses a picture on a horse-car.

Minver, Mrs. "A Memory that Worked Overtime." Once Joe Minver's fiancée, now his wife.

Minver, Richard. "A Presentiment." Minver's father.

Minver, Mrs. "A Presentiment." Minver's mother.

Minver. "The Angel of the Lord," "Braybridge's Offer," "A Case of Metaphantasmia," "The Chick of the Easter Egg," "The Eidolons of Brooks Alford," "The Fulfilment of the Pact," "A Memory that Worked Overtime," "A Presentiment," "Though One Rose from the Dead." A painter, a club member, an often-skeptical listener to the stories told at the club; narrator of "A Presentiment"; he tells Wanhope about Marion Alderling's death in "Though One Rose from the Dead."

Mistress of Royal Langbrith. *The Son of Royal Langbrith.* A Bostonian now living in Paris, with their daughter.

Montgomery, Mrs. *The Coast of Bohemia.* Cornelia Saunders' friendly, slapdash landlady in New York.

Moors, Lady. *Through the Eye of the Needle.* The Thralls' married daughter.

Moors, Lord. *Through the Eye of the Needle.* The Thralls' Oxford-educated son-in-law, on his honeymoon trip around the world on the Thralls' yacht.

Morland, William. *The Landlord at Lion's Head.* A Harvard student in whose rooms Jeff Durgin meets Bessie Lynde.

Morrell, Dr. James. *Annie Kilburn:* an easygoing Hatboro' doctor, aged thirty-six, who eventually marries Annie Kilburn. *The Quality of Mercy:* Putney's tolerant friend.

Morrell, Mrs. *The Quality of Mercy.* The former Annie Kilburn, now the kindly wife of Dr. Morrell.

Morrison, Andy. *A Modern Instance.* Hannah's younger brother, a hostler, and the great admirer of Bartley Hubbard in Equity.

Morrison, Hannah. *A Modern Instance.* Bartley Hubbard's *bête noire;* his pretty, flirtatious employee who causes his downfall in Equity; later a prostitute in Boston whose accidental meeting with Marcia leads to the Hubbards' final quarrel.

Morrison. *A Modern Instance.* A drunken shoemaker in Equity, and father of Andy and Hannah; his squabble with Bartley over Hannah is disastrous to Bartley.

Morrison, Mrs. *A Modern Instance*. Andy and Hannah Morrison's mother.

Morrison. "The Return to Favor." A tailor who is much liked for his work but disliked for his slowness.

Mortimer. *A Woman's Reason*. A Boston auctioneer who sells the Harkness house and later signs a paid confession that the auction was dishonest.

Morton, Rev. *Indian Summer*. A young American who courts Imogene Graham.

Mother, Fanny's. "Not a Love Story." A coarse, sarcastic woman.

Mother, of greedy little girl. "Christmas Every Day."

"Mother-Bird, The." A woman sailing to Europe to join her daughters and always talking about them.

Mulbridge, Dr. *Dr. Breen's Practice*. A harshly forceful man who falls in love with Dr. Grace Breen.

Mulbridge, Mrs. *Dr. Breen's Practice*. The doctor's mother, with whom he lives.

Munger, Jim. *Annie Kilburn*. Mrs. Munger's son, a Harvard student.

Munger, Mrs. *Annie Kilburn, The Quality of Mercy*. A redoubtable social leader in South Hatboro'.

Munt, John. *April Hopes*. A middle-aged Harvard classmate of Elbridge Mavering.

Muse, The Christmas. "Life and Letters." December 14, 1895: a cyclist who visits the narrator. December 19, 1896: helps the narrator write his Christmas essay. December 25, 1897: brings Santa Claus to visit the narrator.

Muse of poetry. "EEC," Jl 12. An apparition who discusses the differences between poetry and prose with the Easy Chair.

Muse, The poet's. "EEC," Jl 07. An apparition who joins in the discussion of age.

Nash, Mrs. *A Modern Instance*. A Boston landlady with whom the Hubbards room in their first months in Boston.

Nathaniel. *The Vacation of the Kelwyns*. A Shaker elder.

Native. "The Rotational Tenants." A seaside resident who tells the Erlcorts that the light in the cottage was a lantern left by a boy.

Native, Philosophic. "EEC," O 14. A New England countryman who

discusses the economics of direct buying with Florindo and
Lindora.

Neighbor. "Buying a Horse." A helper in the attempts of the narrator's friend to buy Frank, a horse.

Nephew of Mrs. Harmon. *The Minister's Charge.* A young man who
runs the furnace at Barker's hotel.

Nephew of the papa. "Butterflyflutterby and Flutterbybutterfly."
The small boy to whom the story is told.

Nevil, Rev. James. *The Shadow of a Dream.* An Episcopalian minister
in a Midwestern city; Douglas Faulkner's closest friend, who
wants to marry Hermia, Faulkner's widow, but is accidentally killed.

Newell. *A Woman's Reason.* A Boston gentleman, a bidder for the
Harkness house.

Newton. "A Case of Metaphantasmia": a man who once had an odd
experience in a Pullman car. "The Chick of the Easter Egg":
the narrator of the story about his family's Easter experience.

Newton, Elbridge. *The Quality of Mercy.* Northwick's rustic coach-
man and handyman.

Newton, Ellen. *The Quality of Mercy.* Newton's wife; their child
dies.

Nichols, Miss. *The Vacation of the Kelwyns.* The bright teacher of a
country school visited by the Kelwyns.

Niece. "EEC," Je 14. A young woman who discusses charities with
her uncle.

Niece of elderly essayist. "EEC," Mr 17. A young lady who discusses solecisms with him.

Niece of the papa. "Butterflyflutterby and Flutterbybutterfly." The
little girl to whom the story is told.

Nina. *A Foregone Conclusion.* The Vervains' servant.

Norah. *The Son of Royal Langbrith.* The Langbriths' Irish maid,
whose cooking James looks down on.

Norey, Dr. "Though One Rose from the Dead." A country doctor
who attends Marion Alderling in her fatal illness.

Northwick, (Miss) Adeline. *Annie Kilburn:* Northwick's older
daughter. *The Quality of Mercy:* an old maid, she dies of nervous prostration.

Northwick, J. Milton. *Annie Kilburn:* a wealthy businessman living
near South Hatboro', Mass. *The Quality of Mercy:* the secre-

tary of a large company who embezzles its money, flees secretly to Canada, and dies while returning voluntarily.

Northwick, Suzette (Sue). *Annie Kilburn, The Quality of Mercy.* Northwick's beautiful, proud younger daughter who eventually marries Matt Hilary.

Novelist. "EEC," S 11. A writer who discusses Havelock Ellis with the Easy Chair.

Novelist, The old. "EEC," O 08. A writer who discusses English and American life with the young novelist.

Novelist, The Veteran. "EEC," Ag 06. A writer who discusses his fiction with his great-niece.

Novelist, A young. "The Critical Bookstore." A writer who comes to the store to see if his bestseller is stocked there.

Novelist, The young. "EEC," O 08. A writer who discusses English and American life with the old novelist.

Nuns. *Their Wedding Journey, A Chance Acquaintance.* Residents of Quebec whom the Marches and Kitty Ellison observe and talk to.

Observer, The veteran. "EEC," Jl 08. An old man who discusses critics with the Easy Chair.

Octogenarians, Older and younger. "EEC," Ap 19. Men who discuss postwar life.

Officer, Unknown Austrian. *A Fearful Responsibility.* A masked officer who dances with Lily Mayhew at a ball.

Officers, Austrian. *A Fearful Responsibility.* Gallant young men who court Lily Mayhew in Venice.

Officers, Custom. *A Foregone Conclusion.* Austrians who make difficulties for Ferris and his party on the lagoon.

Officials, Court. "Butterflyflutterby and Flutterbybutterfly." Distraught courtiers who can't tell the sex of the Khan and the Khant of Tartary.

Oiseau. *The Quality of Mercy.* See Bird.

Olney, Dr. Edward. *An Imperative Duty.* A young nerve specialist just returned to the United States from Italy. Mrs. Meredith tells him the secret of her niece's partially black ancestry, and he eventually marries the girl.

Organ-grinder, Italian. *The Vacation of the Kelwyns.* An itinerant
who entertains the Kelwyns at their summer house.

Organ-grinders. "Doorstep Acquaintance." Friends of the narrator.

Ormond, Jenny. "The Angel of the Lord": Ormond's wife, who fears
his premonitions. "The Fulfilment of the Pact": a widow to
whom Ormond returns after death, as he said he would.

Ormond. "The Angel of the Lord": a middle-aged man who has premonitions of death. "The Fulfilment of the Pact": a spirit
who returns after death to talk to his wife.

Orson, Rev. James B. *Ragged Lady.* Mrs. Lander's elderly relative
who comes out to Venice after her death.

Otterson, Mr. and Mrs. *Their Silver Wedding Journey.* Cheerful Americans whom March meets at Carlsbad.

Overdale, Jacob. *New Leaf Mills.* A surly gristmiller who believes
that the Powells' purchase of the mills will somehow cause
his death.

Overdale, Mrs. *New Leaf Mills.* Overdale's slatternly wife.

Overdale boy. *New Leaf Mills.* A child whom Owen Powell saves
from drowning.

Padrona, The. "EEC," F 20. The narrator's Italian landlady.

Painter, House. "Incident." A train traveler who falls off and is run
over and killed.

Painter, Lady. "Editha." A woman who consoles Editha after Mrs.
Gearson attacks her.

Paolo. *Indian Summer.* The obliging servant at Theodore Colville's
pension in Florence.

Papa, A. "Butterflyflutterby and Flutterbybutterfly," "Christmas
Every Day," "The Pony Engine and the Pacific Express,"
"The Pumpkin-Glory," "Turkeys Turning the Tables." The
narrator of these stories to demanding young audiences.

Parishioner, A wealthy. *The Shadow of a Dream.* One of Nevil's congregation; he takes Nevil to Europe, and later indirectly
causes his death by detaining him on a train.

Paronsina, The. "Tonelli's Marriage." Cenarotti's pretty granddaughter.

Pasmer, Alice. *April Hopes.* A lovely, over-serious, easily insulted
girl, who after many vicissitudes marries Dan Mavering.

Pasmer, Mrs. Jenny Hibbins. *April Hopes.* A class-conscious Bostonian, Pasmer's wife, mother of Alice, whose affair with Dan Mavering she pushes after assuring herself of the Maverings' status.

Pasmer. *April Hopes.* A Bostonian; a silent, indifferent man of leisure.

Passenger, Steamboat. "A Presentiment." A woman rescued from a fire by Uncle Felix.

Passengers, Ship. "The Amigo": they suffer his mischief. "The Mother-Bird": they snub and deride her. *Their Wedding Journey:* some discuss the accident that happens late at night; others flirt.

Paston, John. "An Old-Time Love Affair." A fifteenth-century Englishman who loves Margery Brews.

Pat. *April Hopes.* The Maverings' stableman, a friend of Dan.

Paulo-post-future. See Future, paulo-post.

Pazzelli, Colonel. *The Lady of the* Aroostook. A Venetian *cavaliere* who irritates Lydia Blood.

Pearsall, Miss. "The Critical Bookstore." Erlcort's assistant in the bookstore.

Pearson, Zenas. *A Woman's Reason.* A photographer for whom Helen Harkness colors some photographs.

Peasants. "A Sleep and a Forgetting." Guides for the Americans around the San Remo area.

Peck, Idella. *Annie Kilburn.* Peck's small daughter whom Annie adores and finally gets to keep.

Peck, Rev. Julius W. *Annie Kilburn.* A severe, idealistic Orthodox minister in Hatboro', Mass., who is killed by a train.

Perham, Mrs. *The Undiscovered Country.* A catty fellow boarder of Ford's.

Perkins, Ezra. *The Lady of the* Aroostook. A stage driver who takes Lydia Blood and her grandfather to the train.

Pessimist, American. "EEC," Ag 12. A man who discusses the American *mañana* habit.

Pettrell, Miss. *The Story of a Play.* The actress who makes Maxwell's play a success at last.

Philip. *No Love Lost.* A young American who went off to the Civil War loving Bertha and thinking she loved him.

Phillips. "The Boarders." A divinity student who leaves Mrs. Betterson's boardinghouse because he can't stand the food.

Phillips. *The Undiscovered Country*. A Boston man of leisure, a friend of Ford.

Philosopher. "EEC," S 11. A savant who discusses Havelock Ellis with the Easy Chair.

Philosopher, Eighteenth-century Chinese. "EEC," D 12. An apparition called up by the Easy Chair to discuss the recent election.

Pinney, Hattie. *The Quality of Mercy*. Admiring wife of the reporter.

Pinney, Lorenzo. *The Quality of Mercy*. Brash reporter for the Boston *Events*, who traces Northwick.

Plaisdell. *The Coast of Bohemia*. The decorator of Mrs. Maybough's fashionable apartment.

Planter, A Southern. "A Tale Untold." A steamboat passenger who makes Stephen West brood about slavery.

Plumpton, Jim and Rita. *The Kentons*. Friends of Lottie and Boyne Kenton in New York.

Poet. "EEC," J1 07. A writer who discusses age with the Easy Chair.

Poet. "EEC," S 11. A writer who discusses Havelock Ellis with the Easy Chair.

Poets, Two old. "EEC," Mr 07. Two investigators who conclude that the magazines aren't overlooking any good poems.

Pogis. *The Kentons*. A very young Englishman infatuated with Lottie Kenton on the ship to Europe.

Policeman. *The Minister's Charge*. A Bostonian who captures and later helps Lemuel Barker.

Policeman. "Somebody's Mother." A city man who questions the mysterious old woman.

Policeman. *The World of Chance*. A New Yorker who arrests a man for shoplifting.

Policemen. "EEC," A 20. Men on duty at the Martians' lecture who arrest them after a riot starts.

Polly, Cousin. *New Leaf Mills*. Rosy Hefmyer's cousin, a cook on a canalboat.

Ponto. "How I Lost a Wife." A big dog who rips up the narrator's clothes while he is swimming.

Porter. *A Traveller from Altruria*. A hotel servant whom Homos helps, thus upsetting Twelvemough.

Porter, Pullman. "A Case of Metaphantasmia." A worker who joins the communal nightmare.

Porter, Pullman. *The Day of Their Wedding*. A worker whose air of superiority upsets the two young Shakers.

Powell, Ann. *New Leaf Mills.* Owen Powell's wife, who dislikes frontier living.

Powell, David. *New Leaf Mills.* One of Owen Powell's brothers.

Powell, Felix. *New Leaf Mills.* A prosperous, tubercular merchant whose plan to establish a utopian community with his brother is ended by death.

Powell, Grandmother and Grandfather. *New Leaf Mills.* Parents of David, Felix, Jim, and Owen Powell.

Powell, Jessamy. *New Leaf Mills.* The childless wife of Felix Powell.

Powell, Jim. *New Leaf Mills.* One of Owen Powell's brothers.

Powell, Owen. *New Leaf Mills.* A gentle man (based on Howells' father), an abolitionist and a Swedenborgian, who tries but fails to start a utopian community with his brothers in rural Ohio.

Powell, Richard. *New Leaf Mills.* Owen's oldest son, who helps the family by going to work.

Powell, Sally. *New Leaf Mills.* Jim Powell's wife.

Powell children. *New Leaf Mills.* Boys and girls who greatly enjoy frontier living.

Presence, The nondescript. "EEC," N 16. An apparition called up to discuss republics with the Easy Chair.

Printer, A silent. "The Journeyman's Secret." A miserly, hard-working man who is bullied by the other printers until he tells them that he is saving to help his family.

Printers. "The Journeyman's Secret." Men in a village shop who bully the silent printer because of his unsociability.

Prittiman, Miss. "The Critical Bookstore." A department store sales girl who recommends a bestseller to Erlcort.

Professor, A. "Buying a Horse." A knowing man who gives the narrator's friend advice.

Psychosociologist, The. "EEC," D 15. The spokesman for the old-fashioned Christmas characters.

Pumpkin-seed, Bad. "The Pumpkin-Glory." An ambitious seed who tries to grow like a morning glory.

Pumpkin-seed, Good. "The Pumpkin-Glory." A proper seed who grows into a handsome pumpkin and becomes delicious pies.

Putney, Mrs. Ellen. *Annie Kilburn, The Quality of Mercy.* Annie Kilburn's childhood friend in Hatboro' who marries the lawyer Putney.

Putney, Ralph. *Annie Kilburn* and *The Quality of Mercy*. A brilliant, sardonic, alcoholic lawyer in Hatboro'; friend of Annie Kilburn and enemy of Gerrish and Mrs. Munger.

Putney, Winthrop. *Annie Kilburn*. Putney's little boy; the drunken father crippled him by dropping him downstairs.

Rainford, Lord. *A Woman's Reason*. A shy young Englishman whom Helen Harkness rejects twice.

Ralson, America. *Letters Home*. The temperamental and magnificent daughter of Mr. and Mrs. Ralson.

Ralson. *Letters Home*. The multimillionaire owner of the Cheese and Churn Trust, from Iowa, now living in New York with his family.

Ralson, Mrs. *Letters Home*. The inconspicuous wife of Ralson.

Rangely, Mrs. *The Coast of Bohemia*. A dinner guest at various parties.

Rasmith, Julia. *The Kentons*. A woman of thirty who pursues her minister, Breckon, on the boat to Europe.

Rasmith, Mrs. *The Kentons*. A wealthy New York widow who helps her daughter pursue Breckon.

Ray, Edward. *A Woman's Reason*. A quiet, wealthy Harvard graduate, fiancé and later husband of Marian Butler.

Ray, Percy Bysshe Shelley. *The Story of a Play:* a newspaper critic and author in Midland, a Midwestern town. *The World of Chance:* a fledgling author who comes to New York to try to get his first novel published.

Ray, S. *The World of Chance*. Pseudonym of Shelley Ray.

Reader, The. An invented companion for the Easy Chair. "EEC." My 04: goes to the opera with the Easy Chair. Ap 11, Jl 14: discusses autobiography, and American romance and realism, with the Easy Chair.

Reader, The satirical. "EEC." Ja 08. A man who discusses servants with an editor.

Readers, Volunteer. "The Critical Bookstore." People who help Erlcort select his stock.

Rebecca. *The Undiscovered Country*. A Shaker sister.

Redfield, Jim. *The Leatherwood God*. A hot-tempered but decent youth, leader of the Hounds (the anti-religious young men) in Leatherwood; law student with Squire Braile, leader of campaign against Dylks, successful suitor of Jane Gillespie.

Relatives, The farmer's. "The Pumpkin-Glory." People who come to the family's Thanksgiving celebration.

René. *The Vacation of the Kelwyns.* The Kites' French-Canadian hired man.

Reporter, Girl. *The World of Chance.* The energetic correspondent for a Southern newspaper.

Reporter, Young. "EEC," O 07. The Easy Chair's temporary persona; covers a steamship arrival.

Reverdy, Abel. *The Leatherwood God.* An uncouth young farmer.

Reverdy, Sally. *The Leatherwood God.* The slatternly, friendly wife of Abel.

Reviewer, The. "EEC," My 12, Je 12, Jl 12. A journalist who discusses with the Easy Chair capitalism, publishing, and the differences between poetry and prose.

Richling, Rev. *Ragged Lady.* Clementina Claxon's minister who approves her leaving the country to live with Mrs. Lander.

Richling, Mrs. *Ragged Lady.* The minister's wife, and friend of Clementina Claxon.

Ricker. An able, ethical newspaper editor in Boston. *A Modern Instance:* hires and later drops Bartley Hubbard. *The Quality of Mercy:* edits and prints Maxwell's story about Northwick's flight.

Rivers, Mrs. *The Lady of the Aroostook.* An American woman who sets her cap for Staniford in Messina.

Robert. *Through the Eye of the Needle.* A servant who adjusts well to Altrurian life.

Rock, Mrs. "His Apparition." Miss Hernshaw's ineffectual chaperone.

Rogers, Milton K. *The Rise of Silas Lapham.* Silas Lapham's ex-partner, whom Lapham edged out of the business and who slyly pursues his revenge.

Rogers. *A Woman's Reason.* One of Helen Harkness's creditors.

Rollins, Captain. *A Woman's Reason.* The captain of the ship on which Lt. Fenton is wrecked.

Rondinelli, Don Ippolito. *A Foregone Conclusion.* An unhappy, ineffectual Venetian priest who wants to go to America, falls in love with Florida Vervain, and eventually dies and is forgotten.

Root, Cornelia. *A Woman's Reason.* An art student who tries to help Helen Harkness find work.

Rose-Black. *The Lady of the* Aroostook: an English artist living in Venice. *A Fearful Responsibility:* the same, but insufferably arrogant, and courting Lily Mayhew.

Rueford, Mrs. "The Independent Candidate." Elfred Larker's landlady.

Rueford, Miss. "The Independent Candidate." The daughter of Mrs. Rueford and beloved of Elfred Larker.

Ruffians, Three. "The Bag of Gold." Thieves who entangle Madonna Lucrexia in their crimes.

Rulledge. A genial clubman. "The Angel of the Lord," "Braybridge's Offer," "A Case of Metaphantasmia," "The Chick of the Easter Egg," "The Eidolons of Brooks Alford," "The Fulfilment of the Pact," "A Presentiment": an appreciative listener. "Though One Rose from the Dead": insists that Wanhope go to see Alderling after the death of Mrs. Alderling.

Ryan, Captain. "A Tale Untold." A riverboat pilot who defends slavery.

S——, Ida. "A Tale of Love and Politics." The judge's beautiful daughter, who loves George Wentworth.

S——, Judge. "A Tale of Love and Politics." A New York State man who helps George Wentworth and finally accepts him as a son-in-law.

Sage, A. "EEC," S 17. With the Easy Chair he discusses ways of talking about the war.

Sage, An elder. "EEC," F 16. A man over eighty who talks in Central Park with a younger sage and is met there by his granddaughter.

Sage, Elderly. "EEC," Jl 15. An experienced writer who discusses books with the Easy Chair.

Sage, The. "EEC," N 15. An elderly man who with the Easy Chair discusses recent American fiction.

Sage, The younger. "EEC," F 16. A friend of the elder sage who discusses city life with him.

Sages, Elder and younger. "EEC," Jl 16. Two men just back from Southern resorts who discuss wintering out of New York.

Sages, Older and younger. "EEC," Ja 19. Two literary men who discuss the older sage's passion for happy endings.

Sailors. *The Lady of the* Aroostook. Americans who admire Lydia Blood and her singing.

St. John. "His Apparition." Rich and selfish owner of a Berkshire estate.

Saintsbury, Professor and Mrs. *April Hopes.* A Harvard professor and his wife, who help bring the Maverings and the Pasmers together.

Saleswomen. *The Day of Their Wedding.* Saratoga Springs women who help Althea Brown buy elegant new clothes.

Sallie. "A Day's Pleasure." Frank's wife, who has the sense to stay home from the family outing.

Sanderson. *The World of Chance.* Ray's co-worker and confidant on the Midland *Echo.*

Santa Claus. "Life and Letters," Dec. 25, 1897. A visitor with the Christmas Muse to the narrator.

Saranna. *The Vacation of the Kelwyns.* A Shaker sister.

Saunders, Cornelia. *The Coast of Bohemia.* The heroine; a talented, pretty young girl from Pymantoning, Ohio, who goes to art school in New York and marries Walter Ludlow.

Saunders. "The Boarders." Minervy Betterson's beau.

Saunders, Mrs. *The Coast of Bohemia.* Cornelia's widowed mother.

Saunders, Mrs. *The Quality of Mercy.* The wife of Northwick's tenant farmer.

Savor, Maria. *Annie Kilburn.* A poor woman who blames Annie for her invalid child's death after Annie sends it to the seashore.

Savor, William. *Annie Kilburn.* A Hatboro' worker who regrets his wife's bitterness toward Annie.

Sawyer, Lizzie. *A Modern Instance.* One of the girls in Bartley's newspaper office in Equity.

Scissors grinder. "Doorstep Acquaintance." One of the narrator's friendly visitors.

Scott, Mrs. *Dr. Breen's Practice.* A boarder at Jocelyn's resort hotel.

Self, Our other. "EEC," My 10, F 11. An alter ego of the Easy Chair; discusses with him (1) writers and books about smart society, and (2) E. C. Stedman.

Servants of the Thralls. *Through the Eye of the Needle.* Castaways in Altruria who refuse to work for their food.

Sewell, Alfred. *The Minister's Charge*. Sewell's young son.

Sewell, Rev. David. *The Minister's Charge:* A genteel, earnest Boston minister who becomes involved with Lemuel Barker and bungles the relationship, but eventually realizes his complicity in Barker's fate. *The Quality of Mercy:* attends Hilary's dinner. *The Rise of Silas Lapham:* Lapham meets him at the Coreys' dinner and later turns to him for advice about his daughters' quandary.

Sewell, Edith. *The Minister's Charge*. Sewell's young daughter.

Sewell, Mrs. The minister's wife. *The Minister's Charge:* disapproves of her husband's involvement with Barker. *The Rise of Silas Lapham:* attends the Coreys' dinner with Sewell.

Seymour. *The Rise of Silas Lapham*. An architect who beguiles the Laphams into making their Beacon Street house expensively elegant.

Seyton, Rev. *The Minister's Charge*. A friend of Charles Bellingham.

Shakers. *A Parting and a Meeting*. Earnest people whose example leads Roger Burton to become a Shaker.

Shakers. *The Undiscovered Country*. New Englanders whose life and rituals Dr. Boynton studies with great interest.

Shakespeare. *The Seen and the Unseen at Stratford-on-Avon*. A spirit who appears and talks at length with the narrator.

"She." "EEC," Je 08. A woman who discusses organized charity with "he."

Shirley, Miss. *Fennel and Rue*. A nervous young lady who writes a fake letter to Verrian and suffers from guilt; later the social director at Mrs. Westangle's house party who meets Verrian there.

Shoeman. *Ragged Lady*. A peddler who shows Clementina Claxon shoes that Frank Gregory later secretly buys for her.

Sibyl. *The Minister's Charge*. Miss Vane's pretty, umbrageous niece who causes Barker to lose his job at Miss Vane's.

Simmons, Dr. *A Woman's Reason*. A Navy doctor who treats Lt. Robert Fenton and intercedes for him with the Admiral.

Simpson, Barbara. "The Magic of a Voice." The object of Stephen Langbourne's confused admiration.

Simpson. *A Modern Instance*. An Equity hotel keeper who joins the opposition to Bartley Hubbard.

Simpson. *The Quality of Mercy*. Northwick's groom.

Simpson, Mr. and Mrs. *The World of Chance.* A machinist and his wife who rent an apartment to Mrs. Denton and Peace Hughes.

Sir, The Old. "The Rotational Tenants." The oldest of the natives and the owner of most of the seaside cottages.

Slave women. "A Tale Untold." Passengers on a steamboat whose presence makes Stephen West brood about slavery.

Sliprie. "The Independent Candidate." A slick politician who works both sides in the election.

Smith. "EEC," Mr 10. A Scotch ex-convict.

Smith, Old. "The Independent Candidate." A person who appears suddenly to argue about the story with the narrator "I."

Soldiers, Austrian. *A Foregone Conclusion.* A patrol which challenges the Ferris party in the lagoon at night.

Son, Farmer's. "The Pumpkin-Glory." A boy who makes the bad pumpkin into a jack-o-lantern.

Son, The man's. "Somebody's Mother." A passerby who tries to help the unknown old woman.

Southfield, Mrs. *The Son of Royal Langbrith.* Hope Hawberk's Langbrith-hating grandmother.

Spokesman for the crew of the *Little Sally. Through the Eye of the Needle.* A middle-aged Yankee who knows the harshness of a sailor's life and is glad to be in Altruria.

Stage, Mrs. *Fennel and Rue.* Mrs. Westangle's housekeeper, with whom Miss Shirley arranges house-party tricks.

Stainwell, Mrs. *April Hopes.* One of the chorus of critical ladies on the piazza at Campobello.

Staniford, James. *The Lady of the* Aroostook. An arrogant young Brahmin who despises and then loves Lydia Blood.

Stationmaster, Horsecar. "A Memory that Worked Overtime." A man who is unable to tell Joe Minver anything about a lost painting.

Stephson, Mrs. "A Difficult Case." A farmer's wife who nurses Ransom Hilbrook.

Stevenson, Mrs. *Mrs. Farrell.* A boarder at the Woodward farm.

Stoller. *Their Silver Wedding Journey.* A sour-natured Chicago tycoon, Burnamy's employer in Carlsbad.

Stoller, Misses. *Their Silver Wedding Journey.* Stoller's two raucous daughters, in Europe with him.

Storekeeper, Country. *The World of Chance.* A man in a New York hotel whom Ray overhears telling his friend about his bankruptcy.

Strange, Eveleth. *Through the Eye of the Needle.* See Homos, Eveleth Strange.

Strange, Peter Bellington. *Through the Eye of the Needle.* Mrs. Eveleth Strange's deceased husband, who left her three million dollars.

Stranger, The. "A Tale Untold." A handsome elderly confidence man who sells worthless jewelry.

Strawberry. "The Independent Candidate." The nickname of a printer in Doan's shop.

Strong, Miss. *A Modern Instance.* A music student who boards with Marcia Hubbard after Bartley leaves her.

Stub. "The Independent Candidate." A man in a story within the story whose open umbrella carried him away.

Student, Black divinity. *An Imperative Duty.* The visiting preacher in a black congregation that Rhoda Aldgate drops in on.

Student, Girl. *A Woman's Reason.* A girl who listens sympathetically to Helen Harkness's story and her advice to learn a useful vocation like a man.

Study, The Editor's. "ES." A persona of Howells in the department of the same name written by Howells in *Harper's Monthly,* Jan. 1886–Mar. 1892. D 1890: he watches a vision of authors and critics of future America. D 1891: he observes a similar vision of an Altrurian future. Mr 1892: in the last Study he observes ruefully the paulo-post-future and the Christmas Boy clearing all signs of literary realism out of the study.

Suffragist. "EEC," N 12. A woman who discusses spiritualistic phenomena with the Easy Chair.

Sullivan, Mrs. *A Woman's Reason.* A poor woman who expects to get some of the Harkness family furniture but doesn't.

Swan, Madeline. *The Minister's Charge.* An art student, a boarder at Barker's hotel, who marries Alonzo W. Berry.

Talbert, Cyrus. "The Father." The father of the title, the owner of the Plated-Ware Works in Eastridge, the benevolent despot of the village.

Talbert, Mrs. "The Father." Cyrus Talbert's wife.

Talbert, Peggy. "The Father." A college student, the engaged daughter of the Talberts.

Tedham. "A Circle in the Water." A former Boston business associate of March who serves ten years for embezzlement and then tries to recover his daughter.

Teller, Bank. *The Quality of Mercy.* A Canadian whose information helps Pinney track down Northwick.

Temple, Ned. "The Father." The first-person narrator, the owner of the Eastridge *Banner.*

Temple, Mrs. "The Father." Ned Temple's wife.

Tenant, The Rotational. "The Rotational Tenants." The representative of the first set of rotational tenants.

Tenants, Rotational. "The Rotational Tenants." Unemployed people who live (apparently) in the empty summer cottages.

Theorist. "EEC," N 12. A man who discusses spiritualistic phenomena.

Thomas. *The Lady of the* Aroostook. The cabin boy, devoted to Lydia Blood.

Thorn, Miss. *The Undiscovered Country.* The teacher at a country school near Egerton, Mass., who lends Egeria Boynton a coat.

Thrall, Rebecca. *Through the Eye of the Needle.* Thrall's haughty, snobbish wife, who eventually becomes Altrurianized.

Thrall. *Through the Eye of the Needle.* A New York millionaire whose yacht is stranded on an Altrurian beach.

Ticket sellers. "A Day's Pleasure." Pier workers who are not helpful to the much-harassed family on its outing.

Tinker, Jonathan. "A Romance of Real Life." An ex-sailor and ex-convict who bamboozles the naïve contributor.

Tinker, Julia. "A Romance of Real Life." Tinker's daughter.

Tommy. *A Modern Instance.* Bartley Hubbard's drinking companion in a Boston saloon.

Tonelli, Tomasso. "Tonelli's Marriage." A Venetian notary's assistant.

Townsfolk. *Dr. Breen's Practice.* Loafers at the general store who irritate Dr. Breen with their remarks.

Tradonico, Dr. *Ragged Lady.* Mrs. Lander's Venetian doctor, who can do little with and for her.

Tramp. "The Angel of the Lord." A man who seems to be Ormond's angel of death.

Tramp. *The Vacation of the Kelwyns.* A black man whose sudden appearance frightens the Kelwyns.

Tramp, French-Canadian. *The Vacation of the Kelwyns.* A man who visits the Kelwyns.

Tramps. *The Undiscovered Country.* Men who frighten the Boyntons during their flight through the country.

Trannel. *The Kentons.* A malicious American medical student, vacationing in Scheveningen, who encourages Boyne Kenton's adolescent fantasies about the Dutch Queen.

Traveler, Train. "EEC," O 17. A man whose pocket is picked twice.

Travelers, American and European. "EEC," F 13. Older people who discuss travel in America and Europe.

Travelers, Train. "A Case of Metaphantasmia." People who have a collective walking nightmare in a Pullman car.

Trevor, Mr. and Mrs. *April Hopes.* Owners of a Campobello cottage in which Dan Mavering and Alice Pasmer take part in theatricals.

Triestine. "Doorstep Acquaintance." One of the narrator's visitors.

Trip. *The Flight of Pony Baker.* Pony's faithful dog, who can't understand his master's goings-on.

Triscoe, Agatha. *Their Silver Wedding Journey.* A beautiful, rather haughty young lady who has a complicated affair with Burnamy.

Triscoe, General E. B. *Their Silver Wedding Journey.* A Civil War general, wealthy widower, discontented man of leisure, possessive father of Agatha.

Trooze, John. "The Independent Candidate." The henpecked tavernkeeper in Beauville, and a friend of Larrie.

Trooze, Marquis de Lafayette. "The Independent Candidate." The small son of John Trooze.

Trooze, Sary Ann. "The Independent Candidate." John Trooze's slatternly, bullying wife.

Trufitt. *A Woman's Reason.* An ex-suitor of Helen Harkness who buys her vases from the jeweler's.

Turkeys. "Turkeys Turning the Tables." Angry birds, one being spokesman, which attack a little girl and her family for eating their relatives.

Twelvemough. *A Traveller from Altruria:* the narrator, a writer of trivial romantic novels, a prissy, spiteful snob. *Through the Eye of the Needle:* appears briefly at a New York dinner.

Uccelli, Madame. *Indian Summer*. An American-born hostess in Florence who entertains Colville and the ladies.

Uncle. "EEC," Ja 14. A man overwhelmed with charitable appeals.

Uncle, Arthur's. "Not a Love Story." A bore who teases Arthur and Fanny about Job Green.

Uphill, Mrs. *The Kentons*. A silly young wife with whom Bittridge flirts in Tuskingum.

Vance, Margaret. *A Hazard of New Fortunes*. Mrs. Horn's beautiful, socially concerned niece.

Van der Does, Mrs. *Letters Home*. A New Yorker who introduces Otis Binning, Wallace Ardith, and the Ralsons to each other.

Vane, Miss. *The Minister's Charge*. Sewell's humorous and charitable friend who briefly employs Barker in her home.

Vanecken, Rev. "The Daughter of the Storage." The Presbyterian minister who marries Charlotte Forsyth and Peter Bream in the storage warehouse.

Vanecken, Mrs. "The Daughter of the Storage." The mother of Rev. Vanecken.

Vanecken, The Misses. "The Daughter of the Storage." The old-maid sisters of Rev. Vanecken.

Van Hook, Miss. *April Hopes*. A New Yorker, Julia Anderson's aunt and chaperone.

Veneranda. *A Foregone Conclusion*. Don Ippolito's servant.

Verger. *The Seen and the Unseen at Stratford-on-Avon*. A cleric at Shakespeare's church; discusses him with the narrator.

Veronica. *The Lady of the* Aroostook. Mrs. Erwin's Italian serving woman.

Verrian. *Fennel and Rue*. A serious author of thirty-seven, who has a book published and also becomes romantically entangled with Miss Shirley.

Verrian, Mrs. *Fennel and Rue*. Verrian's possessive mother, with whom he lives.

Vervain, Florida. *A Foregone Conclusion*. A proud, high-strung American girl in Venice with her mother; she loves Ferris and is loved by him and Don Ippolito.

Vervain, Mrs. *A Foregone Conclusion*. The silly widow of an American army officer.

Veterans, War. "Doorstep Acquaintance." One genteel, the other a one-armed starch peddler; both conversational friends of the narrator.

Visitor. "EEC," Je 09. A man who discusses female suffrage with the Easy Chair.

Visitors. *The World of Chance.* People at David Hughes' apartment who argue about utopias, Tolstoy, etc., as Shelley Ray listens.

Vostrand, Genevieve. *The Landlord at Lion's Head.* A genteel young lady, married first to Count Grassi and then to Jeff Durgin.

Vostrand, Mrs. *The Landlord at Lion's Head.* The rich, fatuous mother of Genevieve; the drifting wife of the ever-absent Vostrand.

Wade, Rev. Caryl. *The Quality of Mercy.* A high-minded young Hatboro' minister who helps the Northwick girls.

Waiter. *The World of Chance.* A man in a French restaurant in New York who is friendly to Ray.

Waiters. *The Day of Their Wedding.* Men in Saratoga Springs who are disconsolate when Lorenzo Weaver doesn't tip them.

Waitresses. *A Traveller from Altruria.* Young women at the resort hotel who admire Homos for his opinions and his helpfulness.

Walker. *The Rise of Silas Lapham.* Lapham's bookkeeper, who has much sage advice for Tom Corey.

Wallace. "The Boarders." A medical student who helps his landlady, Mrs. Betterson.

Walters. *New Leaf Mills.* A farmer who buys the Powells' pigs.

Wanhope. A psychologist and "alienist" (psychiatrist), who frequents a city club. "A Case of Metaphantasmia," "The Chick of the Easter Egg," "His Apparition," "A Presentiment": listens to and discusses the stories. "The Angel of the Lord": tells the story of the Ormonds. "The Fulfilment of the Pact": tells the story of Mrs. Ormond. "The Eidolons of Brooks Alford": tells the story and discusses it. "Braybridge's Offer": tells part of the story. "Though One Rose from the Dead": writes down the story.

Wate, Clara. "The Independent Candidate." Robert Wate's little girl, the ward of George Berson.

Wate, Robert. "The Independent Candidate." The drunken husband of George Berson's sister.

Waters, Rev. *Indian Summer.* An elderly, scholarly American in Florence, who seems now contemporary and now aged to Colville.

Watkins. *A Hazard of New Fortunes.* March's pushy clerk in his Boston insurance office.

Watkins. *The Quality of Mercy.* A Canadian whose business discussions Northwick listens to with interest.

Watterson. *The Lady of the* Aroostook. First mate on the ship and Lydia Blood's admirer.

We. "EEC." The Easy Chair, in one of his fictional avatars, in dialogues and colloquia. D 08: discusses American manners. Ja 09: discusses Boston and New York. F 09: discusses the sublimity of New York. Mr 09: discusses the cost of living in New York. Ap 09: discusses rents in New York. Je 09: discusses women's suffrage. F 10: listens to his friend's accounts of European travel. Ap 10: discusses New York as a source of poetry. Jl 10: discusses a pair of lovers. S 10: discusses a couple. Ap 20: is visited by a Martian couple.

We. "Hot." The narrator, who observes a broiling summer day from his newspaper office.

We. *The Seen and the Unseen at Stratford-on-Avon.* The narrator and two other (unnamed) American tourists.

Weatherby. *The Undiscovered Country.* A levitator at Dr. Boynton's séance.

Weaver, Lorenzo. *The Day of Their Wedding.* A handsome young Shaker who leaves the Family at Harshire to marry Althea Brown, but returns with her after their marriage.

Welkin. "Braybridge's Offer." Braybridge's host in the Adirondacks, who told part of Braybridge's story to Wanhope.

Welkin, Mrs. "Braybridge's Offer." A hostess who doesn't allow Braybridge to leave in midweek.

Welwright, Dr. *Ragged Lady.* An American doctor in Italy who proposes to Clementina Claxon.

Wemmel. *The Rise of Silas Lapham.* Zerrilla Dewey's suitor.

Wentworth, George. "A Tale of Love and Politics." An enterprising youth who wins the respect of Judge S—, of the town of G—, New York, along with his daughter Ida.

West, Stephen. A naïve, village-bred young man. "The Pearl": worries about a black cabin boy accused of theft. "A Tale Untold": is cheated by a confidence man.

Westangle, Mrs. *Fennel and Rue.* An ambitious, stupid society woman who has Verrian to her house, Seasands.

Westley, General. *The Coast of Bohemia.* Walter Ludlow's host at dinner.

Westley, Mrs. *The Coast of Bohemia.* General Westley's young and beautiful second wife, Walter Ludlow's confidante.

Westover, Jere. *The Landlord at Lion's Head.* A painter, originally from Wisconsin, twenty-four when the story begins, a resident of Boston, the moral center of the novel, who courts and wins Cynthia Whitwell.

Wetherall. *A Woman's Reason.* A bidder for the Harkness house.

Wetherbee, Dr. "The Independent Candidate." A small-town doctor who treats Clara Wate.

Wetmore. *A Hazard of New Fortunes:* a New York painter in whose studio Alma Leighton studies. *The Coast of Bohemia:* a portrait painter, Walter Ludlow's friend and confidant.

Wetmore, Mrs. *The Coast of Bohemia.* Wetmore's wife.

Wheeler. *A Woman's Reason.* A bidder for the Harkness house.

White. *A Woman's Reason.* A bidder for the Harkness house.

Whittington, Mrs. *April Hopes.* A Washington hostess whose reception Dan Mavering attends with Julia Anderson.

Whitwell, Cynthia. *The Landlord at Lion's Head.* The capable, pretty daughter of Whitwell, who helps run Lion's Head House and is engaged to Jeff Durgin for some time before loving Westover.

Whitwell, Frank. *The Landlord at Lion's Head.* Cynthia's prim younger brother who studies for the ministry.

Whitwell. *The Landlord at Lion's Head.* The garrulous, rustic father of Cynthia and Frank; the resident philosopher at Lion's Head.

Wibbert, A. Lincoln. *Letters Home.* The friend and correspondent of Wallace Ardith.

"Widow." "Doorstep Acquaintance." A woman who claims, to the narrator, to be the widow of one Giovanni Cascamatto.

Willett. *A Modern Instance.* The owner of the logging camp at which Bartley meets Mrs. MacAllister and Witherby.

William. *The Rise of Silas Lapham.* Lapham's office boy.

Williams, Bunty. *The Flight of Pony Baker.* The owner of the watermelon patch which the boys raid.

"Williams." *The Minister's Choice.* Lemuel Barker's cheerful "mate" at the Wayfarer's Lodge, who later embarrasses Barker by stealing while working at Barker's hotel.

Wills, Dr. *A Modern Instance.* An Equity doctor who treats Bird and is very short with Bartley Hubbard.

Willy. "Incident." A little boy, son of a house painter, who bids his father farewell at a country station.

Wilmington, George. *Annie Kilburn.* An elderly, wealthy millowner in Hatboro', Mass.; husband of Lyra Wilmington.

Wilmington, Jack. *Annie Kilburn:* Lyra Wilmington's surly young nephew (by marriage), perhaps her lover. *The Quality of Mercy:* the son of the owner of a Hatboro' stocking mill.

Wilmington, (Mrs.) Lyra. *Annie Kilburn, The Quality of Mercy.* A self-centered, indolent former mill hand who marries a much older man and flirts with her nephew.

Wilson. *A Woman's Reason.* A Bostonian who takes Lord Rainford home and thus causes him to meet Helen Harkness again.

Wilson, Mrs. *A Woman's Reason.* A friend of the Butlers who invites Helen Harkness to lunch.

Wilson, Mr. and Mrs. *New Leaf Mills.* The owners of the bookstore that Owen Powell buys after he gives up the mill.

Wingate, Dr. A Boston nerve specialist. *The Shadow of a Dream:* March's friend and Faulkner's physician, to whom Faulkner confides the dream that Wingate later tells to Faulkner's widow Hermia, to his regret. *An Imperative Duty:* Dr. Olney's absent friend and mentor.

Winterer, Returned. "EEC," Jl 19. A man just back from the South who discusses the American and European plans in hotels.

Witherby. *A Modern Instance, The Rise of Silas Lapham.* The unscrupulous but weak owner of the Boston *Events* and employer of Bartley Hubbard.

Witherby, Mrs. *A Modern Instance.* Witherby's wife.

Witherby, Miss. *A Modern Instance.* Witherby's daughter.

Witheron. "The Independent Candidate." The Beauville schoolmaster, who chats with Wat Larrie.

Woman. "The Critical Bookstore." "The Leading Society Woman at the Intellectual Club," who asks Erlcort to speak there.

Woman. *A Foregone Conclusion.* Ferris's servant, an elderly Venetian.

Woman. *An Imperative Duty.* An old black woman who encourages

Rhoda Aldgate and takes her to a black church service.

Woman. "Somebody's Mother." An unknown old woman on the city street who may be somebody's mother.

Women. "The Eidolons of Brooks Alford." Gossipy women at Alford's summer hotel.

Women and boys, Irish. "Scene." Bystanders whose raucous manner irritates the contributor.

Woodburn, Madison. *A Hazard of New Fortunes*. The charming, vivacious daughter of Colonel Woodburn; she marries Fulkerson.

Woodburn, Colonel. *A Hazard of New Fortunes*. A courtly, elderly, reactionary Virginian who comes to New York to sell his articles and boards with the Leightons.

Woodward, Ben. *Mrs. Farrell*. The earnest, awkward son of the Woodwards, aged nineteen; in love with Mrs. Farrell.

Woodward, Nehemiah. *Mrs. Farrell*. The lackadaisical owner of a rundown farm that his wife saves by taking in boarders.

Woodward, Rachel. *Mrs. Farrell*. The shy but firm-minded, artistically talented daughter, aged twenty, of the Woodwards; a rural schoolteacher.

Woodward, Mrs. *Mrs. Farrell*. The energetic operator of a New England farm that takes summer boarders.

Workers, Railroad. *A Traveller from Altruria*. Enthusiastic listeners to Homos' lecture on Altruria.

Worrell. *The World of Chance*. The substitute reviewer of the *Metropolis* who praises Ray's novel and thus launches its success.

Wrayne, Miss. *April Hopes*. Mrs. Frobisher's sister and a friend of Daniel Mavering; the innocent cause of a quarrel between him and his fiancée, Alice Pasmer.

Wright, Piccolo. *The Flight of Pony Baker*. A boy and friend of Pony Baker in the Boy's Town.

Yarrow, Mrs. "The Eidolons of Brooks Alford." A rich widow who seems to protect Alford from eidolons and whom he eventually marries.

Zeke. "The Journeyman's Secret." A tough printer.